Genealogy Online
FOR DUMMIES®
6TH EDITION

by Matthew L. Helm and April Leigh Helm

WILEY

Wiley Publishing, Inc.

Genealogy Online For Dummies®, 6th Edition

Published by
Wiley Publishing, Inc.
111 River Street
Hoboken, NJ 07030-5774

www.wiley.com

For general information on our other products and services, please contact our Customer Care Department within the U.S. at 877-762-2974, outside the U.S. at 317-572-3993, or fax 317-572-4002.

For technical support, please visit www.wiley.com/techsupport.

Wiley also publishes its books in a variety of electronic formats. Some content that appears in print may not be available in electronic books.

Library of Congress Control Number: 2010942175

ISBN: 978-0-470-91651-3

Manufactured in the United States of America

10 9 8 7 6 5 4 3 2 1

WILEY

About the Authors

Matthew L. Helm is the Chief Executive Officer of Boneyard Creek Heritage, Inc., a family and local history services company. He is also Chief History Officer at HistoryKat, Inc., a company that specializes in digitizing and posting historical records online. He is the creator and maintainer of the award-winning Helm's Genealogy Toolbox, the Helm/Helms Family Research Page, and a variety of other Web sites. Matthew speaks at national genealogical conventions and lectures to genealogical and historical societies. He holds an A.B. in History and an M.S. in Library and Information Science from the University of Illinois at Urbana-Champaign. His full-time job is Director, Business Intelligence and Technology Solutions for Illinois State University.

April Leigh Helm is the President of HistoryKat, Inc. and Boneyard Creek Heritage, Inc. She also works as an Enterprise Systems Coordination Specialist for the University of Illinois. April lectures on genealogy and other topics for various conferences and groups. She holds a B.S. in Journalism and an Ed.M. in Higher Education Administration from the University of Illinois at Urbana-Champaign.

Together, the Helms have coauthored several books in addition to the six editions of *Genealogy Online For Dummies*. These books include *Family Tree Maker For Dummies*, *Your Official America Online Guide to Genealogy Online*, and *Get Your Degree Online*.

Dedication

For Kyleakin and Cambrian: Our future in genealogy.

In loving memory of Viola Reese McSwain (1919–2010): An inspiration to all of us and a valuable resource for anecdotal information about many ancestors.

Authors' Acknowledgments

We want to acknowledge Katie Mohr, Susan Pink, Sharon Mealka, and John Edwards. They've been a great team to work with, and without them this edition would not exist.

Publisher's Acknowledgments

We're proud of this book; please send us your comments at http://dummies.custhelp.com. For other comments, please contact our Customer Care Department within the U.S. at 877-762-2974, outside the U.S. at 317-572-3993, or fax 317-572-4002.

Some of the people who helped bring this book to market include the following:

Acquisitions and Editorial

Project Editor: Susan Pink

Acquisitions Editor: Katie Mohr

Copy Editor: John Edwards

Technical Editor: Sharon Mealka

Editorial Manager: Jodi Jensen

Media Development Assistant Project Manager: Jenny Swisher

Editorial Assistant: Amanda Graham

Sr. Editorial Assistant: Cherie Case

Cartoons: Rich Tennant (www.the5thwave.com)

Composition Services

Project Coordinator: Sheree Montgomery

Layout and Graphics: Timothy C. Detrick

Proofreaders: Cara L. Buitron, Melissa Cossell

Indexer: Infodex Indexing Services, Inc.

Publishing and Editorial for Technology Dummies

Richard Swadley, Vice President and Executive Group Publisher

Andy Cummings, Vice President and Publisher

Mary Bednarek, Executive Acquisitions Director

Mary C. Corder, Editorial Director

Publishing for Consumer Dummies

Diane Graves Steele, Vice President and Publisher

Composition Services

Debbie Stailey, Director of Composition Services

Contents at a Glance

Table of Contents

Introduction

*A*re you a student with an assignment to research your ancestry? Or maybe you're a bit older and recently retired and looking for a hobby. Or perhaps you simply love puzzles and mysteries, and you discovered that genealogy is a lot like solving these. It's even possible that you're an experienced researcher who is just looking for a refresher or wants to see what's new in *Genealogy Online For Dummies.* Regardless of your motivation, you're ready to research, but you're looking for a little guidance or a boost to get you moving. That's where we come in.

About 12 years ago, we wrote the first edition of *Genealogy Online For Dummies.* Internet resources for family history were relatively new, and the advice we gave was pointed to what was available and worked best at the time. Now, here we are, a few years down the road and five editions of *Genealogy Online For Dummies* later, bringing you the sixth edition. The world of online genealogy has changed substantially. With the introduction of smaller and faster technology, and the increased popularity of genetic genealogy, the entire genealogical field — not just the online community — has changed substantially. The whole premise that you can conduct genealogical research from the comfort of your own home and connect with other researchers through a computer is still the same, but some of the resources and methods we recommend have changed.

So if you're a repeat reader of *Genealogy Online For Dummies,* we think you'll be pleased to find all sorts of new and updated information. And if you're brand new to genealogy, we think you'll be equally pleased with easy-to-understand directions and information about the resources that await you.

At this point, we feel obligated to give you a couple of warnings or reminders. First, genealogy is an addictive pursuit. You just might find yourself staying up all hours of the night chasing down that elusive ancestor. Please don't blame us if you start falling asleep at work due to your genealogical research routine. Also, on a more serious note, keep in mind that online research is merely one tool among others for finding information about your family. To thoroughly research your genealogy, you must use a number of tools — many of which we talk about throughout this book.

Now that the disclaimers are out of the way, put the kids to bed, let your pets out, and boot up that computer. Your ancestors are just waiting to be found!

About This Book

Researching your family history online is like being a child in a candy store. So many neat things catch your eye that it's difficult to decide which one to try. That's where this book comes in. We try to help you become a discriminating candy eater — well, a discriminating researcher, anyway — by showing you not only the locations of useful genealogy resources but also how to effectively use them to meet your research goals.

Having said that, you're probably asking yourself how this book differs from the many other genealogy books on the shelf. Some books tell you only the traditional methods of genealogical research — which have you traveling hundreds of miles to visit courthouses and archives in other states. Unfortunately, these books neglect the many opportunities that online research provides. Other books that do cover online genealogy tend to group resources by how users access them (all link-based sites are listed together, all subscription sites are listed together, and so on), rather than telling you how you can integrate the many online resources to achieve your genealogical goal. As genealogists, we understand that researchers don't conduct searches by trying all the link sites, then all the subscription sites. We search by looking for surnames or places anywhere we can find them — through Web sites, blogs, e-mail, or any other source.

Some books become too computer-heavy — overkilling the ins and outs of each kind of Internet resource, and neglecting to help you with basic research techniques online *and offline* that you need to use to successfully meet your goal. We don't want you to have a bad experience online. So rather than focus on just one thing — genealogy *or* online resources — we try to balance the act. In this book, we show you how to integrate genealogical research with the use of online resources so that you can discover how to effectively and efficiently use your computer and the Internet in your family research.

Now that we've explained a bit about the book, are you ready to get started and to become an official genealogist? You might be asking yourself, "What are the requirements for becoming an official genealogist?" It's simple — just say out loud, "I declare myself an official genealogist." It's official — you're a genealogist, and it's time to start pulling together the puzzle pieces of your family history.

Seriously, being a genealogist has no formal requirements. You simply need an interest in your ancestry and a willingness to devote time to pursuing information and documents.

Foolish Assumptions

In writing and revising this book, we made a few assumptions. If you fit one of these assumptions, this book is for you:

- ✔ You've performed at least a little genealogy groundwork, and now you're ready to use the Internet, your phone, DNA testing, and whatever else you can find to pursue (and better prepare yourself for) your genealogy research both online and offline.

- ✔ You have at least a little computer experience, are now interested in pursuing your family tree, and want to know where and how to start.

- ✔ You have a little experience in genealogy and some experience with computers, but you want to find out how to put them together.

You can have a lot of computer experience and be a novice to genealogy or to online genealogy and still benefit from this book. In this case, you may still want to skim some of the basic explanations about computer hardware, software, and the types of Internet resources.

How to Use This Book

We don't expect you to read this book from cover to cover, in the order we wrote it. No, you're not hurting our feelings by skipping through the sections looking only for the information that you're interested in at a particular moment! We want this book to be useful. How you use it is up to you. In fact, we wrote this book to accommodate you. Each section in each chapter can stand alone as a separate entity, so you can pick up the book and flip directly to a section that deals with what you want to know. If we think something relevant in another section can supplement your knowledge on a particular topic, we provide a note or reference telling you the other place(s) we think you should look. However, we tried hard to do this referencing in a manner that isn't obnoxious to those of you who choose to read the book from cover to cover. We hope we've succeeded in addressing both types of readers!

We use a couple of conventions in this book to make it easier for you to follow a set of specific instructions. If you should type something, the **bold type** indicates what you need to type.

Web addresses (or URLs) are in a `different font` to set them apart from the regular text of the book. This way, you can easily see the sites we recommend that you visit to try something or read more online.

How This Book Is Organized

To help you get a better picture of what this book has to offer, this section explains a little about how we organized the book and what you can expect to find in each part.

Part I: Getting Your Act Together

You need to have a good foundation before starting your online genealogical research. This part explores how to form an online research plan, what fundamental family information you need to collect first, and how to start organizing your research and placing it into a genealogical database.

Part II: Focusing on Your Ancestor

Searching online for information about your particular ancestors can be a daunting task. Part II examines resources that are available for locating your ancestor by name and by using worldwide government resources that can assist you in your ancestral hunt.

Part III: Adding Depth to Your Research

Your family history is a lot more than just a list of names and birth dates. You have many details to fill in so that your ancestors' lives are put in context. In Part III, we look at ethnic, religious, and group affiliation resources that provide an insight into the everyday lives of your ancestors. We also examine the use of genetic testing in genealogical research.

Part IV: Share and Share Alike

One of the most important aspects of genealogical research is using a coordinated effort to achieve success. Part IV looks at what goes into this effort, including using all available online resources, cooperating with other researchers, benefiting from groups and societies, and sharing the fruits of your research with the online community.

Part V: The Large Genealogical Sites

Over the past decade, a few genealogical Web sites have grown in content and presence. We believe that Ancestry.com and FamilySearch.org have so many resources to offer that they warrant some special attention.

Part VI: The Part of Tens

Ah, the infamous Part of Tens (infamous because every *Dummies* book has one of these sections with profound advice or lists of things to do). Here you find a series of quick-reference chapters that give you useful genealogical hints and reminders. We provide tools and sites for your research-related travels, some tips for creating a genealogical Web page or blog, a list of sites that offer help to genealogists, and hints to keep your online research sailing smoothly.

Glossary

The glossary provides definitions of many terms that you're likely to encounter in your genealogical research or that you'll see in this book.

Icons Used in This Book

To help you get the most out of this book, we created some icons that tell you at a glance whether a section or paragraph has important information of a particular kind.

The Remember icon marks important genealogical stuff, so don't forget it.

When you see the Tip icon, you know we're offering advice or shortcuts to make your researching easier.

Look out! The Warning icon indicates something tricky or unusual to watch for.

Where to Go from Here

Depending on where you're reading this introduction, your next step is one of the following:

- ✔ You need to go to the front of the bookstore and pay for this book so that you can take it home and use it.

- ✔ If you've already bought the book and you're at home (or wherever), you can go ahead and start reading in depth, following the steps for the online activities in the book as they come along.

Part I
Getting Your Act Together

The 5th Wave — By Rich Tennant

"They came here to help me with my genealogical research, but they stayed for the satellite TV."

In this part . . .

*B*efore wandering online in search of your family history, you should prepare yourself by discovering some of the basics of genealogy and knowing how to form a research plan. Also, you need to know how to organize and preserve what you find both online and offline, as well as ensure that your computer is ready to help. This part starts you off in the right direction.

Chapter 1

Brushing Up on the Basics

. . . .

In This Chapter

▶ Starting your research with yourself

▶ Using the Helm Family Tree Research Cycle

▶ Taking your time

▶ Verifying information

. . . .

You are probably eager to get started researching your family history — we know the feeling. You have a lot to find online, and soon you'll be a pro at locating information. However, we suggest that you do some things first to make your search a whole lot easier.

This chapter is designed to give you a research foundation that will help you spend your time online as efficiently as possible. First, we show you how you can develop research skills by tracking facts about someone very near and dear to you — yourself. Then, we look at how to develop a plan to research your ancestors. In the latter parts of the chapter, we go through some gentle reminders that can help you keep your research as relevant as possible.

Making an Example Out of Yourself

Late one night, you decide to start looking for information on your great-great-grandfather Absalom Looney. After logging on to your service provider, you put good old Absalom's name into a search engine. Within a couple of seconds, a page appears showing 2,140 results for Absalom Looney. But do any of these results apply to the Absalom you're looking for and, if so, which are the magic ones? Well, if you know a little bit about Absalom, you can make some decisions as to which record or site is likely to contain information relevant to him.

At this point, you might be asking yourself how you find information that can confirm whether the Absalom on the screen is the one you're looking for. You're in luck, because that's just what the following sections are all about. But before we go any further, we want to let you in on a little secret: Instead of starting your journey with Absalom, it's better to begin by finding information about someone you already know better — yourself.

Creating a biographical brag book

You already know more about yourself than anyone else knows about you. (Regardless of what your spouse thinks, we're convinced that you're really the expert on you.) You probably know your birth date, place of birth, parents' names, and where you've lived. (We recognize that not everyone knows all this information; adoptions or other extenuating circumstances may require you to do the best you can with what you know until you can discover additional information about yourself.) Knowing some things about yourself, it's time to start sketching out your life.

You can approach the sketch in several ways. Sometimes, the easiest method is to begin with current events and work back through your life. For instance, first note the basics: your current marital or family status, occupation, residence, and activities. Then move back to your last residence, occupation, and so on until you arrive at your birth date. Make sure that you include milestones such as children's birth dates, marriage dates, military service dates, educational experience, religious affiliations, participation in organizations and sports, and other significant events in your life. If you prefer, you can cover your life by beginning with your birth and working forward to the present. Either way is fine, as long as all the important events are listed in the sketch.

You have several ways to store your sketch. Some people prefer to start with index cards, placing a particular event on each card. Others use a spreadsheet or word processor to make notes about things that they recall over a certain period of time. Either way, you can arrange historical events to form the basis of your biographical sketch.

Because this book deals with online resources, we wouldn't be doing our job if we didn't mention an online resource for writing your biographical sketch. One site that uses a set of interview questions to help you author your sketch is arcalife (`www.arcalife.com`). arcalife provides resources for building your family tree online, researching databases, and creating timelines and scrapbooks.

To begin your biographical sketch on arcalife, follow these steps:

1. **Point your browser to `www.arcalife.com`.**

2. **In the right column, fill out your name, e-mail address, password, birth date, gender, and the validation code that appears to the right of the code field.**

   Don't forget to select the check box to agree to the terms of the service.

3. **Click the Sign Up button to continue.**

   You're taken to a new page with links to resources on arcalife. Across the top of the page are tabs for the various sections of the site: Home, My Life, Family Lives, Family Tree, History Search, and Life Showcases.

4. **Click the My Life tab.**

   The next page that you view is titled My Life, with a group of tabbed pages labeled Profile, Memories, Experiences, Timeline, Biography, Comments, and Attachments.

5. **Click the Experiences tab.**

6. **Click the View/Edit link, and type information in the Major Events — Birth — My Birth information area, as shown in Figure 1-1.**

7. **Click Save.**

   You can add more experiences by clicking the New Experience tab. You also find options for adding your experience in a timeline or creating a biography.

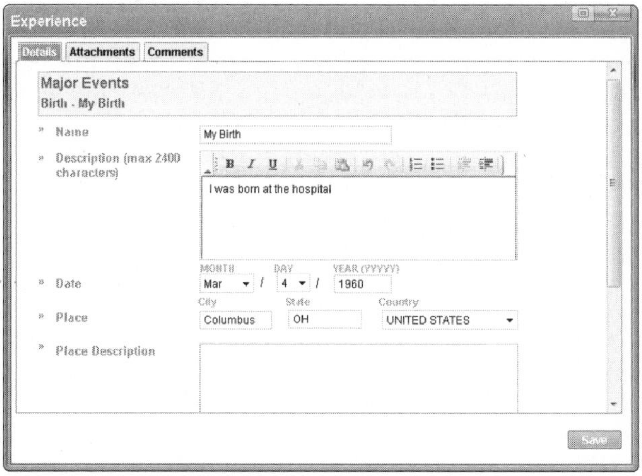

Figure 1-1:
Creating an experience on arcalife.

The biographical sketch that you create now may become an important research tool for one of your descendants who decides to conduct research about you in the future. So, when you have the time, we recommend that you turn that sketch into a full-blown autobiography. This way, your descendants not only know the facts about your life but also gain some insight as to why you chose the paths you did throughout your life.

Finding primary sources

If you're like most of us, you think you know a lot about yourself. If we ask you what your birthday is, you can tell us without batting an eye. But how do you know the birth date? You were obviously there, but you weren't in a condition to be a reliable witness, given that you were a newborn and most likely not fully aware of what was going on. This is where primary sources come in handy. Most likely, witnesses were present who helped create a record of the event.

Primary sources are documents, oral accounts (if the account is made soon after the actual event and witnessed by the person who created the account), photographs, or any other items created at the time of a certain event's occurrence.

For example, a primary source for your birth date is your birth certificate. Typically, a birth certificate is prepared within a few days of the actual event and is signed by one or more witnesses to the birth. Because of the timeliness and involvement of direct witnesses, the information contained on the record (such as the time, date, and parents' names) is usually a reliable firsthand account of the event. It's important to recognize that even if a record was prepared near the time of an event, such a unilateral account doesn't automatically mean that every fact provided on the record is correct. Typographical errors can occur or incorrect information can be provided to the creator of the record. Often these errors are not caught when the certificate application is signed because new parents are preoccupied with things other than government paperwork during their stay at the hospital. For example, when our youngest child was born, the birth certificate application was created and presented to us for signature. After reading it, we discovered three pieces of incorrect data. Fortunately, we were able to correct the birth certificate before it was submitted to the county clerk — even though the hospital clerk wasn't too happy about recreating the document multiple times. So it's always a good idea to try to find other primary records that can corroborate the information found in any record.

Secondary sources are documents, oral accounts, and so on that are created some length of time after the event or for which information is supplied by someone who wasn't an eyewitness to the event. A secondary source can also be a person who was an eyewitness to the event but recalls it after a significant period of time passes.

Some records may be considered both primary and secondary sources. For example, a death certificate contains both primary and secondary source information. The primary source information includes the death date and cause of death. These facts are primary because the certificate was prepared around the time of death, and the information is usually provided by a medical professional who pronounced the person dead. The secondary source information on the death certificate includes the birth date and place of birth of the deceased individual. These details are secondary because the certificate was issued at a time significantly later than the birth (assuming that the birth and death dates are at least a few years apart). Secondary sources don't have the degree of reliability or surety of primary sources. Often secondary source information, such as birth data found on death certificates, is provided by an individual's children or descendants who may or may not know the exact date or place of birth and who may be providing information during a stressful situation. Given the lesser reliability of secondary sources, we recommend backing up your secondary sources with reliable primary sources whenever possible.

Although we've said that secondary sources are not as reliable as primary sources, that doesn't mean that secondary sources are always wrong or aren't useful. A good deal of the time, the information is correct, and such records provide valuable clues to locating primary source information. For example, in the case of a birth date and birthplace on a death certificate, the information provides a place and approximate time frame you can use as a starting point when you search for a birth record.

You can familiarize yourself with primary sources by collecting some information for your own biographical profile. Try to match primary sources for each event in the sketch — for example, birth and marriage certificates, deeds, leases, diplomas or certificates of degree, military records, and tax records. We provide more information on finding some of these types of documents throughout the rest of this book. If you can't locate primary source documents for each event in your life, don't fret! Your biographical sketch can serve as a primary source document because you write it about yourself.

For additional information on primary sources, see The Historian's Sources page at the Library of Congress Web site at `http://lcweb2.loc.gov/ ammem/ndlpedu/lessons/psources/pshome.html`.

For comparisons of primary, secondary, and tertiary sources and examples of each, see James Cook University's overview of primary, secondary, and tertiary sources at `www-public.jcu.edu.au/libcomp/resources/era/ JCUPRD_030412`or William Madison Randall Library's Identifying Primary, Secondary, and Tertiary Sources at `http://library.uncw.edu/web/ research/topic/identifysources.html`.

For strategies on using primary sources online, see the Reference and User Services Association (of the American Library Association) page at `www. ala.org/ala/mgrps/divs/rusa/sections/history/resources/ pubs/usingprimarysources/index.cfm`.

Introducing the Helm Online Family Tree Research Cycle

All great projects start with a plan, right? Starting a genealogical project is no exception. A well-thought-out plan can help you make efficient use of your time and keep you focused on the goals that you have set for a particular research session. Now, we realize that not everyone enjoys coming up with a plan. Finding your ancestors is the fun part — not the planning. So, to help speed things along, we've come up with a basic process that we hope helps you make the most of your research time.

Of course, wanting to take credit for our fabulous model, we like to call it the *Helm Online Family Tree Research Cycle.* Sounds impressive, doesn't it? Well, we have to admit that most of it is common sense. Figure 1-2 shows the five phases of the cycle: planning, collecting, researching, consolidating, and distilling.

Sticking with the *family tree* motif here, we liken the cycle to the steps you take to plant and sustain a tree:

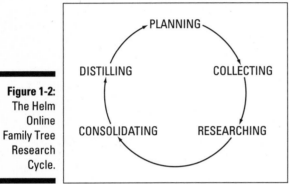

Figure 1-2:
The Helm
Online
Family Tree
Research
Cycle.

✔ **Planning:** The first step in planting a tree is figuring out what kind of tree you want and then finding a good place in your yard for the tree to grow. This step in the cycle is the *planning* phase. In genealogy, you want to select a family that you know enough about to begin a search and then think about the resources that can provide the information that you're looking for.

✔ **Collecting:** After you plan for the tree, you go to a nursery and pick a suitable sapling and other necessary materials to ensure that the tree's roots take hold. The second phase of the cycle, *collecting,* is the same — you collect information on the family that you're researching by conducting interviews in person, on the phone, or through e-mail, and by finding documents in attics, basements, and other home-front repositories.

✔ **Researching:** The next step is to actually plant the tree. You dig a hole, place the tree in it, and then cover the roots. Similarly, you spend the *researching* phase of the cycle digging for clues, finding information that can support your family tree, and obtaining documentation. You can use traditional and technological tools to dig — tools such as libraries, courthouses, your computer, and the Web.

✔ **Consolidating:** You planted the tree and covered its roots. However, to make sure that the tree grows, you put mulch around it and provide the nourishment that the tree needs to survive. The *consolidating* phase of the cycle is similar in that you take the information you find and place it into your computer-based genealogical database or your filing system. These systems protect your findings by keeping them in a centralized location and provide an environment in which you can see the fruits of your labor.

> ✔ **Distilling:** After your tree has taken root and begins to grow, you need to prune the old growth, allowing new growth to appear. Similarly, the *distilling* phase is where you use your computer-based genealogical database to generate reports showing the current state of your research. You can use these reports to prune from your database those individuals you've proven don't fit into your family lines — and perhaps find room for new genealogical growth by finding clues to other lines with which you want to follow up.

We think that using our research model makes looking for genealogical information a lot easier and more fulfilling. However, this model is merely a guide. Feel free to use whatever methods work best for you — as long as those methods make it possible for someone else to verify your research (through sources you cite and so on).

Planning your research

Your computer puts the world at your fingertips. Discovering all the wonderful online resources that exist makes you feel like a kid in a candy store. You click around from site to site with wide eyes, amazed by what you see, tempted to record everything for your genealogy — whether it relates to one of your family lines or not.

Because of the immense wealth of information available to you, putting together a research plan before going online is very important — it can save you a lot of time and frustration by keeping you focused. Millions of pages with genealogical content exist on the Internet. If you don't have a good idea of exactly what you're looking for to fill in the blanks in your family history, you can get lost online. Getting lost is even easier when you see a name that looks familiar and start following its links, only to discover hours later (when you finally get around to pulling out the notes you already had) that you've been tracking the wrong person and family line.

Now that we've convinced you that you need a research plan, you're probably wondering exactly what a research plan is. Basically, a *research plan* is a commonsense approach to looking for information about your ancestors online. A research plan entails knowing what you're looking for and what your priorities are for finding information.

If you're the kind of person who likes detailed organization (such as lists and steps), you can map out your research plan in a spreadsheet or word processor on your computer, write it on paper, or use a genealogical software tool. If you're the kind of person who knows exactly what you want and need at all times, and you have an excellent memory of where you leave off when doing projects, your research plan can exist solely in your mind. In other words, your research plan can be as formal or informal as you like — as long as it helps you plot what you're looking for.

For example, say that you're interested in finding some information on your great-grandmother. Here are some steps you can take to form a research plan:

1. **Write down what you already know about the person you want to research — in this case, your great-grandmother.**

   Include details such as the dates and places of birth, marriage, and death; spouse's name; children's names; and any other details you think may help you distinguish your ancestor from other individuals. Of course, it's possible that all you know at this time is Great-grandma's name.

2. **Survey a comprehensive genealogical index to get an overview of what's available.**

   Visit a site such as Linkpendium (`www.linkpendium.com`) to browse for information by name and location. Using Great-grandma's name and the names of some of the locations where she lived will allow you to see what kinds of resources are available. (Chapter 4 goes into more detail about online tips and searching for this type of information.) Make sure that you make a list of the sites that you find in a word processor document, in a spreadsheet, or on a piece of paper, or bookmark them on your Web browser. Also, given that Web sites come and go frequently, you may want to consider downloading the Web page for future offline browsing.

3. **Prioritize the resources that you want to use.**

   Browsing a comprehensive genealogical index may turn up several types of resources, such as sites featuring digitized copies of original records, transcriptions of records, online genealogy databases, or an online message board with many posts about people with the same last name. We recommend that you prioritize which resources you plan to use first. You may want to visit a Web site that contains specific information on your grandmother's family first — rather than spending a lot of time on a Web site that just contains generic information on her surname. You may also want to visit a site with digitized original records first and leave a site with transcribed records or a database for later use.

4. **Schedule time to use the various resources that you identify.**

   Family history is truly a lifelong pursuit — you can't download every bit of information and documentation that you need all at once. Because researching your genealogy requires time and effort, we recommend that you schedule time to work on specific parts of your research. If you have a particular evening open every week, you can pencil in a research night on your calendar, setting aside 15–30 minutes at the beginning to review what you have and assess your goals, then spending a couple of hours researching, and ending your evening with another 15–30 minutes of review in which you organize what you found.

Collecting useful information

After you generate a research plan (see the preceding section), you may need to fill in a few details such as dates and locations of births, marriages, and deaths. You can collect this information by interviewing family members and by looking through family documents and photographs. (See Chapter 2 for tips on interviewing and using family documents and photographs.) You may also need to look up a few things in an atlas or *gazetteer* (a geographical dictionary), if you aren't sure of certain locations. (Chapter 6 provides more information on online gazetteers.)

For a list of things that may be useful to collect, see Chapter 2. In the meantime, here are a few online resources that can help you get started with your family history:

- **National Genealogical Society Getting Started Page:** www.ngs genealogy.org/cs/getting_started

- **Introduction to Genealogy: First Steps:** http://genealogy.about. com/library/lessons/blintro2a.htm

- **Getting Started in Genealogy and Family History:** www.genuki.org. uk/gs

- **Ancestry.com Learning Center** http://learn.ancestry.com/Home/ HMLND.aspx

Researching: Through the brick wall and beyond

Of course, researching your family history online is the topic of this entire book, so you can find the necessary resources to do a great deal of your online research in these pages.

A time will undoubtedly come when you run into what genealogists affectionately call the *Brick Wall Syndrome* — when you think you have exhausted every possible way of finding an ancestor. The most important thing you can do is to keep the faith — don't give up! Web sites are known to change frequently (especially as more people come online and share their information). Although you may not find exactly what you need today, you may find it next week at a site you've visited several times before or at a new site altogether. The lesson here is to check back at sites that you've visited before.

Another way to get past the brick wall is to ask for help. Don't be afraid to post a message on a mailing list or e-mail other researchers you've corresponded with in the past to see whether they have answers or suggestions for finding answers. We provide more information for using mailing lists and e-mail in Chapter 4. Also, you may be able to use the expertise of members of a genealogical or historical society who can point you to specific resources that you may not have known existed. We talk more about genealogical and historical societies in Chapter 2.

Fortunately, you can also find suggestions posted online on how to get through that brick wall when you run up against it. Check out these sites:

- ✔ **Brick Wall Strategies for Dead-End Family Trees:** `http://genealogy.about.com/od/basics/a/brick_walls.htm`
- ✔ **Brick Wall Research:** `http://genealogypro.com/articles/brick-wall-research.html`
- ✔ **Overcoming "Brick Wall" Problems:** `www.progenealogists.com/brickwall.htm`

Consolidating information in a database

After you get rolling on your research, you often find so much information that it feels like you don't have enough time to put it all into your computer-based genealogical database.

A *genealogical database* is a software program that allows you to enter, organize, store, and use all sorts of genealogical information on your computer.

When possible, try to set aside some time to update your database with information you recently gathered. This process of putting your information together in one central place, which we call *consolidating,* helps you gain a perspective on the work that you've completed and provides a place for you to store all those nuggets you'll need when you begin researching again. By storing your information in a database, you can always refer to it for a quick answer the next time you try to remember something specific, such as where you found a reference to a marriage certificate for your great-great-grandparents, or where your great-grandfather lived during a particular time frame. Placing your information in a genealogical database has a bonus — you can take your research with you when you travel. You can carry your database on your laptop, or you can even find cell phone applications that can display the contents of genealogical databases. We talk more about those options in Chapter 3.

Distilling the information that you gather

The final step in the cycle is distilling the information that you gather into a report, a chart, an organized database, or a detailed research log that you can use to find additional genealogical leads. Frequently, you can complete the distillation process by producing a report from your computer-based genealogical database. Most genealogical software programs allow you to generate reports in a variety of formats. For example, you can pull up a Pedigree chart (a chart showing a primary person with lines representing the relationships to his or her parents, then lines connecting them to their parents, and so on) or an outline of descendants from information that you entered in the database about each ancestor. You can use these reports to see what holes still exist in your research, and you can add these missing pieces to the planning phase for your next research effort — starting the entire cycle over.

Another advantage to genealogical reports is having the information readily available so that you can *toggle* back to look at the report while researching online, which can help you stay focused. (*Toggling* is flipping back and forth between open programs on your computer. For example, in Windows, you press Alt+Tab to toggle, or you can click the appropriate item on the taskbar at the bottom of the screen. On a Macintosh, you can use the Application Switcher in the upper-right corner of the screen.) If you prefer, printing copies of the reports and keeping them next to the computer while you're researching online serves the same purpose.

Too Many Ancestor Irons in the Research Fire

When you begin your research, take your time and don't get in a big hurry. Keep things simple and look for one piece of information at a time. If you try to do too much too fast, you risk getting confused, having no online success, and getting frustrated with online research. This result isn't encouraging and certainly doesn't make you feel like jumping back into your research, which would be a shame because you can find a lot of valuable information and research help online.

Verifying Your Information: Don't Believe Everything You Read!

We have one last piece of advice for you when you're researching. *Don't believe everything you read.* Well, actually, a pure genealogist would say, "Don't believe *anything* that you read." Either way, the point is the same: Always verify any information that you find online — or, for that matter, in print — with primary records. (For more on primary records, see the section "Finding primary sources," earlier in this chapter.) If you can't prove it through a vital record, census record, or some other authoritative record, the information simply may not be as valuable as you think. However, don't discount something just because you can't *immediately* prove it. You might want to hold on to the information and continue to try to prove or disprove it with a primary document. At some time in the future, you may run across a record that does indeed prove the accuracy of the information; in the meantime, it might give you some leads for where to look for more about that person.

You've probably seen the courtroom dramas on television where the lawyer must prove his case before a jury. In family history, researchers go through a similar process to prove that a particular event occurred in the lives of their ancestors. At times, you won't be able to find a record that verifies that your ancestor was born on a certain date. Perhaps the birth record was destroyed in a courthouse fire or the birth was never properly recorded. Or worse yet, you may find two records that contain conflicting information about the same event.

So, how do genealogists and family historians know when they have sufficiently proved something? Well, for the longest time, no published guidelines existed on what constituted sufficient proof. To assist professional genealogists figure out the appropriate level of proof for their clients, the Board for Certification of Genealogists (BCG) created the *Genealogical Proof Standard* as part of the BCG Genealogical Standards Manual (published in 2000 by Ancestry).

The Genealogical Proof Standard is comprised of five steps. If these five steps are completed, sufficient proof exists for a professional genealogist to create a research report stating that a certain event happened. We are going to paraphrase the steps a bit to make them a little easier to understand.

1. Conduct a reasonably exhaustive search for all information related to a particular event.

2. Include a complete and accurate citation of the information that you use for your research.

3. Analyze the quality of the information. (For example, is the information from a primary source or is it from a reliable source?)

4. Resolve conflicts between two sources of information (such as two resources stating two different birth dates for the same person).

5. Arrive at a sound conclusion based on the information related to an event.

   Although these steps were established for professional genealogists, they are good steps for you to follow to make sure that any person reading your research can follow your conclusions. Following these steps does not ensure that your conclusions are accurate 100 percent of the time. You always have the chance that a new piece of evidence will surface that may disprove your conclusions.

If you want to find out more about how the Genealogical Proof Standard relates to the research process, we recommend that you take a look at Mark Tucker's Genealogy Research Process Map at the ThinkGenealogy site (www.thinkgenealogy.com/map). You can download a PDF version of the map from this site.

Chapter 2

Starting Your Ancestral Treasure Hunt

You may not believe it when we tell you this, but one of the first things to do when researching your family history online doesn't involve a computer. That's right: You don't necessarily need to flip the switch on that computer to start your research. Start by collecting some basic information about your family the old-fashioned way: getting family stories from relatives, digging through trunks in the attic, and visiting some traditional places for records. Then you can use some of this basic information to guide your research and help you make decisions about the quality of the information you find online.

In addition to helping you determine whether online information is helpful to your particular research, you need a good foundation in traditional research because you can't complete your entire family history online. We want to make sure that your expectations of online research are appropriate. Although you can find a lot of records online and the number of original records available online increases every day, several sets of crucial records are still not available through the Internet. It's best to think of online genealogy as one of many tools that you use to put together the pieces of your family puzzle.

In this chapter, we give an overview of several hunting grounds where you can gather information before you begin your online genealogical research. You'll probably find yourself returning to these resources over and over as you start researching additional family lines. We also provide some Web sites that can assist you in accessing these resources.

Getting the 4-1-1 from Your Kinfolk

It's likely that you have some valuable but overlooked sources of genealogical gold. You may be looking right through them as they hover around the dessert table at the family reunion, remind you about that embarrassing moment from your childhood, and overstay their welcome in your home. Yes, they are your relatives.

Interviewing your relatives is an important step in the research process. Relatives can provide family records and photographs, give you the dirt on other family members, and identify other people who might be beneficial to talk to about the family history. When talking with relatives, you want to collect the same type of information about their lives that you provided about your own when you wrote your biographical sketch in Chapter 1.

Your parents, brothers, sisters, grandparents, aunts, uncles, and cousins are all good candidates for information sources about your family's most recent generations. Talking to relatives provides you with leads that you can use to find primary sources. (For more information on primary sources, see Chapter 1.) You can complete family interviews in person or through a questionnaire. We strongly recommend that you conduct these interviews in person. However, if meeting your relatives in person is not feasible because they live too far away, by all means, write to them in a letter or an e-mail. A couple of Web sites where you can find example letters and questionnaires follow:

- ✔ **Genealogy.com:** This site has a Request for Genealogical Information from Family Members at www.genealogy.com/00000059.html. A nice thing about Genealogy.com's site is that it offers this letter to family members translated into other languages, including French, German, Italian, and Spanish. You can access these foreign-language versions of the letter from the Genealogy.com Census Abstracts and Form Letters page at www.genealogy.com/00000023.html.
- ✔ **Suite101.com:** See this site's Writing a Genealogy Letter: Free Template for Querying Relatives (www.suite101.com/article.cfm/norwegian_culture/73627), which provides a letter in Norwegian.

If you prefer to write your own letter (without guidance from one of these sites), you can always use an online translator to convert your customized letter or e-mail into another language. For more information about some of these, flip to Chapter 7.

There's no easy way to say this, so please excuse us for being blunt — you may want to begin interviewing some of your older relatives as soon as possible, depending on their ages and health. If a family member passes on before you have the chance to interview him or her, you may miss the opportunity of a lifetime to find out more about his or her personal experiences and knowledge of previous generations.

TIP

Good interviewing questions

Before you conduct a family interview, pull together a set of questions to guide the discussion. A little planning on your part makes the difference between an interview in which the family member stays focused, and a question-and-answer session that invites bouncing from one unrelated topic to another. Here are examples of some questions that you may want to ask:

✔ What is your full name, and do you know why you were named that?

✔ Where were you born and when? Do you remember any stories that your parents told you about your birth?

✔ What do you remember about your childhood? Where did you go to school? Did you finish school? If not, why? (Remember to ask about all levels of schooling through college.)

✔ What were your brothers and sisters like?

✔ Where and when were your parents born? What did they look like? What were their occupations? Did your parents tell you how they met?

✔ Do you remember your grandparents? Do you recall any stories about them? What did they look like? Did you hear any stories about your great-grandparents? Did you ever meet your great-grandparents?

✔ When you were a child, who was the oldest person in your family?

✔ Did any relatives (other than your immediate family) live with you?

✔ Do you remember who your neighbors were when you were a child?

✔ Did your family have any traditions or celebrate any special holidays?

✔ Do you have any items (stories, traditions, or physical items) that have been handed down through several generations of the family?

✔ When did you leave home? Where did you live?

✔ Did you join the military? If so, what branch of service were you in? What units were you a part of? Did you serve overseas?

✔ What occupations have you had? Did you have any special training?

✔ How did you meet your spouse? When and where did you get married? Did you go on a honeymoon? Where?

✔ When were your children born? Do you have any stories about their births?

✔ Do you know who in the family originally immigrated to this country? Where did they come from? Why did they leave their native land?

You can probably think of more questions that are likely to draw responses from your family. If you get stuck and need additional questions identified for you, we recommend taking a look at the Fifty Questions for Family History Interviews at About.com: Genealogy (http://genealogy.about.com/cs/oralhistory/a/interview.htm).

Here are a few tips to remember as you plan a family interview:

- ✔ **Prepare a list of questions that you want to ask.** Knowing what you want to achieve during the discussion helps you get started and keeps your interview focused. (See the nearby sidebar "Good interviewing questions" for some ideas.) However, you also need to be flexible enough to allow the interviewee to take the conversation where he or she wants to go. Often some of the best information comes from memories that occur while the interviewee is talking — rather than being generated strictly in response to a set of questions.

- ✔ **Bring a recorder to the interview.** Use a recorder of your choice, whether it's your computer, an audiocassette recorder, or a video camera. Make sure that you get permission from each participant before you start recording. If the interviewee is agreeable and you have the equipment, we recommend you videotape the session. That way, you can see the expressions on his or her face as he or she talks.

- ✔ **Use photographs and documents to help your family members recall events.** Often photographs can have a dramatic effect on the stories that the interviewee remembers. If you have a lull in the interview, pulling out a photo album is an excellent way to jump-start things.

- ✔ **Try to limit your interviews to two hours or less.** You don't want to be overwhelmed with information, and you don't want the interviewee to get worn out by your visit. Within two hours, you can collect a lot of information to guide your research. And remember, you can always do another interview if you want more information from the family member. (Actually, we strongly encourage you to do subsequent interviews — often the first interview stimulates memories for the individual that you can cover during a later interview. Who knows? It might lead to a regularly scheduled lunch or tea time with a relative whom you genuinely enjoy visiting.)

- ✔ **Be grateful and respectful.** Remember that these are people who have agreed to give you time and answers. Treat them with respect by listening attentively and speaking politely to them. And by all means, be sure to thank them when you've completed the interview.

Striking It Rich in Closets, in Basements, and under Beds

Are you a pack rat, or have you ever been accused of being one? You know what we mean: someone who keeps every little scrap of paper that he or she touches. Recently we heard that such people are not called pack rats anymore —they're *chronic hoarders.* Regardless of what you call yourself, you know who you are. (And we know how to recognize you because — and here's a deep, dark confession — we're *both* pack rats of the serious variety!) If you are, you're well suited for genealogy. In fact, if you're lucky, you descended from a whole family of pack rats who saved all those scraps from the past in their attics or basements. You may be able to share in their treasures — digging to find things that can further your genealogical research. For example, pay a visit to Grandma's attic, and you may discover an old suitcase or cigar box full of documents such as report cards, wartime ration cards, and letters. These items may contain information that you can use to reconstruct part of your ancestor's past or to enhance it.

When you go through old family treasures, look for things that can serve as primary sources for facts that you want to verify. For more information on primary sources, see Chapter 1. Here's a list (although not an exhaustive one) of some specific things to look for:

- ✔ Family Bibles
- ✔ Property-related legal documents (such as mortgages, titles, and deeds)
- ✔ Insurance policies
- ✔ Wills
- ✔ Family letters
- ✔ Obituaries and newspaper articles
- ✔ Diaries
- ✔ Naturalization records
- ✔ Baptismal certificates and other church records
- ✔ Copies of vital records (such as birth, marriage, and death certificates, and divorce decrees)
- ✔ Report cards and other administrative papers from school
- ✔ Occupational or personnel records
- ✔ Membership cards or identification cards with photos

These gems that you find buried around the house contain all sorts of information: names and vital statistics of ancestors, names and addresses of friends of the family and neighbors, military units, religious affiliations, medical conditions and names of doctors or hospitals, work histories, and so many other things that can add color to your family history as well as give you place-names and time frames to guide you in your subsequent research.

For a list of other items to look for around the home, see the Treasures in the Attic page at www.ancestry.com/library/view/ancmag/673.asp.

Dusting Off Old Photo Albums

A picture is worth a thousand words — so the saying goes. That's certainly true in genealogy. Photographs are among the most treasured documents for genealogists. Pictures show how your ancestors looked and what conditions they lived in. Sometimes the flip side of the photo is more important than the picture itself. On the back, you may find crucial information such as names, dates, and descriptions of places.

Photographs are also useful as memory-joggers for family members. Pictures can help others recollect the past and bring up long-forgotten memories. Just be forewarned — sometimes the memories are good, and sometimes they're not so good. Although you may stimulate thoughts of some great moments long ago, you may also open a can of worms when you ask Grandma about a particular person in a picture. On the plus side, in the end, she may give you the low-down on not only that person but also every single individual in the family who has ever made her angry — this can provide lots of genealogical leads.

You may run into several types of photographs in your research. Knowing when certain kinds of photographs were produced can help you associate a time frame with a picture. Here are some examples:

- **Daguerreotypes:** Daguerreotype photos were taken from 1839 to 1860. They required a long exposure time and were taken on silver-plated copper. The photographic image appears to change from a positive to a negative when tilted.

- **Ambrotypes:** Ambrotypes used a much shorter exposure time and were produced from 1858 to 1866. The image was made on thin glass and usually had a black backing.

- **Tintypes:** Tintypes were produced from 1858 to 1910. They were made on a metal sheet, and the image was often coated with a varnish. You can usually find them in a paper cover.

- **Cartes-de-visite:** Cartes-de-visite were small paper prints mounted on a card. They were often bound together into a photo album. They were produced between 1858 and 1891.

- **Cabinet cards:** Cabinet cards were larger versions of cartes-de-visite. They sometimes included dates on the borders of the cards. The pictures themselves were usually mounted on cardboard. They were manufactured primarily between 1865 and 1906.

- **Albumen prints:** These prints were produced on thin pieces of paper that were coated with albumen and silver nitrate. They were usually mounted on cardboard. Albumen prints were used between 1858 and 1910 and were the type of photographs found in cartes-de-visite and cabinet cards.

✔ **Stereographic cards:** Stereographic cards were paired photographs that rendered a three-dimensional effect when used with a stereographic viewer. They were prevalent from 1850 to 1925.

✔ **Platinum prints:** Platinum prints have a matte surface that appears embedded in the paper. The images were often highlighted with artistic chalk. They were produced mainly between 1880 and 1930.

✔ **Glass-plate negatives:** Glass-plate negatives were used between 1848 and 1930. They were made from light-sensitive silver bromide immersed in gelatin.

When you deal with photographs, keep in mind that too much light or humidity can easily destroy them. Oil from your fingerprints isn't the greatest for old photos either, so you might want to keep a pair of light gloves in your research bag to use when handling these treasures. For more information on preserving photographs, see the section "Preserving Your Family Treasures," later in this chapter. Also, some online resources can help you identify types of pictures. See the City Gallery Web site at `www.city-gallery.com/learning` for information about nineteenth-century photography, and visit the Everything You Ever Wanted to Know About Your Family Photographs page at `http://genealogy.about.com/library/authors/ucmishkin1a.htm` for descriptions of several types of photographs.

Organization, Genealogy Style

We bet that you've seen the stereotypical family researcher — the type who walks into the library while trying to balance a stack of binders and loose-leafed papers. This could be you! There's no way to get around it: If you get into genealogy, you're going to collect tons of paper and photographs.

Until now, you've probably used any means possible to take notes while talking with relatives about your ancestors or looking up information in the local library — from notebook paper to receipts you have in your pocket or purse to stick-on notes and paper napkins. You may have used your camera to take pictures of headstones in the cemetery where some of your ancestors are buried or of the old family homestead that's now abandoned and barely standing. And you've probably collected some original source documents, possibly the certified copy of your mother's birth certificate that Grandma gave you, the family Bible from Aunt Lola, and the old photograph of your great-great-grandfather as a child that you found while digging through the attic. Now what are you supposed to do with all these treasures? Organize, organize, organize!

Even if you decide to use genealogical software to track your research progress, you're always going to have paper records and photographs you want to keep. The following sections offer some tips to help you become well organized (genealogically, anyway).

Establishing good organizational skills

You probably already discovered that taking notes on little scraps of paper works adequately at first, but the more notes you take, the harder it becomes to sort through them and make sense of the information on each. To avoid this situation, establish some good note-taking and organizational skills early by being consistent in how you take notes. Write the date, time, and place that you do your research, along with the names of the family members you interview, at the top of each page of your notes. Then place those notes in a binder, perhaps organized by family group. This information can help you later when you return to your notes to look for a particular fact or when you try to make sense of conflicting information.

You want to be as detailed as possible when taking notes on particular events, persons, books, and so on. Just like you were taught in grade school, you should include the who, what, where, when, why, and how. And most importantly, always cite the source of your information, keeping the following guidelines in mind:

- **Person:** If your source is a person, include that person's full name and relationship to you (if any), the information, the contact data (address, phone number, e-mail address), and the date and time that you and this person communicated. As the individual is recounting memories and family stories, be sure to ask his or her age at the time of any events that are being recalled. Also be sure to get the person's age at the time of your interview or communication. This information might help you approximate time frames when looking for documentation to support the story.

- **Record:** Include the name or type of record, record number, book number (if applicable), name and location of the record-keeping agency, and any other pertinent information.

- **Book or magazine:** Include all bibliographic information, including the name of the publication, volume number, date of issue, publisher's name, page number of the applicable article, and the repository where you found the work.

- **Microfilm or microfiche:** Include all bibliographic information, and note the document media (microfilm roll, microfiche), document number, and repository name.

- **Web site or other Internet resource:** Include the name of the copyright holder for the site (or the name of the site's creator and maintainer if no copyright notice appears on it), the name of the site, the address or Uniform Resource Locator (URL) of the site, the date the information was posted or copyrighted, and any notes with traditional contact information for the site's copyright holder or creator.

It's a good idea to print or save a copy of a Web page using a screen-capture utility such as Snagit (www.techsmith.com/screen-capture.asp) or HyperSnap (www.hyperionics.com). A screen-capture utility is software that enables you to take a picture of the computer screen and then use that screen capture as a graphic in a document, a file, or a Web page. You can attach screen-captures as images in your genealogical database or place the paper copies in your research files. Some Web sites have a tendency to disappear over time, so it's best to get documentation of the site while it exists.

You have many ways to cite sources, and even we have a difficult time remembering how to cite each different type of source consistently. Fortunately, Elizabeth Shown Mills has come to the rescue. If you need help citing almost any kind of source, check out *Evidence Explained: Citing History Sources from Artifacts to Cyberspace,* published by the Genealogical Publishing Company (www.genealogical.com). Another handy resource is the Chicago Manual of Style Online at www.chicagomanualofstyle.org/home.html.

Evernote: An alternative to keeping a binder filing system

In the last section, we mention taking notes on paper and placing them in a binder. Although that system works, you have a more efficient way to keep your notes and make them accessible anytime you need them. We like to use a product called Evernote (www.evernote.com), which is a software filing cabinet. You can create a note, attach a picture, scan a document, and clip a Web page and store it in the software, as shown in Figure 2-1. The software then uploads the note to a server, making the information available on any device with the Evernote software. The software supports Windows and Mac computers, iPad, iPhone, iPod touch, Android, BlackBerry, Palm Pre, Palm Pixi, and Windows Mobile phones.

After content is placed into a "notebook" — the virtual filing cabinet — you can further organize it by placing one or more tags on each note. The tags can be used to easily find all content associated with a particular person, place, event, or any other category that you care to make. The content is fully searchable through tags or the full text of the notes.

Also, if you create a note from a mobile device, Evernote can capture your location and add that as an attribute to your note. So, if you are making notes in a cemetery and your phone supports a global positioning system reading, the latitude and longitude of your current position can be attached to your note.

Figure 2-1:
A will transcription clipped from the Web and housed in Evernote.

Understanding genealogical charts and forms

By the time you have information on a few hundred people, it will become nearly impossible to keep all those ancestors straight. Family historians use charts and forms to organize research and make findings easier to understand and share. Allow us to give you a brief lowdown on five of the most common types of genealogical charts and reports:

- ✔ **Pedigree chart**: Flowing horizontally across a page, the *pedigree* chart identifies a primary person by that person's name, date and place of birth, date and place of marriage, and date and place of death. The chart uses lines to show the relationship to the person's father and mother, then each of their parents, then their parents, and so on until the chart runs off the page. See Figure 2-2 for an example of a pedigree chart.

- ✔ **Descendant chart:** A *descendant* chart contains information about an ancestor and spouse (or spouses if more than one exists), their children and their spouses, grandchildren and spouses, and so on down the family line. The chart typically flows vertically on a page and resembles a business organizational chart. To see what a descendant chart looks like, take a gander at Figure 2-3.

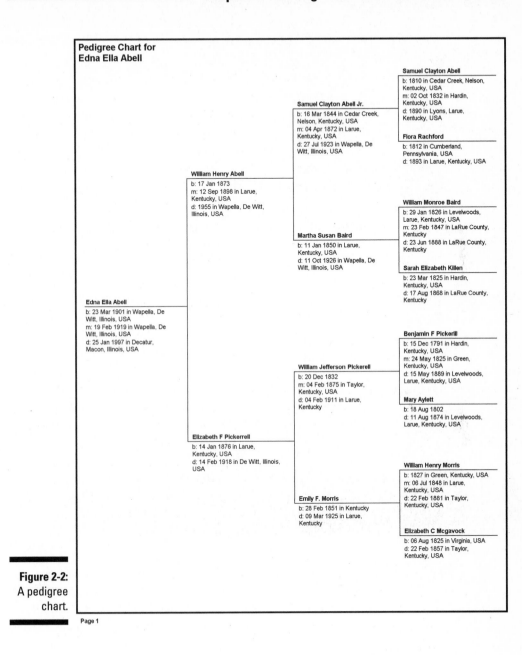

Pedigree Chart for Edna Ella Abell

Samuel Clayton Abell
b: 1810 in Cedar Creek, Nelson, Kentucky, USA
m: 02 Oct 1832 in Hardin, Kentucky, USA
d: 1890 in Lyons, Larue, Kentucky, USA

Samuel Clayton Abell Jr.
b: 16 Mar 1844 in Cedar Creek, Nelson, Kentucky, USA
m: 04 Apr 1872 in Larue, Kentucky, USA
d: 27 Jul 1923 in Wapella, De Witt, Illinois, USA

Flora Rachford
b: 1812 in Cumberland, Pennsylvania, USA
d: 1893 in Larue, Kentucky, USA

William Henry Abell
b: 17 Jan 1873
m: 12 Sep 1898 in Larue, Kentucky, USA
d: 1955 in Wapella, De Witt, Illinois, USA

William Monroe Baird
b: 29 Jan 1826 in Levelwoods, Larue, Kentucky, USA
m: 23 Feb 1847 in LaRue County, Kentucky
d: 23 Jun 1888 in LaRue County, Kentucky

Martha Susan Baird
b: 11 Jan 1850 in Larue, Kentucky, USA
d: 11 Oct 1926 in Wapella, De Witt, Illinois, USA

Sarah Elizabeth Killen
b: 23 Mar 1825 in Hardin, Kentucky, USA
d: 17 Aug 1868 in LaRue County, Kentucky

Edna Ella Abell
b: 23 Mar 1901 in Wapella, De Witt, Illinois, USA
m: 19 Feb 1919 in Wapella, De Witt, Illinois, USA
d: 25 Jan 1997 in Decatur, Macon, Illinois, USA

Benjamin F Pickerill
b: 15 Dec 1791 in Hardin, Kentucky, USA
m: 24 May 1825 in Green, Kentucky, USA
d: 15 May 1889 in Levelwoods, Larue, Kentucky, USA

William Jefferson Pickerell
b: 20 Dec 1832
m: 04 Feb 1875 in Taylor, Kentucky, USA
d: 04 Feb 1911 in Larue, Kentucky

Mary Aylett
b: 18 Aug 1802
d: 11 Aug 1874 in Levelwoods, Larue, Kentucky, USA

Elizabeth F Pickerrell
b: 14 Jan 1876 in Larue, Kentucky, USA
d: 14 Feb 1918 in De Witt, Illinois, USA

William Henry Morris
b: 1827 in Green, Kentucky, USA
m: 06 Jul 1848 in Larue, Kentucky, USA
d: 22 Feb 1881 in Taylor, Kentucky, USA

Emily F. Morris
b: 28 Feb 1851 in Kentucky
d: 09 Mar 1925 in Larue, Kentucky

Elizabeth C Mcgavock
b: 06 Aug 1825 in Virginia, USA
d: 22 Feb 1857 in Taylor, Kentucky, USA

Page 1

Figure 2-2:
A pedigree chart.

Figure 2-3:
A
descendant
chart.

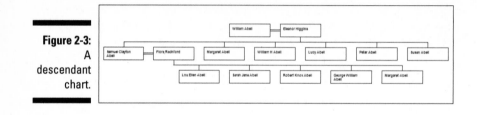

✔ **Outline report:** A family *outline* is a list of the descendants of a particular ancestor. The first numbered line contains the name (and sometimes the years for birth and death) of the primary ancestor. The next line shows a spouse, followed by the next numbered line, which contains the name of the ancestor and spouse's child. If that child is married and has children, the child's spouse follows, as do the names and information on each of that child and spouse's children. Each new generation within the family is indented from the last and is assigned the next number. For example, the focal ancestor is given the number 1; his or her children are all given the number 2 (for the second generation); his or her grandchildren are all given the number 3 (third generation); and so forth. After the first child's entire family is complete, the outline report lists the next child and his or her family in the same manner. See Figure 2-4 for an example of an outline report.

✔ **Family group sheet:** A *family group sheet* is a summary of vital information about a particular family. At the top of the page, it shows the husband, followed by the wife, and then any children of the couple, as well as biographical information (such as dates and places of birth, marriage, and death). In some contemporary family group sheets, you can set the titles for the two main people if the terms *Husband* and *Wife* are not applicable. However, information on the children's spouses and children isn't included on this family group sheet. That information would appear on a separate family group sheet for the child's family in which the child is listed as either the husband or wife. You can get a better understanding of family group sheets from Figure 2-5.

✔ **Kinship report:** A *kinship report* is a list of family members and how they relate directly to one particular ancestor. This report includes the name of the family member, the person's relationship to the primary ancestor, and the civil and canon codes reflecting the degree of relationship between the two people. See Figure 2-6 for an example of a kinship report.

Civil and *canon codes* explain the bloodline relationship in legal terms — in other words, they identify how many *degrees of separation* (or steps) are between two people who are related by blood. Civil law counts each step between two relatives as a degree, so two people who are first cousins have a degree of separation equal to four, which is the total of two steps between one cousin and the common grandparent and two steps between the other cousin and the common grandparent. Canon law counts only the number of steps from the nearest common ancestor of both relatives, so the degree of separation between two first cousins is two. Two steps separate the grandparent from each of the cousins.

Outline Descendant Report for Samuel Abell

..... 1 Samuel Abell b: 1710 in Saint Marys, Maryland, USA, d: 01 Jun 1795 in Rolling Fork, Washington, Kentucky, USA

..... + Susanna Spalding b: 1730 in Leonardstown, Saint Marys, Maryland, USA, d: 1795 in Saint Marys, Maryland, USA

.... 2 Peter Abell b: 1740 in MD, St Mary, Maryland, USA, d: 1785 in Rogers Station, Nelson, Kentucky, USA

.... + Lucy Carman b: 1745 in Saint Marys, Maryland, USA, m: 25 Oct 1769 in Saint Marys, Maryland, USA, d: 22 Jul 1814 in Wilson Creek, Nelson, Kentucky, USA

.... 3 William Abell b: 1770 in Leonardtown, Saint Marys, Maryland, USA, d: 03 Nov 1838 in Cedar Creek, Nelson, Kentucky, USA

.... + Eleanor Higgins b: 1775 in Saint Marys, Maryland, USA, m: 25 Jan 1793 in Nelson, Kentucky, USA, d: 1845 in Cedar Creek, Nelson, Kentucky, USA

.... 4 Samuel Clayton Abell b: 1810 in Cedar Creek, Nelson, Kentucky, USA, d: 1890 in Lyons, Larue, Kentucky, USA

.... + Flora Rachford b: 1812 in Cumberland, Pennsylvania, USA, m: 02 Oct 1832 in Hardin, Kentucky, USA, d: 1893 in Larue, Kentucky, USA

.... 5 Samuel Clayton Abell Jr. b: 16 Mar 1844 in Cedar Creek, Nelson, Kentucky, USA, d: 27 Jul 1923 in Wapella, De Witt, Illinois, USA

.... + Martha Susan Baird b: 11 Jan 1850 in Larue, Kentucky, USA, m: 04 Apr 1872 in Larue, Kentucky, USA, d: 11 Oct 1926 in Wapella, De Witt, Illinois, USA

.... 6 William Henry Abell b: 17 Jan 1873, d: 1955 in Wapella, De Witt, Illinois, USA

.... + Elizabeth F Pickerrell b: 14 Jan 1876 in Larue, Kentucky, USA, m: 12 Sep 1898 in Larue, Kentucky, USA, d: 14 Feb 1918 in De Witt, Illinois, USA

.... 7 Leona Pearl Abell b: 29 Jun 1899, d: 19 Nov 1975 in Decatur, Macon, Illinois, USA

.... + Beauford Helm b: 17 Dec 1898, m: 25 Nov 1922 in Decatur, Illinois, USA, d: Jul 1972 in Tucson, Pima, Arizona, United States of America

.... 8 Donald L Helm b: 07 Jul 1924, d: 26 Dec 1999 in Saint Anne, Kankakee, Illinois, United States of America

.... 9 Living Helm

.... 9 Living Helm

.... 8 Beauford Helm b: 09 Oct 1923, d: 25 Oct 2001 in Decatur, Macon, Illinois, United States of America

.... + Ferne

.... 9 Living Helm

.... 9 Living Helm

.... 9 Living Helm

.... 9 Jeanna Helm

.... 8 Loretta I Helm b: 1928

.... + Living Michael b:, m:

.... 9 Living Michael b:

.... 9 Living Michael b:

.... 9 Living Michael b:

.... 9 Living Michael b:

.... 9 Living Michael b:

.... 8 Living Helm

.... 8 Living Helm

.... 8 Living Helm

.... 8 Living Helm

.... 7 Edna Ella Abell b: 23 Mar 1901 in Wapella, De Witt, Illinois, USA, d: 25 Jan 1997 in Decatur, Macon, Illinois, USA

Figure 2-4:
An outline report.

Family Group Sheet for Peter Abell

Husband:	Peter Abell
Birth:	1740 in MD, St Mary, Maryland, USA
Death:	1785 in Rogers Station, Nelson, Kentucky, USA
Marriage:	25 Oct 1769 in Saint Marys, Maryland, USA
Father:	Samuel Abell
Mother:	Susanna Spalding

Wife:	Lucy Carman
Birth:	1745 in Saint Marys, Maryland, USA
Death:	22 Jul 1814 in Wilson Creek, Nelson, Kentucky, USA
Father:	
Mother:	

Children:

1 M	Name:	William Abell
	Birth:	1770 in Leonardtown, Saint Marys, Maryland, USA
	Death:	03 Nov 1838 in Cedar Creek, Nelson, Kentucky, USA
	Marriage:	25 Jan 1793 in Nelson, Kentucky, USA
	Spouse:	Eleanor Higgins

2 M	Name:	Samuel Abell
	Birth:	11 Feb 1783 in Saint Marys, Maryland, USA
	Death:	22 Mar 1840 in Hardin, Kentucky, USA

3 M	Name:	Ignatius Abell
	Birth:	1775 in Leonardtown, Saint Marys, Maryland, USA
	Death:	16 Aug 1840 in Harrison, Indiana, USA

4 F	Name:	Sarah Sally Abell
	Birth:	25 Oct 1769 in Leonardstown, Saint Marys, Maryland, USA
	Death:	1800 in Nelson, Kentucky, USA

5 F	Name:	Mary Polly Abell
	Birth:	29 Jan 1771 in Leonardtown, Saint Marys, Maryland, USA
	Death:	1850 in Newburg, Phelps, Missouri, USA

6 F	Name:	Nancy Abell
	Birth:	1785 in Nelson, Kentucky, USA
	Death:	Nelson, Kentucky, USA

7 F	Name:	Lucy Abell
	Birth:	25 Oct 1769 in Saint Marys, Maryland, USA
	Death:	Milton, Pike, Illinois, USA

8 F	Name:	Elizabeth Abell
	Birth:	1784

Notes

Figure 2-5:
A family
group sheet.

Kinship Report for Peter Abell

Name:	Birth Date:	Relationship:
Mary	1698	Wife of 4th great grandfather of wife of 2nd great grandson
Abel, Margaret L	Abt. 1908	Wife of 3rd great grandson
Abell, Curtis Ray	08 Aug 1954	4th great grandson
Abell, Cuthbert	1720	Uncle
Abell, Dennis Edward	10 Aug 1922	3rd great grandson
Abell, Edmund	1760	Brother
Abell, Edna Ella	23 Mar 1901	3rd great granddaughter
Abell, Edward	1715	Uncle
Abell, Elizabeth	1750	Sister
Abell, Elizabeth	1784	Daughter
Abell, Elsie Fay	1904	3rd great granddaughter
Abell, Elvin Ray	18 Apr 1905	3rd great grandson
Abell, Enoch	1714	Uncle
Abell, Eugene Coleman	19 May 1913	3rd great grandson
Abell, George William	1848	Great grandson
Abell, Harland Vinson	10 May 1914	3rd great grandson
Abell, Henrietta	1786	Sister
Abell, Ignatius	1741	Brother
Abell, Ignatius	1775	Son
Abell, James Clayton	09 Feb 1916	3rd great grandson
Abell, James M	Abt. 1879	2nd great grandson
Abell, John	1680	Grand uncle
Abell, John	1680	Paternal grandfather
Abell, John	1711	Uncle
Abell, John Barton	1755	Brother
Abell, Joshua	1761	Brother
Abell, Leona Pearl	29 Jun 1899	3rd great granddaughter
Abell, Lillian May	17 May 1905	3rd great granddaughter
Abell, Living		4th great grandchild
Abell, Living		4th great grandchild
Abell, Living		4th great grandchild
Abell, Living		4th great grandchild
Abell, Living		4th great grandchild
Abell, Living		4th great grandchild
Abell, Lou Ellen	1842	Great granddaughter
Abell, Lucy	25 Oct 1769	Daughter
Abell, Lucy	1796	Granddaughter
Abell, Margaret	1797	Granddaughter
Abell, Margaret	1840	Great granddaughter

Page 1 of 19   Tuesday, August 31, 2010 10:17:59 PM

Figure 2-6:
A kinship
report.

If you want to take a look at various genealogical charts and forms, or print some free copies to use when researching, many are available online at sites such as Genealogy Today at `www.genealogytoday.com/genealogy/enoch/forms.html`. Additionally, Chapter 3 explains how to print your own genealogical charts and reports using family history software.

The sooner you become familiar with the most common types of charts and understand how to read them, the sooner you can interpret a lot of the information you receive from other genealogists.

Assigning unique numbers to family members

If you have ancestors who share the same name, or if you've collected a lot of information on several generations of ancestors, you may have trouble distinguishing one person from another. For example, Matthew has an ancestor Samuel Abell, who had a son and two grandsons also named Samuel Abell. To avoid confusion and the problems that can arise from it, you may want to use a commonly accepted numbering system to keep everyone straight. Now genealogical numbering systems can be a bit confusing (and talking about them can be a little boring), but we'll do our best to make it as simple as possible and to give you a few examples to make it a little clearer.

The ahnentafel (Sosa-Stradonitz) system

One well-known numbering system is called *ahnentafel,* which means *ancestor* (*ahnen*) and *table* (*tafel*) in German. You may also hear the ahnentafel system referred to as the *Sosa-Stradonitz* system (the names get easier, trust us) of numbering, because it was first used by a Spanish genealogist named Jerome de Sosa in 1676, and was popularized in 1896 by Stephan Kekule von Stradonitz.

The ahnentafel system is a method of numbering that shows a mathematical relationship between parents and children. Ahnentafel numbering follows this pattern:

1. **The child is assigned a particular number: y**

   Of course, we recognize that y isn't really a number — it's a letter. In our mathematical (that is, algebraic) example, y represents a unique number for that particular person.

2. **The father of that child is assigned the number that is double the child's number: $2y$**

3. **The mother of that child is assigned a number that is double the child's number plus one: $2y + 1$**

4. **The father's father is assigned a number that is double the father's number: 2(2y)**

   The father's mother is assigned the number that is double the father's number plus one: 2(2y) + 1

5. **The mother's father is assigned a number that is double the mother's number: 2(2y + 1)**

   The mother's mother is assigned a number that is double the mother's number plus one: 2(2y + 1) + 1

6. **Continue this pattern through the line of ancestors.**

The mathematical relationship works the same way going forward through the generations — a child's number is one-half the father's number and one-half (minus any remainder) the mother's number.

In a list form, the ahnentafel for April's grandfather looks like the following (see Figure 2-7 for the chart):

1 John Duff Sanders, b. 10 Mar 1914 in Benjamin, Knox Co., TX; d. 15 Mar 1996 in Seymour, Baylor Co., TX; ma. 24 Dec 1939 in Sherman, Grayson Co., TX.

2 John Sanders, b. 19 Oct 1872 in Cotton Plant, Tippah Co., MS; d. 2 Mar 1962 in Morton, Cochran Co., TX; ma. 28 Sep 1902 in Boxelder, Red River Co., TX.

3 Nannie Elizabeth Clifton, b. 1 Apr 1878 in Okolona, MS; d. 27 Apr 1936 in Morton, Cochran Co., TX.

4 Harris Sanders, b. 27 Mar 1824 in Montgomery Co., NC; d. 21 Feb 1917 in Tippah Co., MS; ma. 26 June 1853.

5 Emeline Crump, b. 20 Oct 1836; d. 21 Feb 1920 in Tippah Co., MS.

6 William Clifton, b. 5 Mar 1845 in SC; d. 9 Feb 1923 in Boxelder, Red River Co., TX; ma. 5 Nov 1872 in Birmingham, AL.

7 Martha Jane Looney, b. 8 Mar 1844; d. Boxelder, Red River Co., TX.

John Duff Sanders is number one because he's the base individual for the ahnentafel. His father (John Sanders) is number two (because $2 \times 1 = 2$), and his mother (Nannie Elizabeth Clifton) is number three [$(2 \times 1) + 1 = 3$]. His father's father (Harris Sanders) is four ($2 \times 2 = 4$), and his father's mother (Emeline Crump) is five [$(2 \times 2) + 1 = 5$]. John Sanders's number (2) is one-half his father's number ($4 \div 2 = 2$), or one-half minus any remainder of his mother's number ($5 \div 2 = 2.5$; 2.5 minus remainder of .5 = 2) — well, you get the idea.

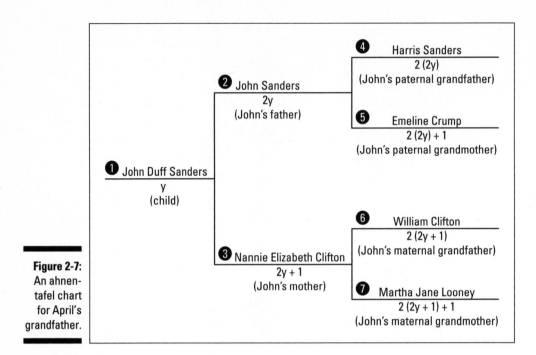

Figure 2-7:
An ahnen-
tafel chart
for April's
grandfather.

As you can imagine, after a while, you begin to tire from all these calculations —
especially if you do them for ten or more generations of people. So, if your genealogy software supports ahnentafel reports, we highly recommend that you run
one — saving you a lot of time and trouble.

The tiny tafel system

Some people confuse ahnentafel with *tiny tafel,* which is a compact way to
show the relationships within a family database. Tiny tafel provides only the
Soundex code for a surname, and the dates and locations where that surname may be found according to the database. (For more on Soundex codes
and how they work, check out Chapter 5.) Computer programs sometimes
use tiny tafels to match the same individual in two different genealogy databases. The following example shows a tiny tafel:

C413	1845	1936	Clifton\South Carolina/Cochran Co. TX
C651	1836	1920	Crump/Mississippi
L500	1844		Looney/Red River Co. TX
S536	1824	1996	Sanders\Montgomery Co. NC/Baylor Co. TX

The Henry system

The *Henry* system is another well-known numbering system. This system
assigns a particular number to the *progenitor,* or the ancestor farthest back
(that you know about) in your family line. Then each of the progenitor's

children is assigned a number in a sequence that starts with his number and adds the numbers 1, 2, 3, and so forth through 9. (If the progenitor had more than nine children, the tenth child is assigned an X, the eleventh an A, the twelfth a B, and so on.) Then the children's children are assigned the parent's number plus a number in sequence (again 1 through 9, then X, A, B, and so on). For example, if progenitor number one (1) had 12 children, his children would be 11, 12, 13, . . . 1X, 1A, and 1B. The eleventh child's children would be assigned the numbers 1A1, 1A2, 1A3, and so on.

For example, suppose that one of your ancestors, John Jones, had 12 children. The names of these children were Joseph, Ann, Mary, Jacob, Arthur, Charles, James, Maria, Esther, Harriett, Thomas, and Sophia. Joseph had one child named Gertrude, and Thomas had three children named Lawrence, Joshua, and David. Under the standard Henry system, the children's children are numbered like this:

1   John Jones

    11   Joseph Jones

        111   Gertrude Jones

    12   Ann Jones

    13   Mary Jones

    14   Jacob Jones

    15   Arthur Jones

    16   Charles Jones

    17   James Jones

    18   Maria Jones

    19   Esther Jones

    1X   Harriett Jones

    1A   Thomas Jones

        1A1   Lawrence Jones

        1A2   Joshua Jones

        1A3   David Jones

    1B   Sophia Jones

By no means are these systems the only genealogical numbering systems in existence. Ahnentafel and Henry are just two of the easier systems to learn. Several others have been designed to display genealogies in book form, such as the Register system (based on the style of the New England Historical and Genealogical Register) and the National Genealogical Society Quarterly system. If you're curious about some of these systems, take a look at the Numbering Systems in Genealogy page at www.saintclair.org/numbers.

There you can find descriptions of each major numbering system and variations of these systems.

If you decide to use a numbering system, you can place the corresponding unique number for each individual in the file that you set up for that person in your paper record-keeping system, as well as in your genealogical software.

Making copies of source documents

You don't want to carry original records with you when you're out and about researching. You have probably gone to a lot of trouble to collect the records and the chances of misplacing or forgetting a document are too great. You have a few options:

- ✔ You can scan the documents and store them on your laptop or notebook computer, or enter the information into a database. Then you can take your laptop with you. (We talk more about using computers in Chapter 3.)

- ✔ You can copy data from your desktop computer to a personal digital assistant (PDA) or a *smartphone* (a mobile phone that has data capabilities).

- ✔ You can copy data from your computer to a CD, DVD, or flash drive (see Chapters 3 and 17 for more information about flash drives). The catch here is that your research destination needs to have a computer that you can use to access the information from your CD, DVD, or flash drive.

- ✔ You can print your data from your computer or make photocopies of the documents that you must have with you for your research.

- ✔ You can upload your information to a site that stores information on servers that are accessible through Web browsers, such as MobileMe (www.mobileme.com).

After you determine which of these solutions works best for you, you can use your notes and copies out in the field, leaving your original documents in the safest place you can think of that is available to you — a lockbox, a fireproof file cabinet or safe, or a safety-deposit box.

Deciding on a storage method

How are you going to store all that information? A filing system is in order! You can set up a good filing system in many ways, and no one system is right or wrong. Just use one that's comfortable for you.

If you're at a loss as to how to start a system, here's one we like: We prefer to have both electronic and physical components to our filing system. To establish an electronic system, enter your ancestors' names into your database. Most genealogical programs enable you to enter numbers for each individual. Use the numbers that you create in the electronic system on file folders for paper documents that you collect on each individual. Although we like to scan all our paper documents, sometimes we get behind, so we set up temporary folders in which we can store the documents until we can scan them. After we scan the documents, we transfer them to permanent folders that we keep in a fireproof container. You may consider saving your scanned images to a notebook computer's hard drive, an external hard drive, or a writable CD-ROM/DVD-ROM so that you can easily transport the images when you go on research trips.

Make backup copies of all your electronic documents as a precaution and store these backups in a location that is off-site from where the originals are stored.

Preserving Your Family Treasures

Time is going to take its toll on every artifact in your possession — whether it is a photograph or an original document. The longer you want your records and pictures to last, the better care you need to take of them now. In this section, we discuss some tips for preserving your family treasures so that you can pass them down to future generations in the best possible shape.

Storing vital records under the right conditions

Place birth certificates, marriage licenses, and other records between sheets of acid-free paper in albums. Keep these albums in a dark, dry, and temperature-consistent place: ideally, a place that is 65 to 70 degrees Fahrenheit year-round, with a relative humidity of less than 50 percent. You may consider placing these albums in a steel file cabinet (but make sure it's rust-free). Also, try to avoid using ink, staples, paper clips, glue, and tape around your documents (unless you use archival products designed for document repair).

For your precious documents (original birth certificates and family papers), rent a safety-deposit box or find another form of secure off-site storage. One of the best ways to ensure the success of your preservation effort is to make electronic copies of your documents using a scanner, and then keep disk backups at a fire-safe, off-site location (again, a safety-deposit box is a good choice).

Protecting your photographs

Fight the urge to put all your photos of every ancestor on display because light can damage them over time. A better option is to scan the photographs and make copies or printouts to hang on the wall. Keep your most-prized pictures in a dark, dry, and temperature-consistent place. If you use a photo album for storage, make sure that it has acid-free paper or chemically safe plastic pockets, and that you affix the pictures to the pages using a safe adhesive. Other storage options include acid-free storage boxes and steel file cabinets. Store the photographs in a place that stays around 65 to 70 degrees Fahrenheit year-round, with a relative humidity of less than 50 percent. Avoid prolonged exposure of photographs to direct sunlight and fluorescent lights. And, by all means, have negatives made of those rare family photos and store them in clearly marked, acid-free envelopes (the kind without gumming or glue).

You can preserve photographs a couple of other ways. First, you can convert photographs from an earlier time to a newer and safer kind of film. A local photograph shop that specializes in preservation can do this for you. Because color photographs fade more quickly than their black-and-white counterparts, you may want to make black-and-white negatives of your color photographs. Also, as with documents, you can always preserve your photographs electronically by scanning them into your computer or by having a photo CD made by your photographic developer.

Of course, you need to store digital photos on a computer or on the camera's memory card. You should still remember to make backup copies and then store the media in a recommended manner. For more on digital media, see Chapter 3.

An electronic version of an old photograph isn't a real substitute for an original. Don't throw away the photos you scan (but you already knew that).

Here are a few Web sites that provide more detailed tips on preserving your family treasures:

- ✔ **Just Black and White's Tips for Preserving Your Photographs and Documents,** by David Mishkin: justblackandwhite.com/tip.htm

- ✔ **Photo Heritage: Guidelines for Preserving Your Photographic Heritage,** by Ralph McNight: http://photoheritage.net/preserving.php

- ✔ **Document and Photo Preservation FAQ,** by Linda Beyea: http://loricase.com/faq.html

And when you're looking for some of the chemically safe archival materials that we've described here (such as albums, paper, boxes, and adhesives), head on over to

      ✔ **Archival Products** at www.archival.com

      ✔ **Light Impressions** at www.lightimpressionsdirect.com/servlet/
      OnlineShopping

Even though you want to preserve everything to the best of your ability, don't be afraid to pull out your albums to show visiting relatives and friends. On the other hand, don't be embarrassed to ask these guests to use caution when looking through your albums. Depending on the age and rarity of some of your documents, you may even want to ask guests to wear latex gloves when handling the albums so that the oil from their hands doesn't get on your treasures. Upon realizing how important these treasures are to you, most guests won't mind using caution.

Visiting Libraries, Archives, and Historical Societies

In Chapter 1, we discuss getting information from living relatives. But your kinfolk aren't the only people who can help you advance your research. You don't want to forget certain institutional-type resources.

Inevitably, a time will come when you need to visit public (and possibly private) libraries in the areas where your ancestor lived. Although local history sections are not generally targeted toward genealogists, the information you can find there is quite valuable. For example, public libraries often have city directories and phone books, past issues of newspapers (good for obituary hunting), and old map collections. Libraries may also have extensive collections of local history books that can give you a flavor of what life was like for your ancestor in that area. And some libraries do have genealogy sections with all sorts of goodies to help you locate records and discover interesting stories about your family. For a list of libraries with online catalogs, see The Library Index site at www.libdex.com.

Archives are another place to find good information. They exist at three levels (national, state, and local) and have different owners (public or private). Each archive varies — some may have a large collection of certain types of documents, whereas others may contain documents from a certain geographical area. To find archives, see the Repositories of Primary Sources page at www.uidaho.edu/special-collections/Other.Repositories.html.

A third place to find information is a historical society. Generally, historical societies have nice collections of maps, documents, and local history books pertaining to the area in which the society is located. They are repositories for collections of papers of people who lived in the community. Often, you can find references to your ancestors in these collections, especially if the person whose personal documents are in the collection wrote a letter or transacted some business with your ancestor. You can find links to historical societies on the Yahoo! site at `http://dir.yahoo.com/arts/humanities/history/organizations/historical_societies`.

Getting Involved with Genealogical Societies

At times, dealing with the many different record sets and methods of researching your family can be overwhelming. On such occasions, it's nice to be able to sit down with people who have similar experiences or more knowledge than you and discuss your research problems. One place that you can find such a group is your local genealogical society. Genealogical societies hold periodic meetings that focus on particular research methods. Some also have weekend seminars where they bring in genealogical lecturers to address topics of interest to their members.

If you have research needs in other areas of the country (or foreign countries for that matter), you might consider joining a society in that area. Although you do not live there, you can still use the resources of the society to find answers to your questions, and you can contribute to the distant organization more than you realize by sharing your findings and experiences. Most societies have people who are well versed in the records that pertain to the area where the society is located. These individuals can be a great resource as you go through the research process.

To find a genealogical society in the United States, check out the Federation of Genealogical Societies Society Hall at `www.familyhistory.com/societyhall/main.asp`.

A general search engine (such as Google or AltaVista) can help you find societies in other countries. In the search field, type the name of the location and the phrase "genealogical society."

We delve into genealogical societies a bit more and explore specific ways you can become active and benefit from them in Chapter 10.

Discovering Family History Centers

If you live in a smaller community, you may be surprised to discover that your hometown has a resource specifically for local genealogical research. Sponsored by the Church of Jesus Christ of Latter-day Saints (LDS), more

than 4,500 Family History Centers worldwide provide support for genealogical research. Microfilms that contain images of records are among the important resources found in Family History Centers.

You are not required to be a member of the LDS church to use a Family
History Center; the resources they contained are available to everyone. Keep
in mind that the workers at a Family History Center cannot research your
genealogy for you, although they're willing to point you in the right direction.
To find a Family History Center, use the FamilySearch search interface, which
you can find at `www.familysearch.org/eng/Library/FHC/frameset_`
`fhc.asp`.

Your local telephone directory will have the Family History Center listed, if
you have one in your area. However, the phone book probably will not list
the hours that the Family History Center is open (like the Web site does), so
it's a good idea to call ahead to determine when it's open.

Selecting a Person to Begin Your Search

Now that you've started collecting and organizing family documents that
can help you put together your overall family history, it's time to focus on
one particular person and start digging deeper through the many online
resources. Selecting a person sounds easy, doesn't it? Just choose your
great-great-grandfather's name, and you're off to the races. But what if your
great-great-grandfather's name was John Smith? You may encounter millions
of sites with information on John Smith — unless you know some facts about
the John Smith you're looking for, we can almost guarantee that you'll have a
frustrating time online.

Trying a unique name

The first time you research online, try to start with a person whose name is,
for lack of a better term, semi-unique. By this we mean a person with a name
that doesn't take up ten pages in your local phone book, but is still common
enough that you can find some information on it the first time you conduct
a search. If you're really brave, you can begin with someone with a common
surname such as Smith or Jones, but you have to do a lot more groundwork
up front so that you can easily determine whether any of the multiple findings relate to your ancestor. (For more on groundwork, return to the preceding sections in this chapter.)

Also, consider any variations in spelling that your ancestor's name may have.
Often, you can find more information on the mainstream spelling of his or her
surname than on one of its rarer variants. For example, if you research someone with the surname Helme, you may have better luck finding information

under the spellings *Helm* or *Helms*. If your family members immigrated to the United States in the last two centuries, they may have *Americanized* their surname. Americanizing a name was often done so that the name could be easily pronounced in English, or sometimes the surname was simply misspelled and subsequently adopted by the family.

To find various spellings of the surname, you may need to dig through some family records or look at a site such as Table of Common Surname Variations & Surname Misspellings (`www.ingeneas.com/alternate.html`).

Narrowing your starting point

If you aren't sure how popular a name is, try visiting a site such as Hamrick Software's surname distribution site (`www.hamrick.com/names`). At Hamrick's site, you can find the distribution of surnames in the United States based on the 1850 Census, 1880 Census, 1920 Census, and phone books from 1990 to the present. Here's what to do:

1. **Open your browser and go to Hamrick Software's surname distribution site (`www.hamrick.com/names`).**

   The Hamrick site appears with instructions and a form to use for searching.

2. **Type the surname you're researching in the Surname field on the search form.**

   For help choosing a surname, see the preceding section.

3. **Use the drop-down menu to select the year(s) for which you want to see the surname distribution.**

   You can choose 1850, 1880, 1920, 1990, or All Years.

4. **Click Display.**

   A color map displaying the distribution of your surname appears.

Figure 2-8 shows a distribution map for the surname Abell in 1990. According to the map, only 1 out of every 1,000 individuals uses this surname in two states. In the remaining states, the name is even rarer. This gives you a good indication that the surname Abell is semi-unique. In contrast, during the same year, the surname Smith was held by at least one 1 of every 300 individuals in each state.

Note: Looking at Figure 2-8, you may find it difficult to determine which two states have one 1 of 1,000 individuals using the surname Abell because the colors show up as black, white, or shades of gray in this book. If you visit Hamrick's site, the maps are displayed in color and are easier to read. (And just in case you're curious, the two states were Maryland and Kentucky.)

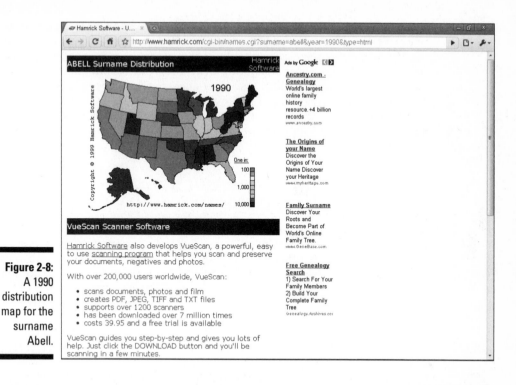

Figure 2-8:
A 1990 distribution map for the surname Abell.

VueScan Scanner Software

Hamrick Software also develops VueScan, a powerful, easy to use scanning program that helps you scan and preserve your documents, negatives and photos.

With over 200,000 users worldwide, VueScan:

- scans documents, photos and film
- creates PDF, JPEG, TIFF and TXT files
- supports over 1200 scanners
- has been downloaded over 7 million times
- costs 39.95 and a free trial is available

VueScan guides you step-by-step and gives you lots of help. Just click the DOWNLOAD button and you'll be scanning in a few minutes.

A good reason to check out distribution maps is that you can use them to identify potential geographic areas where you can look for your family during the years covered by the site. This is especially true for maps generated from 1850 and 1880 Census data. For example, we generated another map on the Abell surname for the 1880 Census. We discovered that the name appeared more frequently in six states than in the rest of the country. If we hit a wall and can't find additional information online about a particular individual or the surname, we know we can start looking at records in these states to find more clues about families with the name. We hope that by doing so, we'll find our branch.

Choosing someone you know about

In addition to choosing a person whom you're likely to have success researching, you want to use a person you already know something about. If you have a family line for which you know some basic information on your great-great-grandparents, use one of their names rather than a name for which you only know a few scattered details. The more details that you know about a person, the more successful your initial search is likely to be.

For example, Matthew used his great-grandfather William Abell because he knew more about that side of his family. His grandmother once mentioned that her father was born in LaRue County, Kentucky, in 1876. This gives him a point of reference for judging whether a site has any relevant information on his family. A site is relevant if it contains any information on Abells who were located in or near LaRue County, Kentucky, before or around the year 1876. Try to use the same technique with your ancestor. For more information on how to extract genealogical information from your family to use in your research, see the section "Getting the 4-1-1 from Your Kinfolk," earlier in this chapter.

Selecting a grandparent's name

Having trouble selecting a name? Why not try one of your grandparent's names? Using a grandparent's name can have several benefits. If you find some information on an individual but you aren't sure whether it's relevant to your family, you can check with relatives to see whether they know any additional information that can help you. This may also spur interest in gene-alogy in other family members who can then assist you with some of your research burden or produce some family documents that you never knew existed.

With a name in hand, you're ready to see how much information is currently available on the Internet about that individual. Because this is just one step in a long journey to discover your family history, keep in mind that you want to begin slowly. *Don't try to examine every resource right from the start.* You're more likely to become overloaded with information if you try to find too many resources too quickly. Your best approach is to begin searching a few sites until you get the hang of how to find information about your ancestors online. And keep in mind that you can always bookmark sites in your Web browser or record the URL in a spreadsheet so that you can easily return to them later, when you're ready for more in-depth researching.

Chapter 3

Equipping Yourself for Success

In This Chapter

▶ Getting your computer up to speed

▶ Determining which software is best for you

▶ Storing your findings in a genealogical database

*F*amily history research is one of the realms where technology can make your life a lot easier. Computers, add-on gadgets, and software can help you organize and quickly access the facts you've collected, prepare charts and summaries of the data about your family, and research for more information. This chapter looks at how to ensure that your computer is ready to help you, as well as how to find and use genealogical software to store and organize information about your ancestors. Additionally, we explore using a handy little gadget that acts as a mobile minicomputer: the smartphone.

Let's Talk Hardware: Is Your Computer Equipped?

After organizing your paper records and photographs, put your computer to work storing and manipulating your family history. We think that a computer may be your best friend when it comes to storing, organizing, and publishing your genealogical information.

Given that computers have become a household staple over the past decade, and the fact that a wide variety of computers are available today, it would be too difficult to tell you exactly what to look for in a base computer system. Instead, we're going to be presumptuous. We presume that you now have access to a computer (whether it's a desktop variety or a notebook) and that you can get online through an Internet service provider (ISP). If these presumptions are incorrect, we advise you to read these recommendations:

✔ cnet Reviews has articles on buying both desktops and laptops:

- Desktop Buying Guide at `http://reviews.cnet.com/desk top-computer-buying-guide`

- Laptop Buying Guide at `http://reviews.cnet.com/laptop-buying-guide`

✔ PC911 offers help in choosing an Internet service provider at `www.pcnineoneone.com/howto/isp1.html`.

As you grow more accustomed to using the information you store in your computer, you may want to consider adding other hardware and peripheral equipment to your system to enhance your genealogy research and the reports that you generate. You may want to start including electronic images of some of the photographs and original documents that you have in your paper filing system. You may think about adding audio of your grandmother reminiscing, or video of your grandchild greeting people at the family reunion. As you find additional documents, you may want to add images of them to your main database as well. So what kind of computer hardware or other equipment do you need to include images and other enhancements with your genealogical information?

You should consider several pieces of equipment as you prepare to enhance your genealogy with audio and video. These include writable CD-ROM or DVD drives, sound cards, video-capture boards, scanners, digital cameras, and external hard drives. As a general rule, before you purchase any equipment for your computer, be sure to check the requirements so that you can determine whether your computer can handle it. Few things are more frustrating than getting home and starting to hook up new hardware only to find out that the item is not compatible with your computer.

Writable CD-ROM or DVD drives

If you're looking to solve both the space needs for storing your files and mobility issues when you'd like to take your database on the road, consider getting a writable CD-ROM/DVD drive. With it, you can burn your own data CDs or DVDs — filling them with family photos (which typically take up a lot of space on your computer) or family files that you want to share at the family reunion — or some of both. Writable CD-ROM/DVD drives are available in internal and external varieties. A writable CD-ROM can hold about 650–700 megabytes of information, and DVDs can hold about 4.7 *gigabytes*. Blu-ray disc writers are also generally available. A double-layer Blu-ray disc can hold up to 50 gigabytes of data, and a single-layer unit can hold up to 25 gigabytes. A double-layer Blu-ray disc can also hold up to 9 hours of high-definition or 23 hours of standard-definition video.

Sound cards

A *sound card* is an internal device that is a standard feature on most computers today. It allows you to hear any audio that comes on software (particularly games) or audio files that you download from the Internet. In most cases, the card also enables you to record audio from your stereo, radio, video camera, or microphone — but you must have software that supports recordings. If your sound card is capable of recording and you have adequate software, you simply plug the sound source into the microphone jack (or the sound-in jack on the back of your computer), set your software to record, and go for it. After you make the recording, you can import it into your genealogical software if your software supports audio.

Is your smartphone the perfect gadget?

You already know a few good reasons to carry your cellular phone with you on research trips, right? It enables you to call relatives in the town you're visiting and to call ahead to ensure that a record exists in a location before traveling there. It also gives you reassurance that you can get help if something goes wrong while you're away from home.

But you have several other reasons why your cellular phone may be the most wonderful gadget to carry on genealogical jaunts. We're talking about the functionality of *smartphones,* cellular phones that can connect to the Internet and have more computing capability than a regular cellular phone. Two common smartphone brands are the iPhone and the BlackBerry. Smartphones also typically have built-in cameras (some with video capability), and many have built-in Global Positioning System (GPS) receivers.

The computing capability of a smartphone enables it to run applications, such as family tree software. Imagine being able to search or add to your genealogical database anywhere, anytime.

The GPS is a satellite system that receives and sends signals to a receiver, enabling the person controlling the receiver to determine his or her exact geographical coordinates. This is a handy system to use when recording the locations of family markers, such as burial plots and old homesteads. After all, natural markers (such as rocks and trees) and man-made markers (such as buildings) may move or disappear after years and years, but the latitude and longitude of a location remain the same. For more information about using GPS for genealogical purposes, check out Chapter 6.

Some smartphones also have built-in voice recorders and video cameras that allow you to easily record interviews with your family members or make notes about your research. Some phone models are now shipping with a front- and rear-facing camera that allows you to video chat with another researcher or create a video research log that you can use to document your research for future generations.

Video-capture devices

Similar to a sound card, a *video-capture device* enables you to grab images from your video camera or VCR. You can use moving images or still pictures, depending on the type of your video-capture device and the accompanying software. Video-capture devices aren't usually a standard feature on computers. They have varying system requirements depending on the manufacturer and the software that's included. Be sure that your computer system can handle a particular video-capture device and software before making your purchase.

Scanners

Scanners remain one of the most popular computer peripherals for genealogists. Everyone wants to include some family photos with his or her genealogy or preserve precious documents electronically. With the cost of scanners decreasing — and the availability of bundled software that allows you to use a scanner not only as a scanner but also as a fax machine and copier — adding a scanner to your equipment collection makes a lot of sense. It can make your genealogical research more colorful and more efficient without putting a big dent in your wallet.

A variety of scanners are available. The most common types are snapshot, sheet-fed, flatbed, and at the high end, microfilm scanners. Although they're harder to find, a few handheld scanners are still around. The system requirements for scanners vary greatly, so carefully read the packaging of any scanner you're considering. Additionally, each scanner requires software to make it work, so carefully check the software's system requirements and capabilities as well. Here's a quick rundown of the major types of scanners:

- ✓ **Photo scanners:** Useful for creating electronic images of photographs that measure 5 x 7 inches or smaller because they're designed to work primarily with that size of photograph. Photo scanners (also called snapshot scanners) are compact and come in external and internal varieties. You feed the photograph into the scanner, and then the scanner captures an image before sending the photo back out. Some photo scanners have a removable top that you can use as a handheld scanner when you want to capture images larger than 5 x 7 inches. One caution with photo scanners: You may not want to use these with old, fragile photographs because the scanner can damage the photograph as it's fed through the scanner.

- ✓ **Film scanners:** Check out a film scanner if you'd like to produce your own photographs directly from negatives. These compact scanners can capture images in color or black and white. You manually feed the negative into the scanner. Some film scanners have optional slide feeders.

✔ **Document scanners:** Document scanners are also sometimes called sheet-fed scanners because they are typically a little wider than a regular sheet of paper (8.5 inches across). They're still rather compact as far as scanners go, but all are external. You feed the photograph or document into the feeder on the scanner, and the scanner captures an image as the document goes through. As do some photo scanners, some document scanners have a removable top that you can use as a handheld scanner to capture images larger than 8.5 inches across. Use caution when using these scanners with fragile photographs.

✔ **Flatbed scanners:** These scanners used to be large and bulky but are now incredibly light and compact. You lift the top of the scanner and place your document or photograph on the bed, close the lid, and tell the scanner (through software) to capture the image. Flatbed scanners are somewhat safer for photographs and old paper records than are other types of scanners because photos are laid on the scanner's glass plate, not fed through the device.

✔ **Handheld scanners:** Although these are great for genealogy because of their flexibility and mobility, they're also more difficult to find. You can use them not only for scanning photographs and paper documents but also for scanning books. Handheld scanners (sometimes called pen or text scanners) are external and compact. They're the perfect size to carry with you when you go on-site for your genealogical research. You scan photos and other objects by holding the scanner and slowly moving it over the object while holding down a button.

✔ **Microfilm scanners:** In the past, microfilm scanners were so costly that they were used only by companies. Now, a few companies are producing microfilm scanners at a more modest cost. However, the cost of these scanners is still significantly more than flatbed or document scanners, so unless you have an extensive personal collection of microfilm, it's probably not worth the cost to invest in a microfilm scanner.

Digital cameras

Digital cameras have become an indispensable tool for genealogists as well as the general public. The ability to take all your photographs with a camera that downloads the images directly to your computer is very appealing. And the fact that you can easily attach digital photos to your genealogical database (or import them) is definitely exciting. Some digital cameras even come with a document setting, so you don't need both a scanner and a digital camera. This feature is extremely convenient when you're on the road researching your ancestors — you can use your digital camera to capture images from cemetery visits, pictures of long-lost cousins at reunions, and copies of rare documents at the local courthouse.

As with every other computer peripheral, if you're considering purchasing a digital camera, carefully read the package and software requirements to make sure that your computer system can support the equipment.

Webcams

While you can find a lot of resources online, it is a good idea to get help from other researchers and even share some of the research workload. Rather than talking for hours on the telephone to share your research, why not use a Webcam to see your fellow researcher. Some computers come with Webcams preinstalled. If yours did not, you can always purchase a Webcam separately. When you do have a Webcam, you can look at products such as Skype (www. skype.com/intl/en-us/home), which allows you to make free video and voice calls to other Skype users. As a bonus, Skype users can make conference calls, share their computer screen, and make inexpensive voice calls to landline and cellular phones.

Finding a Research Mate of the Software Variety

You may think you already have the perfect research mate — that special person who accompanies you to every library, cemetery, and courthouse as you research, right? Wrong! The research mate we're referring to comes on CD-ROMs or is downloadable from the Internet; you install it on your computer and then let it perform all sorts of amazing tasks for you.

Several software programs can store and manipulate your genealogical information. They all have some standard features in common. For instance, most serve as databases for family facts and stories, have reporting functions to generate predesigned charts and forms, and have export capabilities so that you can share your data with others. Each software program also has a few unique features (for example, the capability to take information out of the software and generate online reports at the click of a button) that make it stand out from the others. Here's a list of the features to look for when evaluating software packages:

- **How easy is the software to use?** Is it reasonably intuitive from a graphics standpoint so that you can see how and where to enter particular facts about an ancestor?

- **Does the software generate the reports you need?** For instance, if you're partial to family group sheets, does this software support them?

- **Does the software allow you to export and import a GEDCOM file?** *GEDCOM* is a file format that's widely used for genealogical research. For more info about GEDCOM, see the nearby sidebar "GEDCOM: The genealogist's standard."

✔ **How many names can this software hold?** Make sure that the software can hold an adequate number of names (and accompanying data) to accommodate all the ancestors about whom you have information.

GEDCOM: The genealogist's standard

As you probably have already discovered, genealogy is full of acronyms. One such acronym that you'll hear and see repeatedly is *GEDCOM (GEnealogical Data COMmunication).* GEDCOM is the standard for individuals and software manufacturers for exporting information to and importing information from genealogical databases. Simply put, GEDCOM is a file format intended to make data transferable between different software programs so that people can share their family information easily.

The Church of Jesus Christ of Latter-day Saints developed and introduced GEDCOM in 1987. The first two versions of GEDCOM were released for public discussion only and were not meant to serve as the standard. With the introduction of version 5.*x* and later, however, GEDCOM was accepted as the standard.

Having a standard for formatting files is beneficial to you as a researcher because you can share the information that you collect with others who are interested in some of (or all) your ancestors. It also enables you to import GEDCOM files from other researchers who have information about family lines and ancestors in whom you're interested. And you don't even have to use the same software as the other researchers! You can use Reunion for Macintosh, and someone with whom you want to share information can use Family Tree Maker; having GEDCOM as the standard in both software programs enables each of you to create and exchange GEDCOM files. Similarly, GEDCOM enables you to transfer data from your smartphone genealogical application to your computer at home.

To convert the data in your genealogical database to a GEDCOM file, follow the instructions provided in your software's manual or Help menu. You can create the GEDCOM file relatively easily; most software programs guide you through the process with a series of dialog boxes.

In addition to creating GEDCOM files to exchange one on one with other researchers, you can generate GEDCOM files to submit to larger cooperatives that make the data from many GEDCOM files available to thousands of researchers worldwide. You can also convert your GEDCOM file to HTML so that you can place the data directly on the Web for others to access. Current genealogical software packages make it a snap to convert your GEDCOM file to HTML. (For more information on generating Web pages, see Chapter 11.)

Although GEDCOM has been a reliable standard for quite a while, the implementation of it in some genealogical software products has been less than ideal. As a result, some genealogical software developers have created products that can import files made from one software package into software that uses a different file format — without the need to save the file to GEDCOM. One such product is GenBridge, which is part of the Family Tree SuperTools product from Wholly Genes Software (www.whollygenes.com/Merchant2/merchant.mvc?screen=FTST). Before purchasing a converter product, be sure to check the documentation that came with your genealogical software to ensure that your software doesn't already have the conversion capability built into it.

Keep in mind that your genealogy continues to grow over time.

✔ **Can your current computer system support this software?** If the requirements of the software cause your computer to crash every time you use it, you won't get very far in your genealogical research.

✔ **Does this software provide fields for citing your sources and keeping notes?** Including information about the sources you use to gather your data — with the actual facts, if possible — is a sound genealogical practice. Take a look at Chapter 11 for more information about the importance of citing sources and understanding how to do so.

Entering Information into RootsMagic Essentials

To help you get a better idea of how software can help you organize your records and research, and to help you figure out what features to look for in particular software packages, this section examines how to use RootsMagic, a popular genealogy software program.

You can download a free trial version of RootsMagic Essentials software and install it on your computer as follows:

1. **Open your Web browser and go to the RootsMagic site at** www.roots magic.com/Products.

   The Web site identifying RootsMagic products is displayed.

2. **Scroll down to the RootsMagic Essentials section and click the Free Download button.**

3. **Complete the information fields, including typing your name and your e-mail address. Enter your e-mail address again in the Verify Email field.**

4. **Select the check box if you want to receive e-mails from RootsMagic.**

5. **Click Download.**

   The instructions for downloading the product appear.

6. **Click the RootsMagic Essentials Installer link.**

   The software downloads to a directory on your computer. When the download is complete, the Welcome to RootsMagic Setup Wizard pops up.

7. **Click Next.**

   The license agreement appears.

8. **Read through the licensing agreement. If you agree to its terms, click the I Accept the Agreement option, and then click Next.**

   A window appears in which you can choose where to have the RootsMagic Essentials software stored on your computer.

9. **Identify where to store the software, and then click Next.**

   The Select Start Menu Folder field appears. This enables you to identify where to put shortcuts for the program. The default location is a folder called RootsMagic.

10. **If you want the shortcuts listed in RootsMagic, leave the default location in the field. If you prefer to have shortcuts in another folder, browse and select the folder or enter the location.**

11. **Click Next.**

    The Select Additional Tasks window opens. If you want to set up any additional tasks (such as creating a desktop icon for the program or downloading a gazetteer component), select the appropriate check box.

12. **Click Next.**

    The final information for the installation appears.

13. **Review the installation information and, if everything looks correct, click Install.**

    The software installs on your computer. When it is finished installing, the Completing the RootsMagic Setup Wizard box appears.

14. **If you want to open RootsMagic now, select the Launch RootsMagic check box and click the Finish button.**

    A window opens welcoming you to the software and asking you to identify which version of the product you are opening.

15. **Click the RootsMagic Essentials — Free Version link.**

Now that you have the RootsMagic Essential software installed on your computer, let's get down to the nitty-gritty and start entering data. When you open the application for the very first time, you'll get a RootsMagic News window containing links to various announcements and stories of interest to RootsMagic users. If you want to read any of these, you can click the links. If you don't want to see this News window every time you open RootsMagic, select the Do Not Show Me This Again check box and then click Close. Otherwise, just click Close.

When the RootsMagic News box disappears, you see a Welcome to RootsMagic screen that contains four options. To begin your family tree, follow these steps:

1. **Click Create.**

   A box appears on the screen enabling you to do several things: identify the new filename, determine the location for the file, set any options (including the date format for the file, whether to display a number after a name, whether to display surnames in all capital letters, and whether to set up and support some additional fields for the Latter-day Saints), and choose whether to start a file from scratch or import data from another program.

2. **Enter the new filename in the New File Name box, set any of the optional formatting items, and identify whether you're starting a new file or importing an existing one; then click OK.**

   In our case, we are starting a family tree for the Abell family, so we entered **Abell** as the filename. We set the date format and selected the option for starting a new file.

3. **Click OK.**

   The database is created and the Pedigree view opens, as shown in Figure 3-1.

You can start entering information about yourself in the pedigree chart (presuming that you choose to start with yourself). Then you can add information for five generations of your ancestors.

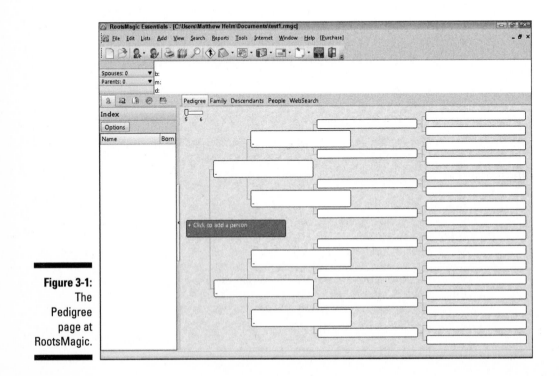

Figure 3-1:
The
Pedigree
page at
RootsMagic.

Completing the Pedigree page

Usually, it's easiest to enter information about yourself, your spouse, and your children, and then work backward through your parents, grandparents, great-grandparents, and so on. After you complete your direct lines back as far as you can, enter information about each of your siblings, nieces and nephews, cousins, and other relatives. Always enter as much information as you can in each of the fields in the Add Person dialog boxes. Follow these steps to fill in the Pedigree page:

1. **Click the box in the pedigree chart that says "Click to add a person."**

   The Add Person dialog box appears, and then you can fill in details about yourself or an ancestor.

2. **Complete the Add Person box and click OK.**

   Type your first and middle names in the Given Name(s) field and your last name in the Surname field. Then complete the remaining fields to the extent that you know the data that belongs in them. Remember to use your maiden name if you're female — regardless of your marital status. Of course, we want to set a good example in this book when it comes to privacy for living relatives, so rather than typing information about one of us, we type in Matthew's great-great-grandfather, Samuel Clayton Abell, Jr.

   After you click OK, the Edit Person dialog box appears.

3. **Complete the Edit Person dialog box and click Save.**

   You can add more facts about yourself or an ancestor by clicking the button for five areas in the edit window — Notes, Sources, Media, Address, and To Do. You can also add or delete facts by clicking the appropriate button and then using the Fact Types functionality. After you finish adding the details, click Save.

   Make sure that you use the four-digit year anytime that you enter dates in RootsMagic. If you inadvertently use only two numerals for the year, the software accepts the year as is, leaving it ambiguous for anyone who references your database in the future.

4. **Click Close.**

After you've entered your first person, you can click the next person box you want to complete or click the Add People to the Database icon on the toolbar, labeled in Figure 3-2, and enter information for people related to the individual, such as spouse, children, and parents. You can keep track of family units by clicking the Family tab.

Add People to the Database

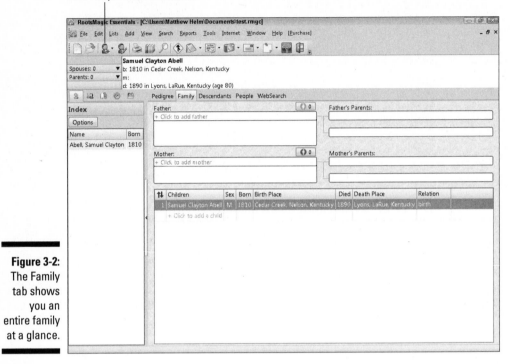

Figure 3-2:
The Family
tab shows
you an
entire family
at a glance.

Sourcing your information

As you enter information about people, it's critical that you cite your data sources. Most genealogical software programs, including RootsMagic, allow you to enter source information. For specific instructions on how to enter info in your particular software, see the Help file or user's manual that comes with the software. In RootsMagic, you add sources through the Edit Person box.

To add a source for your information, follow these steps:

1. **From the pedigree chart view, double-click the person that the source references.**

   We have the source documents for the marriage of Samuel and Martha. So for this example, we double-click Samuel Clayton Abell, Jr. The Edit Person box appears.

2. **Highlight the fact or event that you want to source.**

   We highlight the marriage fact in the left side of the box.

3. **Click the Sources button in the lower-right side of the box.**

   The Citation Manager opens for the marriage fact.

4. Select Add New Source.

The Edit Source box appears, as shown in Figure 3-3.

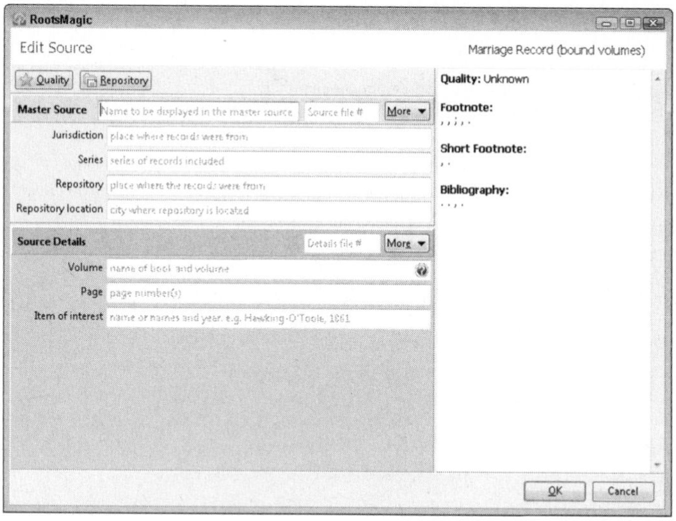

Figure 3-3:
The Edit
Source box.

5. Select from the list of source types.

In our case, we search for the source type Marriage and then select one of the results — Marriage Record (Bound Volumes). If you can't find an existing source type to fit your need, select Free Form and enter your own source type.

6. Click OK.

Enter detailed information about the source of your information. You should complete as many of the information fields as you can for every source.

7. Complete the Edit Source fields and click OK.

You should now see a check mark under the Source icon in the Edit Person box.

You may have noticed that you have another way to get to the Source Manager to add sources. Choose Lists⇨Source List, click the Add a New Source button, and follow the preceding steps. This enables you to add a source that is not necessarily tied to one specific event in that person's life. If your ancestor kept a diary or memoirs of sorts, you might prefer to use this method of citing sources. Similarly, you have functionality to add sources that pertain to more than one person (called Family Sources in the drop-down list accessible from the Sources icon).

After you've used RootsMagic Essentials for a while, you may find that you need more features. You can compare the features between RootsMagic and RootsMagic Essentials at `www.rootsmagic.com/RootsMagic/Features.aspx` to determine whether an upgrade is in order for you.

Mobilizing Your Research

Earlier in this chapter, we extolled about some of the virtues of using a smartphone when traveling. One of those virtues was the ability to use genealogy applications from anywhere. Currently, applications (called *apps* by iPhone users) are available for iPhones that do a variety of genealogy-related functions. Some of them are as follows:

- ✔ **Ancestry.com Tree to Go:** Enables you to log in and interact with a family tree uploaded to the Ancestry.com Web site. Check it out at `landing.ancestry.com/iphone`.

- ✔ **Shrubs:** Imports your GEDCOM file into their database so you can view information on the road. To find out more, visit `http://software.benoitbousquet.com/view.php?app=shrubs`.

- ✔ **FamViewer:** Imports and displays a GEDCOM file. More information on FamViewer is available at `www.astersoftware.biz`.

- ✔ **Reunion and MobileFamilyTree:** Companion apps to regular genealogical databases for Mac computer users. You must have the regular Mac software to use these iPhone applications. More information on Reunion for iPhone is located at `www.leisterpro.com/iphone`. For details on MobileFamilyTree, go to `www.syniumsoftware.com/mobilefamilytree`.

- ✔ **CousinCalc:** Figures out relationships (such as first cousins once removed) up to ten generations of separation. You can find more information about CousinCalc at `www.ackmesoftware.com`.

- ✔ **MobileTree:** Allows registered users to search the "new" FamilySearch.org Web site. Details on the application are at `www.mobiletree.me`.

- ✔ **Traces of the Past:** Sports a search interface to the current FamilySearch.org Web site. You can view records and associated images of documents, if available, on the site. More information on Traces is available at `www.tracesofthepast.net`.

- ✔ **GedView:** Imports your GEDCOM files to your iPhone or iPad. You can import multiple GEDCOM files and maintain them in separate databases. GedView also supports editing of the information after it's imported, and the GPS of the device can be used to record the longitude and latitude of where the entry was made. More on the application is found at `www.ritter.demon.co.uk/Projects/gedview.html`.

✔ **iHeritage:** Lets you enter information about your ancestors on a graphical tree. The current version does not support a GEDCOM import. More details are at `www.ourmountainofideas.com/Our_Mountain_of_Ideas/iHeritage.html`.

✔ **Genealogy Gems Podcast:** Can be received over your iPhone, along with bonus material mentioned in the podcast. Looking for more information about these podcasts? Check out `www.genealogygemspodcast.com`.

These are just some of the applications available for the iPhone. As you might expect, some of them are free and others cost money. You can find specific information about each application at `www.apple.com/itunes`.

Say you have an iPhone and you'd like to download one of these apps. You can download it from iTunes using your computer or you can download directly through your iPhone by clicking the App Store icon. Here's an example of how to download Shrubs. The basic steps are the same for all the apps:

1. **Click the App Store icon.**

   The store site opens.

2. **Scroll through the list of apps and select Shrubs.**

   The information page pops up. You can read about the app before downloading it.

3. **Click the blue button that shows the purchase price.**

   The button changes color and now reads Install.

4. **Click the Buy Now button.**

   The iTunes Password dialog box appears.

5. **Enter your password and click OK.**

   The app downloads and installs.

Many of these apps work not only on an iPhone but also on the iPad. We go into a little more detail about iPads in Chapter 14.

Now that we've identified some iPhone apps, you may be wondering whether anything similar is available for other brands of smartphones (such as the BlackBerry or Android-based phones). We know of nothing specifically for the BlackBerry — although you can view genealogical data that you have placed on a Web site with the BlackBerry. However, we can tell you about a few applications for the Android-based phones:

✔ **Family Bee:** An application that enables you to view your GEDCOM file on your Android-based phone. You can find out more about it at the familytreecircle blog at `www.familytreecircles.com/blog/family-bee-genealogy-app-for-android-phones-51`.

- ✔ **AGeneDB:** Another GEDCOM viewing application for Android-based smartphones. You can download a free copy at androidzoom at `www.androidzoom.com/android_applications/tools/agenedb-alpha_ddg.html`.

- ✔ **Find Grave:** Allows you to use the Find A Grave Web site database through the Android phone. You can find more details on the application at `http://sites.google.com/site/findgrave`.

- ✔ **Genealogy Glossary:** Includes definitions and abbreviations related to family history research. More information is available at `http://uk.androlib.com/android.application.apps-dps-genealogy glossary-jjmtF.aspx`.

- ✔ **MobileTree:** Allows registered users to search the "new" FamilySearch.org Web site. Details on the application are at `www.mobiletree.me`.

For those of you with phones that support the Windows Mobile operating system, the following applications are available:

- ✔ **My Roots:** Allows you to import GEDCOM files, make changes, and then export to a new GEDCOM file. More information on the application is at `www.tapperware.com/MyRoots/ppc/index.html`.

- ✔ **Pocket Genealogist:** A full-featured application that allows the direct import of information from several genealogical databases. It also supports the use of multimedia and comes in several languages. You can find details on Pocket Genealogist at `www.pocketgenealogist.com`.

You can also find the following applications for Palm devices:

- ✔ **GedStar** (`www.ghcssoftware.com/gedstar.htm`)
- ✔ **GedWise** (`www.batteryparksoftware.com/index.html`)
- ✔ **My Roots** (`www.tapperware.com/MyRoots/index.html`)

You have an alternative to storing your genealogical treasures on your phone for mobility. You can upload your information to a Web page and then access it from a browser on your smartphone. For more information about uploading your data to a Web site, head on over to Chapter 11.

Part II
Focusing on Your Ancestor

The 5th Wave   By Rich Tennant

"Well, she now claims she's a descendant of the royal Egyptian line of cats, but I'm not buying that just yet."

In this part . . .

This part covers how to locate resources that provide information on your ancestors by name and location. You can also find search strategies for using a variety of government documents online to substantiate your ancestor's life.

Chapter 4

What's in a Name?

As a genealogist, you may experience sleepless nights trying to figure out all the important things in life — the maiden name of your great-great-grandmother, whether Great-grandpa was really the scoundrel that other relatives say he was, and just how you're related to Daniel Boone. (Well, isn't everyone?) Okay, so you may not have sleepless nights, but you undoubtedly spend a significant amount of time thinking about and trying to find resources that can give you answers to these crucial questions.

In the past, finding information on individual ancestors online was compared with finding a needle in a haystack. You browsed through long lists of links in hopes of finding a site that contained a nugget of information to aid your search. But looking for your ancestors online has become easier than ever. Instead of merely browsing links, you can use search engines and online databases to pinpoint information on your ancestors.

This chapter covers the basics of searching for an ancestor by name, presents some good surname resource sites, and shows you how to combine several different Internet resources to successfully find information on your family.

Letting Your Computer Do the Walking: Using Search Engines

Finding information on an ancestor on the Web can be a challenge. In the past, it was sometimes difficult to find any kind of information about a given individual because online collections were just beginning to grow and become accessible. Now, with the myriad resources available, the challenge is sorting through all the nonrelevant information to find data that can help progress your research. One of the key online resources that you can use to help locate and filter some of the online data is a search engine.

Search engines are programs that examine huge indexes of information generated by Web robots, or simply bots. *Bots* are programs that travel throughout the Internet and collect information on the sites and resources that they run across. You can access the information contained in search engines through an interface, usually through a form on a Web page.

The real strength of search engines is that they allow you to search the full text of Web pages instead of just the title or a brief abstract of the site. This is particularly valuable in a family history because a researcher may be looking for someone who is one of thousands who descended from a particular individual — for whom the Web page may be named. For example, many genealogy Web sites are named for the progenitor of the family. In Matthew's case, the progenitor for his branch of the Helm family was Georg Helm. A Web page might be named something like The Georg and Dorothea Helm Family. If Matthew is looking for one of Georg's great-great-great grandsons, Uriah Helm, he might not know to look under the Georg Helm Web site to find him. Some genealogy programs create Web sites with thousands of pages of information, but only one of which might pertain to Uriah. If a search engine bot happens to index all the pages of the site, Uriah's name becomes visible through the search index.

While search engines offer a lot of coverage of the Web, to find what you're looking for is sometimes more of an art than a science. In the following pages, we look at search strategies, as well as the different kinds of search engines that are available to aid your search.

Using general Internet search engines

General search engines (such as Google or Ask.com) send out bots to catalog the Internet as a whole, regardless of the subject(s) of the site's content. Therefore, on any given search, you're likely to receive a lot of hits, perhaps only a few of which hold any genealogical value — that is, unless you refine your search terms to give you a better chance at receiving relevant results.

You can conduct several types of searches with most search engines. Looking at the Help link for any search engine to see the most effective way to search is always a good idea. Also, search engines often have two search interfaces — a simple search and an advanced search. With the *simple search,* you normally just type your query and click the Submit button. With an *advanced search,* you can use a variety of options to refine your search. The best way to become familiar with using a search engine is to experiment and see what kinds of results you get.

To demonstrate various strategies for using a search engine, we run through some searches using Google for Matthew's ancestor Georg. Before we begin the search, it's a good idea to have some useful facts at hand to help define our search terms. From previous research, Matthew knows that Georg's name is spelled *Georg* on his gravestone — but *George* in land records. He also knows that Georg was born in 1723 and died in 1769 and that he owned land in Winchester, Frederick County, Virginia. He was married to a woman named Dorothea.

Not all search terms are equal

When first using a search engine, a number of people simply type the name of an ancestor, expecting the search engine to take care of the rest. Although search engines do have some default ways of searching, these ways are not always the best for genealogical searches. The following table lists the number of results that we received with different search criteria.

Search Criteria	Number of Results
Georg Helm	31,500,000
George Helm	4,570,000
Georg OR George Helm	5,190,000

The first search, using *Georg Helm,* produces millions of results because it looks for any content containing the words *Georg* and *Helm.* The results include the appearances of words such as *Georg, George, Georgia, Georgeann* with the word *Helm* — which is not only a name but also a common word. The expansion of the search to include variations on the spelling of the word is common in search engines and is referred to as *stemming.* The search for George Helm yields fewer results because the addition of the letter *e* in George precludes the word *Georg* as well as *Georgia.* The third search demonstrates the capability of Google to search for multiple conditions within a single set of search terms. Placing the OR modifier in the search terms allows both Georg and George to be searched and ranked into one set of results. Searching with these dual terms will generate a list that should include all the results from the first (*Georg Helm*) and second (*George Helm*) searches.

Although each of these produced millions of results, only a tiny fraction had anything to do with the Georg Helm that we are looking for. So, we need to refine our search method to get a better selection of more appropriate results.

Searching with phrases

Using quotation marks in Google searches helps to specify the exact form of the word to search. Placing *Georg* in quotation marks means that you want Google to search words that exactly match *Georg* — and that you do not want Google to perform stemming on the name. This would preclude longer words that contain those letters, such as *Georgia* and *Georgeann*. Even with this modifier on the first name, you can see that the results for "Georg" Helm and "George" Helm in the following table still number in the millions because the search engine is looking for any content that contains both the words *Georg* and *Helm*. Incidentally, because Matthew knows that Georg can be spelled either *Georg* or *George,* he can execute a search for both versions of the name at the same time using OR in the search terms — "(Georg OR George) Helm."

Search Criteria	Number of Results
"Georg" Helm	8,150,000
"George" Helm	4,600,000
"(Georg OR George) Helm"	55,200
"Georg Helm"	62,800
"George Helm"	41,300

To further reduce the number and improve the quality of results, you can add quotation marks around the entire name so that Google searches for those two words as a single phrase. Using this strategy, the number of results is reduced from millions to tens of thousands. However, even this many results are too many to research individually.

Performing targeted searches

The search strategies we mention earlier in this chapter are fine for getting a general idea of what is available for a particular name or for searching for a unique name, but they're not necessarily the most efficient for finding information on a specific person. The best strategies involve using specific search terms that include geographic information or other family members associated with the individual.

Using the same example we used earlier — searching for information about Georg Helm — we can find more targeted information on Georg Helm by including geographical terms in the search. The search term

"(Georg OR George) Helm" (Winchester OR "Frederick County") + Virginia

yields 81 results. The search term requires that the online content contain the following:

✔ The words *Georg Helm* or *George Helm*

✔ The word(s) *Winchester* or *Frederick County*

✔ The word *Virginia*

Of these results, less than a quarter of the results have anything to do with the Georg Helm who is the ancestor of Matthew.

Because other George Helms are associated with Frederick County, Virginia, we can further clarify the search terms to include Georg's wife's name — Dorothea. The search term

> "(Georg OR George) Helm" (Winchester OR "Frederick County") + Virginia Dorothea

brings those results with Dorothea in them toward the top of the list.

You can also use targeted searches to meet specific research goals. For example, if Matthew is looking for the will of Georg Helm, he could use the following search terms:

> "(Georg OR George) Helm" (Winchester OR "Frederick County") + Virginia Dorothea + will

The top search result is the transcription of Georg's will on the USGenWeb Archives site.

A few other Google hints

To get the most relevant content to meet your research goals, you have a few other ways to control the results presented by Google. The first is to exclude certain results by using the – (minus) sign. In the case of Matthew's search for George Helm, several of the results that he received in his previous searches dealt with another George Helm who was born in Frederick County, Virginia, and who is unrelated to Matthew's Georg. This second George was married to Sarah Jackman and later moved to Cumberland County, Kentucky. To avoid seeing results for the second George, we can modify our search terms to the following:

> "(Georg OR George) Helm" (Winchester OR "Frederick County") + Virginia – Jackman – "Cumberland County"

Sometimes searching on a phrase can be too exact. If the person you're researching is listed with a middle name, you might not find the content with a phrase search. One way around this is to use the * wildcard term. A search term such as *Georg * Helm* would pick up content containing the name Georg Smith Helm, as well as content containing Georg and Dorothea Helm.

You can also use number ranges within your search terms to push more relevant search results to the top of your results list. Number ranges within Google are specified by placing two periods between the range of numbers.

So, if you want to search on a range of numbers from 1723 to 1769, place two periods between 1723 and 1769. For example, you could use the following search terms:

"(Georg OR George) Helm" 1723..1769

This searches for content with Georg Helm or George Helm with a number between 1723 and 1769.

Google offers a few other useful features for limiting results. If you're searching for a relatively common name, you can try to focus your search on the page titles of content to keep from being overwhelmed by millions of results. To do this, use `intitle` or `allintitle` in your search terms. (Yes, you are seeing those correctly — do not put spaces in the phrases `intitle` [for in title] or `allintitle` [for all in title] when using them in the search term. Google knows how to interpret them without the spaces.) For example, the search terms intitle:Georg Helm Dorothea look for sites that have Georg, Helm, or Dorothea in the page title. However, it doesn't exclude sites that don't have all the search terms in the title (although it does score sites that contain all three higher than those that don't). To do that, use the `allintitle` function — allintitle:Georg Helm Dorothea.

Similarly, you can use the `intext` function to limit the results to search terms that appear in the text of the page. By using the search term intext:Georg Helm Dorothea (or if you want all search terms to appear — allintext:Georg Helm Dorothea), you can search for sites with those specific words in the text of the Web page. If you remember that you found a link on a page that is important to your research but can't remember where you found the link, you can use the `inanchor` function. A search such as inanchor:Georg Helm looks for Georg Helm in links within a page. The search modifier `allinanchor` looks for all the search terms within the link. And finally, if you want to look for search terms within a Uniform Resource Locator, use the `inurl` and `allinurl` search modifiers (such as inurl:Georg Helm).

Google isn't the only general search engine available. Some others include AltaVista (www.altavista.com), Ask.com (www.ask.com), and Bing (www.bing.com).

Looking at general Internet metasearch engines

Wouldn't it be nice if we never had to visit multiple sites to search the Internet? This burning question led directly to the creation of *metasearch engines,* which use a single interface (or form) to execute searches using several search engines. They then return the results of all the individual search engines to a single page that you can use to view the results. The number of results from metasearch engines can be overwhelming, so it's important to have a good search term and to know something substantial about the person you're researching. That way, you can quickly determine whether a result is relevant to your search. You also need to have patience because you may have to trudge through several sets of results before you find something useful. One metasearch engine to experiment with is Dogpile (`www.dogpile.com`). Dogpile uses results from the Google, Bing, Yahoo!, and Ask search engines.

1. **Open your Web browser and go to `www.dogpile.com`.**

   The Dogpile home page contains a search form. Just below the search form is a link to the advanced search.

2. **Click the Advanced Search link.**

   The default search form turns gray, and a new set of search fields are presented.

3. **Type your search terms in the appropriate fields and click the Go Fetch button.**

   Dogpile formats your search terms and executes the search, as shown in Figure 4-1.

Figure 4-1:
Search results from the Dogpile metasearch engine.

Other metasearch engines include

- ✓ **Ixquick:** `http://ixquick.com`
- ✓ **Mamma:** `www.mamma.com`
- ✓ **MetaCrawler:** `www.metacrawler.com`
- ✓ **Search.com:** `www.search.com`

Finding the Site That's Best for You

Your dream as an online genealogist is to find a Web site that contains all the information that you ever wanted to know about your family. Unfortunately, these sites simply don't exist. However, during your search, you may discover a variety of sites that vary greatly in the amount and quality of genealogical information. Before you get too deep into your research, it's a good idea to look at the type of sites that you're likely to encounter.

What about blogs?

Since previous editions of this book were published, the Internet has been inundated by blogging. A *blog* is an online, personal journal of sorts — a site where an individual or even a group of people with a common interest can record their daily, weekly, monthly, or whatever-timed-interval thoughts and experiences. The field of genealogy is no exception! Many genealogy blogs are now available, and they can't be categorized under just one of the groupings we've covered so far in this chapter. In other words, they don't all fit into personal genealogical sites, nor do they all fit into family associations or organizations.

One example of a blog that is genealogical and geographic in nature is the Texas History and Genealogy Blog (`http://texashistory blog.blogspot.com`). As you might imagine, it covers a variety of topics relating to

Texas. At irregular intervals, the host of the blog posts various types of information ranging from cemetery transcriptions, to information about upcoming conferences, to historical markers, to things to see when driving through Texas, to other Web sites or articles that she thinks will interest readers.

A couple of other blogs that are more like personal genealogical sites are Mike's Genealogy Blog (`http://mikegen48.wordpress.com`) and Steve's Genealogy Blog (`www.stephendanko.com`). Both blogs have research findings of the blog hosts.

When you're ready to share your knowledge with the world, you might consider setting up your own genealogical blog. We provide the specific steps for doing so in Chapter 11.

Personal genealogical sites

The majority of pages that you encounter on the Internet are maintained by an individual who is interested in researching a particular person or family line. These pages usually contain information on the site maintainer's ancestry or on particular branches of several different families rather than on a surname as a whole. That doesn't mean valuable information isn't present on these sites — it's just that they have a more personal focus.

You can find a wide variety of information on personal genealogical sites. Some pages list only a few surnames that the maintainer is researching; others contain extensive online genealogical databases and narratives. A site's content depends on the amount of research, time, and computer skills the maintainer possesses. Some common items that you see on most sites include a list of surnames, an online genealogical database, pedigree and descendant charts (for information on these charts, see Chapter 2), family photographs, research blogs, and the obligatory list of the maintainer's favorite genealogical Internet links.

Personal genealogical sites vary not only in content but also in presentation. Some sites are neatly constructed and use plain backgrounds and aesthetically pleasing colors. Other sites, however, require you to bring out your sunglasses to tone down the fluorescent colors, or they use lots of moving graphics and banner advertisements that take up valuable space and make it difficult to navigate through the site. You should also be aware that the JavaScript, music players, and animated icons that some personal sites use can significantly increase your download times.

An example of a personal genealogical site is the Rubi-Lopez Genealogy Page (`http://rubifamilygen.com`), shown in Figure 4-2. The Rubi-Lopez page contains articles on different lines of the family, a photo gallery, and links to other family Web sites.

After you find a site that contains useful information, write down the maintainer's name and e-mail address, and contact him or her as soon as possible, if you have any questions or want to exchange information. Personal genealogical sites have a way of disappearing without a trace as individuals frequently switch Internet service providers or stop maintaining sites.

One-name study sites

If you're looking for a wide range of information on one particular surname, a one-name study site may be worth your while. These sites usually focus on one surname regardless of the geographic location where the surname appears. In other words, they welcome information about people with the surname worldwide. These sites are quite helpful because they contain all sorts of information about the surname, even if they don't have specific information about your branch of a family with that surname. Frequently they have information on the variations in spelling, origins, history, and heraldry of the surname. One-name studies have some of the same resources you find in personal genealogical sites, including online genealogy databases and narratives.

Although one-name study sites welcome all surname information regardless of geographic location, the information presented at one-name study sites is often organized around geographic lines. For example, a one-name study site may categorize all the information about people with the surname by continent or country — such as Helms in the United States, England, Canada, Europe, and Africa. Or, the site may be even more specific and categorize information by state, province, county, or parish. So, you're better off if you have a general idea of where your family originated or migrated from. But if you don't know, browsing through the site may lead to some useful information.

The Bowes Surname Web site (www.bowesonenamestudy.com) is a one-name study site with several resources for the Bowe, Bows, Bow, Boe, and De Bowes surnames. From the home page (see Figure 4-3), you can choose to view news on recent additions to the site, articles on current discoveries, results of the surname DNA project, research in different countries, and information on how to join a mailing list of the surnames.

Figure 4-2:
The Rubi-
Lopez
Genealogy
Page is an
example of
a personal
genealogy
site.

The maintainers of one-name study sites welcome any information you have on the surname. These sites are often a good place to join research groups that can be instrumental in assisting your personal genealogical effort.

To find one-name study sites pertaining to the surnames you're research-ing, you have to go elsewhere. Where, you ask? One site that can help you determine whether any one-name study sites are devoted to surnames you're researching is the Guild of One-Name Studies (www.one-name.org).

Gee, we bet you can't figure out what the Guild of One-Name Studies is! It's exactly as it sounds — an online organization of registered sites, each of which focuses on one particular surname. The Guild has information about more than 7,000 surnames. Follow these steps to find out whether any of the Guild's members focus on the surname of the person you're researching:

1. **Open your Web browser and go to www.one-name.org.**

2. **Click the Reg. Names (Registered Names) link on the navigation menu at the top of the page.**

3. **Choose the letter that corresponds to the first letter of the surname.**

   The resulting page contains a list of names. Those with a link contain more information about the study.

Family associations and organizations

Family association sites are similar to one-name study sites in terms of content, but they usually have an organizational structure (such as a formal association, society, or club) backing them. The association may focus on the surname as a whole or just one branch of a family. The goals for the family association site may differ from those for a one-name study. The maintainers may be creating a family history in book form or a database of all individuals descended from a particular person. Some sites may require you to join the association before you can fully participate in their activities, but this is usually at a minimal cost or free.

The Wingfield Family Society site (`www.wingfield.org`), shown in Figure 4-4, has several items that are common to family association sites. The site's contents include a family history, newsletter subscription details, a membership form, queries, mailing list information, results of a DNA project, and a directory of the society's members who are online. Some of the resources at the Wingfield Family Society site require you to be a member of the society to access them.

To find a family association Web site, your best bet is to use a search engine. For more on search engines, see the section "Using general Internet search engines," earlier in this chapter. Be sure to use search terms that include the surname you're interested in researching and one of these key words: *society, association, group,* or *organization.*

Surnames connected to events or places

Another place where you may discover surnames is a site that has a collection of names connected with a particular event or geographic location. The level of information available on these sites varies greatly among sites and among surnames on the same site. Often, the maintainers of such sites include more information on their personal research interests than other surnames, simply because they have more information on their own lines.

Typically, you need to know events that your ancestors were involved in or geographic areas where they lived to use these sites effectively. Also, you benefit from the site simply because you have a general, historical interest in the particular event or location, even if the Web site contains nothing on your surname. Finding Web sites about events is easiest if you use a search engine, a comprehensive Web site, or a subscription database. Because we devote an entire chapter to researching geographic locations (Chapter 6), we won't delve into that here.

Wingfield Family Soci... ×

http://www.wingfield.org/

Archives
Churches
Coat of Arms
Database
DNA Study
Family Group Sheet
Genealogy Links
Guestbook - Sign
Guestbook - View
History
Immigrants
Jamestowne
Mail List
Membership
Meetings
Newsletter
Obituaries
Officers
Other Links
Photographs
Poll
Publications
Queries
Store
Stones
Title
Tours
Virginia's Founder
Wingfield Links
Home

Wingfield Family Society

The Wingfield Family Society publishes a quarterly newsletter. It is packed with a wide variety of news and information about genealogical searches, queries, Wingfields in history, member profiles, current happenings within the membership, announcements concerning meetings, etc. The newsletter is our primary form of communication with our members.

Newsletter Back Issues

1987 - Spring	1987 - Summer	1987 - Autumn	
1988 - Spring	1988 - Summer	1988 - Autumn	1988 - Winter
1989 - Spring	1989 - Summer		1989 - Winter
1990 - Spring	1990 - Summer	1990 - Autumn	1990 - Winter
1991 - Spring	1991 - Summer	1991 - Autumn	1991 - Winter
1992 - Spring	1992 - Summer	1992 - Autumn	1992 - Winter
	1992 - Special	1992 - Special	
	1993 - Summer	1993 - Autumn	1993 - Winter
	1993 - Special		
1994 - Spring	1994 - Summer		
	1995 - Summer	1995 - Autumn	
		1998 - Autumn	
	2000 - Summer		2000 - Winter
2001 - Spring			2002 - Winter
		2004 - Autumn	
2005 - Spring	2005 - Summer		2005 - Winter

Figure 4-4:
The
Wingfield
Family
Society site.

Taking the Plunge

After you've decided on a particular person to research (for more on selecting a good research candidate, see Chapter 2), it's time to research online. As we've mentioned frequently in this book, it's a good idea to arm yourself with some facts about the individual before venturing online.

Perhaps Matthew wants to research his paternal grandfather's line. His grandfather was Herschel Helm, who lived in Macon County, Illinois. From memory and supported by a copy of a death certificate for Herschel, Matthew knows that his grandfather died in 1985 — information that can be used to distinguish him from another Herschel Helm found online.

Due to privacy laws, the amount of information online on people in the United States after 1930 is limited. However, one source that does provide information on deceased individuals during this time period is the Social Security Death Index (SSDI), also called the Social Security Death Master file — a good place to get your feet wet.

As of 2007, the SSDI contained more than 80 million records of deaths of individuals having a Social Security Number. The vast majority of these records deal with individuals who died after 1962 — although a few scattered records predate that year. Each entry includes the following:

✓ Name of deceased

✓ Birth date

✓ Death date

✓ Last residence

✓ Last benefit received

✓ Social Security Number

✓ State where person lived when Social Security card was issued

Several places exist online where the SSDI can be searched. The most up-to-date version is found at the GenealogyBank.com site at `www.genealogy bank.com/gbnk/ssdi.html`.

However, a membership is required for access. For free access to the SSDI, try visiting `http://ssdi.genealogy.rootsweb.com`.

To search the SSDI, do the following:

1. **Point your browser to `http://ssdi.genealogy.rootsweb.com`.**

   The Social Security Death Index Interactive Search page at Rootsweb. com appears, with a search form near the bottom of the page.

2. **Type the last name and first name of the individual and click Submit.**

   You can search for an exact match on the surname, or use a Soundex or metaphone (a phonetic code algorithm that is similar to Soundex) equivalent for the search. (For more information about Soundex, flip back to Chapter 5.) These sound-based equivalents can be used to find names that are not spelled exactly as you expect them to be. In our case, we type *Helm* in the last name field and *Herschel* in the first name field.

3. **Browse the results page for the appropriate individual.**

   The results are presented in a table with nine columns. Our search yielded four results, and only one of those has the last residence of Macon County and a death date of 1985.

Whenever you use this database and find someone for whom you're searching, you have the opportunity to generate a letter to order the original Social Security application (Form SS-5) from the Social Security Administration.

Family Trees Ripe for the Picking: Finding Compiled Resources

Using online databases to pick pieces of genealogical fruit is wonderful. But you want more, right? Not satisfied with just having Social Security information on his grandfather, Matthew is eager to know more — in particular, he'd like to know who Herschel's grandfather was. You have a few research tactics to explore at this point. Perhaps the first is to see whether someone has already completed some research on Herschel and his ancestors.

When someone publishes his or her genealogical findings (whether online or in print), the resulting work is called a *compiled genealogy*.

Compiled genealogies can give you a lot of information about your ancestors in a nice, neat format. When you find one with information relevant to your family, you get this overwhelming feeling of instantaneous gratification. Wait! Don't get too excited yet! When you use compiled genealogies, it's important to remember that you need to verify any information in them that you're adding to your own findings. Even when sources are cited, it's wise to get your own copies of the actual sources to ensure that the author's interpretation of the sources was correct and that no other errors occurred in the publication of the compiled genealogy.

Compiled genealogies take two shapes online. One is the traditional narrative format — the kind of thing that you typically see in a book at the library. The second is in the form of information exported from an individual's genealogical database and posted online in a lineage-linked format (*lineage-linked* means that the database is organized by the relationships between people).

Narrative compiled genealogies

Narrative compiled genealogies usually have more substance than their exported database counterparts. Authors sometimes add color to the narratives by including local history and other text and facts that can help researchers get an idea of the time in which the ancestor lived. An excellent example of a narrative genealogy is found at The Carpenters of Carpenter's Station, Kentucky, at `http://freepages.genealogy.rootsweb.ancestry.com/~carpenter`.

The site maintainer, Kathleen Carpenter, has posted a copy of her mother's historical manuscript on the Carpenter family, as well as some photos and a map of Carpenter's Station. You can view the documents directly through the Web or download PDF copies.

To locate narrative genealogies, try using a search engine or comprehensive genealogical index. (For more information on using these resources, see the sections later in this chapter.) Often, compiled genealogies are part of a personal or family association Web site.

Compiled genealogical databases

Although many people don't think of lineage-linked, online genealogical databases as compiled genealogies, these databases serve the same role as narrative compiled genealogies — they show the results of someone's research in a neatly organized, printed format.

For example, the Simpson History site (`http://simpsonhistory.com/_main_page.html`) is a personal site that contains a compiled genealogical database providing information on John "The Scotsman" Simpson and his descendants. You can navigate through descendant charts and family group sheets, clicking particular individuals to access more information about them. (Descendant charts and family group sheets are two ways to present genealogical information about a person. For more information about them, check out Chapter 2.)

Finding information in compiled genealogical databases can sometimes be tough. There isn't a grand database that indexes all the individual databases available online. Although general Internet search engines have indexed quite a few, some very large collections are still accessible only through a database search — something that general Internet search engines don't normally do.

In the preceding section, we conducted a search on Matthew's grandfather, Herschel Helm. Now we want to find out more about his ancestry. We can jump-start our research by using a lineage-linked database in hopes of finding some information compiled from other researchers that can help us discover who his ancestors were (perhaps even several generations' worth). From documents such as his birth and death certificates, we find out that Herschel's father was named Emanuel Helm. And from interviews with family members, we also learn that Emanuel was born in Fayette County, Illinois, in the early 1860s. Armed with this information, we can search a compiled genealogical database.

The FamilySearch Internet Genealogy Service (`www.familysearch.org`) is the official research site for the Church of Jesus Christ of Latter-day Saints (LDS). This free Web site allows you to search several LDS databases including the Ancestral File, International Genealogical Index, Pedigree Resource File, vital records index, census records, and a collection of abstracted Web sites — all of which are free. The two resources that function much like lineage-linked databases are the Ancestral File and the Pedigree Resource File. Fortunately, you don't have to search each of these resources separately. A master search is available that allows you to search all seven resources on the site at once.

To search the FamilySearch site, follow these steps:

1. **Open your Web browser and go to `www.familysearch.org`.**

2. **In the Search Records for Your Ancestors section (near the upper left of the main Web page), type the first and last name of the ancestor you're researching in the First Name and Last Name fields, respectively.**

   You can complete optional fields such as Life Event, Year, Year Range, or Country. (Keep in mind that filling in any of these fields may reduce the overall number of results you receive.) We typed *Emanuel* in the First Name box and *Helm* in the Last Name box.

   If you're researching a common name and know more information about the individual, you might want to click the Advanced Search link. This takes you to a page showing several additional fields, including names for father, mother, and spouse. It also enables you to restrict your search by state and to use the exact spelling of the ancestor's name that you provide. If you decide to use the advanced search and include information on the spouse or mother or father and you don't receive adequate results, try doing the search on only the name of the ancestor.

3. **After you select your search criteria (first and last names), click Search.**

   The Results page contains links (with descriptions) to the resources that meet your search criteria. For example, our search for Emanuel Helm yields 53 results. These results come from eight resources on the site. The far-right column, Sources Searched, provides a breakdown of the number of results you received from each FamilySearch resource, as shown in Figure 4-5.

4. **Click the link of any result to see more information.**

   A few results jump out at us. The second record is an Emanuel Helm born about 1863 in Fayette, Illinois. Looking for other records from Illinois, we find Manuel Helm in the 1870 U.S. Census and an Emanuel Helm born about 1863 in Fayette, Illinois, in the International Genealogical Index. As it turns out, these are the same person — in the 1870 Census, his name was misspelled as *Manuel.*

If we select the Ancestral File entry for Emanuel Helm, we are taken to the individual record page. This page shows the sex of the individual, the event prompting the record, the parent names (if known), and information on the submitter of the record. From this record, we see that someone submitted a record showing Emanuel's parents as Uriah Helm and Rebecca Norris. The source information for this is not here, so it would be worthwhile to contact the submitter to locate the source. The other links on the page allow us to generate a pedigree chart of Emanuel's ancestors or a family group sheet of his immediate family. Looking at the family group sheet, the submission shows that Uriah and Rebecca had six children and that Uriah's parents' names were William Helm and Elizabeth Guffey. Clicking the Pedigree link generates a chart that shows ancestors of Emanuel going back five generations to George Helm (born in 1723 in Virginia). Matthew can use this information to look for primary records to document these generations.

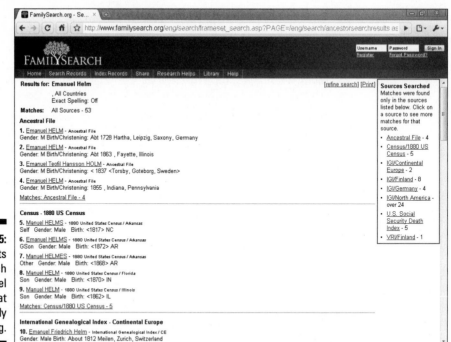

Figure 4-5:
The results
of a search
for Emanuel
Helm at
Family
Search.org.

Although the LDS Church is well known for its large genealogical collection, don't expect to find the complete collection online — the vast majority of LDS resources reside in its library and Family History Centers. Also, you need to verify — with the help of the *original* records — any information that you do find online. Much of the information currently on the site was contributed by other family-history researchers, who may or may not have been careful in researching and diligent in documenting their family history.

You can find several other lineage-linked collections that may contain useful information, including WorldConnect (`wc.rootsweb.ancestry.com`), OneGreatFamily.com (`www.onegreatfamily.com`), and MyTrees.com (`www.mytrees.com`). The following list gives you details on some of the better-known collections:

- **Ancestry World Tree:** The Ancestry.com site (`www.ancestry.com/trees/awt/main.aspx`) contains a free area where researchers can contribute GEDCOM files from their individual databases, as well as search through the files of other researchers. Another part of the Ancestry.com subscription site has a more sophisticated search engine for family trees kept on the site. This search engine, OneWorldTree, is located at `www.ancestry.com/search/rectype/trees/owt`.

- ✔ **WorldConnect:** The WorldConnect Project (worldconnect.roots web.com) is part of the RootsWeb.com site. The Project has more than 575 million names in its database.

- ✔ **MyTrees.com:** MyTrees.com (www.mytrees.com) is a site maintained by Kindred Konnections. The site has a lineage-linked database numbering 513 million records. The site is available only by subscription.

- ✔ **OneGreatFamily.com:** OneGreatFamily.com (www.onegreatfamily.com) hosts a subscription-based, lineage-linked database. The database contains 190 million unique names contributed by users in 170 countries.

- ✔ **GenCircles:** GenCircles (www.gencircles.com) is a free, lineage-linked database site with a twist. Its SmartMatching feature compares individuals from different files and attempts to match them together. Thus, a researcher who contributes to GenCircles can get in contact with another who may be working on the same family lines.

Online Subscription Databases: Goldmines of Genealogy?

Some of your ancestors may have been prospectors. You know the type — they roamed from place to place in search of the mother lode. Often, they may have found a small nugget here or there, but they never seemed to locate that one mine that provided a lifetime supply of gold. When searching on the Internet, you become the prospector. You pan through results from search engines only to find small nuggets of information here and there. However, don't lose hope. There may be some gold mines waiting for you if you can only stumble upon the right site to dig — and the right site may be in the form of an online subscription database.

Online subscription databases are repositories of information that you can retrieve by paying a monthly, quarterly, or yearly fee. Most online subscription databases are searchable and allow you to type your ancestor's name and execute a search to determine whether any information stored in the database relates to that particular name. Databases can be large or small; they can focus on a small geographic area or have a broad scope that encompasses many different areas. Each database may also have its own unique search method and present information in its own format. The online subscription database sites vary in the types of content they offer and the amounts and quality of background or historical information they provide about each of the databases within their collections.

You can find online subscription databases in many ways. You can locate references to them through search engines, comprehensive genealogical indexes, and links that appear on personal and geographic-specific Web sites. For examples of the types of data available on subscription sites, see Chapters 12 and 13.

Browsing Comprehensive Genealogical Indexes

If you're unable to find information on your ancestor through a search engine or online database, or if you're looking for additional information, another resource to try is a comprehensive genealogical index. A *comprehensive genealogical index* is a site that contains a categorized listing of links to online resources for family history research. Comprehensive genealogical indexes can be organized in a variety of ways, including by subject, alphabetically, or by resource type. No matter how the links are organized, they usually appear hierarchically — you click your way down from category to subcategory until you find the link for which you're looking.

Some examples of comprehensive genealogical indexes include the following:

- **Cyndi's List of Genealogy Sites on the Internet:** www.cyndislist.com

- **Helm's Genealogy Toolbox:** www.genealogytoolbox.com

- **Linkpendium:** www.linkpendium.com

To give you an idea of how comprehensive genealogical indexes work, try the following example:

1. **Fire up your browser and go to Linkpendium (www.linkpendium.com).**

   This launches the home page for Linkpendium.

2. **Scroll down to the portion of the main page with the links to surnames.**

3. **Click a link with a letter for your surname.**

   For example, we're looking for Helm, so we click the H surnames link.

4. **Click the link that contains the first three letters of the surname you're researching.**

   We click the link entitled Hel Families: Surname Genealogy, Family History, Family Tree, Family Crest.

5. **Click the link to your surname.**

   We click the Helm Family: Surname Genealogy, Family History, Family Tree, Family Crest link. Figure 4-6 shows the links for the Helm surname.

One drawback to comprehensive genealogical indexes is that they can be time-consuming to browse. It sometimes takes several clicks to get down to the area where you believe links that interest you may be located. And, after several clicks, you may find that no relevant links are in that area. This may be because the maintainer of the site has not yet indexed a relevant site or the site may be listed somewhere else in the index.

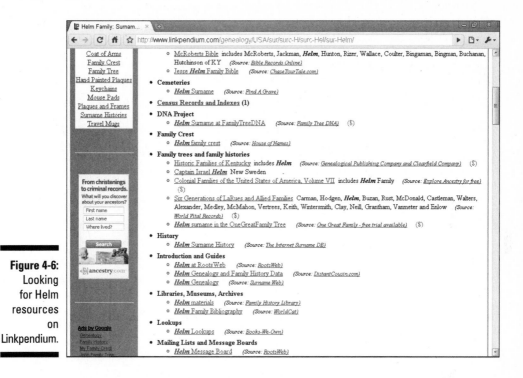

Figure 4-6:
Looking
for Helm
resources
on
Linkpendium.

Query for One: Seeking Answers to Your Surname Questions

Even if you can't find any surname-specific sites on your particular family, you still have hope! This hope comes in the form of queries. *Queries* are research questions that you post to a particular Web site, mailing list, or newsgroup so that other researchers can help you solve your research problems. Other researchers may have information that they haven't yet made available about a family, or they may have seen some information on your family, even though it isn't a branch that they're actively researching.

Web queries

One of the quickest ways to reach a wide audience with your query is through a query site on the Web. For an example of a query site, try GenForum:

1. **Open your Web browser and go to** www.genforum.com.

2. **In the field below Forum Finder, type the surname you're looking for and click Find.**

   We entered *Helm*. But feel free to enter a surname that interests you. If you feel like browsing the forums, you can also select a letter below the word *Surnames*.

   Don't worry if your surname doesn't have a forum. The GenForum section is constantly growing and adding surnames, so you should check back every so often to see whether one has been added, or you may consider requesting that a new forum be added for your surname. (Look for the Add Forum link near the bottom of the GenForum pages.)

   You may also want to search other forums to see whether the name is included in a variant spelling or whether someone else mentioned the name in a passing reference in another forum. (See the next section for details.)

3. **After you find a forum, read a message by clicking its link.**

   As soon as your browser loads the message board page, you should see a list of bulleted messages to choose from, as shown in Figure 4-7. You can also navigate to other pages of the message board if the messages don't fit on a single page. If you don't want to read all the messages, you have the option to see only the latest messages, only today's messages, or any messages posted in the last seven days. These options are available at the top of the list of posted messages.

4. **To post a new query, click Post New Message at the top of the list of posted messages.**

   If you're not already a registered user of GenForum, you see a page with instructions on registering.

   If you're already a registered user or after you become one, a page containing the fields that generate your message pops up. This page includes the name of the forum to which you're posting, your name and e-mail address, the subject of the posting, and a free-form text field where you can enter your message.

5. **Fill out the appropriate fields and then click Preview Message.**

   Make sure that your message contains enough information for other researchers to determine whether they can assist you. Include full names, birth and death dates and places (if known), and geographic locations where your ancestors lived (if known).

   Clicking the Preview Message button is an important step because you can see how the message will look when it's posted. This option can prevent you from posting a message filled with those embarrassing typos.

6. **When you're satisfied with the way the message looks, click Post Message.**

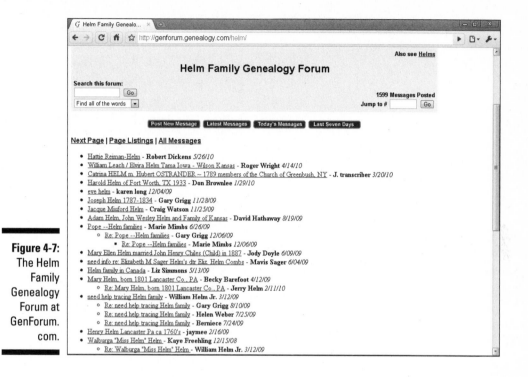

Figure 4-7:
The Helm
Family
Genealogy
Forum at
GenForum.
com.

Mailing list queries

When you think of mailing lists, you may have nightmares of the endless stream of junk mail that you receive every day as a result of some company selling your name to a mailing list. Well, fear no more. The type of mailing list we refer to delivers mail that you request. Such lists also provide a way that you can post queries and messages about your surnames and genealogical research in general.

Mailing lists are formed by groups of people who share common interests, whether those interests are surnames, specific geographic areas, particular topics, or ethnic groups. A list consists of the e-mail addresses of every person who joins (subscribes to) the group. When you want to send a message to the entire group, you send it to a single e-mail address that in turn forwards the message to everyone on the list. To join a mailing list, you send an e-mail to a designated address with a subscription message. You should then receive a confirmation e-mail that lets you know you're subscribed to the list and tells you where to send an e-mail if you want to send a message to everyone on the list.

Okay, even when you're hip to what a mailing list is, how do you find one of interest to you? One way is to consult the Mailing Lists page at RootsWeb (http://lists.rootsweb.ancestry.com), or you can look at a comprehensive genealogical index.

Chapter 5

Bureaucracy at Its Best: Using Government Sources

As we all know, governments love paper. Sometimes it seems that government workers can't do anything without a form. Luckily for genealogists, governments have been this way for a number of years — otherwise, it might be next to impossible to conduct family history research. In fact, the number of useful government records available online has exploded in the past decade. Not only have government entities been placing records and indexes online — private companies have put great effort into digitizing and indexing government records for online use.

In this chapter, we show you what kinds of records are currently available and describe some of the major projects that you can use as keys for unlocking government treasure chests of genealogical information.

These Records Are Vital

It seems that some kind of government record accompanies every major event in our lives. One is generated when we are born, another when we get married (as well as get divorced), another when we have a child, and still another when we pass on. *Vital records* is the collective name for records of these events. Traditionally, these records have been kept at the local level — in the county, parish, or in some cases, the town where the event occurred. However, over time, some state-level government agencies began making an effort to collect and centralize the holdings of vital records.

Reading vital records

Vital records are among the first sets of primary sources typically used by genealogists (for more on primary sources, see Chapter 1). That's because these records contain key and usually reliable information because they were produced near the time that the event occurred, and a witness to the event provided the information. (Outside the United States, vital records are often called *civil registrations*.) We explore the four types of vital records in this section.

Birth records

Birth records are good primary sources for verifying — at a minimum — the date of birth, birthplace, and names of an individual's parents. Depending on the information requirements for a particular birth certificate, you may also discover the birthplace of the parents, their ages, occupations, addresses at the time of the birth, whether the mother had given birth previously, date of marriage of the parents, and the names and ages of any previous children. Sometimes, instead of a birth certificate, you may find another record in the family's possession that verifies the existence of the birth record. For example, instead of having a certified copy of a birth certificate, Matthew's grandmother had a Certificate of Record of Birth. This certificate attests to the fact that the county has a certificate of birth and notes its location. These certificates were used primarily before photocopiers became commonplace, and it became easier to get a certified copy of the original record.

Birth records were less formal in earlier times. Before modern record-keeping, a simple handwritten entry in a book sufficed as an official record of an individual's birth. So be very specific when citing a birth record in your genealogical notes. Include any numbers you find in the record and where the record is located (including not only the physical location of the building, but also the book number and page number of the information, and even the record number if one is present).

Marriage records

Marriage records come in several forms. Early marriage records may include the following:

- **Marriage bonds:** Financial guarantees that a marriage was going to take place
- **Marriage banns:** Proclamations of the intent to marry someone in front of a church congregation
- **Marriage licenses:** Documents granting permission to marry
- **Marriage records or certificates:** Documents certifying the union of two people

These records usually contain the groom's name, the bride's name, and the location of the ceremony. They may also contain occupation information, birthplaces of the bride and groom, parents' names and birthplaces, names of witnesses, and information on previous marriages.

When using marriage records, don't confuse the date of the marriage with the date of the marriage bond, bann, or license. The latter records were often filed anywhere from a few days to several weeks *before* the actual marriage date. Also, do not assume that because you found a bond, bann, or license, a marriage took place. Some people got cold feet then (as they do today) and backed out of the marriage at the last minute.

If you have trouble finding a marriage record in the area where your ancestors lived, try looking in surrounding counties or parishes or possibly even states. Like today, destination weddings did occur! Lucky for those of us researching in the twenty-first century — most of our ancestors' destinations were nearby towns instead of exotic, far-off places. Typically, the reason some ancestors traveled to another location was to have the wedding at a particular relative's house or church. So if the record isn't in the location you expect, be sure to look in the areas where the parents of the ancestors lived.

Divorce records

One type of vital record that may be easy to overlook is a divorce decree. Later generations may not be aware that an early ancestor was divorced, and the records recounting the event can be difficult to find. However, divorce records can be valuable. They contain many important facts, including the age of the petitioners, birthplace, address, occupations, names and ages of children, property, and the grounds for the divorce.

Death records

Death records are excellent resources for verifying the date of death but are less reliable for other data elements such as birth date and birthplace, because people who were not witnesses to the birth often supply that information. However, information on the death record can point you in the right direction for records to verify other events. More recent death records include the name of the individual, place of death, residence, parents' names, spouse's name, occupation, and cause of death. Early death records may only contain the date of death, cause, and residence.

Gauging vitals online

Historically, researchers were required to contact the county, parish, or town clerk to receive a copy of a vital record. This meant either traveling to the location where the record was housed or ordering the record through the mail (and waiting several weeks for it to arrive). With the advent of online research, most sites covering vital records are geared toward providing addresses of repositories, rather than information on the vital records of particular individuals. The reason for this is the traditional sensitivity of vital records — and the reluctance of repositories to place vital records online due to identity theft and privacy concerns.

A few years ago, the number of resources containing information about specific vital records, including indexes and digitized records, began to greatly increase. Today, the vast majority of resources are indexes to vital records, but digitized records are starting to appear more frequently.

To get a better idea of how to search for vital records, we'll use members of Matthew's family as examples as we look at the different types of records that you will encounter online.

Vital record indexes

A good first place to start in your quest for vital records is to search for a vital records index for the place where you suspect your ancestor was born, married, or died. Vital record indexes serve much the same purpose as census indexes: They point to the locations of original records. You can use indexes to confirm that an ancestor's vital records are available prior to submitting a request for the record — or in some cases, you can use the index to lead you to a digitized copy of the record (typically on subscription sites). And knowing the exact location of the record can often make retrieval of the record a lot easier.

Although the majority of indexes are on subscription sites, sometimes you can find them on free genealogy project sites. To find these sites, you can conduct a search in a search engine for the locality, and then use the site search engine to find the individual you are looking for.

For example, Matthew is interested in acquiring a copy of the death certificate for his great-grandfather, William Henry Abell, who died in Kentucky. According to his headstone, William was born in 1873 and died in 1955. With this information, Matthew can begin to search for a vital records index.

To find an online index, you can use a search engine such as Google (www. google.com). For example, to find a death index for Kentucky, type the following search into Google:

> +"death index" +Kentucky

At the top of the results list is a link to RootsWeb Presents Kentucky Death Records 1911–2000. To find information on William Henry Abell, we go through the following steps:

1. **Go to the Kentucky Death Records site (`http://vitals.rootsweb.ancestry.com/ky/death/search.cgi`).**

   You see search fields in the middle of the page.

2. **In the Last Name field, type the surname of your ancestor. In the First Name field, type his or her given name.**

3. **If you want to restrict your search to a particular place of death, residence, or year, type those values in the appropriate fields.**

   Sticking with the example, we typed **Abell** and **William H.**

4. **Click Search.**

   Wait for the results to return.

5. **Scan the results of your query.**

   In our case, the results page contained two individuals named William H. Abell, as shown in Figure 5-1. One died in LaRue County and the other in Jefferson County. The location seems right for the William from LaRue County. The death date — September 7, 1955 — and the age, 82, is consistent with the information on the gravestone. The database also supplies us with the record volume number and certificate number, which we can use to obtain a copy of the certificate.

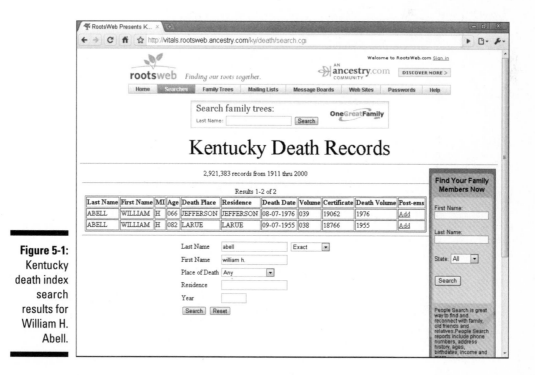

Figure 5-1: Kentucky death index search results for William H. Abell.

The following are some free sites containing state-wide vital records indexes:

- **California:** Death Records, 1940–1997, at `http://vitals.rootsweb.com/ca/death/search.cgi`

- **Idaho:** Death Index, 1911–1956, at `www.rootsweb.com/~idgenweb/deaths/search.htm`

- **Illinois:** Death Index, 1916–1950, at `www.cyberdriveillinois.com/departments/archives/idphdeathindex.html`

- **Kentucky:** Death Index, 1911–2000, at `http://vitals.rootsweb.com/ky/death/search.cgi`

- **Maine:** Marriage History Search at `http://portal.maine.gov/marriage/archdev.marriage_archive.search_form`

- **Maryland:** Death Index, 1898–1951, at `http://mdvitalrec.net/cfm/dsp_search.cfm`

- **Massachusetts:** Vital Records, 1600–1849, at `www.ma-vitalrecords.org`

- **Michigan:** Genealogical Death Indexing System, 1867–1897, at `www.mdch.state.mi.us/pha/osr/gendisx/search2.htm`

- **Minnesota:** Death Certificates Index, 1904–2001, at `http://people.mnhs.org/dci/Search.cfm?bhcp=1`

- **Missouri:** Death Certificates, 1910–1956, at `www.sos.mo.gov/archives/resources/deathcertificates`

- **Montana:** Death Registry Index, pre-1954 and 1954–2002, at `www.rootsweb.com/~mtmsgs/death_records.htm`

- **North Dakota:** Public Death Index Project, 1881–present, at `https://secure.apps.state.nd.us/doh/certificates/deathCertSearch.htm`

- **Ohio:** Death Certificate Index, 1913–1944, at `www.ohiohistory.org/dindex`

- **Oregon:** Death Index, 1903–1930, at `www.heritagetrailpress.com/Death_Index`

- **South Carolina:** Death Indexes, 1915–1956, at `www.scdhec.net/administration/vr/vrdi.htm`

- **South Dakota:** Birth Record Search Site for South Dakota Birth Records, with Birth Dates Over 100 Years, at `http://apps.sd.gov/applications/PH14Over100BirthRec/index.asp`

- **Tennessee:** Index to Tennessee Death Records, 1908–1912, at `www.tennessee.gov/tsla/history/vital/death2.htm`

- **Tennessee:** Index to Tennessee Death Records, 1914–1931, at `www.tennessee.gov/tsla/history/vital/tndeath.htm`

- ✔ **Tennessee:** Partial Index to Tennessee Death Records, 1914–1925, at `www.tennessee.gov/tsla/history/vital/death.htm`

- ✔ **Texas:** Texas Death Records, 1964–1998, at `http://vitals.roots web.com/tx/death/search.cgi`

- ✔ **Virginia:** Death Records Index, 1853–1896, at `http://ajax.lva. lib.va.us/F/?func=file&file_name=find-b-clas29&local_ base=clas29`

- ✔ **Wisconsin:** Wisconsin Genealogy Index, pre-1907 birth, death, and marriage records, at `www.wisconsinhistory.org/vitalrecords`

A number of free vital records indexes are available on the FamilySearch. org Records Search site at `http://search.labs.familysearch.org/ recordsearch/start.html#p=allCollections&r=0`. These indexes include the following:

- ✔ **Alabama:** Births and Christenings, 1881–1930; Deaths and Burials, 1881–1952; Deaths, 1908–1974; Marriages, 1816–1957

- ✔ **Arizona:** Births and Christenings, 1909–1917; Deaths and Burials, 1910–1911 and 1933–1994; Deaths, 1870–1951; Marriages, 1888–1908

- ✔ **Arkansas:** Births and Christenings, 1880–1893; Deaths and Burials, 1882–1929 and 1945–1963; County Marriages, 1837–1957; Marriages, 1837–1944

- ✔ **Connecticut:** Births and Christenings, 1649–1906; Deaths and Burials, 1772–1934; Marriages, 1729–1867

- ✔ **Delaware:** Births and Christenings, 1710–1896; Deaths and Burials, 1815–1955; State Birth Records, 1861–1922; Marriages, 1713–1953

- ✔ **District of Columbia:** Births and Christenings, 1830–1955; Deaths and Burials, 1840–1964; Marriages, 1830–1921

- ✔ **Florida:** Births and Christenings, 1880–1935; Deaths and Burials, 1900–1921; Deaths, 1877–1939; Marriages, 1837–1974

- ✔ **Georgia:** Deaths, 1914–1927; Marriages, 1928–1930

- ✔ **Hawaii:** Births and Christenings, 1852–1933; Deaths and Burials, 1862–1919; Marriages, 1826–1922

- ✔ **Idaho:** Births and Christenings, 1856–1965; Death Certificates, 1911–1937; Deaths and Burials, 1907–1965; Marriages, 1878–1898

- ✔ **Illinois:** Cook County Birth Certificates, 1878–1922; Cook County Deaths 1878–1922; Cook County Marriages, 1871–1920; Cook County Birth Registers, 1871–1915

- ✔ **Indiana:** Marriages, 1780–1992 and 1811–1959

- ✔ **Iowa:** Births and Christenings, 1830–1950; Deaths and Burials, 1850–1990; Marriages, 1809–1922

- ✔ **Kansas:** Births and Christenings, 1818–1936; Deaths and Burials, 1885–1930; Marriages, 1840–1935

- ✔ **Kentucky:** Births and Christenings, 1839–1960; Deaths and Burials, 1843–1970; Marriages, 1785–1979

- ✔ **Louisiana:** Births and Christenings, 1811–1830, 1854–1934; Deaths and Burials, 1850–1875, 1894–1954; Marriages, 1816–1906

- ✔ **Maine:** Births and Christenings, 1739–1900; Deaths and Burials, 1841–1910; Marriages, 1771–1907

- ✔ **Maryland:** Births and Christenings, 1650–1995; Deaths and Burials, 1877–1992; Marriages, 1666–1970

- ✔ **Massachusetts:** Births and Christenings, 1639–1915; Deaths and Burials, 1795–1910; Marriages, 1841–1915

- ✔ **Michigan:** Births and Christenings, 1775–1995; Deaths and Burials, 1800–1995; Marriages, 1822–1995

- ✔ **Minnesota:** Births and Christenings, 1840–1980; Deaths and Burials, 1835–1990; Marriages, 1849–1950

- ✔ **Missouri:** Deaths and Burials, 1867–1976

- ✔ **Montana:** Marriages, 1889–1947

- ✔ **Nebraska:** Marriages, 1855–1995

- ✔ **New Hampshire:** Births and Christenings, 1714–1904; Deaths and Burials, 1784–1949; Marriages, 1720–1920

- ✔ **New Jersey:** Births and Christenings, 1660–1980; Deaths and Burials, 1720–1988; Marriages, 1678–1985

- ✔ **New Mexico:** Births and Christenings, 1726–1918; Deaths and Burials, 1788–1798, 1838–1955; Marriages, 1751–1918

- ✔ **New York:** Births and Christenings, 1640–1962; Deaths and Burials, 1795–1952; Marriages, 1686–1980

- ✔ **North Carolina:** Births and Christenings, 1866–1964; Deaths and Burials, 1898–1994; Marriages, 1759–1979

- ✔ **Ohio:** Births and Christenings, 1821–1962; Deaths and Burials, 1854–1997; Marriages, 1800–1958

- ✔ **Oregon:** Births and Christenings, 1868–1929; Deaths and Burials, 1903–1947; Marriages, 1853–1935

- ✔ **Pennsylvania:** Philadelphia City Death Certificates, 1803–1915; Philadelphia Marriage Indexes, 1885–1951

- ✔ **Rhode Island:** Births and Christenings, 1878–1914; Deaths and Burials, 1802–1950; Marriages, 1724–1916

✔ **Tennessee:** Births and Christenings, 1828–1939; Deaths and Burials, 1874–1955; Marriages, 1796–1950

✔ **Texas:** Births and Christenings, 1840–1981; Deaths and Burials, 1903–1973; Marriages, 1837–1973

✔ **Utah:** Births and Christenings, 1892–1941; Deaths and Burials, 1888–1946; Marriages, 1887–1966

✔ **Vermont:** Births and Christenings, 1765–1908; Deaths and Burials, 1871–1965; Marriages, 1791–1974

✔ **Virginia:** Deaths and Burials, 1853–1912; Marriages, 1785–1940

✔ **Washington:** Death Certificates, 1907–1960; State County Marriages, 1858–1950

✔ **West Virginia:** Births and Christenings, 1853–1928; Deaths and Burials, 1854–1932; Marriages, 1854–1932

✔ **Wisconsin:** Births and Christenings, 1826–1926; Deaths and Burials, 1835–1968; Marriages, 1836–1930

✔ **Wyoming:** Marriages, 1877–1920

You can also find free sites with smaller collections of vital records, such as birth records for a particular county. To find these, use your favorite general search engine.

You can also find an abundant selection of vital records indexes at subscription sites. For example, WorldVitalRecords.com has built a collection of vital record indexes for many states in the United States, as well as a growing collection of international records (see Figure 5-2).

Examples of vital record indexes on WorldVitalRecords.com follow:

✔ Frederick County, Virginia: Marriages 1771–1825

✔ Parish Register of Kingston, Upper Canada, 1785–1811

✔ Tennessee Deaths, 1908–1912

✔ Vital Records of Weymouth, Massachusetts: to the year 1850

Digital images of vital records

One of the newest areas in the digitization of primary sources has been in the area of vital records. In the past, archives that house vital records have been reluctant to digitize them due to privacy concerns. However, as more and more requests come in for vital records, these archives have allowed companies to place those records that fall outside the provisions of the privacy act online.

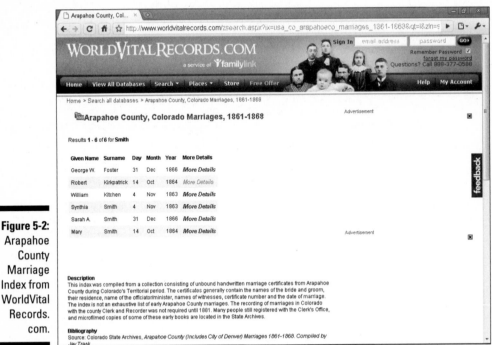

Figure 5-2:
Arapahoe
County
Marriage
Index from
WorldVital
Records.
com.

Through family interviews, Matthew knows that John C. Martin, his great-great grandfather on another side of his family, was married to Emma Temperance Gardiner in Missouri. Let's suppose that you too are interested in finding a copy of the record documenting the marriage. (It's more likely that you just want to learn the method for finding such a record for one of your ancestors.) To find digitized vital records, try this:

1. **Go to the search engine Bing (www.bing.com) and type the search term** Missouri Marriage Records.

   You might prefer to use a different state name, depending on whether your ancestor was from Missouri or somewhere else.

2. **Click the Missouri Marriage Records, 1805–2002 — Ancestry.com link.**

   The resulting screen includes a search form requesting name, spouse, and marriage information.

3. **Type** John Martin **in the name field and** Emma Gardiner **in the spouse field, and then clicked the Search button.**

   Again, you might want to substitute your own ancestors' names. If so, your results will vary a bit. A table containing search results was displayed. The top two results contained a record for John C. Martin who married an Emma Gardiner. Both records have the marriage occurring in Lafayette County. The difference is that Emma's middle initial is different.

4. **Click the icon on the far right of the row below the View Images column.**

    A page appeared with subscription information. If you already have a subscription, you can log in to your account at the upper-right corner of the screen. If not, you have to follow the prompts to get a free 14-day trial. We filled in the login information and clicked the Sign In button. After the login, the page displayed the image of the marriage record.

5. **After the image pops up, click the Zoom In button to see the image more clearly.**

    Figure 5-3 shows the image of the marriage record. We found two entries in the index because Emma's middle initial is not entirely clear. It could have been either a *T* or an *S*. From the image, we can see that William C. Dawson married John and Emma on 27 August 1868.

Here is a list of examples of the vital records now available online:

- ✔ **Arizona:** Arizona Genealogy Birth and Death Certificates (births 1887–1931; deaths 1878–1956) at `http://genealogy.az.gov`

- ✔ **Colorado:** Arapahoe County (includes City of Denver) Marriages 1861–1868 at `www.colorado.gov/dpa/doit/archives/DenMarriage/denver_and_arapahoe_county_marri.htm`

- ✔ **Georgia:** Death Certificates, 1919–1927, at `http://content.sos.state.ga.us/cdm4/gadeaths.php`

- ✔ **Kentucky:** Death Certificates, 1852–1953 (subscription site), at `http://content.ancestry.com/iexec/?htx=List&dbid=1222&offerid=0%3a7858%3a0`

- ✔ **Utah:** Death Certificates, 1904–1959, at `http://archives.utah.gov/research/indexes/20842.htm`

- ✔ **West Virginia:** Birth, Death, and Marriage Certificates at `www.wvculture.org/vrr/va_select.aspx`

General information sites

If you've had only a little luck finding a digitized vital record or index (or you need a record that is within the range of the privacy act), your next step might be to visit a general information site. If you're looking for information on how to order vital records in the United States, you can choose among a few sites. Several commercial sites have addresses for vital records repositories. Unfortunately, some of them are full of advertisements for subscription sites, making it difficult to determine which links will lead you to useful information and what is going to lead you to a third-party site to make a sale.

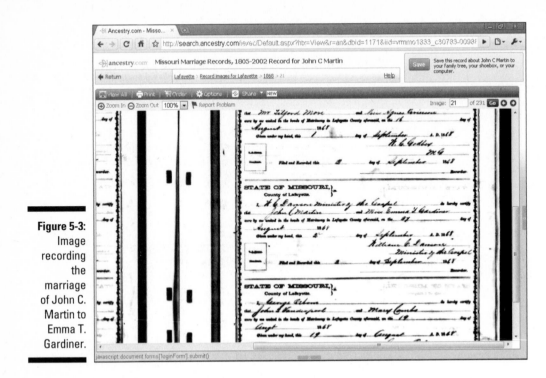

Figure 5-3:
Image
recording
the
marriage
of John C.
Martin to
Emma T.
Gardiner.

One site that contains useful information without the advertisements is the Where to Write for Vital Records page on the Centers for Disease Control and Prevention site (www.cdc.gov/nchs/w2w.htm). To locate information, simply click a state and you see a table listing details on how to order records from state-level repositories.

Coming to Your Census

A lot of key dates in a person's life are recorded in vital records (see the section "These Records Are Vital," earlier in this chapter, for more details). However, unless your ancestors were consistently encountering life events that resulted in numerous vital records, you'll still have some gaps to fill in while researching. Census records are one of the most valuable tools to a genealogist, at least in the United States. *Census records* are periodic counts of a population by a government or organization. These counts can be conducted at regular intervals (such as every ten years) or special one-time counts made for a specific reason.

Census records are valuable for tying a person to a place and for discovering relationships between individuals. For example, suppose you have a great-great-great-grandfather by the name of Nimrod Sanders. You're not sure who his father was, but you do know that he was born in North Carolina. By using a census index, you may be able to find a Nimrod Sanders listed in a North Carolina census index as a member of someone's household. If the information about Nimrod in that record (age, location, and siblings' names) fits what you know from family legend, you may have found one more generations to add to your genealogy. You can use the name of the head of household and his or her spouse as a lead to investigate in identifying Nimrod's parents.

Often a census includes information such as a person's age, sex, occupation, birthplace, and relationship to the head of the household. Sometimes the *enumerators* (the people who conduct the census) added comments to the census record (such as a comment on the physical condition of an individual or an indication of the person's wealth) that may give you further insight into the person's life.

But before we launch into how to find census records online, it's a good idea to have some background on how the records were used. So, here we go.

United States census schedules

Federal census records in the United States have been around since 1790. Censuses were conducted every ten years to count the population for a couple of reasons — to correctly divide the number of seats in the U.S. House of Representatives and to assess federal taxes. Although census collections are still performed, privacy restrictions prevent the release of any detailed census information on individuals for 72 years. Currently, you can find federal census data on individuals only for the census years 1790 to 1930 (with the 1940 census due out in 2012). However, practically all the 1890 Census was destroyed due to actions taken after a fire in the Commerce Building in 1921 — for more on this, see "First in the Path of the Firemen," The Fate of the 1890 Population Census, at www.archives.gov/publications/prologue/1996/spring/1890-census-1.html.

Federal census records are valuable in that you can use them to take historical snapshots of your ancestors in ten-year increments. These snapshots enable you to track your ancestors as they moved from county to county or state to state, and to identify the names of parents and siblings of your ancestors who you may not have previously known.

Each census year contains a different amount of information, with more modern census returns (also called *schedules*) containing the most information. Schedules from 1790 to 1840 list only the head of household for each family, along with the number of people living in the household broken down by age classifications. Schedules from 1850 on have the names and ages of all members of the household.

Using American Soundex to search U. S. census records

For the censuses conducted from 1880 to 1920, you can use microfilmed indexes organized under the American Soundex system.

The *American Soundex* system is an indexing method that groups names that are pronounced in a similar way but are spelled differently. This indexing procedure allows you to find ancestors who may have changed the spelling of their names over the years. For example, you find names such as Helm, Helme, Holm, and Holme grouped in the American Soundex.

The American Soundex code for a name consists of a letter and then three numbers. (Double letters count for only one number, and if your surname is short or has a lot of vowels in it, you use zeros on the end to bring the total number to three.) To convert your surname to American Soundex, use the first letter of your surname as the first letter of the American Soundex code and then substitute numbers for the next three consonants according to the following list. (For example, the American Soundex code for the surname *Helm* is H450.)

1	B, P, F, V
2	C, S, K, G, J, Q, X, Z
3	D, T
4	L
5	M, N
6	R

That explanation probably sounds confusing, so just follow these steps to convert your surname to an American Soundex code:

1. **Write down your surname on a piece of paper.**

   As an example, we will convert the surname *Abell*.

2. **Keep the first letter of the surname, and then cross out any remaining vowels (A, E, I, O, U) and the letters *W, Y,* and *H.***

   If your surname begins with a vowel, keep the first vowel. If your surname does not begin with a vowel, cross out all the vowels in the surname. So, in the surname *Abell,* we keep the letters *A, B, L,* and *L.*

3. **If the surname has double letters, cross out the second letter.**

   For example, the surname Abell has a double *L,* so we cross out the second *L,* which leaves us with the letters *A, B,* and *L.*

4. **Convert your letters to the American Soundex code numbers according to the preceding list.**

   Because *A* is the first letter of the surname, it remains an *A*. The *B* converts to the number 1 and the *L* to the number 4. That leaves us with A14.

5. **Cross out the second occurrence of any repeated numbers that are side by side, including a number that repeats the value that the letter at the beginning would have.**

   The remaining numbers of the Abell (A14) surname do not have the same numerical code next to each other. But it could happen with a name such as Schaefer. Ordinarily, the name Schaefer would have the American Soundex code of S216. However, because the *S* and the *C* would both have the code of 2 and are side by side, you would eliminate the second 2, resulting in an American Soundex code of S160.

6. **If you do not have three numbers remaining, fill in the rest with zeros.**

   Only two numbers remain in the Abell surname after we cross out the vowels and double letters. Because the American Soundex system requires a total of three numbers to complete the code, we fill in the remaining numerical spot with a 0. Thus, our result for Abell is A140.

If you're like we are, you want the most efficient way to do things. Although figuring out an American Soundex is not overly complicated, it can be a little time-consuming if you have several names to calculate. Fortunately, some free online sites are available to calculate American Soundex codes. Here are a few:

✔ **Yet Another Soundex Converter:** www.bradandkathy.com/genealogy/yasc.html

✔ **Surname to Soundex Code:** http://resources.rootsweb.com/cgi-bin/soundexconverter

✔ **Surname to Soundex Converter:** www.searchforancestors.com/soundex.html

American Soundex indexes are subject to human error and, in some cases, are incomplete. For example, the 1880 Federal Census American Soundex primarily focuses on indexing those households with children age 10 years or younger. And those who carried out the actual indexing did not always handle American Soundex codes correctly or consistently. So the indexer may have made a coding error or failed to include some information. Therefore, if you're relatively certain that an ancestor *should* show up in a particular county in a census that uses American Soundex, but the American Soundex microfilm doesn't reflect that person, you may want to go through the census microfilm for that county anyway and look line by line for your ancestor. This process may seem tedious, but the results can be worthwhile.

Soundex improvements

Many of you have heard of the Soundex system — especially if you've worked with the United States census in the past, if you live in a state that uses the Soundex as part of your driver's license number, or if you're just a nut for indexing systems. However, you might not realize that more than one Soundex System exists. The American Soundex, which is the one used for the U. S. census and the one most widely recognized, is not the only one, nor was it the first system developed.

The Russell Soundex system: Robert C. Russell patented the first Soundex system in 1918. The Russell Soundex system categorizes the alphabet phonetically and assigns numbers to the categories. You find eight categories and four other rules to follow. The odd-looking terms that refer to parts of the mouth are technical descriptions of how to make the sounds; just try making the sounds of the letters shown with each one, and you'll get the idea. Here's what they look (and sound) like:

Categories:

1. Vowels or oral resonants: *a, e, i, o, u, y*

2. Labials and labio-dentals: *b, f, p, v*

3. Gutturals and sibilants: *c, g, k, s, x, z*

4. Dental-mutes: *d, t*

5. Palatal-fricative: *l*

6. Labio-nasal: *m*

7. Dento- or lingua-nasal: *n*

8. Dental-fricative: *r*

Other rules:

- The code always begins with the first letter of the word.

- If you have two letters in a row that are the same, they are represented in the code as one letter (for example, *rr,* is represented as *r*).

- If the word ends in *gh, s,* or *z,* those letters are ignored.

- Vowels are considered only the first time they appear.

The American Soundex system: The American Soundex system, the system with which most people are familiar, modified the Russell Soundex system. The changes include these:

- The code disregards vowels altogether, unless the first letter of the word is a vowel.

- The letters *m* and *n* are categorized together and represented by the same number.

- Words ending in *gh, s,* and *z* are treated the same as other words, and those letters are assigned values.

The American Soundex code begins with the first letter of the word and has three numbers following. Zeros are added to the code to ensure that it has three numbers. You can see the categories of letters and numbers assigned to them in the section "Using American Soundex to search U. S. census records," earlier in this chapter.

The Daitch-Mokotoff Soundex system: The Daitch-Mokotoff Soundex system builds on the Russell and American Soundex systems, and addresses difficulties in categorizing many Germanic and Slavic names that the other two systems encounter. The major points of this system are as follows:

- The code is made up of six numbers.

- The first letter of the word is also represented by a number. If the first letter is a vowel, it has the code 0.

- Some double-letter combinations that sound like single letters are coded as single.

- If a letter or letter combination can have two sounds, it is coded twice.

If you want more detailed information about the various Soundex systems, take a gander at the Soundexing and Genealogy Web site at `www.avotaynu.com/soundex.html`.

The Beider-Morse Phonetic Matching system: A problem with the various Soundex systems is that they often match names that are not really closely related. The goal of Phonetic Matching is to remove the irrelevant name matches, while not losing matches that are closely related. The features of the system include the following:

✔ Because the pronunciation of a name depends on the language that the name comes from, the system includes pronunciation tables for several languages, including Catalan, Czech, Dutch, English, French, German, Greek, Hebrew, Hungarian, Italian, Polish, Portuguese, Romanian, Russian, Spanish, and Turkish.

✔ After the language of the name is known, the name is converted to a sequence of phonetic tokens that are compared to other names that have been converted to tokens.

✔ Some double-letter combinations that sound like single letters are coded as single.

You can find more details on phonetic matching on the Phonetic Matching: A Better Soundex page at `http://stevemorse.org/phonetics/bmpm2.htm`.

And if you want to run some names through the American Soundex, Daitch-Mokotoff Soundex, and Beider-Morse Phonetic Matching systems at the same time, we recommend you visit the Generating Soundex Codes and Phonetic Tokens in One Step converter at `http://stevemorse.org/census/soundex.html`.

Regular population schedules were not the only product of the federal censuses. Special schedules, including census returns for particular populations such as slaves, mortality, agriculture, manufacturing, and veterans, were also conducted. Each type of special schedule contains information pertaining to a specific group or occupation. In the case of slave schedules (used in the 1850 and 1860 censuses), slaves were listed under the names of the slave owner, and information was provided on the age, gender, and race of the slave. If the slave was more than 100 years old, his or her name was listed on the schedules (although names may have been included for other slaves if the enumerator felt inclined to list them).

Mortality schedules (used in 1850, 1860, 1870, and 1880) include information on people who died in the 12 months previous to the start of the census. Agricultural schedules were used between 1840 and 1910. However, only the schedules from 1840 to 1880 survive. They contain detailed demographic and financial information on farm owners. Manufacturing schedules (taken infrequently between 1810 and 1880) contain information on business owners and their business interests. Veteran schedules include the Revolutionary pensioner census, which was taken as part of the 1840 Census, and the special census for Union veterans and their widows (taken in 1890).

State, territorial, and other census records

Federal census records are not the only population enumerations you can find for ancestors in the United States. You may also find census records at the state, territorial, and local level for certain areas of the United States.

Several state and territorial censuses have become available online. Ancestry.com (www.ancestry.com) has state and territorial censuses for Alabama (1820–1866), Colorado (1885), Florida (1867–1945), Illinois (1825–1865), Iowa (1836–1925), Kansas (1855–1925), Michigan (1894); Minnesota (1849–1905), Mississippi (1792–1866), Missouri (1844–1881), Nebraska (1860–1885), New Jersey (1895), New York (1880, 1892, 1905), North Dakota (1915, 1925), Oklahoma (1890, 1907), Washington (1857–1892), and Wisconsin (1895, 1905), as well as a host of other census records including images of the U.S. Indian Census schedules from 1885 to 1940.

Another source for state and territorial census images is at HistoryKat (www.historykat.com). HistoryKat has images for Colorado (1885), Florida (1885), Illinois (1820–1865), Iowa (1836), Minnesota (1857), New Mexico (1885), Oklahoma (1890, 1907), and Wisconsin (1836–1847). Figure 5-4 shows an image from the 1840 Illinois State Census for Calhoun County.

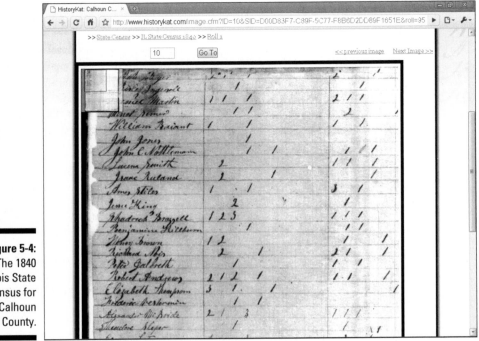

Figure 5-4: The 1840 Illinois State Census for Calhoun County.

Non-federal census records can often help you piece together your ancestors' migration patterns or account for ancestors who may not have been
enumerated in the federal censuses. Sometimes, these censuses can also provide more detail about your ancestors than the federal census schedules can.

Finding your ancestors in census records

Imagine that you're ready to look for your ancestors in census records. You
hop in the car and drive to the nearest library, archives, or Family History
Center. On arrival, you find the microfilm roll for the area where you believe
your ancestors lived. You then go into a dimly lit room, insert the microfilm into the reader, and begin your search. After a few hours of rolling the
microfilm, the back pain begins to set in, cramping in your hands becomes
more severe, and the handwritten census documents become blurry as your
eyes strain from reading each entry line by line. You come to the end of the
roll and still haven't found your elusive ancestor. At this point, you begin to
wonder whether a better way exists.

Fortunately, a better way *does* exist for a lot of census records: census
indexes. A *census index* contains a listing of the people who are included in
particular census records, along with references indicating where you can
find the actual census record. Traditionally, these indexes come in book
form, but you can now find these indexes online. Although no single Web site
contains indexes of all available census records for all countries (at least not
yet), some sites contain substantial collections of census indexes.

So how do you find these online indexes? Well, you have a few ways, depending on whether you want to use a free site or a subscription site. First, you
can check a comprehensive index site, a search engine, or a site listing links
to census indexes to find an index that was placed on a free site by an individual or a group project.

If you don't want to pay a fee to access census indexes online, you can find
some census indexes under the USGenWeb Archives Census Project at www.
rootsweb.com/~usgenweb/census. The Census Project is a volunteer
effort to index the United States censuses and provide them online for free. If
you can't find an index there, try a site dedicated to providing links to online
census resources, such as Census Online (www.census-online.com) or
CensusLinks (www.censuslinks.com), or a geographic-specific site, such
as the county-level pages in the USGenWeb Project (www.usgenweb.org).
Also, a number of independent sites have census indexes; typically you can
find them by using a search engine such as Google (www.google.com).

Say you want to find Samuel Abell (Matthew's sixth great-grandfather), who lived
in St. Mary's County, Maryland, in 1790. Your first step is to see whether an index
is available for that county during the 1790 Census. To do this, try the following:

1. **Fire up your Web browser and go to Census Online (`www.census-online.com`).**

2. **Click Links to Online Census Records.**

   This page contains a number of links represented by a state or province (depending on whether it's a state in the United States or a province in Canada).

3. **Click the Maryland Census Records link.**

   A page appears, showing a column (on the left) with state-wide links to censuses and the names of counties for the state, and a second column containing a map of the state.

4. **Select a county from the left column or from the map.**

   In our case, we selected St. Mary's County. The resulting page for St. Mary's County has nine links.

5. **Scroll down and click the Index to 1790 Federal Census link.**

   This takes you to a text file on the USGenWeb Census Project containing the index. The sixteenth person on the list is Samuel Abell, as shown in Figure 5-5.

Another free index that you may want to take a look at is the 1880 U.S. Census index at FamilySearch. This index contains more than 50 million names. Among those names is Matthew's third great-grandfather, Samuel Clayton Abell. Here's how to find him:

1. **Point your Web browser to `www.familysearch.org`.**

2. **Click the Search Records tab at the top of the page**

   In the left column (colored tan), you see a list of resources to refine the search.

3. **Click the Census link.**

4. **Use the Census drop-down list to select the 1880 United States Census.**

   New search criteria are displayed.

5. **Type your search criteria in the appropriate fields and click Search.**

   Type **Samuel** in the First Name field and **Abell** in the Last Name field. To further refine the search, we selected Kentucky in the Census State drop-down list. Because different spellings of his name exist, make sure that the Use Exact Spelling option is deselected.

   The search results show 11 Samuels with last names spelled either Abell or Able in Kentucky in the 1880 Census. We select the first one, because he has a middle initial of *C* — Samuel normally included his middle name or initial on government records. Figure 5-6 shows the record for Samuel C. Able, along with a link to the digital image of the census at Ancestry.com. To see the actual image, you must be a subscriber to Ancestry.com.

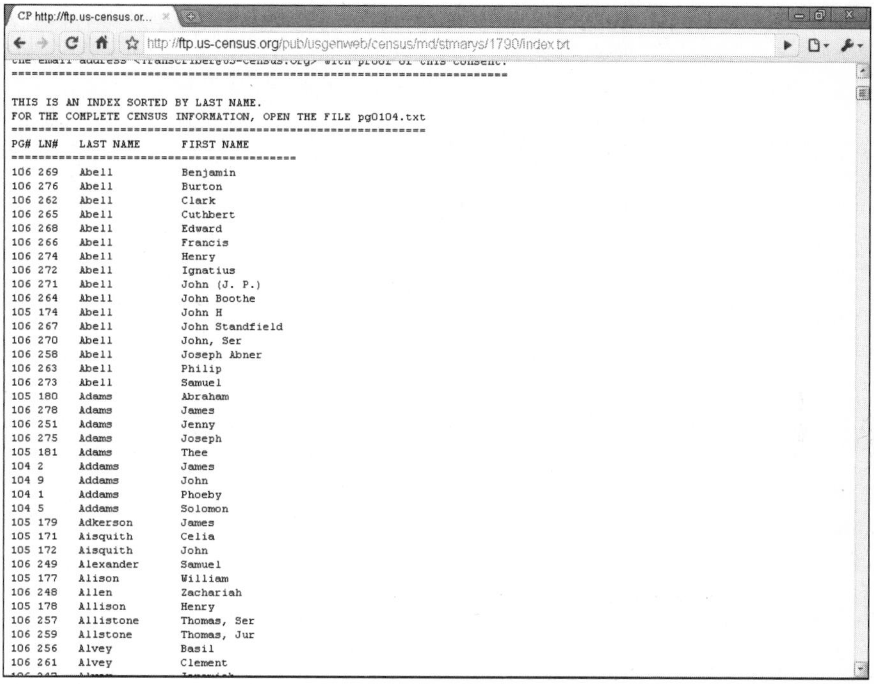

Figure 5-5:
Scrolling through the Index to 1790 Federal Census, we see that Samuel Abell is listed.

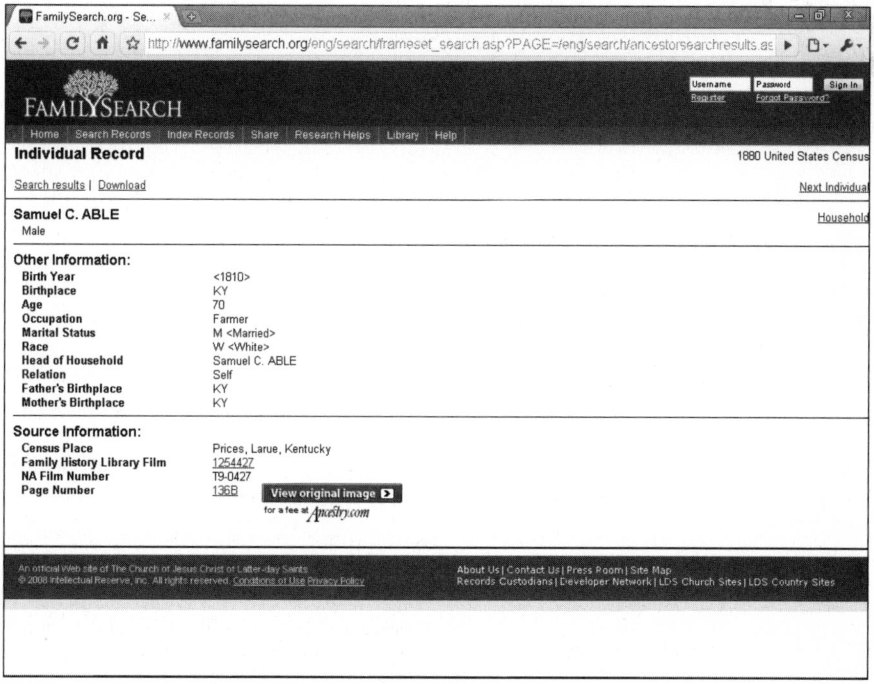

Figure 5-6:
The entry for Samuel C. Able in the 1880 U.S. Census.

Finding individuals in subscription indexes

Currently, the largest United States Census population schedule index collections are found on the subscription-based Ancestry.com (available to individuals, libraries, and other institutions) and HeritageQuest Online (available only to libraries and other institutions). Ancestry.com (www.ancestry.com) has census indexes for the years 1790 through 1870, generated from print indexes. Ancestry.com also has reindexed population schedules from 1790 to 1870 and from 1900 to 1930. The site uses the 1880 index produced by the Church of Jesus Christ of Latter-day Saints and has indexed the census fragment for 1890. HeritageQuest Online (www.heritagequestonline.com) has reindexed census entries for the years 1790 through 1930.

Recently, Ancestry.com and FamilySearch.org (www.familysearch.org) announced a partnership where FamilySearch volunteers will create a second set of census indexes for United States censuses from 1790 to 1930. After the new indexes are available, they will be posted free of charge on the FamilySearch.org site. A similar agreement has been negotiated between FamilySearch.org and Findmypast.com (www.findmypast.co.uk) to index United Kingdom censuses from 1841 to 1901.

Footnote.com (www.footnote.com) has also begun to index the United States censuses. Work is under way on the 1860, 1900, 1910, 1920, and 1930 censuses.

Be careful when using these indexes. Not all indexes include every person in the census. Some are merely head-of-household indexes. So, it's a good idea to read the description that comes with the index to see how complete it is. Also, the same quality control may not be there for every census year, even within the same index-producing company. If you do not find your ancestor in one of these indexes, don't automatically assume that he or she is not in the census. Also remember that many indexes were created outside the United States by people who were not native English speakers and who were under time constraints. It is quite possible that the indexer was incorrect in indexing a particular entry — possibly the person you are searching for.

One of the benefits of using a subscription census index is the value-added features built into the search mechanism. For example, if we do a search for the same Samuel Abell as we did in the last section on Ancestry.com, we see some of the additional features of the search engine. Figure 5-7 shows the search results for Samuel Abell, limiting the search to the 1790 Census. The first column is the match quality, which is a visual representation of how close the search result is to the search terms. In this case, Samuel Abell ranks first based on his name and his location in St. Mary's County, Maryland. From this same search results page, you can view a textual record of the individual, as well as a link to see a digital image of the census record. In addition to presenting results based on your search criteria, this search mechanism displays other results that are similar — such as individuals with the same last name or people who have a name that sounds similar to the search criteria.

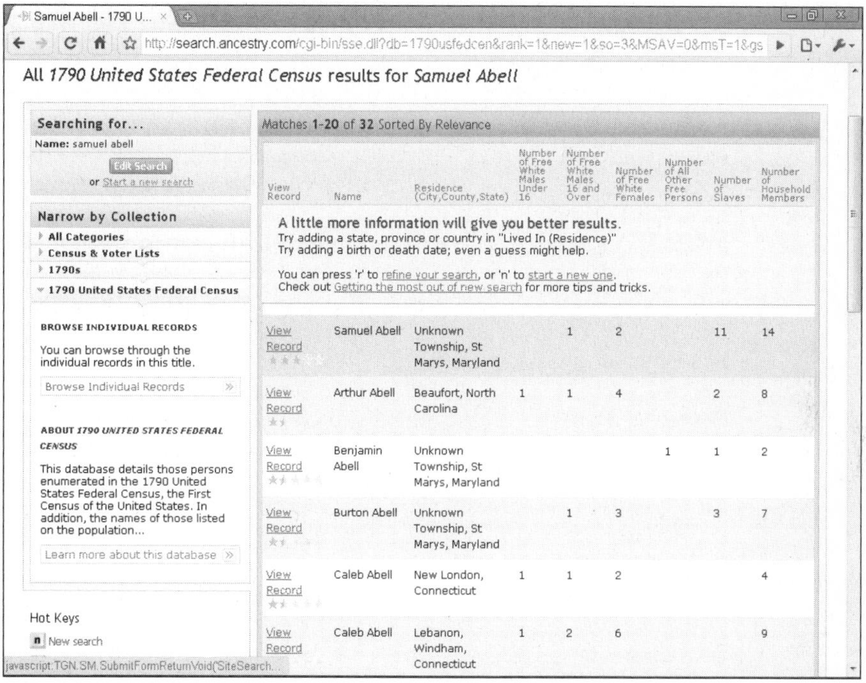

Figure 5-7:
Search
results for
Samuel
Abell in
the 1790
Census.

If you widen the search criteria to more than 1790 (such as in Figure 5-8), you can see entries for Samuel not only in the 1790 Census but also in the 1800 Census and 1810 Census, along with some rent roll records.

Using a transcribed online census

Although finding census indexes is a start, they don't show you enough to let you determine whether that record is that of the person for whom you're look-ing. Often you need additional information such as the age of the individual or the number of people in the individual's household. With the number of census images available online, we advise you to consult those after finding someone in an index. Even if you don't want to pay for a subscription site, several libraries hold subscriptions to the major genealogy sites. But, if you don't have access to a subscription site, census transcriptions can get you on the correct path. Most of the free online transcriptions cover only a portion of a census area dealing with a particular family or are complete transcriptions for a county.

As with any transcribed record, you should always verify your findings with a digitized or microfilm copy of the original record. Often, census records are difficult to read because of their age, the quality of the handwriting, and so on — so mistakes do occur in the transcription process. But these transcribed records are better than nothing.

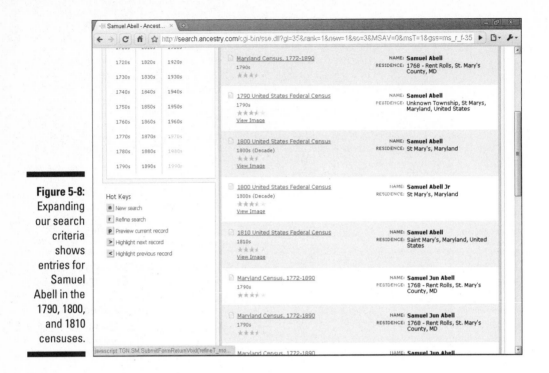

Finding transcribed records on the Internet is similar to finding census indexes. You can try one of the comprehensive genealogical sites under a geographical category or a search engine. To see a step-by-step walk-through of a search using a comprehensive site or search engine, see Chapter 4.

Census records in the United States are a mainstay of genealogists, so most transcribed censuses that you see on the Internet come from the United States (although that doesn't mean that censuses from other countries aren't online — as we explain in the next chapter). A couple of projects are undertaken by USGenWeb volunteers to systematically transcribe census records. You can find the USGenWeb Archives Census Project at www.rootsweb.com/~us genweb/census and the USGenWeb Census Project On-Line Inventory of Transcribed Censuses at www.us-census.org/inventory/inventory.htm. Individuals simply transcribed those censuses in which they are interested or those associated with a geographical area they are researching. This fact doesn't diminish the importance of these efforts; it only explains why you may see a census record for one county but not for the county right next to it.

Here's a sample search on the USGenWeb Archives Census Project site:

1. **Go to the USGenWeb Census Project site (www.rootsweb. com/~census/states.htm).**

   You see a page with a map and list of states and territories for which census transcriptions are available.

2. **Select a state for your search by clicking the state on the map or its link in the list.**

   For our example, we're looking for census information on Isaac Metcalf, who lived in Baylor County, Texas, around 1880, so we selected Texas. A list of available census schedules for the state appears.

3. **Click a year or type of schedule that interests you.**

   We selected 1880. The resulting page contains a table listing the location, roll number, status of the project, and transcriber's name.

4. **Click the Status button for an available census.**

   We choose the transcription for Baylor County by clicking the Online link, which takes us to the Information on Baylor County Web page.

5. **Scroll down and click the 1880 Baylor County Federal Census link.**

   A page of transcribed census entries is displayed, and we can scroll down to an individual named Isaac Metcalf. You can also use your browser's Find in Page option to find the name you're looking for.

The transcriptions you can use at this site are the works of volunteers; you might find errors here and there. Typographical errors may crop up, some censuses may not be indexed, or the status of the project for a particular county may be incorrect.

The most plentiful type of transcribed census records you're likely to encounter is what we refer to as the *plain-text census,* which is a Web page or text file that's simply a transcription of the actual census record without any kind of search function. You either have to skim the page or use your Web browser's Find in Page option to find the person you're looking for. The 1850 Census for Stark County, Illinois, at `www.rootsweb.ancestry.com/~cenfiles/il/stark/1850/indx-a-g.txt`, is an example of this type of census return (see Figure 5-9). For each individual, the record includes the house number of the household, last name, first name, age, sex, race, occupation, real-estate value, personal-property value, and birthplace. This site is also typical of smaller census sites in its focus on the records on one county (actually, one township in one county).

Some sites contain collections of several census returns for a specific geographic area (over an extended period of time). A good example of this type of site is the Transcribed Census Records for Vernon County, Missouri, at `http://freepages.genealogy.rootsweb.com/~jrbakerjr/census/census1.htm`, which has several transcribed census returns for the county from 1860 to 1930.

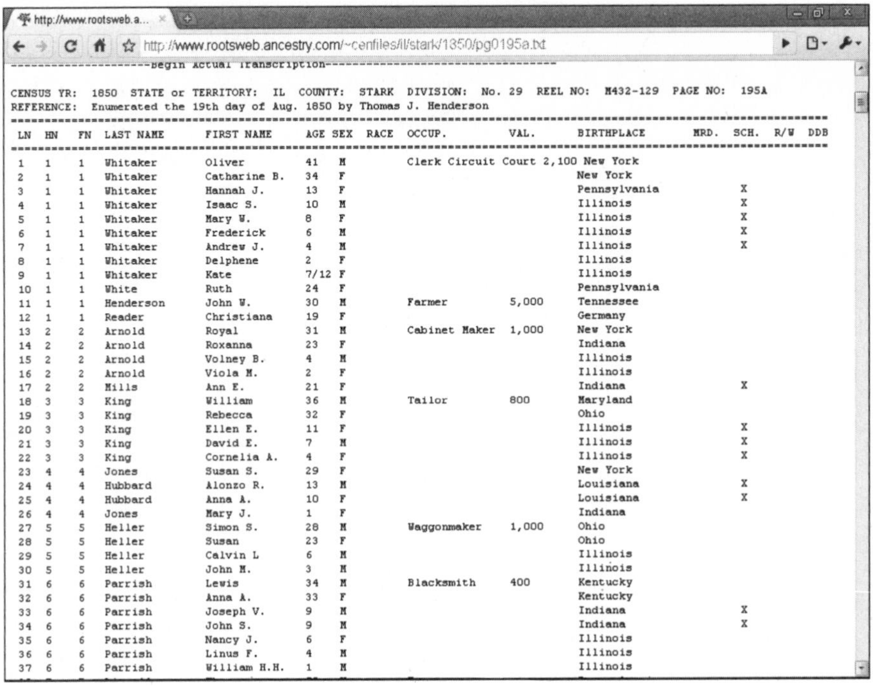

--------------------Begin Actual Transcription--------------------

CENSUS YR: 1850 STATE or TERRITORY: IL COUNTY: STARK DIVISION: No. 29 REEL NO: M432-129 PAGE NO: 195A
REFERENCE: Enumerated the 19th day of Aug. 1850 by Thomas J. Henderson

LN	HN	FN	LAST NAME	FIRST NAME	AGE	SEX	RACE	OCCUP.	VAL.	BIRTHPLACE	MRD.	SCH.	R/W	DDB
1	1	1	Whitaker	Oliver	41	M		Clerk Circuit Court	2,100	New York				
2	1	1	Whitaker	Catharine B.	34	F				New York				
3	1	1	Whitaker	Hannah J.	13	F				Pennsylvania		X		
4	1	1	Whitaker	Isaac S.	10	M				Illinois		X		
5	1	1	Whitaker	Mary W.	8	F				Illinois		X		
6	1	1	Whitaker	Frederick	6	M				Illinois		X		
7	1	1	Whitaker	Andrew J.	4	M				Illinois		X		
8	1	1	Whitaker	Delphene	2	F				Illinois				
9	1	1	Whitaker	Kate	7/12	F				Illinois				
10	1	1	White	Ruth	24	F				Pennsylvania				
11	1	1	Henderson	John W.	30	M		Farmer	5,000	Tennessee				
12	1	1	Reader	Christiana	19	F				Germany				
13	2	2	Arnold	Royal	31	M		Cabinet Maker	1,000	New York				
14	2	2	Arnold	Roxanna	23	F				Indiana				
15	2	2	Arnold	Volney B.	4	M				Illinois				
16	2	2	Arnold	Viola M.	2	F				Illinois				
17	2	2	Mills	Ann E.	21	F				Indiana		X		
18	3	3	King	William	36	M		Tailor	800	Maryland				
19	3	3	King	Rebecca	32	F				Ohio				
20	3	3	King	Ellen E.	11	F				Illinois		X		
21	3	3	King	David E.	7	M				Illinois		X		
22	3	3	King	Cornelia A.	4	F				Illinois		X		
23	4	4	Jones	Susan S.	29	F				New York				
24	4	4	Hubbard	Alonzo R.	13	M				Louisiana		X		
25	4	4	Hubbard	Anna A.	10	F				Louisiana		X		
26	4	4	Jones	Mary J.	1	F				Indiana				
27	5	5	Heller	Simon S.	28	M		Waggonmaker	1,000	Ohio				
28	5	5	Heller	Susan	23	F				Ohio				
29	5	5	Heller	Calvin L	6	M				Illinois				
30	5	5	Heller	John M.	3	M				Illinois				
31	6	6	Parrish	Lewis	34	M		Blacksmith	400	Kentucky				
32	6	6	Parrish	Anna A.	33	F				Kentucky				
33	6	6	Parrish	Joseph V.	9	M				Indiana		X		
34	6	6	Parrish	John S.	9	M				Indiana		X		
35	6	6	Parrish	Nancy J.	6	F				Illinois				
36	6	6	Parrish	Linus F.	4	M				Illinois				
37	6	6	Parrish	William H.H.	1	M				Illinois				

Figure 5-9: A plain-text census page for Stark County, Illinois.

Investigating Immigration and Naturalization Records

You may have heard the old stories about your great-great-grandparents who left their homeland in search of a more prosperous life. Some of these stories may include details about where they were born and how they arrived at their new home. Although these are great stories, as a genealogist, you want to verify this information with documentation.

Often the document you're looking for is an immigration or naturalization record. *Immigration records* are documents that show when a person moved to a particular country to reside. They include passenger lists and port-entry records for ships, and border-crossing papers for land entry into a country. *Naturalization records* are documents showing that a person became a citizen of a country without being born in that country. Sometimes an immigrant will reside in a country without becoming a naturalized citizen, and you can find paperwork on him or her too. You can look for alien registration paperwork and visas. A *visa* is a document permitting a noncitizen to live or travel in a country.

Immigration and naturalization documents can prove challenging to find, especially if you don't know where to begin looking. Unless you have some evidence in your attic or have a reliable family account of the immigration, you may need a record or something else to point you in the right direction. Census records are useful. (For more information about census records, see the section "Coming to Your Census," earlier in this chapter.) Depending on the year your ancestors immigrated, census records may contain the location of birth and tell you the year of immigration and the year of naturalization of your immigrant ancestor.

Emigration records — documents that reflect when a person moved out of a particular country to take up residence elsewhere — are also useful to researchers. You find these records in the country your ancestor left. They can often help when you can't find immigration or naturalization records in the new country.

To find more information on research using immigration records in the United States, we recommend taking a look at the National Archives: Immigration Records (Ship Passenger Arrival Records) site at www.archives.gov/ genealogy/immigration. This site provides general information on using immigration records and also identifies the types of immigration records held by the National Archives. The Olive Tree Genealogy: NaturalizationRecords. com site (www.naturalizationrecords.com) provides an overview of what you might glean from naturalization records in the United States and Canada.

You can also check out Chapter 13, "Immigration: Finding Important Immigrant Origins," written by Kory L. Meyerink and Loretto Dennis Szucs, in *The Source: A Guidebook of American Genealogy,* edited by Szucs and Sandra Hargreaves Luebking (Ancestry Publishing, Inc.). Other sources to refer to include *They Became Americans,* written by Loretto Dennis Szucs (Ancestry Publishing), and *They Came in Ships,* Third Edition, written by John Philip Colletta (Ancestry Publishing). Both provide more information about immigration and naturalization within the United States.

Locating immigration, emigration, and naturalization records online can be challenging. But some good news is that the common types of records that genealogists use to locate immigrants — passenger lists, immigration papers, and emigration records — have increased in availability on the Internet over the past decade and will likely continue to increase in numbers. A good starting point for determining an ancestor's homeland is to look at census records. (Again, for more information about census records, see the section "Coming to Your Census," earlier in this chapter.) Because a great deal of early immigration and naturalization processing occurred at the local level, census records may give you an indication of where to look for immigration records.

Some examples of online records, indexes, and databases include the following:

- ✔ **McLean County Circuit Clerk:** McLean County, Illinois, Immigration Records (www.co.mclean.il.us/CircuitClerk/imgrecs/ imgrecs.html)

- ✔ **inGeneas.com:** Library and Archives Canada Miscellaneous Immigration Index (www.ingeneas.com/free/index.html)

> ✔ **New Mexico Genealogical Society:** Passport Records, 1828–1836: Mexican Records from the Port of Entry at Santa Fe, New Mexico Territory (www.nmgs.org/artpass.htm)
>
> ✔ **MayflowerHistory.com:** Complete Mayflower Passenger List (www.mayflowerhistory.com/Passengers/passengers.php)
>
> ✔ **Iron Range Research Center:** 1918 Minnesota Alien Registration Records (`www.ironrangeresearchcenter.org/genealogy/collections/alienregistration/index.htm`)

If you don't have a lot of details on when your ancestor may have immigrated but have a general idea of the time or place of immigration, you may want to consider looking for information in a comprehensive genealogical index. As you look at comprehensive genealogy sites, you're likely to find these types of records categorized under immigration, under naturalization, under passenger lists, or by geographical area. If you know more details, try using a search engine and restricting your search by using several keywords in your search term, such as the type of record you're looking for (passenger list, port of entry, alien registration, and so on), the time frame, and the location.

Passenger lists

One type of immigration record that you can find on the Web is passenger lists. Passenger lists are manifests of who traveled on a particular ship. You can use passenger lists not only to see who immigrated on a particular ship, but you can also see citizens of the United States who were merely traveling on a ship (perhaps coming back from vacation in Europe).

To find passenger lists, you can try using a general search engine or a genealogically focused search engine. This is a particularly good strategy if you don't know what the name of the ship was or the year that they immigrated. If you do know the name of the ship, a comprehensive genealogical index may be more appropriate.

As an example, suppose that you have a family legend that Martin Saunders immigrated to America on a ship called *Planter* sometime in the first part of the 17th century. The following steps show you how to search for a passenger list to confirm the legend:

1. **Go to the Ask.com search engine (`www.ask.com`).**

   On the home page, the search box is located at the top of the page.

2. **In the Search the Web field, type your search terms and then click Search.**

   For this example, we typed **Martin Saunders on the ship Planter.**

3. **Click a promising link from the list of results.**

   The results page shows the first 10 links of more than 2,000 links found for these search terms. One of the top links goes to a transcription of the passengers on the *Planter,* which sailed on April 6, 1635 — the first on the list being "Martin Saunders, aged 40 years." Another link on the results page reads "Ships Passenger List — PLANTER of London for Boston Massachusetts." In the abstract that you access by clicking the link, you see that a Martin Saunders, age 40, sailed on the *Planter.*

Another source for passenger lists is the Immigrant Ships Transcribers Guild passenger-list transcription project (www.immigrantships.net). Currently, the Guild has transcribed more than 11,000 passenger manifests. The passenger lists are organized by date, ship's name, port of departure, port of arrival, passenger's surname, and captain's name. You can also search the site to find the person or ship that interests you. Other pages containing links to passenger lists include

- **Rootsweb.com Passenger Lists:** http://userdb.rootsweb.com/passenger
- **Olive Tree Genealogy:** www.olivetreegenealogy.com/ships/index.shtml
- **Castle Garden (the precursor to Ellis Island):** www.castlegarden.org
- **Famine Irish Passenger Record Data File:** http://aad.archives.gov/aad/fielded-search.jsp?dt=180&tf=F&cat=SB302&bc=sb,sl
- **Ship Passenger List Index for New Netherlands:** www.rootsweb.com/~nycoloni/nnimmdex.html
- **Boston Passenger Manifests (1848–1891):** www.sec.state.ma.us/arc/arcsrch/PassengerManifestSearchContents.html
- **Maine Passenger Lists:** www.mainegenealogy.net/passenger_search.asp
- **Partial Transcription of Inward Slave Manifests:** www.afrigeneas.com/slavedata/manifests.html
- **Maritime Heritage Project: San Francisco:** www.maritimeheritage.org/log.htm
- **Galveston Immigration Database:** www.galvestonhistory.org/Galveston_Immigration_Database.asp

You can also find some significant commercial database collections of immigration records. Ancestry.com's U.S. Immigration Collection contains information on millions of names and immigration records from more than 100 countries. Highlights of the collection include

✔ U.S. passport applications, 1795–1925

✔ Passenger lists from several U.S. cities (including Boston, Philadelphia, New Orleans, Seattle, and Honolulu), as well as countries (such as Australia, Wales, Germany, Canada, and Latvia)

✔ Naturalization records (1700s–1900s)

We delve into Ancestry.com's extensive collection in Chapter 12, if you're looking for more about what the site offers.

If you know (or even suspect) that your family came through Ellis Island, your first stop should be the Ellis Island Foundation site. The site contains a collection of 25 million passengers, along with ship manifests and images of certain ships.

To illustrate how the Ellis Island Foundation site works, look for Harry Houdini, who passed through the port a few times:

1. **Go to the Ellis Island site at `www.ellisislandrecords.org/default.asp`.**

   The search box is located just under the main header in a tan box.

2. **Type the passenger's name in the search boxes and click Start Search.**

   You should see a results box with the name of the passenger, residence (if stated), arrival year, age, and some links to the passenger record, ship manifest, and the ship's image (if available).

3. **Click the ship manifest link.**

   Figure 5-10 shows the manifest for the ship *Imperator* that sailed from Southampton on 3 July 1920 and arrived on 11 July 1920. If you scroll through the manifest online, you can see that Harry was traveling with his wife.

It's worthwhile to note that you must register with the Ellis Island site to see the actual digitized documents. However, this registration is free. You can follow the site's steps online to register.

Naturalization records

The road to citizenship was paved with paper, which is a good thing for researchers. On the Footnote.com site (`www.footnote.com`), you can find naturalization records housed in the National Archives online. Figure 5-11 shows a naturalization record from Footnote.com.

Footnote.com has more than 7.6 million naturalization records in a variety of collections, including the following:

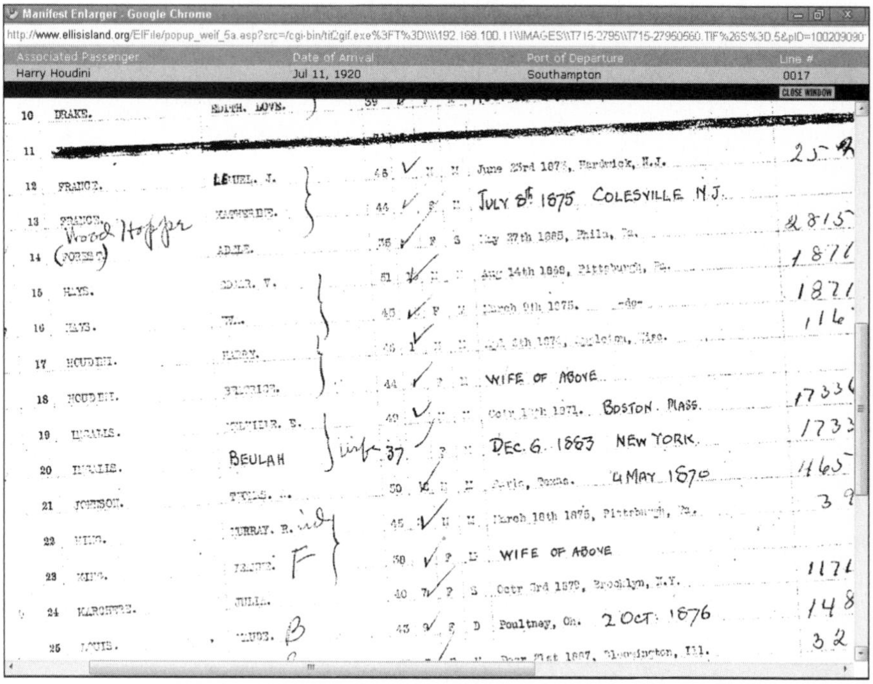

Figure 5-10:
Harry
Houdini's
entry in a
passenger
list at the
Ellis Island
site.

Figure 5-11:
A natu-
ralization
petition at
Footnote.
com.

- Naturalization Petitions for the Southern District of California, 1887–1940

- Records of the U.S. Circuit Court for the Eastern District of Louisiana, New Orleans Division: Petitions, 1838–1861

- Petitions and Records of Naturalizations of the U.S. District and Circuit Courts of the District of Massachusetts, 1906–1929

- Naturalization Petitions of the U.S. District Court for the District of Maryland, 1906–1930

- Naturalization Petitions for the Eastern District of Pennsylvania, 1795–1930

- Naturalization Petitions of the U.S. Circuit and District Courts for the Middle District of Pennsylvania, 1906–1930

- Naturalization Petitions of the U.S. District Court, 1820–1930, and Circuit Court, 1820–1911, for the Western District of Pennsylvania

- Index to Naturalizations of World War I Soldiers, 1918

For more about Footnote.com and all its records, flip to Chapter 16.

You can also find some database indexes of naturalizations online. Here are some examples:

- **Arkansas:** Arkansas Naturalization Records Index, 1809–1906, at `www.naturalizationrecords.com/usa/ar_natrecind-a.shtml`

- **California:** Index to Naturalization Records in Sonoma County, California, 1841–1906, at `www.rootsweb.com/~cascgs/nat.htm`

- **California:** Index to Naturalization Records in Sonoma County, California, Volume II, 1906–1930, at `www.rootsweb.com/~cascgs/nat2.htm`

- **Colorado:** Colorado State Archives Naturalization Records at `www.colorado.gov/dpa/doit/archives/natural.html`

- **Delaware:** Naturalization Records Database at `http://archives.delaware.gov/collections/natrlzndb/nat-index.shtml`

- **Indiana:** Indiana Commission on Public Records Naturalization Index at `www.state.in.us/serv/icpr_naturalization`

- **Kansas:** Index of the Petitions for Naturalization at the Osage County Courthouse at `http://skyways.lib.ks.us/towns/Lyndon/genealogy/natindex1.htm`

- **Missouri:** Naturalization Records, 1816–1955, at `www.sos.mo.gov/archives/naturalization`

- **New York:** Albany County Clerk's Office Naturalization Index at `www.albanycounty.com/departments/achor/naturalizationindexes.asp?id=856&SearchType=ExactPhrase&terms=naturalization%20records`

- ✔ **New York:** Eastern District Court of New York Naturalization Project at www.italiangen.org/EDN.stm

- ✔ **New York:** Kings County Clerk's Office Index to Naturalization Records at www.jgsny.org/kingsintro1.htm

- ✔ **North Dakota:** North Dakota Naturalization Records Index at http://library.ndsu.edu/db/naturalization

- ✔ **Ohio:** Miami County Naturalization Papers, 1860–1872, at www.tdn-net.com/genealogy/m-county/natural.htm

- ✔ **Pennsylvania:** Centre County Naturalization Records, 1802–1929, (includes images of the records) at www.co.centre.pa.us/hrip/natrecs/default.asp

- ✔ **Washington:** Digital Archives at www.digitalarchives.wa.gov/default.aspx

Land Ho! Researching Land Records

In the past, an individual's success could be measured by the ownership of land. The more land your ancestors possessed, the more powerful and wealthy they were. This concept often encouraged people to migrate to new countries in the quest to obtain land.

In addition to giving you information about the property your ancestor owned, land records may tell you where your ancestor lived before purchasing the land, the spouse's name, and the names of children, grandchildren, parents, or siblings. To use land records effectively, however, you need to have a general idea of where your ancestors lived and possess a little background information on the history of the areas in which they lived. Land records are especially useful for tracking the migration of families in the United States before the 1790 Census.

Most land records are maintained at the local level — in the town, county, or parish where the property was located. These records can come in multiple forms that reflect various types of land records and the locations in which they exist. Getting a foundation in the history of land records before conducting a lot of research is a good idea because the practices of land transfers differed by location and time period. A good place to begin your research is at the Land Record Reference page at www.directlinesoftware.com/landref.htm. This page contains links to articles on patents and grants, bounty lands, the Homestead Act, property description methods, and how land transactions were conducted. For a more general treatment of land records, see "Research in Land and Tax Records," by Sandra Hargreaves Luebking, in *The Source: A Guidebook of American Genealogy*, edited by Loretto Dennis Szucs and Luebking (Ancestry Publishing, Inc.).

Surveying land lovers in the United States

Land resources are among the most plentiful sources of information on your ancestors in the United States. Although a census would have occurred only once every ten years on average, land transactions may have taken place multiple times during that decade, depending on how much land your ancestor possessed. These records don't always contain a great deal of demographic information, but they do place your ancestor in a time and location, and sometimes in a historical context as well. For example, you may discover that your ancestors were granted military bounty lands. This discovery may tell you where and when your ancestors acquired the land, as well as what war they fought in. You may also find out how litigious your ancestors were by the number of lawsuits they filed or had filed against them as a result of land claims.

Your ancestors may have received land in the early United States in several ways. Knowing more about the ways in which people acquired land historically can aid you in your research.

Your ancestor may have purchased land or received a grant of land in the public domain — often called *bounty lands* — in exchange for military service or some other service for the country. Either way, the process probably started when your ancestor petitioned (or submitted an application) for the land. Your ancestor may have also laid claim to the land, rather than petitioning for it.

If the application was approved, your ancestor was given a *warrant* — a certificate that allowed him or her to receive an amount of land. (Sometimes a warrant was called a *right.*) After your ancestor presented the warrant to a land office, an individual was appointed to make a *survey* — a detailed drawing and legal description of the boundaries — of the land. The land office then recorded your ancestor's name and information from the survey into a *tract book* (a book describing the lots within a township or other geographic area) and on a *plat map* (a map of lots within a tract).

After the land was recorded in the tract book, your ancestors may have been required to meet certain conditions, such as living on the land for a certain period of time or making payments on the land. After they met the requirements, they were eligible for a *patent* — a document that conveyed title of the land to the new owner.

If your ancestors received bounty lands in the United States, you might be in luck. The Bureau of Land Management, Eastern States Land Office (www. glorecords.blm.gov) holds more than 3 million federal land title records for the Eastern States office (for lands east of the Mississippi River) issued between 1820 and 1908.

Follow these steps to search the records on this site:

1. Go to the Land Patents Records Site (www.glorecords.blm.gov).

2. **In the left green bar at the top of the page, click Search Land Patents. On the following page, enter your zip code in the appropriate space and click Continue.**

   This brings you to a page displaying a form that you can fill out to search the patents. Matthew's interest, for example, is in finding land that one of his ancestors, Jacob Helm, owned in Illinois.

3. **Select the state that you're interested in from the State drop-down list.**

   We selected Illinois.

4. **Type a first name and last name in the text boxes in the section where you enter the name of the patentee or warrantee, and then click Search.**

   We typed **Helm** in the Last Name text box, typed **Jacob** in the First Name text box, and then clicked Search. A page listed one result for Jacob Helm, with the name of the patentee, state, county, issue date, land office, document number, and accession number, as well as a link for details on the entry and a button to view the image (the button looks like a piece of paper).

5. **Click the Patentee Name or Warrantee Name link.**

   The Land Patent Details page loads, displaying the Patent Description. From this information, we can obtain the document number of the purchase, how many acres were purchased, how and when the land was purchased, and which land office recorded the transaction. Most databases stop here, but this site offers more, as you can see from the four tabs — Patent Description (which you're currently viewing), Legal Land Description, Document Image, and Certified Copy.

6. **Click the Document Image tab to view a digitized copy of the patent.**

   You can view the document as a small GIF image, a large GIF image, a TIFF image, or a PDF document. We can then save the copy of the document on your computer. Figure 5-12 shows the patent for Jacob Helm.

The National Archives (`www.archives.gov/research_room/federal_records_guide/bureau_of_land_management_rg049.html`) holds the land records for the Western states. For secondary land transactions (those made after the original grant of land), you probably need to contact the recorder of deeds for the county in which the land was held.

Several online sites contain indexes to land transactions in the United States. Some of these are free, and other broader collections require a subscription. The easiest way to find these sites is to consult a comprehensive genealogical index site and look under the appropriate geographical area. What you are likely to encounter in a land index is the name of the purchaser or warrantee, the name of the buyer (if applicable), the location of the land, the number of acres, and the date of the land transfer. In some cases, you may see the residence of the person who acquired the land. Figure 5-13 shows an example of a land entry in the index to Texas Land Grants at `wwwdb.glo.state.tx.us/central/LandGrants/LandGrantsSearch.cfm`.

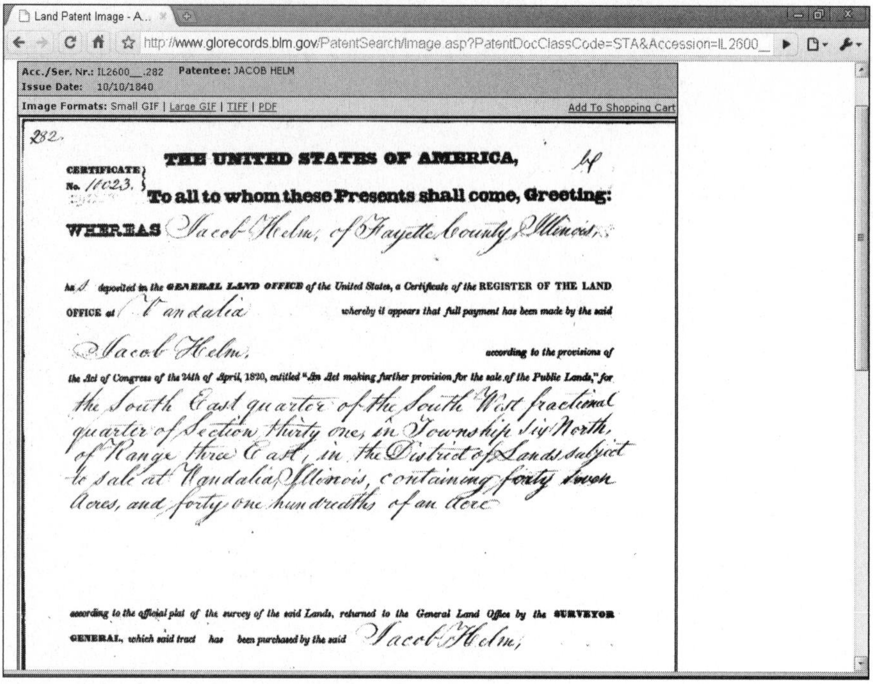

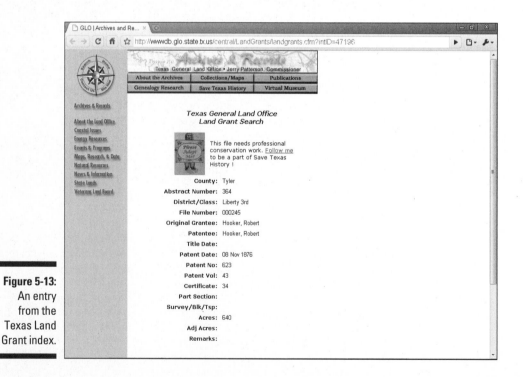

Figure 5-12:
The land patent for Jacob Helm at the General Land Office site.

Figure 5-13:
An entry from the Texas Land Grant index.

Here are some Web sites with information on land records:

- **Legal Land Descriptions in the USA:** www.outfitters.com/genealogy/land/land.html

- **Alabama:** Land Records at www.sos.state.al.us/govtrecords/land.aspx

- **Arkansas:** Land Records at http://searches.rootsweb.com/cgi-bin/arkland/arkland.pl

- **California:** Early Sonoma County, California, Land Grants, 1846–1850, at www.rootsweb.com/~cascgs/intro.htm

- **Colorado:** Kit Carson County Land Registration Receipts 1913–1919 at www.colorado.gov/dpa/doit/archives/land/kit_carson_land_index.html

- **Florida:** Spanish Land Grant Claims at www.floridamemory.com/Collections/SpanishLandGrants

- **Georgia:** Chatham County Deed Books, 1785–1806, at http://content.sos.state.ga.us/cdm4/chathamdeed.php

- **Illinois:** Illinois Public Domain Land Tract Sales at www.sos.state.il.us/departments/archives/data_lan.html

- **Indiana:** Land Office Records at the Indiana State Archives at www.in.gov/icpr/2585.htm

- **Kentucky:** Kentucky Land Office at http://sos.ky.gov/land

- **Louisiana:** Office of State Lands at www.doa.la.gov/SLO/DocumentAccess.htm

- **Louisiana:** Acadian Memorial Archive Land Grants at www.acadianmemorial.org/ensemble_encore/landgrants.htm

- **Maryland:** Land Records in Maryland at www.mdarchives.state.md.us/msa/refserv/genealogy/html/land.html

- **New York:** Ulster County Deed Books 1, 2 & 3 Index at http://archives.co.ulster.ny.us/deedsearchscreen.htm

- **North Carolina:** Alamance County Land Grant Recipients at www.rootsweb.com/~ncacgs/ala_nc_land_grants.html

- **Ohio:** Introduction to Ohio Land History at www.directlinesoftware.com/ohio.htm

- **Oklahoma:** Federal Tract Books of Oklahoma Territory at www.sirinet.net/~lgarris/swogs/tract.html

- **Oregon:** Oregon State Archives Land Records at http://arcweb.sos.state.or.us/land.html

- **Texas:** Texas General Land Office Archives at www.glo.state.tx.us/archives/archives.html

✔ **Texas:** Land Grant Database at www.db.glo.state.tx.us/central/
LandGrants/LandGrantsSearch.cfm

✔ **Virginia:** Land Office Grants at http://ajax.lva.lib.va.us/
F/?func=file&file_name=find-b-clas30&local_base=CLAS30

✔ **Wisconsin:** Wisconsin Public Land Survey Records: Original Field
Notes and Plat Maps at http://digicoll.library.wisc.edu/
SurveyNotes

Because the topic of land records is so expansive, many books have been
devoted to the subject. When you're ready to tackle land records in more
depth, you may want to look at William Thorndale's "Land and Tax Records"
in *The Source: A Guidebook of American Genealogy,* edited by Loretto Dennis
Szucs and Sandra Hargreaves Luebking (Ancestry Publishing).

In addition to the methods we mention in this section, you may want to check
out geography-related resources, such as the USGenWeb project (www.usgen
web.org) or the WorldGenWeb project (www.worldgenweb.org). These
sites organize their resources by location (country, state, county, or all three,
depending on which you use). Of course, if your attempts to find land records
and information through comprehensive sites and geography-related sites
don't prove as fruitful as you'd like, you can always turn to a search engine
such as AltaVista (www.altavista.com) or Google (www.google.com).

Marching to a Different Drummer: Searching for Military Records

Although your ancestors may not have marched to a different drummer,
at least one of them probably kept pace with a military beat at some point.
Military records contain a variety of information. The major types of records
that you're likely to find are service, pension, and bounty land records. Draft
or conscription records may also surface in your exploration.

Service records chronicle the military career of an individual. They often
contain details about where your ancestors lived, when they enlisted or were
drafted (or *conscripted*, enrolled for compulsory service), their ages, their discharge dates, and in some instances, their birthplaces and occupations. You
may also find pay records (including muster records that state when your
ancestors had to report to military units) and notes on any injuries that they
sustained while serving in the military. You can use these records to determine
the unit in which your ancestor served and the time periods of their service.
This information can lead you to pension records that can contain significant
genealogical information because of the level of detail required to prove service to receive a pension. Also, service records can give you an appreciation of
your ancestor's place within history — especially the dates and places where
your ancestor fought or served as a member of the armed forces.

Pensions were often granted to veterans who were disabled or who demonstrated financial need after service in a particular war or campaign; widows or orphans of veterans also may have received benefits. These records are valuable because, to receive pensions, your ancestors had to prove that they served in the military. Proof entailed a discharge certificate or the sworn testimony of the veteran and witnesses. Pieces of information that you can find in pension records include your ancestor's rank, period of service, unit, residence at the time of the pension application, age, marriage date, spouse's name, names of children, and the nature of the veteran's financial need or disability. If a widow submitted a pension application, you may also find records verifying her marriage to the veteran and death records (depending on when the veteran ancestor died).

Bounty lands are those lands granted by the government in exchange for military service that occurred between 1775 and 1855. Wars covered during this period include the American Revolution, War of 1812, Old Indian Wars, and the Mexican Wars. To receive bounty lands, soldiers were required to file an application. These applications often contain information useful to genealogical researchers.

If you are new to researching United States military records, take a look at the Research in Military Records page at the National Archives site (`www.archives.gov/genealogy/military`). It contains information on the types of military records held by the archives, how you can use them in your research, and information on records for specific wars. Also, for the historical context of the time period that your ancestor served, see the U.S. Army Center of Military History Research Material page at `www.army.mil/cmh-pg/html/bookshelves/resmat/resmat.html`. This site contains links to chapters from *American Military History,* which covers military actions from the Colonial period through the war on terrorism.

The largest collections for military records are currently housed in subscription sites. Here we give you a quick rundown on what several subscription sites have within their collections. And in Chapters 12 and 13, we dig through some of these sites and give you the nitty-gritty.

Footnote.com (`www.footnote.com`) has partnered with the National Archives to place digitized images of microfilm held by the archives. As a result, most of the military records on Footnote are federal. Here are some examples of available record sets:

- Compiled Service Records of Soldiers Who Served in the American Army During the Revolutionary War

- Revolutionary War Pension and Bounty-Land Warrant Application Files

- Revolutionary War Rolls, 1775–1783 (includes muster rolls, payrolls, and personnel records of American Army Units)

- Organization Index to Pension Files of Veterans Who Served Between 1861 and 1900

✔ Compiled Service Records of Confederate Soldiers

✔ Mathew B. Brady Collection of Civil War Photographs

✔ Case Files of Approved Pension Applications of Widows and Other Dependents of Civil War and Later Navy Veterans (Navy Widows' Certificates), 1861–1910

✔ Records of the American Section of the Supreme War Council, 1917–1919

Ancestry.com (www.ancestry.com) has a number of indexes for American Revolution records, including

✔ American Revolutionary War Rejected Pensions

✔ Loyalists in the American Revolution: Miscellaneous Records

✔ U.S. Revolutionary War Miscellaneous Records (Manuscript File), 1775–1790s

✔ U.S. Civil War Soldiers, 1861–1865

✔ Confederate Service Records, 1861–1865

✔ Civil War POW Records

✔ U.S. Colored Troops Military Service Records, 1861–1865

✔ U.S. Marine Corps Muster Rolls

✔ World War I Draft Registration Cards

✔ U.S. World War II Army Enlistment Records

HistoryKat (www.historykat.com) features digital images from the following:

✔ Historical Register of Officers of the Continental Army during the War of the Revolution, April, 1775, to December, 1783

✔ Historical Register and Dictionary of the United States Army

✔ War of 1812 Military Bounty Land Warrants

✔ Returns of Killed and Wounded in Battles or Engagements with Indians and British and Mexican Troops, 1790–1848

✔ Military entries from A Register of Officers and Agents, Civil, Military, and Naval, in the Service of the United States 1829 and 1831

At WorldVitalRecords.com (http://worldvitalrecords.com), you can find textual records, including

✔ List of Officials, Civil, Military, and Ecclesiastical of Connecticut Colony, 1636–1677

✔ Spanish American War Volunteers — Colorado

✔ Korean War Casualties

✔ Army Casualties 1956–2003

✔ Muster Rolls of the Soldiers of the War of 1812: Detached from the Militia of North Carolina in 1812 and 1814

Here is a sampling of the different types of records that are available on free sites:

✔ **Muster Rolls and Other Records of Service of Maryland Troops in the American Revolution:** www.msa.md.gov/megafile/msa/speccol/sc2900/sc2908/000001/000018/html/index.html

✔ **Ohio Historical Society War of 1812 Roster of Ohio Soldiers:** www.ohiohistory.org/resource/database/rosters.html

✔ **Illinois Black Hawk War Veterans Database:** www.cyberdrive illinois.com/departments/archives/blkhawk.html

✔ **South Carolina Confederate Pension Applications 1919–1926:** www.archivesindex.sc.gov

✔ **Annual Report of the Adjutant General of Missouri, December 31, 1863:** http://digital.library.umsystem.edu/cgi/t/text/text-idx?sid=d580ce6aa5df1d2b7af19a7357bb672d;c=umlib;idno=umlk000033

✔ **Colorado Volunteers in the Spanish American War (1898):** www.colorado.gov/dpa/doit/archives/military/span_am_war

✔ **National World War II Memorial Registry:** www.wwiimemorial.com/default.asp?page=registry.asp&subpage=intro

Another set of valuable resources for researching an ancestor that partici-pated in a war is information provided by a lineage society. Some examples include the Daughters of the American Revolution (www.dar.org), Sons of the American Revolution (www.sar.org), Society of the Cincinnati (www.societyofthecincinnati.org), United Empire Loyalists' Association of Canada (www.uelac.org), National Society United States Daughters of 1812 (www.usdaughters1812.org), Daughters of Union Veterans of the Civil War (www.duvcw.org), and Sons of Confederate Veterans (www.scv.org).

One of the largest collections of military records at a free site is the Civil War Soldiers and Sailors System (CWSS). The CWSS site is a joint project of the National Park Service, the Genealogical Society of Utah, and the Federation of Genealogical Societies. The site contains an index of more than 6.3 million soldier records of both Union and Confederate soldiers. Also available at the site are regimental histories and descriptions of 384 battles.

Follow these steps to search the records on this site:

1. **Point your browser to the Civil War Soldier and Sailors System (www. itd.nps.gov/cwss).**

   On the right side of the screen are links to information on the site, including links to soldiers, sailors, regiments, cemeteries, battles, prisoners, Medals of Honor, and National Parks.

2. **Click the appropriate link for the person you are looking for.**

   We're looking for a soldier who served, so we clicked the Soldier link.

3. **Type the name of the soldier or sailor in the appropriate field and click Submit Query.**

   If you know additional details, you can select the side on which side your ancestor fought, the state they were from, the unit, and the function that they performed. We typed **Helm** in the Last Name field, **Uriah** in the First Name field, **Union** in the Union or Confederate field, and **Illinois** in the State field. One search result appeared with that information.

4. **Click the name of the soldier or sailor to see the Detailed Soldier Record.**

   The soldier record showed that Uriah served in Company G, 7th Illinois Cavalry (see Figure 5-14). He entered and left the service as a private. His information is located on National Archives series M539 microfilm, roll 39.

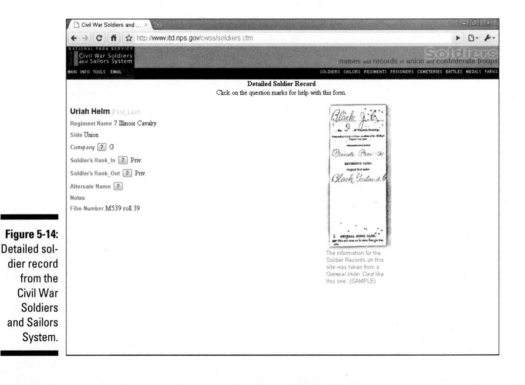

Figure 5-14: Detailed soldier record from the Civil War Soldiers and Sailors System.

Taxation with Notation

Some of the oldest records available for research are tax records — including property and inheritance records. Although several local governments have placed tax records online, these records are usually very recent documents rather than historical tax records. Most early tax records you encounter were likely collected locally (that is, at the county level). However, many local tax records have since been turned over to state or county archives — some of which now make tax records available on microfilm, as do Family History Centers. (If you have a Family History Center in your area, you may be able to save yourself a trip, call, or letter to the state archives — check with the Family History Center to see whether it keeps copies of tax records for the area in which you're interested.) And a few maintainers of tax records — including archives and Family History Centers — are starting to make information about their holdings available online. Generally, either indexes or transcriptions of these microfilm records are what you find online, and a lot of these are located on subscription sites.

Here are just a few examples of the types of resources that you can find pertaining to tax records:

- **General Information:** Chapter 8, "Research in Land and Tax Records," by Sandra Hargreaves Luebking, in *The Source: A Guidebook of American Genealogy,* edited by Luebking and Loretto Dennis Szucs (Ancestry Publishing).

- **Tax List:** 1790–1800 County Tax Lists of Virginia at www.binns genealogy.com/VirginiaTaxListCensuses

- **Land and Poll Tax:** Benton County, Tennessee 1836 Land and Poll Tax List at www.tngenweb.org/benton/databas2.htm

If you're locating records in the United States, try the USGenWeb site for the state or county. Here's what to do:

1. **Go to the USGenWeb site (www.usgenweb.org).**

2. **Click a state in the left column.**

   We clicked the Pennsylvania link because we're looking for tax records in Lancaster County.

   As a shortcut, you can always get to any USGenWeb state page by typing www.usgenweb.org and the two-letter postal code for the state. For example, for Pennsylvania, you could type **www.usgenweb.org/pa**.

3. **From the USGenWeb state page (for the state that you choose), find a link to the county in which you're interested.**

   On the Pennsylvania Counties page, we clicked the Lancaster link to get to the Lancaster County GenWeb site.

4. **Scroll through the main page for the state you've selected and click any tax-related links that look promising.**

   We clicked the link for Proprietary and State Tax Lists of the County of Lancaster for the Years 1771, 1772, 1773, 1779, and 1782; edited by William Henry Egle, M.D. (1898) under the Documents section.

The state and county Web sites in the USGenWeb Project vary immensely. Some have more information available than the Pennsylvania and Lancaster County pages, while others have less. The amount of information that's available at a particular USGenWeb site affects the number of links you have to click through to find what you're looking for. Don't be afraid to take a little time to explore and become familiar with the sites for the states and counties in which your ancestors lived.

One other strategy for finding tax assessment information is to search local newspapers for the time period in which your ancestor lived. A tax list was published on a yearly basis in some localities. To find out more about searching newspapers online, see Chapter 8.

Trial and Error at the Courthouse

Do you have an ancestor who was on the wrong side of the law? If so, you may find some colorful information at the courthouse in the civil and criminal court records. Even if you don't have an ancestor with a law-breaking past, you can find valuable genealogical records at your local courthouse, given that even upstanding citizens may have civil records on file or may have been called as witnesses. Typical records you can find there include land deeds, birth and death certificates, divorce decrees, wills and probate records, tax records, and some military records (provided the ancestors who were veterans deposited their records locally).

Court cases and trials aren't just a phenomenon of today's world. Your ancestor may have participated in the judicial system as a plaintiff, defendant, or witness. Some court records can provide a glimpse into the character of your ancestors — whether they were frequently on trial for misbehavior or called as character witnesses. You can also find a lot of information on your ancestors if they were involved in land disputes — a common problem in some areas where land transferred hands often. Again, your ancestor may not have been directly involved in a dispute but may have been called as a witness. Another type of court record that may involve your ancestor is a probate case. Often, members of families contested wills or were called upon as executors or witnesses, and the resulting file of testimonies and rulings can be found in a probate record. Court records may also reflect appointments of ancestors to positions of public trust such as sheriff, inspector of tobacco, and justice of the peace.

Finding court records online can be tricky. They can be found using a general search engine, such as Lycos (www.lycos.com), or a subscription database service. Note, however, that good data can also be tucked away inside free databases that are not indexed by search engines. In this case, you will have to search on a general term such as "Berks County wills" or "Berks County court records." Here is an example:

1. **Go to the Lycos search engine site (www.lycos.com).**

   The search box is near the top of the page.

2. **Type your search terms in the search box and click Go Get It.**

   The results page is displayed. We typed **Berks County wills** and received 231,080 results. Please note that this number changes often as new sites are added to the Lycos database. If the number of results you get is too large to reasonably sort through, you can narrow your search with additional terms, such as specific years or town names.

3. **Click a link that looks relevant to your search.**

   We selected the link to the Berks County Register of Wills at www. co.berks.pa.us/rwills/site/default.asp. This site contains a database where you can search more than 1 million records covering a variety of areas, including birth, death, marriage, and estate.

Chapter 6

Discovering Ancestral Homelands

. . . .

In This Chapter

▶ Identifying where your ancestors lived

▶ Locating places on maps and in history

▶ Using maps in your research

▶ Getting information from local sources

. . . .

Say you dig up an old letter addressed to your great-great-great-grand-father in Winchester, Virginia. But where is Winchester? What was the town like? Where exactly did he live in the town? What was life like when he lived there? To answer these questions, you need to go a little further than just retrieving documents — you need to look at the life of your ancestor within the context of where he lived.

Geography played a major role in the lives of our ancestors. It often determined where they lived, worked, and migrated (as early settlers often migrated to lands that were similar to their home state or country). It can also play a major role in how you research your ancestor. Concentrating on where your ancestor lived can often point you to area-specific record sets or offer clues about where to research next. In this chapter, we look at several ways to use geographical resources to provide a boost to your family history research.

Are We There Yet?: Researching Where "There" Was to Your Ancestors

What did "there" mean for your ancestors? You have to answer this question to know where to look for genealogical information. These days, a family that lives in the same general area for more than two or three generations is rare. If you're a member of such a family, you may be in luck when it comes to researching. However, if you come from a family that moved around at least every few generations (or not all members of the family remained in the same location), you may be in for a challenge.

How do you find out where your ancestors lived? In this section, we look at several resources you can use to establish locations: using known records, interviewing relatives, consulting gazetteers, looking at maps, using GPS devices, and charting locations using geographical software. As we go through these resources, we use a real-life example to show how the resources can be used together to solve a research problem — finding the location of the final resting place of Matthew's great-great-grandfather.

Using documents that you already possess

When you attempt to locate your ancestors geographically, start by using any copies of records or online data that you or someone else has already collected. Sifting through all those photocopies and original documents from the attic and printouts from online sites provides a good starting point for locating places to look for additional information about your ancestors. Pay particular attention to any material that provides definite whereabouts during a specific time period. You can use these details as a springboard for your geographical search.

For example, Matthew's great-great-grandfather, Uriah Helm, is listed in the family trees at the WorldConnect Web site (for more on the WorldConnect project — http://wc.rootsweb.ancestry.com — see Chapter 4). In the record, the submitter states that Uriah was buried in the German Reformed Cemetery in Fayette County, Illinois. The mention of Fayette County, Illinois, gives us a place to begin our search.

If you have information about places where your ancestors lived but not necessarily the time frame, you can still be reasonably successful in tracking your ancestors. Aids are available to help you approximate time frames, such as the Period Approximation Chart (www.pennyparker2.com/appxchart.html). For example, say you know the birth dates of your great-great-grandmother's children, but you don't know when Great-great-grandma and Great-great-grandpa were married. You can use the Period Approximation Chart to calculate a date range in which you can look for the marriage record. The Period Approximation Chart uses average ages for events in history and the typical lifespan during certain periods of time to make the calculations.

Grilling your relatives

Your notes from interviews with family members or from other resources you've found on your ancestors, most likely contain some information about locations where the family lived and, we hope, the approximate time frames.

Chances are you have at least some notes with statements such as "Uncle Zeke recalled stories about the old homestead in Red River County, Texas." Of course, whether he recalled stories firsthand (those that he lived through or participated in) or his recollections were stories he heard from those before him has an effect on the time frames within which you look for records in Red River County. Either way, these stories give you a starting point.

For details on interviewing your family members, see Chapter 2.

Where is Llandrindod, anyway?

At some point during your research, you're bound to run across something that says an ancestor lived in a particular town or county, or was associated with a specific place, but contains no details of where that place was — no state or province or other identifiers. How do you find out where that place was located?

A *gazetteer,* or geographical dictionary, provides information about places. By looking up the name of the town, county, or some other kind of place, you can narrow your search for your ancestor. The gazetteer identifies every place by a particular name and provides varying information (depending on the gazetteer itself) about each. Typically, gazetteers provide at least the names of the principal region where the place is located. Many contemporary gazetteers also provide the latitude and longitude of the place.

By adding the information you get from the online gazetteer to the other pieces of your puzzle, you can reduce the list of common place-names to just those you think are plausible for your ancestors. By pinpointing the location of a place, you can look for more records to prove whether your ancestors really lived there and even visit those locations to get pictures of burial plots or old properties.

For research in the United States, a first stop is the U.S. Geological Survey's Geographic Names Information System (GNIS) Web site. The GNIS site contains information on more than 2 million places within the United States and its territories (the site also includes data for Antarctica).

To find the precise location of the cemetery where Uriah Helm is buried, we can use the Geographic Names Information System (GNIS) site. Follow these steps:

1. **Start your Web browser and head to the U.S. Geological Survey's Geographic Names Information System (GNIS) at `http://geonames. usgs.gov/pls/gnispublic`.**

   This page contains the search form for the United States and its territories (see Figure 6-1).

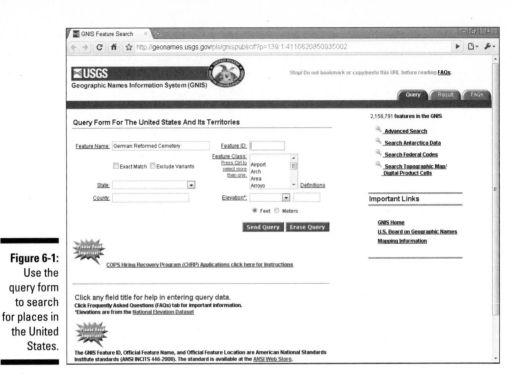

Figure 6-1:
Use the
query form
to search
for places in
the United
States.

2. Enter any information that you have, tabbing or clicking between fields.

We're looking for a cemetery in Illinois where we believe Uriah Helm is buried, so we entered *German Reformed Cemetery* in the Feature Name field and selected Illinois from the state drop-down box.

If you're not sure what a particular field asks for but you think you may want to enter something in it, click the title of the field for an explanation.

3. When you're finished, click Send Query.

The result of the search shows one result for the German Reformed Cemetery in Fayette County, Illinois. The cemetery is located at a latitude of 38 degrees, 55 minutes, 58 seconds north and a longitude of 88 degrees, 54 minutes, 18 seconds west. We can then use an online map to plot the longitude and latitude to see the actual location of the cemetery.

In addition to using the GNIS database, you might want to see some online gazetteers that identify places in other countries as well as places in the United States. One that builds on worldwide data available through Google Maps is Maplandia.com: Google Maps World Gazetteer. To use this gazetteer, follow these steps:

1. **Using your Web browser, go to Maplandia.com at `www.maplandia.com`.**

   You see the welcome page, which has search fields to look for locations by place-name or region.

2. **In the World Places field, type the name of the place you're trying to locate.**

   If you're trying to identify an entire region, you may prefer to use the World Regions field instead.

   We entered the *Llandrindod* place-name.

3. **Click Search.**

   Figure 6-2 shows the results of the search. The only result was a place called Llandrindod Wells in Powys, Wales, in the United Kingdom. Clicking the result takes you to a page that contains the longitude and latitude of Llandrindod Wells and a map of the town.

Figure 6-2:
Results for a search on Llandrindod at Maplandia. com.

Following are some gazetteer sites for you to check out. You can use some for worldwide searches; others are country specific:

- **Alexandria Digital Library Gazetteer Server**: `www.alexandria.ucsb.edu` (this site has a worldwide focus).
- **Belgian Place Names**: `http://belgium.rootsweb.ancestry.com/bel/_places/index.html`.
- **Geoscience Australia Place Name Search**: `www.ga.gov.au/map/names`.
- **Canada's Geographical Names**: `http://geonames.nrcan.gc.ca/search/search_e.php`.
- **Gazetteer for Scotland**: `www.scottish-places.info`.
- **Gazetteer of British Place Names**: `www.gazetteer.co.uk`.
- **German Genealogy Gazetteer (in German)**: `http://gov.genealogy.net`.
- **Institut Géographique National**: `www.ign.fr`. The main page is in French; if you want to see the site in English, just click the little EN in the upper-right corner.)
- **IreAtlas Townland Data Base (Ireland)**: `www.seanruad.com`.
- **Metatopos.org (in Dutch)**: `www.metatopos.org`.
- **National Gazetteer of Wales**: `http://homepage.ntlworld.com/geogdata/ngw/home.htm`.
- **Land Information New Zealand (LINZ)**: `www.linz.govt.nz/placenames/index.aspx`.
- **KNAB, the Place Names Database of EKI (Estonia)**: `www.eki.ee/knab/knab.htm`.
- **Registro de Nombres Geograficos (in Spanish)**: `http://mapserver.inegi.gob.mx/rnng/?c=730`.
- **Statens Kartverk**: `kart.statkart.no/adaptive2/default.aspx?gui=1&lang=2`. This site is in Norwegian; however, if you'd like to see an English version, just click the English Bokmal Nynorsk link in the upper-left corner.
- **Swedish Gazetteer**: `www.sna.se/gazetteer.html`.
- **World Gazetteer**: `http://world-gazetteer.com`.
- **GPS Data Team: Coordinate Finder**: `www.gps-data-team.com/map`.

Most online gazetteers are organized on a national level and provide information about all the places (towns, cities, counties, landmarks, and so on) within that country. However, you find some exceptions. Some unique gazetteers list information about places within one state or province. One such example is the Kentucky Atlas and Gazetteer (`www.uky.edu/KentuckyAtlas`), which has information only about places within — you guessed it — Kentucky. For each place, it provides the name of the place, county, type of the place (civil division, school, cemetery, airport, and so on), source of information, an identification number, topoquad (topographic-map quadrangle that contains the feature), latitude, longitude, elevation, population (if applicable), area (if applicable), date of establishment, and the URL for a map showing you the location of the place. The name of the place is typically a link that goes directly to the map.

In addition to online gazetteers, you also find a number of software gazetteers. One such gazetteer geared toward genealogists is the World Place Finder by Progeny Software (`www.progenygenealogy.com/place finder.html`).

If you can't find a location in current gazetteers, you may need to consult a historical gazetteer. A couple of examples of these include A Vision of Britain through Time (British), available at `www.visionofbritain.org.uk`, and the Digital Gazetteer of the Song Dynasty, at `http://songgis.ucmerced library.info`. One way to find a historical gazetteer is to visit a general search engine (such as Google, at `www.google.com`) and search the location-name plus the words *historical gazetteer*.

Mapping your ancestor's way

After you determine where a place is located, it's time to dig out the maps. Maps can be an invaluable resource in your genealogical research. Not only do maps help you track your ancestors' locations at various points in their lives, but they also enhance your published genealogy by illustrating some of your findings.

Different types of online sites have maps that may be useful in your genealogical research.

✔ **Historical maps:** Several Web sites contain scanned or digitized images of historic maps. In a lot of cases, you can download or print copies of these maps. Such sites include

- David Rumsey Map Collection: `www.davidrumsey.com`
- Perry-Castañeda Library Map Collection, University of Texas at Austin: `www.lib.utexas.edu/maps/index.html`
- American Memory Map Collections of the Library of Congress: `http://memory.loc.gov/ammem/gmdhtml/gmdhome.html`

You can also find local collections of maps at several university and historical society sites. A few examples are

- Cartography: Historical Maps of New Jersey (Rutgers University): `http://mapmaker.rutgers.edu/MAPS.html`

- Ohio Historical Maps (The Ohio State University): `http://library.osu.edu/find/subjects/maps/ohio-historical-maps`

- Massachusetts Maps (The Massachusetts Historical Society): `www.masshist.org/online/massmaps`

- L.C. Bishop Emigrant Trail Map Series (Wyoming State Historical Society): `http://wyshs.org/content/wyoming-historical-maps`

✔ **Digitized historical atlases:** In addition to map sites, individuals have scanned portions or the entire contents of atlases, particularly those from the 19th century. Examples include

- Countrywide atlases: An example is the 1895 U.S. Atlas at `www.livgenmi.com/1895`.

- County atlases: The 1904 Maps from the New Century Atlas of Cayuga County, New York, are a good example at `www.rootsweb.com/~nycayuga/maps/1904`.

- Specialty atlases: An occupational example is the 1948 U.S. Railroad Atlas at `http://trains.rockycrater.org/pfmsig/atlas.php`.

✔ **Interactive map sites:** A few sites have interactive maps that you can use to find and zoom in on areas. After you have the view you want of the location, you can print a copy of the map to keep with your genealogical records. Some of these sites are

- Google Maps (`http://maps.google.com`): This site includes road and satellite maps for countries around the world. You can also get directions for places within the United States and Canada.

- MapQuest (`www.mapquest.com`): You can find interactive maps for more than 200 countries, although some of these look down from too high a level to get much detail. Street-level maps are available for the United States and Canada. Driving directions are available for the United States, Canada, and a few European countries.

- Bing Maps (`www.bing.com/maps`): This site features road and aerial maps of North and South America. In some areas, an aerial view is available, which is a close-up satellite view of the area.

- National Geographic MapMachine (`http://maps.nationalgeographic.com/maps`): You'll find a world atlas with road, satellite, and physical maps.

- The U.K. Street Map Page (`www.streetmap.co.uk`): This page identifies streets in London or places in the United Kingdom.

Interactive maps are especially helpful when you're trying to pinpoint the location of a cemetery or town you plan to visit for your genealogical research, but they're limited in their historical helpfulness because they typically offer only current information about places.

✔ **Specialized maps:** You can view specialized maps on Web sites such as:

- AnyPlace America (www.anyplaceamerica.com), which has free topographic maps for the United States.

- OffRoute.com (www.offroute.com), which lets you order custom-made waterproof topographical maps, perfect for those cemetery trips.

Zeroing in

We've looked at a few types of maps, but the real promise of mapping technology is the ability to use different maps together to see the whole picture of where your ancestors lived. One of the ways of doing this is by using mapping layers.

A good example of mapping layers is the Google Earth technology. Google Earth (www.google.com/earth/index.html) is a downloadable program that combines Google searches with geographic information. When you launch the program, you see the Earth represented as a globe. Enter a place-name or a longitude and latitude coordinate, and the system maps it for you. Then you can add additional map layers to see other information about that particular place.

Here's an example of how the layering works: In the cemetery example used in the previous sections, we know two pieces of information about where that cemetery is located. The WorldConnect entry states that the cemetery is in Fayette, Illinois; the GNIS tells us that the cemetery is in Fayette County, Illinois, at a specific latitude and longitude. Because Matthew wants to see the gravestone for himself, we can use Google Earth to give us an idea of how to get to the cemetery and what that area looked like at the time his ancestors lived there.

Here is how to generate a Google Earth map by latitude and longitude (you need to download the Google Earth program from www.google.com/earth/index.html to your computer before following these steps):

1. **Open the Google Earth program.**

   When Google Earth launches, you see the Earth as viewed from space, as shown in Figure 6-3. In the upper-left corner of the screen is the Search area, where you can click the Fly To tab and enter coordinates for latitude and longitude.

2. **On the Fly To tab, enter the latitude and longitude of the location and click the Begin Search icon (the magnifying glass).**

   We entered the latitude and longitude from the GNIS entry for the cemetery — 38 55.58 N, 088 54.18' W. The Google Earth application "flies" to the location on the map.

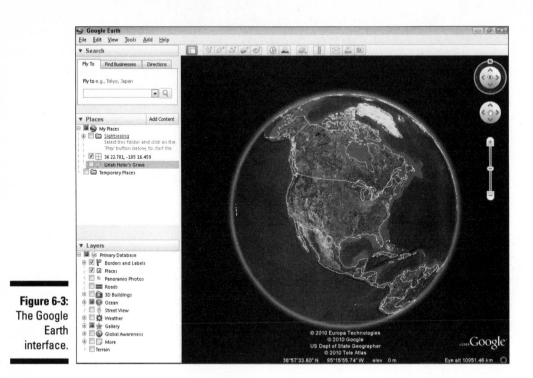

Figure 6-3:
The Google
Earth
interface.

The location is marked with a crosshair, and the latitude and longitude label appears to the right. If the map zooms in too far, you can use the scale in the upper-right corner of the map to zoom out. Just move your cursor to the area containing the circle with the *N*. Using your cursor on the N moves the map in a circle. Clicking in the circle below it moves the map up, down, right, and left so that you can see different areas. Next to the compass is a scale with plus and minus signs — clicking the plus and minus signs allows you to zoom the map in and out.

3. **Add a place mark to label the location.**

Move your cursor to the top of the screen and click the Placemark icon (the yellow pushpin). When you click the icon, a dialog box appears where you can title the place mark, add a description, and change attributes of the place mark. We entered *Uriah Helm's Grave* in the Name field and a brief description on the Description tab. The resulting image is seen in Figure 6-4.

4. **Overlay the roads layer.**

The bottom area in the left column contains a list of available layers. We clicked the Roads layer. From this layer, we can see that Illinois Route 185 runs past the cemetery.

5. **Add the Rumsey Historical Maps layer, under the Gallery directory of the Layers section.**

Visiting the Layers area again, we clicked the Gallery item and then clicked Rumsey Historical Maps. To add a map, you need to click the MapFinder option, activating it. Zoom out (using the zooming tools explained in Step 2) until you see compass roses (little sun-looking icons) all over the map. Each compass rose represents a historical map that you can select to overlay your location. After selecting one, you can zoom in again to see your location up close.

Using the Rumsey Historical Maps layer, we selected the United States 1833 layer — the compass rose is near Columbus, Ohio, when we zoomed out on the map of the United States. The 1833 map of the United States appears; then we zoomed in again to Uriah's gravesite. Although Uriah Helm lived several decades after the map was made, his grandfather moved into the area around 1840 — so we can see roughly what the area looked like when the family arrived, as shown in Figure 6-5.

Although interactive maps are good for getting a general idea of the location of a place, more specific maps are sometimes necessary for feature types such as creeks or ridges. Topographic maps are an especially good set to use for these purposes; they contain not only place-names but also information on features of the terrain (such as watercourses, elevation, vegetation density, and, yes, even cemeteries). At the USGS National Map site (www.anyplaceamerica.com), you can view a variety of map layers, including topographical maps.

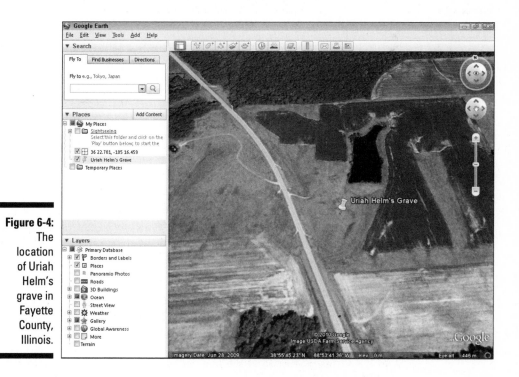

Figure 6-4: The location of Uriah Helm's grave in Fayette County, Illinois.

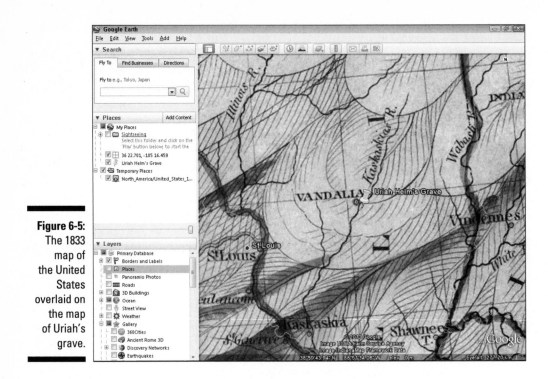

Figure 6-5:
The 1833
map of
the United
States
overlaid on
the map
of Uriah's
grave.

To view a topographic map at the National Map, follow these steps:

1. **Direct your browser to `http://nationalmap.gov/viewers.html`.**

2. **Near the top of the page on the right side, click the Click Here to Open Viewer link.**

   After a few moments, a map of the United States appears.

3. **At the top of the page, type a place or longitude and latitude and click Search.**

   We typed *German Reformed Cemetery*. A Tasks/Results pane appeared on the right, with ten results — the top result was the German Reformed Cemetery in Illinois. The map opened automatically to the first result. You can close the Tasks/Results pane by clicking the arrow just below the Tasks/Results label.

4. **Click the Overlays link on the left side of the headline.**

   The Overlays page appears, with the Content tab displaying a list of layers that can be overlaid on top of the base map.

5. **Select the Scanned Topo Maps overlay by clicking the box next to the name.**

   The topographic map appears on the screen, as shown in Figure 6-6.

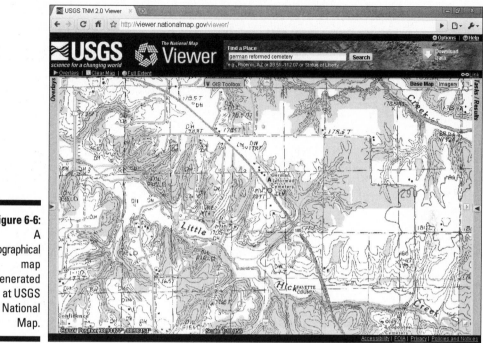

Figure 6-6:
A topographical map generated at USGS National Map.

Crossing the line

Just as maps help you track your ancestors' movements and where they lived, they can also help you track when your ancestors *didn't* really move. Boundaries for towns, districts, and even states have changed over time. Additionally, towns and counties sometimes change names. Knowing whether your ancestors really moved or just appeared to move because a boundary or town name changed is important when you try to locate records for them.

To determine whether a town or county changed names at some point, check a gazetteer or historical text on the area. (Gazetteers are discussed earlier in this chapter, in the "Where is Llandrindod, anyway?" section.) Finding boundary changes can be a little more challenging, but resources are available to help you. For example, historical atlases illustrate land and boundary changes. You can also use online sites that have maps for the same areas over time, and a few sites deal specifically with boundary changes in particular locations. Several examples are

- ✔ **NationalAtlas.gov: Where We Are:** `www.nationalatlas.gov/index.html`

- ✔ **Atlas of Historical County Boundaries:** `http://publications.newberry.org/ahcbp`

- ✔ **The Counties of England, Scotland, and Wales Prior to the 1974 Boundary Changes:** `www.genuki.org.uk/big/Britain.html`

You can also use software designed to show boundary changes over time. Programs like these can help you find places that have disappeared altogether:

- **The Centennial Historical Atlas** tracks boundary changes in Europe. Its Web site is www.clockwk.com.

- **AniMap Plus** tracks boundary changes in the United States. Its Web site is www.goldbug.com/AniMap.html.

Following is a quick walk-through using the AniMap Plus demonstration to see how some counties have changed over time. You can download a demonstration version of this software at the AniMap Web site.

1. **Open the demonstration version of AniMap Plus that you downloaded from www.goldbug.com/AniMap.html.**

2. **Double-click Start Demo in the upper-left corner of the screen.**

   AniMap opens to a 1683 map that shows the 12 original counties of New York. All counties are named in the upper-left corner of the map. Abbreviations of each are explained in the County Codes box; you can see the county boundaries on the map.

3. **Click Next to advance to the next map of New York to see changes that took place between 1683 and 1686.**

   The box in the upper-left corner briefly explains the changes that took place and which counties still existed in New York in 1686.

4. **You can advance through the maps in sequential order by clicking the Next button, or you can skip to other years by double-clicking the years identified in the Go To box.**

Positioning your family: Using global positioning systems

After discovering the location of the final resting place of Great-great-great-grandpa Nimrod (yes, that is the name of one of April's ancestors), you just might get the notion to travel to the cemetery. Now, finding the cemetery on the map is one thing, but often finding the cemetery "on the ground" is a completely different thing. That is where global positioning systems come into play.

A *global positioning system (GPS)* is a device that uses satellites to determine the exact location of the user. The technology is sophisticated, but in simple terms, satellites send out radio signals that are collected by the GPS receiver — the device that you use to determine your location. The receiver then calculates the distances between the satellites and the receiver to determine your location. Receivers can come in many forms, ranging from vehicle-mounted receivers to those that fit in your hand. (We frequently use a GPS receiver mounted inside Matthew's cell phone for quick readings.)

While on research trips, we use GPS receivers not only to locate a particular place but also to document the location of a specific object within that place. For example, when we visit a cemetery, we take GPS readings of the gravesites of ancestors and then enter those readings into our genealogical databases. That way, if the marker is ever destroyed, we still have a way to locate the grave. As a final step, we take that information and plot the specific location of the sites on a map, using geographical information systems software. (See the following section for more details on geographical information systems.)

A project is under way that combines genealogy with the use of GPS devices. The U.S. GeoGen project (`http://geogen.org/welcome.htm`) was established to create county-level pages with coordinates of some places of interest to genealogists (such as cemeteries, mines, homesteads, and historical post offices). At present, these resources are being developed for 20 states.

If you don't want to lug around a separate GPS device, several smartphones contain GPS capability beyond just simple location services. For example, the iPhone app MotionX-GPS (`www.motionx.com`) contains a variety of tools that are useful for the genealogist in the field. It can show your position on the street, topographic maps, and satellite maps. You can also set the application to track your movements and set waypoints along the way. The application also has a built-in compass and the capability to take a picture and automatically associate it with a latitude and longitude.

Plotting against the family

Although finding the location where your ancestors lived on a map is interesting, it's even more exciting to create maps specific to your family history. One way genealogists produce their own maps is by plotting land records: They take the legal description of the land from a record and place it into land-plotting software, which then creates a map showing the land boundaries. A couple of programs for plotting boundaries are DeedMapper, by Direct Line Software (`www.directlinesoftware.com/factsht.htm`), and Metes and Bounds, by Sandy Knoll Software (`www.tabberer.com/sandyknoll/more/metesandbounds/metes.html`). You can also find a number of commercial plotting programs by using a search engine such as Google (`www.google.com`).

Another way to create custom maps is through geographical information systems (GIS) software. GIS software allows you to create maps based on layers of information. For example, you may start with a map that is just an outline of a county. Then you might add a second layer that shows the township sections of the county as they were originally platted. A third layer might show the location of your ancestor's homestead based on the legal description of a land record. A fourth layer might show watercourses or other terrain features within the area. The resulting map can give you a great appreciation of the environment in which your ancestor lived.

To begin using GIS resources, you first have to acquire a GIS data viewer. This software comes in many forms, including free software and commercial packages. One popular piece of free software is ArcReader, which is available on the ESRI site at `www.esri.com/software/arcgis/arcreader/download.html`. Then you download (or create) geographical data to use with the viewer. A number of sites contain data, both free and commercial. Starting points for finding data include ArcGIS Online (`www.arcgis.com/home`), GIS Data Depot (`http://data.geocomm.com`), and Geodata.gov (`http://gos2.geodata.gov/wps/portal/gos`). For more information on GIS software, see GIS.com at `www.gis.com`.

You can also use maps from other sources and integrate them into a GIS map. When visiting cemeteries, we like to use GIS resources to generate an aerial photograph of the cemetery and plot the location of the grave markers on it. When we get back home, we use the aerial photograph as the base template and then overlay the grave locations on it electronically to show their exact positions.

For example, when grave hunting for the German Reformed Cemetery (discussed earlier in the chapter), we generated an aerial view of the area at Bing.com (`www.bing.com`). In the search field, we entered the place-name (German Reformed Cemetery Illinois), then clicked the magnifying glass icon and selected Aerial in the upper-left corner of the resulting map.

Figure 6-7 shows the photograph at its maximum zoom. The cemetery is the slightly lighter, triangular gray area near the center of the photograph (it's bordered on the west by the highway and on the east by a grove of trees). This view of the cemetery helps a lot when we try to find it "on the ground."

From the photograph, we know that the cemetery is right off the highway, between two farms, and across from a triangular lake (although we have to keep in mind that the aerial photograph may have been taken long ago — some things might have changed since then).

After plotting the gravestone locations based on GPS readings at the cemetery, we generate the picture shown in Figure 6-8. We store that picture in our genealogical database so that it's easy to find gravestones at that cemetery should we (or anyone else) want to visit it in the future.

There's No Place Like Home: Using Local Resources

A time will come (possibly early in your research) when you need information that's maintained on a local level — say, a copy of a record stored in a local courthouse, confirmation that an ancestor is buried in a particular cemetery, or just a photo of the old homestead. So how can you find and get what you need?

Figure 6-7:
An aerial
map
generated
at Bing.com.

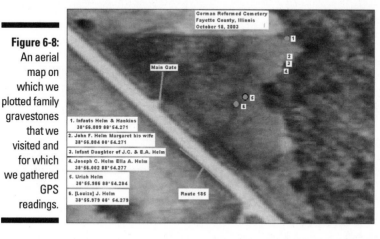

Figure 6-8:
An aerial
map on
which we
plotted family
gravestones
that we
visited and
for which
we gathered
GPS
readings.

Finding this information is relatively easy if you live in or near the county where the information is maintained — you decide what you need and where it's stored, and then go get a copy. Getting locally held information isn't quite as easy, however, if you live in another county, state, or country. Although you can determine what information you need and where it may be stored, finding out whether the information is truly kept where you think it is and then getting a copy is another thing. Of course, if this situation weren't such a common occurrence for genealogists, you could just make a vacation out of it — travel to the location to finish researching there and get the copy you need while sightseeing along the way. But unfortunately, needing records from distant places is a common occurrence, and most of us can't afford to pack our bags and hit the road every time we need a record or item from a faraway place — which is why it's nice to know that resources are available to help.

From geographic-specific Web sites to local genealogical and historical societies to libraries with research services to individuals who are willing to do lookups in public records, a lot of resources are available to help you locate local documents and obtain copies. Some resources are free, others may charge you a fee for their time, and still others will bill you only for copying or other direct costs.

Geographic-specific Web sites

Geographic-specific Web sites are those pages that contain information only about a particular town, county, state, country, or other locality. They typically provide information about local resources, such as genealogical and historical societies, government agencies and courthouses, cemeteries, and civic organizations. Some sites have local histories and biographies of prominent residents online. Often, they list and have links to other Web pages that have resources for the area. Sometimes they even have a place where you can post *queries* (or questions) about the area or families from there, in the hope that someone who reads your query will have some answers for you.

You can find several good examples of general geographic-specific Web sites:

- ✔ **The USGenWeb Project** (www.usgenweb.org) conveys information about the United States. The USGenWeb Project is an all-volunteer online effort to provide a central genealogical resource for information (records and reference materials) pertaining to counties within each state. (See the sidebar "The USGenWeb Project," later in this chapter, for more information.)

- ✔ **GENUKI: UK + Ireland Genealogy** (www.genuki.org.uk) is an online reference site that contains primary historical and genealogical information in the United Kingdom and Ireland. It links to sites containing indexes, transcriptions, or digitized images of actual records. All the information is categorized by locality — by country, then county, then parish.

- ✔ **The American Local History Network** (www.alhn.org) organizes its resources by state and by topic.

- ✔ **National Library of Australia** (www.nla.gov.au/oz/genelist.html) has a listing of all sorts of state and territory resources in Australia, including archives, libraries, societies, and cemeteries. It also has links directly to indexes and records at some local levels.

- ✔ **The WorldGenWeb Project** (www.worldgenweb.org) attempts the same type of undertaking as USGenWeb, only on a global scale.

Genealogical and historical societies

Most genealogical and historical societies exist on a local level and attempt to preserve documents and history for the area in which they are located. Genealogical societies also have another purpose — to help their members research their ancestors whether they lived in the local area or elsewhere. (Granted, some surname-based genealogical societies, and even a few virtual societies, are exceptions because they aren't specific to one particular place.) Although historical societies usually don't have a stated purpose of aiding their members in genealogical research, they are helpful to genealogists anyway. Often, if you don't live in the area from which you need a record or information, you can contact a local genealogical or historical society to get help. Help varies from lookup services in books and documents the society maintains in its library to volunteers who actually locate records for you and get copies to send you. Before you contact a local genealogical or historical society for help, be sure you know what services it offers.

Many local genealogical and historical societies have Web pages and identify exactly which services they offer to members and nonmembers online. To find a society in an area you're researching, you can try a search in a search engine, such as the following:

> Frederick County Virginia society genealogy OR historical

Or, you can find an index of genealogical and historical societies — such as the Society Hill Directory (www.daddezio.com/society). You might try this if a search engine search yields nothing — because some societies still do not maintain Web pages. The Society Hill Directory contains directories for societies in the United States, Canada, and Australia. To find a society in the directory, try this:

1. **Using your Web browser, go to Society Hill Directory at www.daddezio.com/society.**

2. **Select the link to the country where the society resides.**

   We selected United States Historical & Genealogical Societies.

3. **Click a state.**

   You have two ways to search after you're on the state page. You can use the search form to search by a society name, or you can browse through the alphabetical listings.

4. **Type a name in the search box and click Go.**

   We typed *Frederick*. The results page contained a link to the Winchester-Frederick County Historical Society.

Libraries and archives

Often, the holdings in local libraries and archives can be of great value to you — even if you can't physically visit the library or archive to do your research. If the library or archive has an Internet site, go online to determine whether that repository has the book or document you need. (Most libraries and archives have Web pages with their card catalogs or another listing of their holdings.) After seeing whether the repository has what you need, you can contact it to borrow the book or document (if it participates in an inter-library loan program) or to get a copy of what you need. (Most libraries and archives have services to copy information for people at a minimal cost.)

To find online catalogs for libraries in particular places, follow these steps:

1. **Using your Web browser, go to LibDex: The Library Index at www. libdex.com.**

2. **Scroll down to the bottom of the page and click the Browse by Country link.**

   A geographic index of links sorted by country is displayed. For example, you can look for the National Library of Australia to see whether its collection has books that would help your Australian research.

3. **Scroll down and click the link for Australia.**

   Clicking the link for Australia takes you to a page that lists regions in Australia.

4. **Click a region and browse through the list to find a library of interest.**

   Depending on the link you select, you are taken to a page for that particular location. For example, clicking the Tasmania link takes us to the Geographic: Countries: Australia: Tasmania page, where we can scroll through a list of catalogs.

5. **Click the State Library of Tasmania link.**

   Selecting the State Library of Tasmania link takes you to a description page with a link to the State Library's catalog online. From this point, follow the site's instructions to search for books of interest and applicability to your particular research.

Professional researchers

Professional researchers are people who research your genealogy — or particular family lines — for a fee. If you're looking for someone to do all the research necessary to put together a complete family history, some do so. If you're just looking for records in a particular area to substantiate claims in your genealogy, professional researchers can usually locate the records for you and get you copies. Their services, rates, experience, and reputations vary, so be careful when selecting a professional researcher to help you. Look for someone who has quite a bit of experience in the area in which you need help. Asking for references or a list of satisfied customers isn't out of the question. (That way, you know who you're dealing with before you send the researcher money.) Chapter 10 provides a list of questions we recommend you ask when looking for a professional researcher to hire, as well as provides some steps to follow in finding a professional researcher online.

To find a researcher in a particular location, you can do a search by geographic specialty on the Association of Professional Genealogists Web site at www.apgen.org/directory/search.html?type=geo_specialty&new_search=true.

The USGenWeb Project

The USGenWeb Project provides a central resource for genealogical information (records and reference materials) pertaining to counties within each state. USGenWeb offers state-level pages for each state within the United States that has links to pages for each county, as well as links to other online resources about the state. At the county level, the pages have links to resources about the county.

In addition to links to other Web sites with genealogical resources that are geographic-specific, most of the county-level pages have histories of the county or places within that county and a query section where you can post or read queries (or questions) about researching in that county. Some of the county-level pages offer other services in addition to the query section, such as online records (transcribed or digitized), information about ongoing projects for that county, a surname registry for anyone researching in the county, and a lookup section that identifies people who are willing to look up information for others.

Although some states have uniform-looking county pages with the same standard resources

for each county, other states don't. The content and look of USGenWeb state and county pages vary tremendously from state to state.

In addition to state- and county-level pages, the USGenWeb Project includes special projects that cross state and county lines. Some of these projects include the following:

- A project to collect and transcribe tombstone inscriptions so that genealogists can access the information online

- An undertaking to transcribe all federal census data for the United States and make it available online

- The Pension project — an attempt to transcribe pensions for all wars before 1900

- The Digital Map Library project, which provides free, high-quality digital maps to researchers

The various pages and projects that make up the USGenWeb Project are designed and maintained by volunteers. If you're interested in becoming involved, visit the USGenWeb home page (www.usgenweb.org).

Looking at directories and newspapers

If you have a general idea of where your family lived at a particular time but no conclusive proof, city and county directories and newspapers from the area may help. (Census records, which we discuss in Chapter 5, are quite helpful for this purpose, too.) Directories and newspapers can help you confirm whether your ancestors indeed lived in a particular area, and in some cases, they can provide even more information than you expect. A friend of ours has a great story — morbid as it is — that illustrates just this point. He was looking through newspapers for an obituary about one of his great-uncles. He knew when his great-uncle died but couldn't find mention of it in the obituary section of the newspaper. As he set the newspaper down (probably in despair), he glanced at the front page — only to find a graphic description of how a local man had been killed in a freak elevator accident. And guess who that local man was? That's right! He was our friend's great-uncle. The newspaper not only confirmed for him that his great-uncle lived there but also gave our friend a lot more information than he ever expected.

Directories

Like today's telephone books, the directories of yesteryear contained basic information about the persons who lived in particular areas, whether the areas were towns, cities, districts, or counties. Typically, the directory identified at least the head of the household and the location of the house. Some directories also included the names and ages of everyone in the household and occupations of any members of the household who were employed.

When looking for a city directory, make your first stop the City Directories of the United States of America at www.uscitydirectories.com. The intent of this site is to identify repositories of city directories online and offline, and to guide you to them. And other sites can direct you to directories for particular geographic areas too. You can find a list of city directories available on microfilm at the Library of Congress for nearly 700 American towns and states through the U.S. City Directories on Microfilm in the Microform Reading Room Web page (www.loc.gov/rr/microform/uscity). If you're looking for city directories for England and Wales, look at the Historical Directories site (www.historicaldirectories.org). The site contains digitized directories from 1750 to 1919. You can also often find lists of city directories on the Web sites of local and state libraries.

Some individuals have also posted city directories in their areas. An example of this is the Fredericksburg, Virginia, City Directory 1938 page at departments.umw.edu/hipr/www/fredericksburg/1938directory.htm.

And a commercial effort from Ancestry.com is attempting to re-create the 1890 Census through city directories. For more information on this subscription-based project, see Chapter 12, or jump on over to Ancestry.com's Web site at www.ancestry.com/search/rectype/census/1890sub/main.htm.

For tips on using city directories, see the article "City Directories," by Brian Andersson, at www.ancestry.com/learn/library/article. aspx?article=2634.

Also, some genealogical and historical societies and associations have made a commitment to post the contents of directories for their areas or at least an index of what their libraries hold online so that you know before you contact them whether they have something useful to you. Check out the section "Genealogical and historical societies," earlier in this chapter, for more information on how to find these organizations.

Newspapers

Unlike directories that list almost everyone in a community, newspapers are helpful only if your ancestors did something newsworthy — but you'd be surprised at what was considered newsworthy in the past. Your ancestor didn't necessarily have to be a politician or a criminal to get his or her picture and story in the paper. Just like today, obituaries, birth and marriage announcements, public records of land transactions, advertisements, and gossip sections were all relatively common in newspapers of the past.

Finding copies online of those newspapers from the past is a challenge. Most of the newspaper sites currently on the Web are for contemporary publications. Although you can read about wedding anniversaries and birthdays in England and Sweden today, you can't necessarily access online information about your ancestor's death in the 1800s in one of those countries. Many researchers are beginning to recognize the potential that the Web holds for making historical information from newspapers available worldwide. However, the lack of committed resources (time and money, primarily) prevents them from doing so as quickly as we'd like.

Here's what you're likely to find online pertaining to newspapers:

✔ **Indexes:** A variety of sites serve as indexes of newspapers that are available at particular libraries, archives, and universities. Most of these list the names and dates of the periodicals that are held in the newspaper or special collections. Examples of index sites include the following:

- The Newspapers at Library and Archives Canada page: www. collectionscanada.ca/8/16/index-e.html

- The Newspaper Collection at the State Library of Victoria, Australia: www.slv.vic.gov.au/our-collections/what-we-collect/newspapers

- New England Old Newspaper Index Project of Maine: www.roots web.com/~megenweb/newspaper/project

- The Online Newspaper Indexes Available in the Newspaper and Current Periodical Reading Room of the Library of Congress: www. loc.gov/rr/news/npindex2.html

✔ **Transcriptions:** A few sites contain actual transcriptions of newspaper articles, entire issues, or excerpts. Typically, the contents at these sites are limited to the topic and geographic interests of the person who transcribed the information and posted it for public access on the Web. Here are a few examples:

- Old Newspaper Articles of Henderson County, Texas: `www.txgenweb7.org/txhenderson/Newspapers.htm`

- The Knoxville Gazette: `www.rootsweb.com/~tnnews/kgmain.htm`

- Ireland Old News: `www.irelandoldnews.com`

✔ **Collectors' issues for sale:** Although they don't provide information directly from the newspaper online for you to use in your genealogical pursuits, these sites can help you find out about collectors' editions of newspapers and possibly even buy them online. The sites that sell old newspapers generally market their papers as good gift ideas for birthdays and anniversaries. For the services to be useful to you as a genealogist, you have to know the date and place of the event you want to document (and a newspaper name helps, too), as well as be willing to pay for a copy of that paper. Here are a couple of newspaper collector sites to check out:

- HistoryBuff.com: `www.historybuff.com`

- Simply Personalized: Newspaper Gifts: `www.simplypersonalized.com/newspaper-gifts`

✔ **Online newspaper projects:** Many people are beginning to recognize the important role newspapers play in recording history and the value of putting newspaper information on the Web. We've seen an increasing number of online projects to catalog or transcribe newspapers — some of the projects are organized on a state level, and others are for cities or particular newspapers. The Web sites for these projects explain the purpose of the project, its current status, and how to find the newspapers if they've been transcribed or digitized and placed online. Here are a few examples:

- Chronicling America: Historic American Newspapers (see Figure 6-9 for an example of a newspaper on this site): `www.loc.gov/chroniclingamerica`

- GenealogyBank.com: `www.genealogybank.com`

- NewspaperArchive.com: `www.newspaperarchive.com`

- Ancestry.com: `www.ancestry.com`

Now you know what newspaper resources you may find online, but how do you find these sites? One option is to use a geographic category in a comprehensive genealogical site (though most may not list newspaper transcriptions if the transcriptions are buried under a larger site). Another option is to use a general Internet search engine such as Google.com or Bing.com — especially if you know the location and timeframe for the newspaper.

Figure 6-9:
An image of the Weekly Kansas Chief from 1872 on the Chronicling America Web site.

Localizing your search

To find a lot of detail about a specific area and what it was like during a particular timeframe, local histories are the answer. Local histories often contain information about when and how a particular place was settled and may have biographical information on earlier settlers or principal people within the community who sponsored the creation of the history.

Online local histories can be tucked away in geographically specific Web sites, historical society pages, library sites, and Web-based bookstores. You can also find a few sites that feature local histories:

✔ Ancestry.com (www.ancestry.com) features several thousand works in its Stories, Memories, and Histories collection.

✔ A collection of Canadian local histories is available at Our Roots/Nos Racines (www.ourroots.ca).

✔ You can search by location and find a growing collection of local histories on Google Books (http://books.google.com).

For an example of a local history site, take a gander at Figure 6-10, which shows an example page of the History of Sangamon County, Illinois, on Google Books.

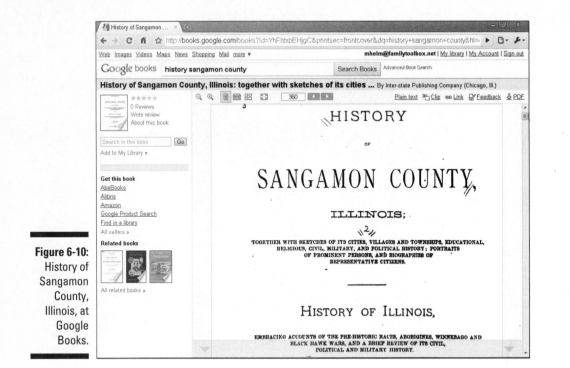

Figure 6-10:
History of
Sangamon
County,
Illinois, at
Google
Books.

Part III
Adding Depth to Your Research

The 5th Wave
By Rich Tennant

"The good news is that I've located Pinnochio's natural mother. The bad news is she's part of the parquet flooring at a bowling alley in upstate New York."

In this part . . .

These chapters help you add some pizzazz to your research by examining how to find ethnic-based resources. These types of resources often offer perspectives into your ancestors' lives. We also explore some interesting genealogical byways, such as adoption records, molecular genealogy, and records associated with religious groups and fraternal orders.

Chapter 7

Going Beyond Borders: International and Ethnic Records

At some point in your research, you will encounter an ancestor who was born outside the United States (or before the United States was a country) or who is associated with a particular ethnicity that requires you to use a specific set of sources. These records often have characteristics that make them very different from the typical records found in the United States. Even if you can't find the actual records online (a lot of international records have been placed online over the past few years), certain sites can help identify what records are available in archives and how to use them to benefit your research. In this chapter, we look at strategies to find these resources online as well as provide links to some key sites to consult.

Fishing for International and Ethnic Sources

You can use a number of strategies when attempting to locate international and ethnic resources online. These strategies range from using genealogical wikis to search engines and comprehensive genealogical indexes.

Wiki-ing for answers

When beginning to research in a new geographical area, we always like to start by seeing what is available in that area at the FamilySearch Wiki (`https://wiki.familysearch.org`). You can type the country or locality in the search box at the top of the page, or you can browse articles by country. At the time that we wrote this book, we found articles on 237 countries in the browsable list, although not all the articles were fully complete. Some of the topics contained in the articles were Getting Started with Research, Jurisdictions, Research Tools, Help Wanted (ways that users can contribute what they know about the country), Featured Content, and Did You Know. Embedded in the left-side navigation of an article are links to other articles that might be relevant to the country or geographical area, as shown in Figure 7-1.

Figure 7-1:
The Netherlands topic on the Family-Search Wiki.

You can also search for ethnic entries in the FamilySearch Wiki through the search box. Topics on ethnic articles might include Records and Databases, Related Web Sites, Help Near You, presentations regarding the ethnic group, Helpful Guides, FamilySearch Forums, Research Aids, Forms, FamilySearch Indexing Projects, and LDS Church Service Resources.

While you're at the FamilySearch site, you might want to check out the Research Helps section found at `www.familysearch.org/eng/search/RG/frameset_rhelps.asp`. Included in this section are links to geographical and topic-specific resources. For example, the topics addressed in the outline for Latin America include Search Strategies, Records at the Family History Library, Family History Library Catalog, Archives and Libraries, Cemeteries, Census,

Church Records, Civil Registration, Emigration and Immigration, Gazetteers, History, Land and Property, Military Records, Native Races, Nobility, Notarial Records, Periodicals, Probate Records, Societies, and For Further Reading.

Surveying sites with comprehensive genealogy indexes

To get an idea of what is generally available online, a comprehensive genealogy index is always a good start. These indexes have the benefit of being genealogically focused, so you don't have to wade through a lot of links that are not relevant to genealogy or history. Typically, these sites also categorize the links in such a way that you can get to what you're looking for in a few clicks.

For example, if you're interested in researching an ancestor who lived in the Netherlands, you could visit Cyndi's List (`www.cyndislist.com`), select the Netherlands/Nederland category, and see links to 338 resources, organized into 17 groups.

Using search engines

If you haven't found what you are looking for in a comprehensive genealogy index, your next stop should be a general search engine. Similar to searches for information on particular individuals, you need to ensure that your search criteria is fairly specific, or you risk receiving too many search results — most of which might be irrelevant to your search. For example, when we typed the search term *Belgium genealogy,* we received 1,240,000 results in Google and 4,390,000 results in Bing.

Search engines are a good resource when you're looking for information on records in a specific locality. So, instead of *Belgium genealogy,* if we use the search criteria *Hainaut baptism records,* we receive a fraction of the results — only 69,700.

WorldGenWeb

The WorldGenWeb Project (`www.worldgenweb.org`) contains links to Web sites for more than 400 countries and areas in the world. To find a specific country, follow these steps:

1. **Go to the WorldGenWeb Project site (`www.worldgenweb.org`).**

   You see a page with a map and a list of resources along the left side of the page (below the map).

2. **Click the link to the Country Index under the Main Menu column.**

   For our example, we're looking for information on civil registrations in Jamaica.

3. **Click the link in the WorldGenWeb Region column for your target country.**

   We clicked the CaribbeanGenWeb link next to the entry for Jamaica. This link took us to the region project page. In our case, the CaribbeanGenWeb page had three versions — in English, French, and Spanish. We chose the English version.

4. **From the region page, find a link to the countries represented in the project.**

   On the CaribbeanGenWeb page, we clicked the Island Links link located near the top of the page in the second column. If you didn't choose the same region, you have to find the appropriate link on your particular region page.

5. **Select the link to your country.**

   We clicked the Jamaica link, which took us to the Genealogy of Jamaica page.

6. **Choose a link to a resource that interests you.**

   On the Genealogy of Jamaica home page, we found a list of resources available on the site. We clicked the Civil Registration link, which displayed the Civil Registrations of Jamaicans page, as shown in Figure 7-2.

Figure 7-2:
Page for Civil Registrations of Jamaicans.

REMEMBER

When researching your European roots, keep in mind that due to the number of European countries, no single European GenWeb Project site exists. Instead, you find the following four European region sites:

- **BritishIslesGenWeb** (www.britishislesgenweb.org) contains projects for Caribbean Islands, Channel Islands, England, Falkland Islands, Gibraltar, Ireland, Isle of Man, Northern Ireland, Scotland, St. Helena, and Wales.

- **CenEuroGenWeb** (www.rootsweb.ancestry.com/~ceneurgw) lists pages for Belgium, Denmark, Greenland, Germany, Iceland, Latvia, Liechtenstein, Lithuania, Luxembourg, Netherlands, Norway, Poland, Sweden, and Switzerland.

- **EastEuropeGenWeb** (www.rootsweb.ancestry.com/~easeurgw) contains sites for Albania, Austria, Croatia, Czech Republic, Estonia, Finland, Montenegro, Serbia, Slovak Republic, Slovenia, and Yugoslavia.

- **MediterraneanGenWeb** (www.mediterraneangenweb.com/indexe.html) has project pages for Azores, France, Italy, Madeira, Portugal, and Spain.

Another place to look for help in getting started is the International Internet Genealogical Society site, at www.iigs.org/index.htm.en. Although the site is currently limited in the areas that it covers, you can find global village representatives that can help you with specific countries. You can also find a list of current projects by group members and some online courses that provide an introduction to genealogy in Australia, New Zealand, Canada, Germany, and South Africa.

Translating sites

Within this chapter (and when you search online), you will encounter several sites in languages other than English. Due to advancements in translation Web sites and Web browser translators, the fact that the site is in a different language doesn't mean that it is not useful in your research. The translation site Yahoo! Babel Fish, at http://babelfish.yahoo.com, has the capability to translate a block of text, or you can enter a URL to translate an entire Web page.

Rather than going to the Babel Fish Web page each time we encounter a site in a foreign language, we prefer to have that functionality built into our browser. The Google Chrome browser (www.google.com/chrome/intl/en/landing_chrome.html?hl=en) has the Google Translate functionality built in. When you reach a site in a foreign language, the Translate toolbar appears and suggests the language that the site is authored in. It then asks whether you want the site translated. If you say yes, the page is translated — that is, the text that is not part of a graphic is translated. Although the translation isn't perfect, it's usually good enough to give you a good idea of the meaning of the text.

Records from the English-Speaking World

Currently, the most prolific number of records available on the Web are from countries with English as their native language. In the following sections, we look at records in the United Kingdom, Ireland, and Canada.

Gathering information from England and Wales

To become familiar with records in England and Wales, visit the National Archives site (www.nationalarchives.gov.uk). By clicking the Catalogues and Online Records link below the Records tab, you find links to the following resources:

- ✔ **The Catalogue** (formerly PROCAT) contains descriptions of 11 million documents generated by the government.

- ✔ **DocumentsOnline** includes downloadable documents digitized by the National Archives, such as wills and medal index cards.

- ✔ **Equity Pleadings** focus on civil court cases in the late 17th and early 18th centuries.

- ✔ **Library Catalogue** lists the works contained in the National Archives research library.

- ✔ **Taxation Records** contains descriptions of documents that relate to medieval and early-modern tax records.

- ✔ **Trafalgar Ancestors Database** includes records of everyone who served on the British side in the Battle of Trafalgar.

Census records

Since 1801, censuses have been taken in England and Wales every ten years (except 1941). Most of the returns from 1801 to 1831 were statistical and did not contain names, making them useless for genealogists. Beginning in 1841, the administration of the census became the responsibility of the Registrar General and the Superintendent Registrars, who were responsible for recording civil registrations (vital records). This changed the focus of the census from the size of the population to details on individuals and families. The National Archives releases information in the census only after 100 years.

For general information on census records, see the National Archives Looking for Records of the Census page at www.nationalarchives.gov.uk/records/looking-for-person/recordscensus.htm. You can find online versions of the following censuses:

✔ **Images** of the 1841 through 1911 Censuses are available at 1901CensusOnline.com (www.1901censusonline.com), Ancestry. uk (www.ancestry.co.uk), FindMyPast.co.uk (www.findmypast. co.uk), and Genes Reunited (www.genesreunited.co.uk). British Origins (www.britishorigins.com) contains images of the 1841, 1861, and 1871 Censuses.

✔ **Transcriptions** are sporadic for the 1841 through 1891 Censuses at the FreeCEN site (http://freecen.rootsweb.com). Also, partial transcriptions are available at TheGenealogist.co.uk (www.thegenealogist.co.uk).

✔ **Indices** for the complete 1881 Census are available at the FamilySearch site (www.familysearch.org).

✔ **Maps** of the registration districts for the 1871 Census are available at the Cassini site (www.cassinimaps.co.uk/shop/tna1. asp?id=166&page=ce).

Birth, marriage, and death records

A number of online sources are available for transcribed and digitized documents. BMD Registers (www.bmdregisters.co.uk) features images of birth, baptism, marriage, and death records taken from nonparish sources from 1534 to 1865. You can conduct a search of its database; however, you must purchase credits before being able to view an image of the digitized document. The subscription site, The Genealogist (www.thegenealogist.co.uk), has a complete index of birth, marriage, and death records for England and Wales. If you're looking for free birth, marriage, and death records, see the FreeBMD project at www.freebmd.org.uk. This volunteer effort has transcribed more than 189 million records — although the collection is still not complete.

The subscription sites 1901CensusOnline.com, Ancestry.uk, FindMyPast. co.uk, and Genes Reunited also have birth, marriage, and death records. For links to subscription and free birth, marriage, and death resources online, see the UK BMD site (www.ukbmd.org.uk).

Other records

A number of records (and pointers to records housed in archives) are available on both subscription and government sites. These sites include the following:

✔ **Access to Archives** (www.a2a.org.uk) is a consortium of archives in England and Wales. The Access to Archives site features a database with descriptions of the holdings of 418 record offices and repositories.

✔ **British Origins** (www.britishorigins.com) includes Boyd's Marriage Index, a marriage license allegation index, wills indexes, probate indexes, apprenticeship records, court records, burial records, militia records, and passenger lists.

✔ **British Library — India Office Family History Search** (http://india family.bl.uk/UI) holds records of the government of pre-1949 India.

The site features a bibliographical index that contains more than 300,000 entries.

- **Commonwealth War Graves Commission** (`www.cwgc.org`) is responsible for maintaining the 1.7 million graves of those who died in the two world wars. The CWGC Web site includes the Debt of Honour Register, which provides basic information on those covered by the Commission.

- **General Register Office** (`www.direct.gov.uk/en/Governmentcitizensandrights/Registeringlifeevents/index.htm`) holds birth, marriage, and death records in England and Wales from July 1, 1837, up to one year ago. The GRO Web site details how to get copies of certificates and has some basic guides on researching genealogy.

- **Imperial War Museum** (`www.iwm.org.uk`) chronicles the wars of the 20th century from 1914. Its Web site contains fact sheets on tracing ancestors who served in the armed forces and an inventory of war memorials.

- **National Library of Wales/Llyfrgell Genedlaethol Cymru** (`www.llgc.org.uk/index.php?id=2`) holds documents such as electoral lists, marriage bonds, probate and estate records, and tithe maps. The Library's Web site contains a list of independent researchers, and you can search databases including an index to the gaol files (*gaol* is the British word for *jail*), applicants for marriage licenses, and descriptions of the library's archival holdings.

Finding help

To contact other genealogists interested in British genealogical research, see the Society of Genealogists (`www.sog.org.uk`). The site includes information on membership, publications, and the Society's online library catalog.

For societies at a local level, consult the list of members of the Federation of Family History Societies (`www.ffhs.org.uk`). The Federation's site includes information on its current projects and on upcoming events, as well as a set of subscription databases.

If you are not finding what you are looking for in one of the previously mentioned sites, your next stop should be the GENUKI: United Kingdom and Ireland Genealogy site, at `www.genuki.org.uk`. The GENUKI site is similar to the GenWeb sites in that it contains subsites for the various counties. You can find a variety of guides, transcribed records, and other useful data on the GENUKI sites.

A lot more than haggis — finding Scottish records

The ScotlandsPeople site (www.scotlandspeople.gov.uk) is the official government site for Scottish records. The subscription site contains statutory registers of births (1855–1906), marriages (1855–1931), and deaths (1855–1956); old parish registers of births and baptisms (1553–1854) and banns and marriages (1553–1854); census records (1841–1901); and wills and testaments (1513–1901).

Other sites that can assist you in tracking down Scottish ancestors follow:

- ✔ **General Register Office for Scotland** (www.gro-scotland.gov.uk) holds birth, marriage, divorce, adoption, and death records in Scotland from 1855. The GROS is also responsible for the periodic censuses for Scotland.

- ✔ **National Archives of Scotland** (www.nas.gov.uk) contains records of when Scotland was its own kingdom as well as those of modern Scotland. Records housed there include land transfers, records of the Church of Scotland parishes, estate papers, court papers, and taxation lists.

- ✔ **Scottish Archives Network** (www.scan.org.uk) is a joint project between the National Archives of Scotland, the Heritage Lottery Fund, and the Genealogical Society of Utah. The project has placed the holdings of 50 Scottish archives into an online catalog and has digitized more than 2 million records.

- ✔ **Scottish Genealogy Society** (www.scotsgenealogy.com) provides assistance for individuals researching their Scottish roots. The Web site contains information on the Society's library and annual conference.

- ✔ **Scottish Register of Tartans** (www.tartanregister.gov.uk), part of the National Archives of Scotland, houses a repository of tartans. On the Web site, you can search for tartans by name and view an image of the material.

Researching the north o' Ireland

If you're looking for ancestors in Northern Ireland (specifically, the counties of Antrim, Armagh, Down, Fermanagh, Londonderry, and Tyrone), you have a few places to check. If you want a brief introduction to the different record types and resources available, consult the Northern Ireland Online Genealogy Centre at www.nireland.com/genealogy.

The Public Record Office of Northern Ireland (`www.proni.gov.uk`) holds items such as estate, church, business, valuation and tithe, school, and wills records. The Web site includes online databases that contain signatories to the Ulster Covenant, Freeholders records, street directories, and will calendars. You can also find guides to some of the more popular collections at PRONI on its Online Guides and Indexes page at `www.proni.gov.uk/index/research_and_records_held/catalogues_guides_indexes_and_leaflets/online_guides_and_indexes.htm`.

The General Register Office for Northern Ireland (`www.groni.gov.uk`) maintains registrations of births, stillbirths, adoptions, deaths, marriages, and civil partnerships. The Web site contains summaries of these record types and a family history guide that can assist you with your research in Northern Ireland at `www.groni.gov.uk/family_research.pdf`.

Also, take a look at the North of Ireland Family History Society site (`www.nifhs.org`). The site contains details on the Society's Research Centre, branches, publications, and meeting calendar. For books on genealogy in Northern Ireland and for research services, see the Web page for the Ulster Historical Foundation at `www.ancestryireland.com`. This site also contains pay-per-view and members-only online databases, including indexes to birth, marriage, and death records for County Antrim and County Down, index to the 1796 Flaxgrowers Bounty List, directories, sporadic census and education records, emigration records, wills, election records, and estate records.

Emerald Ancestors (`www.emeraldancestors.com`) maintains subscription databases on over 1 million ancestors from Northern Ireland, including birth, marriage, death, and census records. For free resources, see the Northern IrelandGenWeb site at `www.rootsweb.ancestry.com/~nirwgw`. The site contains a resource listing and links to a variety of helpful online resources. The Ireland page on GENUKI also contains links to resources in the counties of Northern Ireland at `www.genuki.org.uk/big/irl`.

Because some of the resources overlap between Northern Ireland and Ireland, you might also look at some of the resources described in the following section.

Traversing the Emerald Isle

As we mention in the previous section, the GENUKI site (`www.genuki.org.uk`) contains information on a variety of geographic areas in the United Kingdom and Ireland. You see pages for all 32 counties of Ireland, and you can find brief articles on a variety of topics, including cemeteries, censuses, church records, civil registrations, court records, emigration and immigration, land and property, newspapers, probate records, and taxation. You can also find county pages at the Ireland Genealogy Projects site (`http://irelandgenealogyprojects.rootsweb.ancestry.com`) and the Ireland Genealogy Project and Ireland Genealogy Project Archives at `www.igp-web.com`.

To get an overview of Irish genealogy, take a look at the Directory of Irish Genealogy at `http://homepage.eircom.net/~seanjmurphy/dir`. In particular, look at A Primer in Irish Genealogy, available as a link at the top of the site's home page. You can also find information on genealogy courses and articles on Irish genealogy on this site. On the parent page to this site, the Centre for Irish Genealogical and Historical Studies (`http://homepage.tinet.ie/~seanjmurphy`), you find guides to the National Archives to Ireland and the General Register Office of Ireland. Another resource for those new to Irish research is the Irish Ancestors pages hosted by the Irish Times at `www.ireland.com/ancestor`. The site provides guides on sources of genealogical information in Ireland, a list of county heritage centers, record sources, and useful addresses.

Census records

Countrywide census enumerations have been conducted every ten years since 1821. Unfortunately, the census returns from 1821 to 1851 were largely destroyed in a fire at the Public Record Office in 1922. Fragments of these census returns are available at the National Archives of Ireland.

The government destroyed the returns from 1861 and 1871. Returns for 1901 and 1911 still survive and are available at the National Archives of Ireland. The 1901 and 1911 Censuses are available online at `www.nationalarchives.ie`.

Historical statistics for Irish censuses can be found on the census page maintained by the Central Statistics Office Ireland at `www.cso.ie/census`. No names are included in the publications, but the data can be used to gain some historical perspective on a particular area.

Other resources

A few sites contain databases and transcriptions of Irish records of interest to genealogists. Irish Family Research (`www.irishfamilyresearch.co.uk`) contains both free and subscription content, including a directory of headstones, electoral registers, city directories, Griffith's Valuation, hearth rolls, school records, and a variety of other sources. My Irish Ancestry (`http://myirishancestry.com`) allows users to search Griffith's Valuation at no cost. The Department of Tourism, Culture, and Sport sponsors the Irish Genealogy site (`www.irishgenealogy.ie`), which contains an index of church records and provides tips for planning a research trip to Ireland.

In addition to census records, the National Archives of Ireland (`www.nationalarchives.ie`) houses other records of interest to researchers, including Tithe Applotment books and Griffith's Valuation, wills, estate records, private source records, parish records and marriage licenses, and Crown and Peace records. However, these are not currently offered online. A database that is offered online on the site is the Ireland-Australia transportation records (1791–1853).

If you're looking for maps, check out Past Homes (www.pasthomes.com), which has a subscription site with Irish townland maps. The maps on the site were surveyed between 1829 and 1843. Another useful site for geographical data is the IreAtlas Townland Database at www.seanruad.com. Typing a townland name provides you with alternate names, number of acres, county, barony, civil parish, and province for the townland.

The Irish Family History Foundation hosts an online database of 17 million records, including birth, marriage, and death records, at its RootsIreland.ie site (www.rootsireland.ie). The Foundation also provides research services for a fee. Additional online databases can be found at the Irish Origins site (www.irishorigins.com). The site includes census, electoral register, marriage, will, burial, military, passenger list, and directory records.

At some point, you may need help with a specific area in Ireland. One site that may help is Ireland Roots at www.irelandroots.com. The site features message boards for each Irish county, where you can post queries about your family or questions about research in that particular county. If you need professional assistance, take a look at the Association of Professional Genealogists in Ireland site at www.apgi.ie. The Association establishes standards for its members to help ensure quality research. The Web site includes a member directory listing its areas of specialization.

Heading north for Canadian records

So you want to research your ancestors from Canada, eh? Well, a place to start is the Canadian Genealogy Centre (www.collectionscanada.gc.ca/genealogy/index-e.html), maintained by Library and Archives Canada. The site contains information for beginners, including what to do first and search strategies for a variety of record types. In the Guides section, see the online version of the Tracing Your Ancestors in Canada brochure (www.collectionscanada.gc.ca/genealogy/022-607.001-e.html), if you're new to Canadian resources. Also, at the top of the Canadian Genealogy Centre Web page, you can find a search engine that provides results for the databases maintained by Library and Archives Canada.

To get an idea of what online resources are available for Canadian research, some genealogical link sites specialize in Canada. These include Canadian Genealogy & History Links (www.islandnet.com/~cghl), CanGenealogy (www.cangenealogy.com), and Canadian Genealogy Resources (www.canadiangenealogy.net).

Census records

Canadian census returns are available for the years 1851, 1861, 1871, 1881, 1891, and 1901. The returns from 1851 to 1891 contain the individual's name, age, sex, province or country of birth, religion, race, occupation, marital status, and education. The returns for 1901 also include birth date, year of immigration, and address. For more information on data elements in the 1901 census, see the Description of Columns on the 1901 Census Schedule page at `http://freepages.genealogy.rootsweb.ancestry.com/~wjmartin/census.htm`.

Library and Archives Canada maintains information on the 1851, 1871, 1881, 1891, 1901, 1906, and 1911 censuses online at `www.collectionscanada.gc.ca/census/index-e.html`). Part of the collection includes images of the census returns, as shown in Figure 7-3.

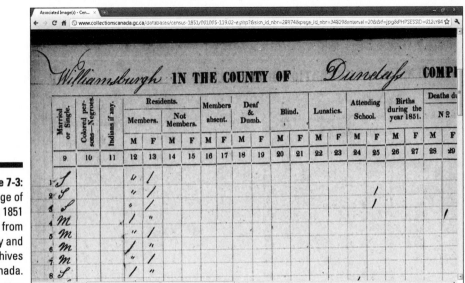

Figure 7-3:
Image of the 1851 census from Library and Archives Canada.

If you're looking for online information on specific census records, see the Virtual Reference Library at `www.virtualreferencelibrary.ca`.

Scroll down the Subject Directory and select Genealogy. Then click the Census Records link to get to a list of sites specifically about — you guessed it — census records. The list includes sites about the 1752 Laroque census (Isle Royale and Isle St. Jean), 1872 Victoria census, the First Census of New France (Quebec), and the 1901 and 1911 censuses for several provinces.

Automated Genealogy (`http://automatedgenealogy.com`) has indexes to the 1851, 1901, 1906 (a special census that included only the provinces of Alberta, Saskatchewan, and Manitoba), and 1911 censuses. The FamilySearch. org Record Search (`http://pilot.familysearch.org/recordsearch/start.html#start`) contains indexes to the 1851, 1871, 1881, and 1891 censuses. To search a specific census year, choose a link from the Browse Collections page at `http://pilot.familysearch.org/recordsearch/start.html#p=allCollections&r=1`.

Ancestry.ca (www.ancestry.ca) contains name indexes and images for the 1851 to 1911 censuses as well as the 1906 and 1916 censuses of Manitoba, Saskatchewan, and Alberta. It also contains indexes to various censuses conducted in Ontario and Nova Scotia from 1800 to 1842 and the 1770 census of Nova Scotia.

You might be interested in presenting some context to your research by using some statistical information from past censuses. For example, you may want to include in your research how many people lived in a particular province during a given census year. You can find this kind of information in the Historical Statistics of Canada at the Statistics Canada site (www.statcan.gc.ca).

Local resources

For resources on a more local basis, go to the Canada GenWeb Project site at www.rootsweb.ancestry.com/~canwgw. The project site includes links to genealogical sites, research queries, lookups, and a timeline. You also find a branch of the site that is oriented to kids at www.rootsweb.ancestry.com/~cangwkid. The following provinces also have a GenWeb Project page:

- **Alberta:** www.rootsweb.ancestry.com/~canab/index.html
- **British Columbia:** www.rootsweb.ancestry.com/~canbc
- **Manitoba:** www.rootsweb.ancestry.com/~canmb/index.htm
- **New Brunswick:** www.rootsweb.ancestry.com/~cannb
- **Newfoundland/Labrador:** www.rootsweb.ancestry.com/~cannf/index.html
- **Nova Scotia:** www.rootsweb.ancestry.com/~canns/index.html
- **Northwest Territories and Nunavut:** www.rootsweb.ancestry.com/~cannt
- **Ontario:** www.geneofun.on.ca/ongenweb
- **Québec:** www.rootsweb.ancestry.com/~canqc/index.htm
- **Saskatchewan:** www.rootsweb.ancestry.com/~cansk/Saskatchewan
- **Yukon:** www.rootsweb.ancestry.com/~canyk

Although Acadia is not a province, you can also find an Acadian GenWeb site at http://acadian-genweb.acadian-home.org/frames.html.

Other records and resources

The Library and Archives Canada site not only has images of census records but also houses images of the following records:

- Chinese Immigration Registers, 1887–1908
- Canadians in the South African War, 1899–1902

✔ Attestation Papers of Soldiers of the First World War, 1914–1918

✔ Upper Canada and Canada West Naturalization Records, 1828–1850

✔ Ward Chipman, Muster Master's Office, 1777–1785 (Loyalist registers)

✔ Immigrants from the Russian Empire

✔ Canadian Patents, 1869–1894

✔ Passenger Lists, 1865–1935

The Ancestry.ca subscription site maintains a variety of record sets, including census and voter lists; birth, marriage, and death records; military records; newspapers; maps and gazetteers; school and church histories; tax records; and wills. For more on the content of Ancestry.ca, see Chapter 12.

When it comes time to do some on-site research, you can look at the directory of archives at the Canadian Council of Archives. The Web site search interface (`www.cdncouncilarchives.ca/directory_adv.html`) allows you to search by an archive name or by province. The information on the site includes an overview of the collections of each archive, along with its hours of operation. To get more detailed information on the holdings in various archives across Canada, consult the ArchivesCanada.ca site (`www.archivescanada.ca`) — part of the Canadian Archival Information Network (CAIN). You can use a single search form to search by keyword for descriptions of collections, or you can use a separate form to find online exhibits. For published items held in the Library and Archives Canada and more than 1,300 other Canadian libraries, you can search the AMICUS national catalog at `http://amicus.collections canada.gc.ca/aaweb/aalogine.htm`. To make things even easier to find, the Library and Archives Canada has created a search engine that brings together several resources to make searching for genealogical data easier. The That's My Family site (`www.thatsmyfamily.info`) features a search form that allows you to specify what resources you want to search (either federal or by individual provinces) by keyword. Figure 7-4 shows the results page for a search on the surname Helm.

A number of sites contain abstracts of Canadian records. Olive Tree Genealogy (`www.olivetreegenealogy.com`) has free databases of ship and passenger lists, civil registrations, and cemetery records. inGeneas (`www.ingeneas.com`) is a pay site that offers access to passenger, immigration, census, vital statistic, land, and military records. For pointers to military records, you can search the catalog of the Canadian War Museum at `http://catalogue.warmuseum.ca/musvw/Vubis. csp?Profile=Profile`. This catalog contains entries (and in some cases abstracts) for textual and photographic records.

FamilySearch.org has a freely searchable International Genealogical Index online that contains data extracted from various original records — such as birth, christening, death, burial, and marriage dates. The Record Search collection contains indexes to many collections, including the following:

✔ British Columbia Birth, Marriage, and Death Registrations

✔ Canada Births and Baptisms, 1661–1959

✔ Canada Marriages, 1661–1949

✔ New Brunswick Census, 1861

✔ Nova Scotia Antigonish Catholic Diocese, 1823–1905

✔ Quebec Catholic Parish Registers, 1621–1900 (browsable images only)

If your family immigrated to Canada between 1928 and 1971, take a look at the Pier 21 Immigration Museum site (www.pier21.ca). The site gives a brief overview of the function of Pier 21 and information on the research services available on site. From 1869 to 1948, more than 100,000 British children were sent to Canada as laborers until they reached the age of 21. A site dedicated to these children is the Canadian Centre for Home Children, at www.canadianhomechildren.ca. A searchable database of Home Children is on the Library and Archives Canada site at www.collectionscanada.gc.ca/databases/home-children/001015-100.01-e.php.

Not able to travel to a distant cemetery in Canada to see the headstone of your ancestor? Then visit the Canadian Headstone Photo Project (www.canadianheadstones.com) to see whether someone has already snapped a photo or transcribed the headstone. This site currently boasts more than 117,000 photos from across Canada.

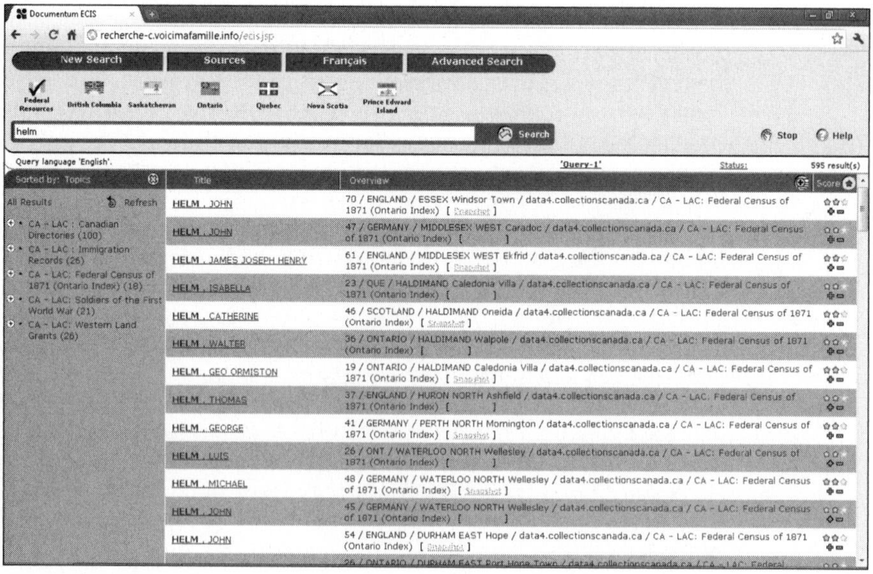

Figure 7-4: The search results for Helm at That's My Family.

While searching through records, you may run into a place name that you don't recognize. The Atlas of Canada (http://atlas.nrcan.gc.ca/site/english/index.html), at the Natural Resources Canada site, contains a variety of geographical resources including a place-name finder, satellite maps, and topographical maps. For a searchable database of Canadian geographical names, see the Geographical Names of Canada page at http://geonames.nrcan.gc.ca/index_e.php. If you want a historical perspective on the geography of Canada, look at the Historical Atlas of Canada project at www.historicalatlas.ca/website/hacolp.

Getting help

If you're looking for local genealogical experts, you can turn to a number of genealogical societies in Canada. An example of a society Web site is Alberta Family Histories Society (www.afhs.ab.ca). The site includes the monthly schedule of meetings of the society, publications for sale, document transcriptions, research aids, queries, and information about the society library.

Because Canada has a history of immigration of a number of different ethnicities, you might also check to see whether a site is dedicated to the ethnic group that you're researching. For example, the Chinese-Canadian Genealogy site (www.vpl.ca/ccg), maintained by the Vancouver Public Library, contains information on the early Chinese immigrations, Chinese name characteristics, biographic resources, and a survey of the types of record sets associated with the Canadian Chinese population.

Accessing Australian sources

When researching Australian ancestors, you find two distinct paths — aboriginal records and the sources for later settlers. For an introduction to aboriginal records, see Australian Aboriginal Genealogy Resources at http://mc2.vicnet.net.au/home/pmackett/web/index.html. The Australian Family History Compendium (www.cohsoft.com.au/afhc) offers information on a wider range of record types, as well as information on archives, maps, glossary, and societies.

Although Australia has taken a census every ten years since 1901, the first Australia-wide census was conducted in 1911. Now for some bad news — every return has been destroyed, in accordance with law. You can substitute other records for census returns in the form of convict returns and musters and post office directories. These returns are available for some states for the years 1788, 1792, 1796, 1800, 1801, 1805, 1806, 1811, 1814, 1816, 1817 through 1823, 1825, 1826, and 1837. Some of these records can be found at these locations:

✔ The New South Wales Government, Department of Commerce, State Records Authority of New South Wales site, at www.records.nsw.gov.au/state-archives/indexes-online

- The Archives Office of Tasmania at `http://portal.archives.tas.gov.au/menu.aspx?search=10`
- The Public Records Office of Victoria at `www.prov.vic.gov.au`

An index to the 1841 census is maintained by the New South Wales Government at `www.records.nsw.gov.au/state-archives/indexes-online/census-records/index-to-the-1841-census/index-to-the-1841-census/?searchterm=1841%20census`. The index contains only the name of the head of household and has a little more than 9,000 entries. For more information on locating census returns, see the Census in Australia page at `www.jaunay.com/auscensus.html`.

A transcription of the convicts on Australia's first three fleets and the Irish convicts that came to New South Wales from 1791 to 1834 is located at `http://members.pcug.org.au/~pdownes`.

The Heraldry and Genealogy Society of Canberra maintains a database of Australian memorials of Australians in the Boer War (1899–1902) at `www.hagsoc.org.au/sagraves/abwmdb/abwm-search.php`. The Metropolitan Cemeteries Board of Western Australia has a database of internments in five cemeteries at `www.mcb.wa.gov.au`.

The Donegal Relief Fund site (`http://freepages.genealogy.rootsweb.ancestry.com/~donegal/relief.htm`) includes a description of the background of the Relief Fund, passenger lists, and subscription lists for those who donated to the Fund. A searchable index of birth, marriage, and death records for New South Wales is available at `www.bdm.nsw.gov.au/familyHistory/searchHistoricalRecords.htm`.

Ancestry.com.au (`www.ancestry.com.au`) features more than 970 databases of use in Australian research. Several of these databases relate to England and Wales rather than Australia.

Hispanic (and Portuguese) Roots

A growing number of genealogists are researching their Hispanic and Portuguese roots. If you have these ancestors, you can use several types of records to pursue your genealogy, depending on when your ancestor immigrated.

If your ancestor immigrated in the 19th or 20th century, look for vital records, military records, photographs, passports, church records, passenger lists, naturalization papers, diaries, or other items that can give you an idea of the birthplace of your ancestor. For those ancestors who immigrated before the 19th century, you may want to consult Spanish or Portuguese Colonial records after you exhaust any local records in the region where your ancestor lived.

If you aren't sure where to begin your research, check out the messages that people post to the GEN-HISPANIC-L mailing list at `http://lists.roots web.ancestry.com/index/intl/ESP/?GEN-HISPANIC.html`.

For more information on researching Hispanic records, see the following:

✔ *The Source: A Guidebook of American Genealogy,* edited by Loretto Dennis Szucs and Sandra Hargreaves (Ancestry, Inc.). In particular, see Chapter 16, "Tracking Hispanic Family History," written by George Ryskamp. You can find this online at `www.ancestry.com/wiki/index.php?title=Overview_of_Hispanic_Research`.

✔ *Hispanic Family History Research in a L.D.S. Family History Center,* written by George R. Ryskamp (Hispanic Family History Research).

Within the United States

Individuals of Hispanic descent have been in present-day United States since St. Augustine was founded in 1565. Consult some of the following helpful resources when conducting research on your Spanish-speaking ancestors:

✔ **Hispanic Genealogy Center (`www.hispanicgenealogy.com`):** Maintained by the Hispanic Genealogical Society of New York, the site contains information on Society events and publications, including the newsletter *Nuestra Herencia* and the Workbook of Hispanic Genealogy.

✔ **Hispanic Genealogical Society (`www.hispanicgs.org`):** The Society maintains a list of online resources for Hispanic research and hosts the annual Texas State Hispanic Genealogical and Historical Conference.

✔ **Hispanic Genealogical Research Center of New Mexico (`www.hgrc-nm.org`):** The Center maintains the Great New Mexico Pedigree Database and publishes the journal *Herencia*.

✔ **Society of Hispanic Historical and Ancestral Research (`http://shhar.net`):** The Society is based in Orange County, California, and publishes the online newsletter *Somos Primos*.

✔ **Puerto Rican/Hispanic Genealogical Society (`www.rootsweb.ancestry.com/~prhgs`):** The site contains a transcription of the 1935 Census of Puerto Rico and a query page.

✔ **Colorado Society of Hispanic Genealogy (`www.hispanicgen.org`):** The Society hosts a surname list and information in its publication *Colorado Hispanic Genealogist*.

✔ **La Genealogia de Puerto Rico (`www.rootsweb.ancestry.com/~prwgw/index.html`):** The site contains a number of resources, including message boards, surname databases, links to personal pages, microfilm index, and a partial transcription of the 1910 census.

If you are going to Puerto Rico for research, you might consider visiting the Web sites of the Archivo General de Puerto Rico (www.icp.gobierno.pr/agp) and the Biblioteca Nacional (www.icp.gobierno.pr/bge) for information on their holdings.

Exploring south of the border: Mexican sources

To get your feet wet with resources from Mexico, take a look at the Mexico Research Outline at the FamilySearch site (www.familysearch.org/eng/Search/RG/frameset_rg.asp?Dest=G1&Aid=&Gid=&Lid=&Sid=&Did=&Juris1=&Event=&Year=&Gloss=&Sub=&Tab=&Entry=&Guide=Mexico.ASP). The outline covers archives and libraries, cemeteries, church records, emigration and immigration, gazetteers, land and property, military records, probate records, and societies. Another FamilySearch resource to try is the Mexico page on the Wiki at https://wiki.familysearch.org/en/Mexico. You can find a primer on tracing your ancestors on the Mexico Genealogy 101 page at the About.com genealogy site (http://genealogy.about.com/od/mexico/a/records.htm).

The MexicoGenWeb site (www.worldgenweb.org/~mexwgw) contains links to a few Mexican genealogical resources. Only a few of the state pages have been "adopted" by volunteers. These include

- ✔ **Baja California Norte:** www.californiagenealogy.org/labaja
- ✔ **Baja California Sur:** www.californiagenealogy.org/labaja
- ✔ **Chihuahua:** www.worldgenweb.org/~mexchh
- ✔ **Coahuila:** www.worldgenweb.org/~mexcoa
- ✔ **Durango:** www.rootsweb.ancestry.com/~mexdur/Durango.html
- ✔ **Morelos:** www.rootsweb.ancestry.com/~mexmorel/Morelos.html
- ✔ **San Luis Potosí:** www.rootsweb.ancestry.com/~mexsanlu
- ✔ **Sonora:** homepages.rootsweb.ancestry.com/~windmill/sonora
- ✔ **Tabasco:** www.rootsweb.ancestry.com/~mextab
- ✔ **Tamaulipas:** www.rootsweb.ancestry.com/~mextam

The Genealogy of Mexico site (http://garyfelix.tripod.com/index1.htm) features several sets of transcribed records, including lists of individuals who accompanied Cortez, early entrants into New Spain, surnames contained in literature on Mexico, and a DNA project.

An index to vital records from Mexico is available on the FamilySearch. org site (`www.familysearch.org/Eng/Search/frameset_search. asp?PAGE=vr/search_VR.asp&clear_form=true`). After entering the name that you are researching, make sure that you set the country to Mexico before executing the search. The search results contain information on the vital record, including the date of the event, individuals involved, age of the individual, the film or fiche number containing the record, and the collection housing the record. For example, Figure 7-5 shows an entry for a marriage between Jose Lopez and Adelaida Ortiz in 1876. Jose was 20 years old when the marriage took place in Mineral del Chico, Hidalgo, Mexico. The record is in the La Purisima Concepcion, Catolica collection and is located on LDS Film Number 638889.

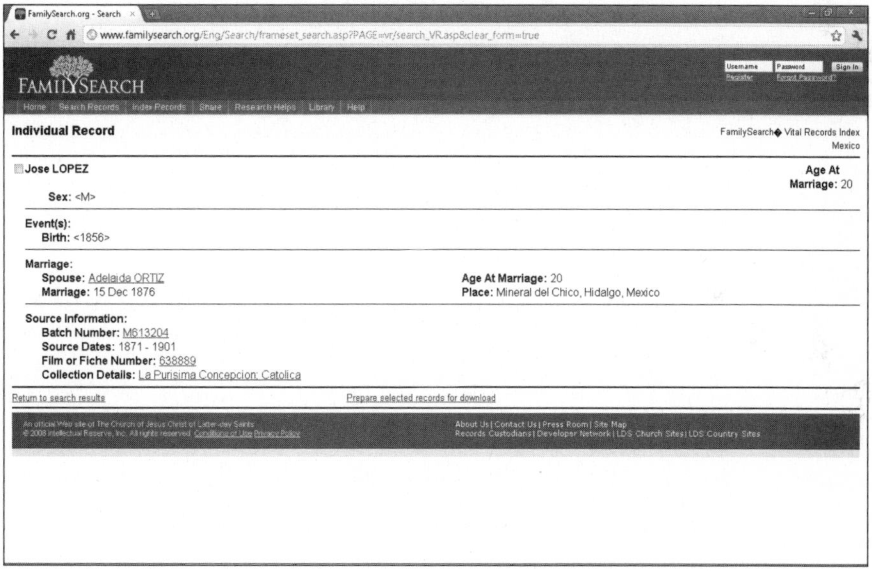

Figure 7-5: Entry from the Vital Records Index at Family-Search.

FamilySearch.org Record Search (`http://pilot.familysearch.org/ recordsearch/start.html#p=allCollections&r=0`) has also begun placing online records related to Mexico, including the following:

- ✔ Mexico Baptisms, 1560–1950
- ✔ Mexico Census, 1930
- ✔ Mexico Deaths, 1680–1940
- ✔ Mexico Marriages, 1570–1950
- ✔ Mexico Catholic Church Records
- ✔ Mexico Civil Registrations, 1860–1950
- ✔ Mexico Distrito Federal Catholic Church Records, 1886–1933

A mailing list is available for anyone with an interest in genealogy in Mexico. To subscribe to the mailing list, send a message to `mexico-l-request@rootsweb.com` with only the word *subscribe* in the body of the message.

Transcribed records are also available on sites that focus on Hispanic ancestors. For example, you can view transcribed records from the 1750 and 1753 Censuses of the village of Guerrero at `www.hispanicgs.com/census.html`.

If you are planning a research trip to Mexico, you may want to visit the Web site for the Achivo General de la Nación at `www.agn.gob.mx` or the Biblioteca Nacional de México at `http://biblional.bibliog.unam.mx/bibn`.

Continental resources

Eventually, your research may take you across the Atlantic, back to the Iberian Peninsula to Spain or Portugal. If you're researching Spain, stop by the Genealogía Española – España GenWeb site at `www.genealogia-es.com`. The site contains an introduction to research, links to surname databases, and links to provincial Web pages. The Asociación de Genealogía Hispana (`www.hispagen.es`) also maintains a Web site dedicated to helping those who are researching their Spanish roots.

For official records, point your Web browser to the Portal de Archivos Españoles site at `http://pares.mcu.es`. The Portal is designed to point to resources housed in many different national and local archives. A large project housed on the site is the Portal de Movimientos Migratorios Iberoamericanos (`http://pares.mcu.es/MovimientosMigratorios/staticContent.form?viewName=presentacion`). The goal of the project is to provide access to information on individuals who emigrated from Spain to Central America in modern times. The project is a partnership between the Archivo General de la Administración de España, Archivo General de la Nación de México, Archivo General de la Nación de la República Dominicana, and Archivo Nacional de la República de Cuba.

Portuguese official records are housed in a network of national and 16 regional archives coordinated by the Direcção Geral de Arquivos (`http://dgarq.gov.pt`). The organizations are cooperating in the construction of the Portal Português de Arquivos at `http://portal.arquivos.pt`. The Portal is designed to allow keyword searches of all the collections of the participating archives. Another resource to check out is the Biblioteca Nacional de Portugal (`www.bnportugal.pt`). For a more focused search on genealogy, you may want to search the catalogs on the Biblioteca Genealogica de Lisboa Web site, at `www.biblioteca-genealogica-lisboa.org`.

Those with Basque ancestors may find the resources at the Basque Genealogy home page (`http://home.earthlink.net/~fybarra/index.html`) useful. You find a list of surnames contained within the author's database and information on fee-based research services.

A few mailing lists apply to the Iberian Peninsula. These include the following:

- **Basque-L:** This list discusses Basque culture and periodically includes genealogical postings. To subscribe to the mailing list, type **SUBSCRIBE BASQUE-L** *your first name your last name* in the body of an e-mail message and send it to `listserv@cunyvm.cuny.edu`.

- **Portugal:** This list is devoted to anyone with a genealogical interest in Portugal. Send a message to `portugal-l-request@ rootsweb.com` with only the word *subscribe* in the body of the message to subscribe to the list.

- **Spain:** This list is devoted to people who have a genealogical interest in Spain. Send a message to `spain-l-request@ rootsweb.com` with only the word *subscribe* in the body of the message to subscribe to the list.

Central and South American research

Research in Central and South America has been a rapidly growing area recently. The following resources, broken down by country, should help you along your way:

- **Argentina:** Although the Argentina WorldGenWeb site has limited resources, you may want to visit the site at `www.worldgenweb.org/~argwgw`. A few links to provincial query pages are available. Another option is the Archivo General de la Nación (`www.mininterior.gov.ar/archivo/archivo.php?idName=arc&idNameSubMenu=&idNameSubMenuDer=`) or the Instituto de Estudios Genealógicos y Heráldicos de la Provincia de Buenos Aires (`www.genproba.com.ar`). You can also search information on deceased individuals who lived in Argentina in the International Genealogical Index at FamilySearch.org (`http://pilot.familysearch.org/recordsearch/start.html#p=allCollections&r=2`).

- **Brazil:** BrazilGenWeb (`www.rootsweb.ancestry.com/~brawgw`) has a how-to guide and links to individual Brazilian states. To see records available in Brazil, visit the Arquivo Nacional Web site (`www.arquivonacional.gov.br/cgi/cgilua.exe/sys/start.htm`). If you're looking for help with Brazilian research, try one of the mailing lists described at `www.rootsweb.ancestry.com/~jfuller/gen_mail_country-bra.html`. Entries for those who lived in Brazil can also be found in the International Genealogical Index at FamilySearch.org (`http://pilot.familysearch.org/recordsearch/start.html#p=allCollections&r=2`).

- **Belize:** The BelizeGenWeb page (`www.worldgenweb.org/index.php/north-america/belize`) has a few links to general resources. The Web site for the Belize Archives and Records Service, at `www.belizearchives.gov.bz`, contains some general information on accessing records. To subscribe to a mailing list, send a message to `belize-l-request@rootsweb.com` with only the word *subscribe* in the body of the message.

- **Chile:** A site with several compiled genealogies of Chilean families is the Genealogia de Chile site, at `http://genealog.cl`. See the Web page for the Archivo Nacional (`www.dibam.cl/archivo_nacional`) for Chilean records. To subscribe to a mailing list, send a message to `chile-l-request@rootsweb.com` with only the word *subscribe* in the body of the message. Chilean records are available also on FamilySearch. org at `http://pilot.familysearch.org/record search/start. html#p=allCollections&r=2`.

- **Columbia:** COLEXT is a general mailing list on Columbia. To subscribe to the mailing list, type **SUBSCRIBE COLEXT *your first name your last name*** in the body of an e-mail message and send it to `listserv@cuvmb. columbia.edu`. Columbian records are available on FamilySearch.org at `http://pilot.familysearch.org/record search/start. html#p=allCollections&r=2`.

- **Costa Rica:** A mailing list is available for those people who have a genealogical interest in Costa Rica. To subscribe to the mailing list, send a message to `costa-rica-l-request@rootsweb.com` with only the word *subscribe* in the body of the message. The GenWeb page for Costa Rica is located at `www.worldgenweb.org/index.php/north-america/costa-rica`, and the Web page for the Archivo Nacional de Costa Rica is at `www.archivonacional.go.cr`. Costa Rican records are available on FamilySearch.org at `http://pilot.familysearch. org/recordsearch/start.html#p=allCollections&r=2`.

- **Cuba:** You can find links to Cuban genealogical resources at the CubaGenWeb.org Web site (`www.cubagenweb.org`). This mailing list is devoted to people who have a genealogical interest in Cuba. To subscribe to the mailing list, send a message to `cuba-l-request@roots web.com` with only the word *subscribe* in the body of the message. To find records in Cuba, see the Web site for the Archivo Nacional de la República de Cuba (`www.arnac.cu`).

- **Dominican Republic:** República Dominicana en el proyecto CaribbeanGenWeb (`www.rootsweb.ancestry.com/~domwgw/ mhhbcgw.htm`) contains a few links to resources for the Dominican Republic. A mailing list is available for people with a genealogical interest in the Dominican Republic. To subscribe to the mailing list, send a message to `republica-dominicana-l-request@rootsweb.com` with only the word *subscribe* in the body of the message. Records for the country are held at the Archivo General de la Nación (`http://agn. gov.do`). Dominican Republic records are available on FamilySearch. org at `http://pilot.familysearch.org/recordsearch/start. html#p=allCollections&r=2`.

- **Ecuador:** A mailing list is devoted to people who have a genealogical interest in Ecuador. To subscribe to the mailing list, send a message to `ecuador-l-request@rootsweb.com` with only the word *subscribe* in the body of the message. Discover more about records in Ecuador at the Archivo Nacional del Ecuador site, at `www.ane.gov.ec`. Records from Ecuador are available on FamilySearch.org at `http://pilot.familysearch.org/recordsearch/start.html#p=allCollections&r=2`.

✔ **El Salvador:** A mailing list is devoted to people who have a genealogical interest in El Salvador. To subscribe to the mailing list, send a message to `elsalvador-l-request@rootsweb.com` with only the word *subscribe* in the body of the message. Information on records is found at the Archivo General de la Nación Web site (`www.agn.gob.sv`). El Salvadoran records are available on FamilySearch.org at `http://pilot.familysearch.org/recordsearch/start.html#p=allCollections&r=2`.

✔ **Guatemala:** A mailing list is devoted to people who have a genealogical interest in Guatemala. To subscribe to the mailing list, send a message to `guatemala-l-request@rootsweb.com` with only the word *subscribe* in the body of the message. See also the GuatemalaGenWeb page, at `www.worldgenweb.org/~gtmwgw/indexen.html`, and the Archivo General de Centro América page (`www.archivogeneraldecentroamerica.com`). Guatemalan records are available on FamilySearch.org at `http://pilot.familysearch.org/recordsearch/start.html#p=allCollections&r=2`.

✔ **Haiti:** The Genealogie d'Haiti et de Saint-Domingue, at `www.rootsweb.ancestry.com/~htiwgw`, contains information on the history and geography of the country. It also has links to other Haiti resources. For further information, see the Archives Nationales D'Haïti site, at `www.anhhaiti.org`, and L'Association de Généalogie d'Haïti (`www.agh.qc.ca`).

✔ **Honduras:** A mailing list is devoted to people who have a genealogical interest in Honduras. To subscribe to the mailing list, send a message to `honduras-l-request@rootsweb.com` with only the word *subscribe* in the body of the message. Some basic information is available on the Honduras WorldGenWeb project page at `www.worldgenweb.org/index.php/north-america/honduras`. You can find baptism and marriage records on the FamilySearch.org site at `http://pilot.familysearch.org/recordsearch/start.html#p=allCollections&r=2`.

✔ **Nicaragua:** A mailing list is devoted to people who have a genealogical interest in Nicaragua. To subscribe to the mailing list, send a message to `nicaragua-l-request@rootsweb.com` with only the word *subscribe* in the body of the message. The GenWeb page for Nicaragua is at `www.rootsweb.ancestry.com/~nicwgw`. A brief description of the Archivo General de la Nación can be found at `www.inc.gob.ni/index.php?option=com_content&task=view&id=14&Itemid=29`. Nicaraguan records are available on FamilySearch.org at `http://pilot.familysearch.org/recordsearch/start.html#p=allCollections&r=2`.

✔ **Panama:** A mailing list is devoted to people who lived in the Panama Canal Zone. To subscribe to the mailing list, send a message to `panama-canal-l-request@rootsweb.com` with only the word *subscribe* in the body of the message. Some brief information on the National Archives is available at the Archivo Nacional de Panamá site, at www.archivonacional.gob.pa. You can find records for baptisms, deaths, and marriages on FamilySearch.org at `http://pilot.familysearch.org/record search/start.html#p=allCollections&r=2`.

✔ **Paraguay:** A mailing list is available for anyone with an interest in genealogy in Paraguay. To subscribe to the mailing list, send a message to paraguay-l-request@rootsweb.com with only the word *subscribe* in the body of the message. Information on the holdings of the Archivo Nacional de Asunción is available at http://archivonacionaldeasuncion.org/Bienvenida.html. Records for baptisms and marriages are available on FamilySearch.org at `http://pilot.familysearch.org/record search/start.html#p=allCollections&r=2`.

✔ **Peru:** Peru — The WorldGenWeb Project, at `www.worldgenweb.org/~perwgw`, contains a few links to genealogy sites involving individuals from Peru. A mailing list is devoted to people who are interested in genealogy in Peru. To subscribe to the mailing list, send a message to `peru-l-request@rootsweb.com` with only the word *subscribe* in the body of the message. For records regarding Peru, see the Archivo General de la Nación site, at `www.archivogeneral.gob.pe`. Peruvian records are available on FamilySearch.org at `http://pilot.familysearch.org/recordsearch/start.html#p=allCollections&r=2`.

✔ **Uruguay:** A mailing list is devoted to people who have a genealogical interest in Uruguay. To subscribe to the mailing list, send a message to `uruguay-l-request@rootsweb.com` with only the word *subscribe* in the body of the message. Records for Uruguay can be found at the Archivo General de la Nación page (`www.agn.gub.uy`). Baptism and marriage records are available on FamilySearch.org at `http://pilot.familysearch.org/recordsearch/start.html#p=allCollections&r=2`.

✔ **Venezuela:** A mailing list is available for anyone with an interest in genealogy in Venezuela. Send a message to `venezuela-l-request@rootsweb.com` with only the word *subscribe* in the body of the message to subscribe to the mailing list. Information on the Archivo General de la Nación can be found at `http://agn.gob.ve`.

You can see a list of archives and libraries in Central American and Caribbean countries at the Repositories of Primary Sources page (`www.uidaho.edu/special-collections/latam.html`).

Swimming through Caribbean genealogy

To be successful in researching Caribbean genealogy, you have to be aware of the history of the particular island that you're researching. Some islands have a variety of record sets that may differ significantly depending on what country was in control of the island.

A place to start your research is the CaribbeanGenWeb Project page, at www. rootsweb.ancestry.com/~caribgw. The project is an umbrella site for each of the individual islands that have their own project pages. The site contains a list of the transcribed data sets held within the CaribbeanGenWeb Archives portion of the project, along with a global search engine for searching those data sets; descriptions of the mailing lists available for each island; links to surname resources; and some research tips. The individual island pages include

- ✔ **Anguilla:** www.britishislesgenweb.org/~anguilla
- ✔ **Antigua and Barbuda:** www.rootsweb.ancestry.com/~atgwgw
- ✔ **Bahamas:** www.rootsweb.ancestry.com/~bhswgw
- ✔ **Bermuda:** www.rootsweb.ancestry.com/~bmuwgw/bermuda.htm
- ✔ **Cuba:** www.cubagenweb.org
- ✔ **Dominica:** www.britishislesgenweb.org/~dominica
- ✔ **Grenada:** www.britishislesgenweb.org/grenada
- ✔ **Haiti:** www.rootsweb.ancestry.com/~htiwgw
- ✔ **Jamaica:** www.rootsweb.ancestry.com/~jamwgw/index.htm
- ✔ **St. Kitts and Nevis:** www.tc.umn.edu/~terre011/genhome.html
- ✔ **St. Vincent & the Grenadines:** www.rootsweb.ancestry.com/~vctwgw
- ✔ **Trinidad and Tobago:** www.rootsweb.ancestry.com/~ttowgw
- ✔ **U.S. Virgin Islands:** www.rootsweb.ancestry.com/~usvi

You can also find information on some islands on the GenWeb Project page of the mother country. For example, Guadeloupe and Martinique genealogical data can be found on the FranceGenWeb Project page, at www.francegen web.org/~sitesdgw/outremer. Another resource for the French islands is the Généalogie et Histoire de la Caraïbe (www.ghcaraibe.org). The site contains some transcribed records and articles on the history of the area.

If you have a question about a specific individual, you can post a query on the Caribbean Surname Index (CARSURDEX), at www.candoo.com/surnames/index.php. The site has message boards based on the first letter of the surname and has research specialty boards for the French West Indies, Dutch West Indies, and Spanish West Indies.

Auchtung! Using Sites for the German-Speaking World

As German-speaking peoples have migrated to several places in Europe, as well as to the United States, you could very well encounter an ancestor of German descent. GermanRoots (www.germanroots.com) contains a variety of information to help you get started in researching your German roots. It contains a directory of Web sites, a basic research guide, and links to articles on record sets that are useful in completing your research.

To get a bird's-eye view of available German genealogical sites, a good place to start is Genealogy.net (www.genealogy.net/genealogy.html). The site includes home pages for German genealogical societies, general information on research, a gazetteer, a ships database, a passenger database, and a list of links to Web sites. Ahnenforschung.net (http://ahnenforschung.net) is a German-language, genealogically focused search engine and index to genealogy Web sites.

Along the beautiful Danube: Austrian roots

A place to begin your Austrian journey is the AustriaGenWeb site (www.roots web.ancestry.com/~autwgw). The site contains some general information on Austria as well as links to Austrian resources. From the home page of this site, you can access links to the provinces of Austria. These links are divided into two types — provinces of modern Austria (since 1918) and areas of the Austrian Empire and Austro-Hungarian Empire (until 1918). Areas listed under the second group are covered in other GenWeb projects, such as KüstenlandGenWeb, CzechGenWeb, RomanianGenWeb, UkraineGenWeb, SloveniaGenWeb, CroatiaGenWeb, PolishGenWeb, ItalianGenWeb, and FranceGenWeb.

Austrian censuses were taken in the years 1857, 1869, 1880, 1890, 1900, and 1910. The first census that listed individuals by name was the 1869 census. These returns include surname, sex, year of birth, place of birth, district, religion, marital status, language, occupation, literacy, mental and physical defects, residence, and whether the household had farm animals. Some general information is available on the content of the Galicia censuses and is contained in two articles on the Federation of East European Family History Societies site — Austrian Census Returns 1869–1890 (www.feefhs.org/links/galicia/shea.html) and Austrian Census for Galicia (www.feefhs.org/links/galicia/1880-gal.html).

If you're looking for help with your Austrian research, check out the Familia Austria Web site (www.familia-austria.at) maintained by the Österreichische Gesellschaft für Genealogie und Geschichte. The site contains links to a variety of Austrian resources, including maps, cemetery databases, and a Wiki covering many topics related to individual provinces. It also has databases developed by the Association, including a family name finder; a birth, marriage, and death index for Wiener Zeitung; a marriage index before 1784; and directories of individuals holding particular occupations.

To get information on records available in the national archives, see the Austrian State Archives page, at `www.oesta.gv.at/DesktopDefault. aspx?alias=oestaen&init`. Another site to visit is the Österreichische Nationalbibliothek (National Library), at `www.onb.ac.at/ev/index.php`. If you need professional help, you might look at the Historiker Kanzlei research firm (`www.historiker.at`), which specializes in Austrian research. You can also get help from other researchers through mailing lists. The Austria page at Genealogy Resources on the Internet (`www.rootsweb.ancestry. com/~jfuller/gen_mail_country-aut.html`) lists those that are pertinent to your research.

Consulting German resources

A place to start finding out about the research process for German records is the Genealogical Handbook of German Research, available on the FamilySearch site (`www.familysearch.org/Eng/Search/RG/frame set_rg.asp?Dest=G1&Aid=&Gid=&Lid=&Sid=&Did=&Juris1=&Eve nt=&Year=&Gloss=&Sub=&Tab=&Entry=&Guide=Ger_BMD_RefDoc_ HandbookGermanResearch.ASP`). The German GenWeb project site (`www. rootsweb.ancestry.com/~wggerman`) has a few resources such as maps and links to other sites. The German Genealogy Group (`www.german genealogygroup.com`) was formed to help individuals research their German roots. The Web site contains descriptions on the various databases that the Group maintains and some presentations on research in Germany.

The German central government held censuses in 1871, 1880, 1885, 1890, 1895, 1900, 1905, 1910, 1919, 1925, 1933, and 1939. Unfortunately, these census returns do not have much genealogical value because they were statistical in nature. Some local censuses are available. The collection at Ancestry.de (`www.ancestry.de`) contains the Mecklenburg-Schwerin censuses of 1819, 1867, 1890, and 1900.

The German Emigrants Database (`www.dad-recherche.de/hmb/ index.html`), maintained by the Historisches Museum Bremerhaven, contains information on emigrants who left Europe for the United States from German ports between 1820 and 1939. At the time this book was written, the database contained more than 4.4 million emigrants. The site allows users to search an index of individuals and order records for a fee based on the results. For more information on emigrants from the port of Hamburg, see Ballinstadt Hamburg (`www.ballinstadt.net/`

BallinStadt_emigration_museum_Hamburg/english_BallinStadt_
das_Auswanderermuseum_Hamburg_besonderes_Ausflugsziel_
Ausflugsort_Erlebnisort_Freizeit_leisureworkgroup_
Geschaeftsfuehrer_Jens_Nitschke_Berater_Museen_Fachmann_
Entwicklung_Konzeption_Design_Erlebniswelt_Erlebnismuseum.
html), a site that describes the emigrant experience at the Hamburg port.

An important group of records in German research are church records. The Association of Church Archives created the Kirchenbuchportal site (www.kirchenbuchportal.de) to post detailed inventories of parish registers in their collections. A collection of Lutheran church registers is available at Matricula (http://matricula-online.eu/pages/en/home.php?lang=EN).

Ancestry.com has a subscription site for German genealogy at www.ancestry.de. Ancestry.de provides access to more than 1,800 databases, including census records; birth, marriage, and death records; military records; immigration and emigration records; and local and family histories. Examples of databases are the Hamburg Passenger lists (1850–1934), Bremen sailor registers (1837–1873), and Bremen ship lists (1821–1873).

For descriptions of records held in archives, see the Bundesarchiv site at www.bundesarchiv.de/index.html.en. If you need research help, see the Germany/Prussia page at the Genealogy Resources on the Internet site at www.rootsweb.ancestry.com/~jfuller/gen_mail_country-ger.html.

You can find resources for other Germanic areas on the Federation of East European Family History Societies site at http://feefhs.org and on the following sites:

- ✔ **Liechtenstein:** LiechGen (www.rootsweb.ancestry.com/~liewgw)
- ✔ **Luxembourg:** Luxembourg home page (www.rootsweb.ancestry.com/~luxwgw)
- ✔ **Swiss:** Swiss Genealogy on the Internet (www.eye.ch/swissgen/gener-e.htm)

Focusing on French Resources

For an overview of genealogy in French-speaking regions, drop by the FrancoGene site, at www.francogene.com/genealogy. The site features resources for Quebec, Acadia, the United States, France, Belgium, Switzerland, and Italy. If you're not familiar with French surnames, you might want to see how common a surname is in France. At Geopatronyme.com (www.geopatronyme.com), you can view the surname distribution of more than 1.3 million names.

GeneaBank (www.geneabank.org) contains transcribed records created by French genealogical societies. To access the information in the site's databases, you must be a member of a society participating in the project. GeneaNet (www.geneanet.org) is a fee-based site that has transcriptions of some civil registers. The Lecture et Informatisation des Sources Archivistiques site (www.lisa90.org) contains a database with more than 360,000 transcribed parish records covering the 18th and 19th centuries, and Migranet (www.francegenweb.org/~migranet/accueil.php) houses a database of more than 45,000 French marriages where one of the participants was listed as a migrant.

Ancestry.fr (www.ancestry.fr) has a collection of more than 600 subscription databases. This collection includes birth, marriage, death, military, and immigration and emigration records as well as maps.

Scanning Scandinavian Countries

For a general overview of Scandinavian research, see the Scandinavia portal at the FamilySearch Wiki (https://wiki.familysearch.org/en/Portal:Scandinavia). A key database to consult when beginning your research is the Vital Records Index at FamilySearch.org (www.family search.org/Eng/Search/frameset_search.asp? PAGE=vr/search_VR.asp). The Index includes records for Denmark, Norway, Sweden, and Finland.

Denmark

An article to launch your Danish research is Genealogy Research in Denmark (www.progenealogists.com/denmark), found on the ProGenealogists Web site. It offers a brief introduction to every major record type that you might use during your research. MyDanishRoots.com (http://mydanish roots.com) contains articles on vital records, census lists, place names, emigration, and Danish history.

The Danish Archives has census returns for the years 1787, 1801, 1834, 1840, 1845, 1850, 1855, 1860, 1870, 1880, 1890, 1901, 1906, 1911, 1916, 1921, and 1925. You can find information from these censuses at the Statens Arkiver site (www.sa.dk/ao/) and the Dansk Demografisk Database (http://ddd.dda.dk/kiplink_en.htm). The returns contain name, age, occupation, and relationship for each individual in the household. After 1845, census returns include information on the individual's place of birth. Census returns for Denmark are available after 80 years. The Dansk Demografisk Database also includes censuses and lists of emigrants and immigrants for Denmark.

DIS-Danmark (www.dis-danmark.dk/dis-english.asp) is a group of genealogists using computing in their research. The Web site includes information on the districts and parishes of Denmark, data on indexed church books, and a database of Danish online records. The Statens Arkiver is also digitizing church books and placing them online at www.sa.dk/ao.

Finding another researcher who is researching the same family as you can make your research life a lot easier. Sending a GEDCOM file to the GEDCOMP site, at www.lklundin.dk/gedcomp/english.php, allows it to be compared with other researchers' files to see where overlaps exist. Other members of GEDCOMP can then contact you for further research.

If you're planning a research trip to Denmark, you may want to visit the collection at the Statens Arkiver (State Archives). You can find a list of resources available, as well as descriptions of records that are critical to Danish research, at www.sa.dk/content/us.

Finland

The Finland Genealogy Web site has a small number of biographies, some transcribed United States census records of individuals of Finnish descent, a few obituaries of people who were born in Finland and died in the United States, and links to Web pages of those interested in Finnish research.

The Genealogical Society of Finland site (www.genealogia.fi) contains some advice on getting started in your research, membership information, blogs, and links to member pages.

You can find transcriptions of passport lists for the Åland Islands in Finland at the Transcription of the Borough Administrator's Passport List 1882–1903 (www.genealogia.fi/emi/magistrat/indexe.htm) and Sheriff's Passport List 1863–1916 (www.genealogia.fi/emi/krono/indexe.htm) sites. The database at DISBYT Finland (www.dis.se/search_fi_index_e.htm) contains more than 160,000 individuals who lived in Finland prior to 1913. The Genealogy Society of Finland maintains a list of christenings, marriages, burials, and moves as part of its HisKi Project at http://hiski.genealogia.fi/historia/indexe.htm.

The Institute of Migration/Siirtolaisuusinstituutti (www.migration institute.fi/index_e.php) maintains a database of more than 550,000 emigrants from Finland.

Keep in mind that up to 1809, Finland was a part of Sweden. So, you may need to consult Swedish records to get a complete picture of your ancestors.

Norway

For help with your Norwegian ancestors, see the article "Basics of Norwegian Research," at www.rootsweb.ancestry.com/~wgnorway/list-basics.htm. Also, a useful guide entitled "How to Trace Your Ancestors in Norway" (http://digitalarkivet.uib.no/sab/howto.html) is housed on the site for the National Archives of Norway. The Velkommen to Norway Genealogy site (www.roots web.ancestry.com/~wgnorway), part of the WorldGenWeb project, contains a Getting Started article and links to several Norwegian online resources.

The first census in Norway was conducted in 1769, and statistical censuses were also conducted in 1815, 1835, 1845, and 1855. Censuses by name were conducted in 1801, 1865, 1870, 1875, 1885, 1891, and 1900. Censuses by name were also taken in 1910, 1920, 1930, 1946, and 1950 — but research on these can be performed only for statistical purposes, due to privacy restrictions. Each census after 1865 contained information such as name, sex, age, relationship to head of household, civil status, occupation, religion, and place of birth. For more details on the censuses, see "Documenting the Norwegian Censuses," at www.rhd.uit.no/nhdc/census.html. An online searchable index of the 1801, 1865, 1875, and 1900 censuses of Norway is available at http://digitalarkivet.uib.no/cgi-win/WebFront.exe?slag=vis &tekst=meldingar&spraak=e.

The 1865, 1875, and 1900 censuses of Norway are also available from the Norwegian Historical Data Centre. Some parish registers are also available on the site (www.rhd.uit.no/indexeng.html).

The National Archives of Norway hosts a digital archive at http://digital arkivet.uib.no/cgi-win/WebFront.exe?slag=vis&tekst=meldin gar&spraak=e. The site includes digitized parish registers, real estate registers, and probate records, It also has a tutorial on Gothic handwriting, a photo album of farms, and information on the Archive's holdings.

If you're looking for research help, the DIS-Norge site (www.disnorge.no/cms/en/eng/english-pages) has a message board to answer questions, a Nordic dictionary to help with common terms, and a database containing genealogists who are working in a specific geographic area.

Sweden

The Federation of Swedish Genealogical Societies/Sveriges Släktforskarförbund hosts the site Finding Your Swedish Roots (www.genealogi.se/roots) that includes helpful articles on church, legal, and tax records; information on the collection in the Swedish Archives; and a brief history of Sweden.

The Swedish DISBYT database (www.dis.se) contains 22.2 million Swedes who lived before 1910. Genline.com (www.genline.com), now part of Ancestry.com, has more than 18 million scanned Swedish church records from 1860. Ancestry.se (www.ancestry.se) is a subscription site that contains emigration lists from 1783 to 1751, passenger and immigration lists from the 1500s to 1900s, and some local histories and published genealogies.

Censuses have been taken in Sweden since 1749. A database of the 1890 Census for the counties of Norrbotten, Västerbotten, Västernorrland, Jämtland, and Värmland is available online at www.foark.umu.se/census/about.htm. The subscription portion of the Svensk Arkivinformation site (www.svar.ra.se), hosted by the Riksarkivet, holds the full censuses from 1880 to 1900 and partial censuses for 1860 and 1910. Other subscription databases on the Svensk Arkivinformation site include births, convicts, deaths, inventories, marriages, seamen's records, and a village and farm database. The site also contains scanned images of church and tax records. The Sweden Genealogy (www.rootsweb.ancestry.com/~wgsweden) contains queries, a list of surnames, and links to other Swedish resources.

Iceland

A few resources are available for Icelandic research. The IcelandGenWeb site (www.rootsweb.ancestry.com/~islwgw) contains a few links to resources for your research. The Íslenski Ættfræðivefurinn site (www.halfdan.is/aett) contains links to personal Web pages of people interested in Icelandic genealogy.

A transcription of the 1816 Icelandic Census is available at www.halfdan.is/vestur/census.htm, The Þjóðskjalasafn Íslands site (www.archives.is/index.php?node=english) contains information about the holdings of the National Archives. You can search the indexes of the 1703, 1835, 1840, 1845, 1850, 1855, 1860, 1870, and 1890 censuses at the National Archives Census Database page, at www.manntal.is.

Italian Cooking

A place to begin your Italian research is the Italian Genealogy home page, at www.daddezio.com. The site contains useful articles on family history research as well as links to other Italian genealogical resources. The Italian Genealogy home page (www.italgen.com) features message boards that cover topics such as genealogy, immigration, geography, and the Italian language.

The Italian Genealogical Group (www.italiangen.org) is based in New York City. Resources on its Web site include naturalization and vital records databases. Ancestry.it (www.ancestry.it) contains 95 databases related to Italian genealogy. The bulk of these databases contain birth, marriage, and death records — although some maps and newspapers are available.

The Italian State Archives contains national censuses for the years 1861, 1871, 1881, 1891, and 1901. Its Web site is `www.archivi.beniculturali.it`.

Other European Sites

Several other sites cover European countries and ethnic groups. These include the following:

- **Belarusian:** Belarusian Genealogy (`www.belarusguide.com/genealogy1/index.html`).

- **Bosnia-Herzegovina:** Bosnia-Herzegovina Web Genealogy Project (`www.rootsweb.ancestry.com/~bihwgw`).

- **Bulgarian:** Bulgarian GenWeb (`www.rootsweb.ancestry.com/~bgrwgw`).

- **Croatian:** CroatiaGenWeb (`www.rootsweb.ancestry.com/~hrvwgw`).

- **Czech:** Czech Republic Genealogy (`www.rootsweb.ancestry.com/~czewgw`).

- **Estonian:** Estonian GenWeb (`www.fortunecity.com/meltingpot/estonia/200/genweb.html`).

- **Federation of East European Family History Societies (FEEFHS):** If you're looking for research guides for Eastern Europe, start here. The federation's pages (`http://feefhs.org`) have information on the Albanian, Armenian, Austrian, Belarusian, Bohemian, Bulgarian, Carpatho-Rusyn, Croatian, Czech, Danish, Finnish, Galician, German, Hutterite, Hungarian, Latvian, Lithuanian, Polish, Moravian, Pomeranian, Romanian, Russian, Silesian, Slavic, Slavonian, Slovak, Slovenian, Transylvanian, Ukrainian, and Volhynian ethnic groups.

- **Greek:** GreeceGenWeb (`www.rootsweb.ancestry.com/~grcwgw`).

- **Hungarian:** HungaryGenWeb (`www.rootsweb.ancestry.com/~wghungar`).

- **Latvian:** LatvianGenWeb (`www.rootsweb.ancestry.com/~lvawgw`).

- **Maltese:** MaltaGenWeb (`www.rootsweb.ancestry.com/~mltwgw`).

- **Moldava:** MoldavaGenWeb (`www.rootsweb.ancestry.com/~mdawgw`).

- **Polish:** PolandGenWeb (`www.rootsweb.ancestry.com/~polwgw`).

- **Romanian:** Romania World GenWeb (`www.rootsweb.ancestry.com/~romwgw`).

- **Russian:** RussiaGenWeb (`www.rootsweb.ancestry.com/~ruswgw`).

- **Serbian:** SerbiaGenWeb (`www.rootsweb.ancestry.com/~serwgw`).

- **Slovak:** Slovak Republic Genealogy (`www.rootsweb.ancestry.com/~svkwgw`).

- **Slovenia:** Genealogy and Heraldry in Slovenia (`www.rootsweb.ancestry.com/~svnwgw`).

- **Ukrainian:** Ukraine WorldGenWeb (`www.rootsweb.ancestry.com/~ukrwgw`).

Asian Resources

If your ancestors came from Asia or the Pacific Rim, your success at finding records greatly depends on the history of the ancestor's ethnic group and its record-keeping procedures. Currently, you don't find much online genealogical information that pertains to these areas and peoples. Here's a sampling of Asian and Pacific Rim resources:

- **Bangladesh:** Bangladesh Genealogy (`www.rootsweb.ancestry.com/~bgdwgw`)

- **Bhutan:** Bhutan Genealogy (`www.rootsweb.ancestry.com/~btnwgw`)

- **China:** ChinaGenWeb (`www.rootsweb.ancestry.com/~chnwgw`)

- **Japan:** Japan GenWeb (`www.rootsweb.ancestry.com/~jpnwgw`)

- **Lebanon:** Lebanon GenWeb (`www.rootsweb.ancestry.com/~lbnwgw`)

- **Melanesia:** MelanesiaGenWeb (`www.rootsweb.ancestry.com/~melwgw`)

- **Polynesia:** PolynesiaGenWeb (`www.rootsweb.ancestry.com/~pyfwgw`)

- **Saudi Arabia:** Saudi Arabia GenWeb (`www.angelfire.com/tn/BattlePride/Saudi.html`)

- **South Korea:** South Korea GenWeb (`www.rootsweb.ancestry.com/~korwgw-s`)

- **Syria:** Syria GenWeb (`www.rootsweb.ancestry.com/~syrwgw`)

- **Sri Lanka:** Sri Lanka GenWeb (`www.rootsweb.ancestry.com/~lkawgw`)

- **Taiwan:** TaiwanGenWeb (`www.rootsweb.ancestry.com/~twnwgw`)

- **Tibet:** TibetGenWeb (`www.rootsweb.ancestry.com/~tibetwgw`)

✔ **Turkey:** Turkish Genealogy (`www.rootsweb.ancestry.com/~turwgw`)

✔ **Vietnam:** Vietnamese Genealogy (`www.rootsweb.ancestry.com/~vnmwgw`)

✔ **Various:** Genealogical Gleanings (genealogies of the rulers of India, Burma, Cambodia, Thailand, Fiji, Tonga, Hawaii, and Malaysia; `www.uq.net.au/~zzhsoszy/index.html`)

Ancestry.com recently launched a new Web site dedicated to Chinese genealogy — Jiapu.com (`www.jiapu.com/index_new2`). The site allows users to create their own family tree online and see the origins of their surname.

Researching African Ancestry

It's a common misconception that tracing African ancestry is impossible. In the past decade or so, much has been done to dispel that perception. If your ancestors lived in the United States, you can use many of the same research techniques and records (census schedules, vital records, and other primary resources) that genealogists of other ethnic groups consult, back to 1870. Prior to 1870, your research resources become more limited, depending on whether your ancestor was a freedman or a slave. To make that determination, you may want to interview some of your relatives. They often possess oral traditions that can point you in the right direction.

If your ancestor was a slave, try consulting the slave owners' probate records (which you can usually find in local courthouses), deed books (slave transactions were often recorded in deed books — which you can also find in local courthouses), tax records, plantation records, Freedman's Bureau records, and runaway-slave records. These types of records can be helpful because they identify persons by name.

Although your first inclination may be to turn to a slave schedule in the U.S. Census (slave schedules show the owner's name and the age, sex, and color of slaves), such schedules are not as useful as other sources in your research because the *enumerators* who collected the census information didn't record the names of slaves, nor did the government require them to do so. This fact doesn't mean that looking at slave schedules is a total waste of time; the schedules simply don't identify your ancestor by name. You need to find other resources that name your ancestor specifically.

If your ancestors served in the American Civil War, they may have service and pension records. You can begin a search for service records in an index to Civil War records of the United States Colored Troops or, if your ancestor joined a state regiment, in an Adjutant General's report. (An *Adjutant General's report* is a published account of the actions of military units from a particular state during a war; these reports are usually available at libraries or archives.) A good place to begin your search for Civil War records is the Civil War Soldiers and Sailors System at www.itd.nps.gov/cwss.

Two other sources of records to keep in mind are the Freedmen's Bureau and the Freedmen's Savings and Trust. Following are a few sites that contain information from these two organizations.

- ✔ **The Freedmen's Bureau** (its full name was the Bureau of Refugees, Freedmen and Abandoned Lands) was established in 1865 to assist ex-slaves after the American Civil War. For more on the Bureau, see the article by Elaine Everly at www.archives.gov/publications/prologue/1997/summer/freedmens-bureau-records.html.

- ✔ **The Freedmen's Bureau Online** offers examples of Freedmen's Bureau records at www.freedmensbureau.com.

- ✔ **The Freedman's Savings and Trust Company** was also established in 1865 as a bank for ex-slaves. For more information, see the article by Reginald Washington at www.archives.gov/publications/prologue/1997/summer/freedmans-savings-and-trust.html. Several of the bank's contributors were members of the United States Colored Troops during the American Civil War. The company failed in 1874; its records are now kept at the National Archives and Records Administration, along with the records for the Freedmen's Bureau. You can also find information on the Freedman's Bank Records CD-ROM available from the FamilySearch.org store (www.ldscatalog.com/webapp/wcs/stores/servlet/CategoryDisplay?catalogId=10151&storeId=10151&categoryId=13706&langId=-1&cg1=13701&cg2=&cg3=&cg4=&cg5=).

- ✔ **The National Archives and Records Administration** provides information about Freedman's Savings records (and their availability on microfilm) at www.archives.gov/research/guide-fed-records/groups/105.html.

For more information on using records to research your African ancestry, try the resources that follow.

- ✔ *The Source: A Guidebook of American Genealogy,* edited by Loretto Dennis Szucs and Sandra Hargreaves Luebking (Ancestry, Inc.). In particular, see Chapter 15, "African American Research," written by Tony Burroughs. This is available online at www.ancestry.com/wiki/index.php?title=Overview_of_African_American_Research.

- ✔ *Black Roots: A Beginner's Guide to Tracing the African American Family Tree*, written by Tony Burroughs (Fireside).

- ✔ *Black Family Research: Records of Post-Civil War Federal Agencies at the National Archives,* available online at www.archives.gov/publications/ref-info-papers/108.

✔ *Slave Genealogy: A Research Guide with Case Studies,* written by David H. Streets (Heritage Books).

Mailing lists focusing on African research

When you look for key records specific to African ancestral research, it's a good idea to interact with other researchers who may already be knowledgeable about such resources. One place to start is the AfriGeneas mailing list. This mailing list focuses primarily on African genealogical research methods (see Figure 7-6). On the Web page for the mailing list (`www.afrigeneas.com`), you find the following resources:

✔ A beginner's guide to researching genealogy

✔ Links to census schedules and slave data on the Internet

✔ A digital library of transcribed resources

✔ A link to a database of African-American surnames and their corresponding researchers

Figure 7-6: The AfriGeneas site aids in finding your African ancestors.

Here's how to subscribe to the AfriGeneas mailing list:

1. **Start your favorite e-mail program.**

2. **Create a new e-mail message.**

3. **Type** majordomo@lists.msstate.edu **in the To line.**

   Make sure that you type *only* **majordomo@lists.msstate.edu** in the To line. You subscribe to AfriGeneas at this listserv e-mail account. If you type anything more, your e-mail message won't be delivered and your attempt to subscribe fails.

4. **Make sure that your e-mail address is in the From line.**

   Most e-mail programs automatically fill in your e-mail address in the From line. In that case, just make sure that it's correct. Otherwise, type the e-mail address where you want to receive postings to the AfriGeneas mailing list.

5. **In the body of the message, type** subscribe afrigeneas **or** subscribe afrigeneas-digest. **You can leave the subject line blank.**

   Use **subscribe afrigeneas-digest** if you want to receive fewer e-mail messages a day from the list. In the digest form, the listserver compiles all the messages that people post throughout the day into one e-mail. For example, if April subscribes to the mailing list in its regular format, where each posting arrives separately, she'd type **subscribe afrigeneas** in the body of her message. Again, don't type anything more than this line in the message body or you confuse the automatic program that adds you to the mailing list — and it rejects your attempt to subscribe.

6. **Send the e-mail message.**

Another resource is the Ethnic-African Mailing Lists page, at `http://lists.rootsweb.ancestry.com/index/other/Ethnic-African`. This page identifies more than 80 mailing lists of interest to those conducting African research. For mailing lists with a little broader focus, see the list at Genealogy Resources on the Internet, at `www.rootsweb.ancestry.com/~jfuller/gen_mail_african.html`.

Genealogical resource pages on the Web

In addition to the AfriGeneas Web site, a number of online resources are available to assist you in finding your African ancestry.

You can find a high-level overview of the subject at African American Lives (`www.pbs.org/wnet/aalives`). The site is the companion to the PBS show that originally aired in early 2006 (see Figure 7-7). Items on the site include

- ✔ Profiles of individuals featured on the show
- ✔ Tips on how to effectively use documentation in researching African ancestral roots
- ✔ A brief primer on DNA testing
- ✔ An introduction to some of the issues and pitfalls surrounding research
- ✔ A list of stories from other researchers

Figure 7-7:
African
American
Lives Web
site.

For a brief list of resources that you can use, see the University of Pennsylvania African Studies Center bibliography page, at `www.africa.upenn.edu/Bibliography/menu_Biblio.html`.

Other sites with helpful content include

- Sankofa's Slave Genealogy Wiki (`www.sankofagen.com`)
- Slave Archival Collection Database (`http://rootsweb.ancestry.com/~ilissdsa/text_files/database_intro2.htm`)

Transcribed records pertaining to ancestors with African roots

Many genealogists recognize the benefits of making transcribed and digitized records available for other researchers. More and more of these Web sites are popping up every day. A few Web sites have transcribed records that are unique to the study of African ancestry online. Some examples are

- **Cemetery records:** For a transcribed list of cemeteries, see African American Cemeteries Online at `http://africanamericancemeteries.com`.
- **Freedman's Bureau records:** You can find transcribed Freedman's Bureau records at the Freedman's Bureau Online at `www.freedmensbureau.com/index.html`.

- **Manumission papers:** For examples of manumission papers (documents that reflect that a slave was granted freedom), see the Bourbon County Deeds of Manumission Abstracts site at `www.rootsweb.ancestry.com/~kyafamer/Bourbon/manumissions.htm`.

- **Registers:** At the Valley of the Shadow site, you can view transcribed Registers of Free Blacks in Augusta County, Virginia at `http://valley.lib.virginia.edu/VoS/govdoc/free.html`.

- **Slave schedules:** You can find transcriptions of slave schedules (lists of slave owners and the number of slaves owned by them) at the African American Census Schedules Online site at `www.afrigeneas.com/aacensus`. Although some of these schedules don't identify ancestors by name, they're useful if you know the name of the slave owner.

- **Wills and probate records:** Slaves were often mentioned in the disposition of wills. A list of slaves mentioned in probate records of Noxubee County, Mississippi, can be found at `http://earphoto.tripod.com/SlaveNames.html`.

The preceding sites are a few examples of transcribed records that you can find on the Internet. To see whether online records exist that pertain specifically to your research, visit a comprehensive genealogical site and look under the appropriate category.

Special ethnic pages about African ancestry

Many Web sites include information on a particular subset of individuals of African ancestry. Here are some you may want to visit.

- The African-Native Genealogy home page provides details on the Estelusti, a tribe of Black Indians in Oklahoma (`www.african-nativeamerican.com`).

- You can find information on French Creoles on the French Creoles Free People of Color Web site (`www.frenchcreoles.com/CreoleCulture/freepeopleofcolor/freepeopleofcolor.htm`).

Original records

You can find digitized original records online at some subscription sites. For example, Ancestry.com (`www.ancestry.com`) has images of the 1850 and 1860 Slave Schedules. This collection includes both the images and an index of names. Footnote (`www.footnote.com`) has the federal and Supreme Court case files for the case involving the seizure of the Amistad, a ship carrying slaves seized by the U.S. Navy in 1839 (see Figure 7-8).

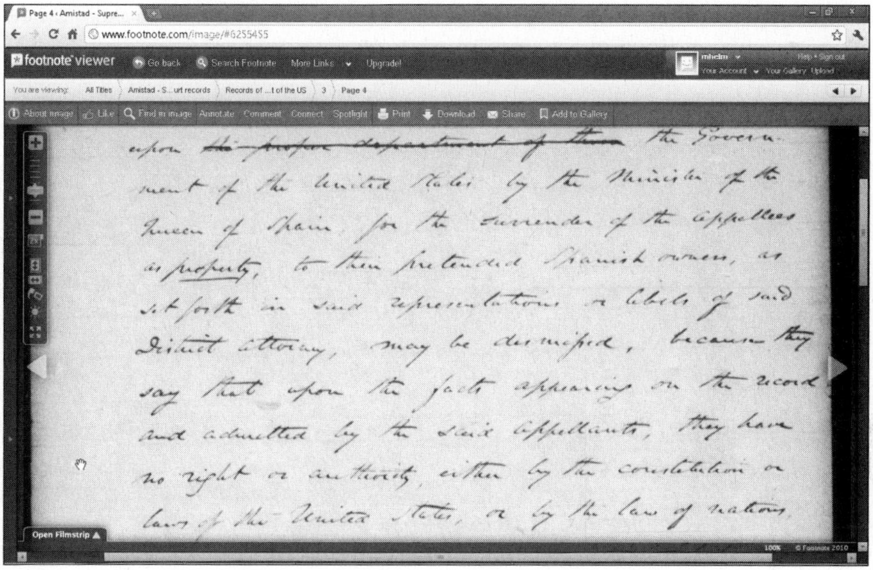

Figure 7-8:
A record
from the
Amistad
case on
Footnote.
com.

American Indian Resources

Tracing your American Indian heritage can be challenging. Your ancestor may have moved frequently, and most likely, few written records were kept. However, your task isn't impossible. With a good research strategy, you may be able to narrow your search area and find primary resources to unlock some of the mysteries of your ancestors.

One key to your research is old family stories that have been passed down from generation to generation. Interviewing your family members is a good way to find out what tribe your ancestor belonged to and the geographic area in which that ancestor lived. After you have this information, a trip to your local library is well worth the effort to find a history of the tribe and where it migrated throughout time. From this research, you can then concentrate your search on a specific geographic area and gain a much better chance of success in finding records of genealogical value.

Fortunately, the government of the United States did compile some records on American Indians. For example, you can find annual census lists of American Indians, dating from 1885 to 1940, in the National Archives — as well as digitized copies of the censuses on Ancestry.com (see Figure 7-9). You can also find probate and land records at the federal level, especially for transactions occurring on reservations. In federal repositories, you can also find school records for those who attended schools on reservations. Additionally, the Bureau of Indian Affairs has a vast collection of records on American Indians. For more information about American Indian resources that are available from the National Archives and Records Administration, visit www.archives.gov/research/alic/reference/native-americans.html.

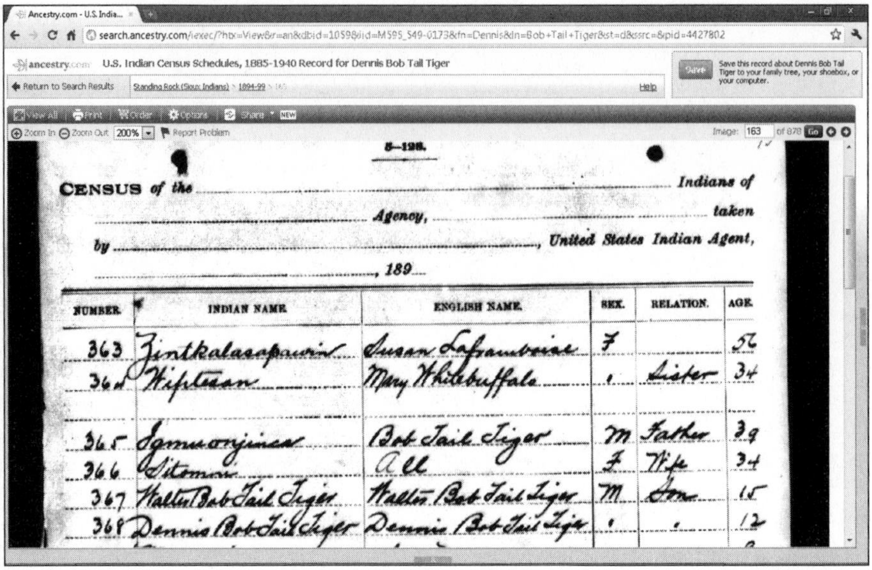

Figure 7-9:
Image of an
Indian cen-
sus record
at Ancestry.
com.

You may also be able to find records on your ancestor in one of the many
tribal associations in existence. To find out how to contact tribes recognized
in the United States, go to the American Indian Tribal Directory, at www.
indians.org/Resource/FedTribes99/fedtribes99.html.

For more information about researching American Indian records, see the
following resources:

- *The Source: A Guidebook of American Genealogy,* edited by Loretto
  Dennis Szucs and Sandra Hargreaves Luebking (Ancestry, Inc.). In particular, see Chapter 14, "Tracking Native American Family History," written
  by Curt B. Witcher and George J. Nixon. You can find this online at www.
  ancestry.com/wiki/index.php?title=Overview_of_Native_
  American_Research.

- *Native American Genealogical Sourcebook,* edited by Paula K. Byers and
  published by Gale Research.

- *Guide to Records in the National Archives of the United States Relating
  to American Indians,* written by Edward E. Hill and published by the
  National Archives and Records Services Administration.

Where to begin looking for information about American Indians

For a general look at what Internet resources are available on American Indians, see the NativeWeb site (www.nativeweb.org). NativeWeb includes a resource center with hundreds of links to other Internet sites on native peoples around the world.

When you're ready to dive into research, you may want to join the INDIAN-ROOTS-L mailing list, which is devoted to discussing American Indian research methods. To subscribe to the list, type **SUB INDIAN-ROOTS-L** *your first name your last name* in the body of an e-mail message and send it to listserv@listserv.indiana.edu.

Another resource worth exploring is the National Archives and Records Administration's Archival Research Catalog (ARC), at www.archives.gov/research_room/arc/index.html. ARC contains indexes to a small portion of the archive's holdings. Among the Native American collections in ARC are

- ✔ Images of the Index to the Final Rolls of the Citizens and Freedmen of the Five Civilized Tribes in Indian Territory
- ✔ Images of the Index to Applications Submitted for the Eastern Cherokee Roll of 1909 (Guion Miller Roll)
- ✔ Records of the Bureau of Indian Affairs Truxton Canon Agency
- ✔ Record of Applications under the Act of 1896 (1896 Citizenship Applications) received by the Dawes Commission
- ✔ Descriptions for records of the Cherokee Indian Agency and the Seminole Indian Agency
- ✔ Descriptions for records of the Navajo Area Office, the Navajo Agency, and the Window Rock Area Office of the Bureau of Indian Affairs
- ✔ Some images of Cherokee, Chickasaw, Creek, and Seminole Applications for Enrollment to the Five Civilized Tribes (Dawes Commission)
- ✔ Images of the Kern-Clifton Roll of Cherokee Freedmen
- ✔ Images of the Wallace Roll of Cherokee Freedmen in Indian Territory
- ✔ Surveys of Indian Industry, 1922
- ✔ Classified Files of the Extension and Credit Office, 1931–1946
- ✔ Selected Documents from the Records of the Bureau of Indian Affairs, 1793–1989
- ✔ American Indians, 1881–1885

To search ARC, try this:

1. **Go to www.archives.gov/research_room/arc/index.html.**

2. **Click the Search button located near the ARC logo.**

   This link takes you to the ARC Basic Search interface.

3. **Type the name or keyword you're looking for and click Go.**

   For example, if April is looking for a person with the name Annie Abbott, she simply types **Annie Abbott** in the blank text box and then clicks Go. After you submit the search, you are taken to the ARC Search Results page. Each result contains the title of the document, creator, type of material, description level, and physical location.

4. **Click the link to see the full record description.**

   A screen displays the available information on the document, including a description of its content.

At this point, ARC contains descriptions of only a portion of the Archives' total holdings. So, if you don't find something, it does not mean it doesn't exist.

You can find a brief outline of how to trace American Indian ancestry at the U.S. Department of the Interior site (www.doi.gov/tribes/trace-ancestry.cfm).

American Indian resource pages on the Web

Researching American Indian roots would be much easier if some sites were dedicated to the genealogical research of specific tribes. If your ancestor's tribe passed through the state of Oklahoma, you may be in luck. Volunteers with the Oklahoma USGenWeb project developed the Twin Territories site, at www.okgenweb.org/~itgenweb. (For more information about USGenWeb, see Chapter 6.)

Some links to various tribes available on the Web are

- ✔ Cherokee Nation Indian Territory (www.rootsweb.ancestry.com/~itcherok)

- ✔ Cherokee Archival Project (www.rootsweb.ancestry.com/~cherokee)

- ✔ NC Cherokee Reservation Genealogy (www.ncgenweb.us/cherokee reservation)

- ✔ Cheyenne-Arapaho Lands Indian Territory (www.rootsweb.ancestry.com/~itcheyen)

- Chickasaw Nation, Indian Territory, 1837–1907 (`www.rootsweb.ancestry.com/~itchicka`)

- Choctaw Nation, Indian Territory (`www.felihkatubbe.com/ChoctawNation/index.html`)

- Kiowa, Comanche, Apache Lands Indian Territory (`www.genealogynation.com/kiowa`)

- Muscogee (Creek) Nation of Oklahoma (`www.genealogynation.com/creek`)

- Native Genealogy People of the Three Fires (Chippewa, Ottawa, and Potawatomi; `www.rootsweb.ancestry.com/~minatam`)

- Osage Nation Genealogical Web site (`www.felihkatubbe.com/OsageNation`)

- Quapaw Agency Lands Indian Territory (`www.rootsweb.ancestry.com/~itquapaw`)

- Seminole Nation in Indian Territory (`www.seminolenation-indianterritory.org`)

- Sovereign Nation of the Kaw (`www.okgenweb.org/~itkaw/KanzaNation.html`)

Transcribed American Indian records

Some Web sites have transcribed records that are unique to researching American Indian roots. Two examples are

- **The Chickasaw Historical Research Page:** This page contains transcriptions of marriage records, a partial census roll of 1818, land sale records, court records, treaty letters, and guardianship records, all at `www.chickasawhistory.com`.

  - **1851 Census of Cherokees East of the Mississippi:** This site provides a transcription of the census, including names, family numbers, ages, and relationships to head of household, all at `http://freepages.genealogy.rootsweb.ancestry.com/~gilmercountyrecords/1851silerrollforgilmercounty.htm`.

Many families have legends that they are descended from famous American Indians. These claims should always be researched carefully and backed up with appropriate proof. One of the most prolific legends is descent from Pocahontas. If that legend runs through your family, you may want to visit the Pocahontas Descendants page for resources that can help you prove your heritage. You can find it at `http://pocahontas.morenus.org/poca_gen.html`.

Chapter 8

Records off the Beaten Path

*M*any people who are familiar with genealogy know to use vital records, census returns, tax lists, and wills to find information about their ancestors. These records offer historical snapshots of an individual's life at particular points in time. But as a family historian, you want to know more than just when your ancestors paid their taxes — you want to know something about them as people.

For example, April once came across a photograph of her great-great-grandfather while she was looking through an old box full of pictures and letters. He was dressed in a uniform with a sash and sword, and he was holding a plumed hat. As far as April knew, her great-great-grandfather hadn't been in the military, so she decided to dig for some information about the uniform. Although part of the picture was blurry, she could make out three crosses on the uniform. One was on his sleeve, the second was on the buckle of his belt, and the third was a different kind of cross that was attached to his sash. April suspected that the symbols were Masonic. She visited a few Masonic sites on the Web and found that the crosses indicated that her great-great-grandfather had been a member of the Order of the Temple in the Masonic organization. She would never have known that he was a member of that organization had she depended solely upon the usual group of records used by genealogists.

This chapter looks at some examples of unique or hard-to-find records that can be useful in family history research, including records kept by religious groups and fraternal orders, photographs, and adoption records.

Researching Religious Group Records

In the past, several countries required attendance at church services or the payment of taxes to an ecclesiastical authority. Although your ancestors may not have appreciated those laws at the time, the records that were kept to ensure their compliance can benefit you as a genealogist. In fact, before governments started recording births, marriages, and deaths, churches kept the official records of these and other events (such as baptisms and lists of vestrymen). You can use a variety of records kept by church authorities or congregations to develop a sketch of the everyday life of your ancestor.

Some common records that you may encounter include baptismal records, parish registers, lists of people holding positions in the church (vestrymen, deacons, elders, lay ministers), marriage records, death or burial records, tithes, welfare rolls, meeting minutes, and congregation photographs. Each type of record may include several different bits of information. For example, a baptismal record may include the date of birth, date of baptism, parents' names, and where the parents lived. Parish registers may have names of household members and addresses, and possibly an accounting of their tithes to the church. The amount of data present on the records depends on the church.

Several sites provide general information and links to all sorts of resources that pertain to specific religions and sects. Here are a few examples:

- **Anabaptist:** The Global Anabaptist Mennonite Encyclopedia Online (GAMEO) site (www.gameo.org) has an extensive collection of articles related to Amish, Mennonite, Hutterite, and Brethren in Christ congregations, as well as confessions and faith statements from some church members. It also has links to other resources for Anabaptist-Mennonite research. Additionally, you can find genealogical databases of Anabaptists at the Swiss Anabaptist Genealogical Association site (www.omii.org).

- **Baptist:** The American Baptist Historical Society site (www.baptist history.us) contains an overview of its collections and the services that the Society provides.

- **Catholic:** The Local Catholic Church History & Genealogy Research Guide (http://localcatholic.webs.com) includes links to information on diocese and genealogy, categorized by location. If you're looking for British resources, see www.catholic-genealogy.com.

- **Church of the Brethren:** The Fellowship of Brethren Genealogists Web site (www.cob-net.org/fobg) contains information on the organization and the current projects sponsored by the Fellowship.

- **Church of Scotland:** The General Register Office for Scotland site (www.scotlandspeople.gov.uk) features searchable indexes of births, baptisms, banns, marriages, deaths, and burials from the Old Parish Registers dating from 1553 to 1854.

✔ **Huguenot:** The Huguenots of France and Elsewhere site (`http://huguenots-france.org/english.htm`) contains genealogies of several Huguenot families. For information on Huguenots in America, see Experiences of the French Huguenots in America at `http://pages.prodigy.net/royjnagy/ressegui.htm`. Also, you find a surname index at the Australian Family Tree Connections site (`www.aftc.com.au/Huguenot/Hug.html`).

✔ **Hutterite:** The Hutterite Genealogy Home Page (`www.feefhs.org/links/hutterites.html`) gives an introduction and links to resources for this denomination found in Austria, Bohemia, Moravia, Slovakia, Hungary, Romania, Canada, the United States, and the Ukraine. For links to a variety of Hutterite resources, see Hutterite Reference Links at `http://home.westman.wave.ca/~hillmans/BU/hutterite.html`.

✔ **Jewish:** The JewishGen site (`www.jewishgen.org`) has information about the JewishGen organization and FAQs about Jewish genealogy, as well as indices of other Internet resources, including searchable databases, special interest groups, and JewishGen family home pages.

✔ **Lutheran:** The Lutheran Roots Genealogy Exchange (`www.lutheransonline.com/lutheransonline/genealogy`) has a registry of researchers looking for information about Lutheran ancestors and a message board to which you can post questions about your research.

✔ **Mennonite:** The Mennonite Research Corner (`www.ristenbatt.com/genealogy/mennonit.htm`) features general information about Mennonites and a collection of online resources for researchers. For a Canadian perspective, visit the Mennonite Genealogy Data Index at `www.mennonites.ca`.

✔ **Methodist:** The Researching Your United Methodist Ancestors site (`www.gcah.org/site/pp.aspx?c=ghKJI0PHIoE&b=2901109`) contains general advice on getting started with your research and links to online resources.

✔ **Moravian Church:** The Moravian Church Genealogy Links page (`www.enter.net/~smschlack`) features links to articles on the history of the church, as well as links to genealogical resources.

✔ **Quaker:** The Quaker Corner (`www.rootsweb.com/~quakers`) contains a query board, a list of research resources, and links to other Quaker pages on the Web.

✔ **Seventh-day Adventist:** The Center for Adventist Research at Andrews University site (`www.andrews.edu/library/car`) contains information on the university's archives and research center and databases including a periodical index, obituary index, bibliographies, and photographs.

A few church organizations have online descriptions of their archives' holdings:

- **Archives of Brethren in Christ Church:** `www.messiah.edu/archives/archives_bic.html`
- **Catholic Archives of Texas:** `www.onr.com/user/cat`
- **Center for Mennonite Brethren Studies in Fresno, California:** `www.fresno.edu/library/cmbs/genealogical_resources.asp`
- **Concordia Historical Institute Department of Archives and History (Lutheran):** `http://chi.lcms.org`
- **General Commission on Archives and History for the United Methodist Church:** `www.gcah.org/index.htm`
- **Greek Orthodox Archdiocese of America Department of Archives:** `www.goarch.org/archdiocese/departments/archives`
- **Moravian Archives:** `http://moravianchurcharchives.org`
- **United Church of Canada Archives:** `www.united-church.ca/local/archives/on`

The following sites can give you a better idea of the types of information available on the Internet for religious groups:

- **Baptism records:** You can find a list of those baptized in the Wesleyan Methodist Baptismal Register at `http://freepages.genealogy.rootsweb.ancestry.com/~wjmartin/wm-index.htm`.
- **Cemetery records:** The Quaker Burying Ground Cemetery, Galesville, Anne Arundel County, Maryland, site is `www.interment.net/data/us/md/anne_arundel/quaker.htm`. This Web page is part of the Interment.net: Cemetery Records Online site, which provides transcribed burial information, including the person's name and dates of birth and death, as well as some other information, as shown in Figure 8-1.
- **Marriage records:** The Moravian Church, Lititz Marriages 1742–1800 page (`http://files.usgwarchives.net/pa/lancaster/church/moravianlititz.txt`) contains a list of marriage dates along with the names of the bride and groom married in the church located in Lancaster County, Pennsylvania.
- **Parish directories:** The Holy Trinity Church, Boston, Massachusetts, site (`http://homepages.rootsweb.com/~mvreid/bgrc/htc.html`) has a searchable 1895 parish directory, an ongoing project to identify and post information about church members who served in the Civil War, and a list of church members who served in World War I.

In addition to sites that focus specifically on one type of record, you may run across sites that collect digitized copies of all sorts of records pertaining to a particular church. For example, the goal of the Genline Project (`www.genline.com`) is to place all digital copies of Swedish church records online.

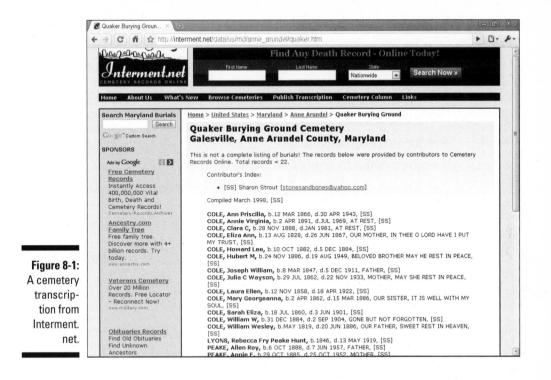

Figure 8-1:
A cemetery transcription from Interment. net.

Finding Fraternal Orders and Service Clubs

Were any of your ancestors members of fraternal orders or service clubs? These groups are organized around a feature or attribute (such as a religion, military service, occupation, and so forth) and generally worked toward a common good. Many such organizations exist and, chances are, you have at least one ancestor who was a member of an order or club. Although most of the better-known organizations are for men, affiliated organizations for women exist too. A few general-information sites on fraternal orders and service clubs are

✔ **American Legion:** www.legion.org

✔ **Ancient and Mystical Order Rosae Crucis:** www.amorc.org

✔ **Ancient Order of Hibernians in America:** www.aoh.com

✔ **Catholic Knights:** www.catholicknights.org/Home.htm

✔ **DeMolay International:** www.demolay.org/home/index.shtml

✔ **Eagles (Fraternal Order of Eagles):** www.foe.com

✔ **Elks (Benevolent Protective Order of the Elks):** www.elks.org

- **Freemasonry:** The Philalethes Society (www.freemasonry.org) and A Page About Freemasonry (http://web.mit.edu/dryfoo/www/Masons/index.html)
- **Improved Order of Red Men:** www.redmen.org
- **Job's Daughters (International Order of Job's Daughters):** www.iojd.org
- **Kiwanis International:** www.kiwanis.org
- **Knights of Columbus:** www.kofc.org/un/eb/en/index.html
- **Lions Clubs:** LionNet (www.lionnet.com)
- **Military Order of the Loyal Legion of the United States:** www.suvcw.org/mollus/mollus.htm
- **Modern Woodmen of America:** www.modern-woodmen.org/Public/AboutUs/History/
- **Moose International:** www.mooseintl.org/public/default.asp
- **Odd Fellows (Independent Order of Odd Fellows):** www.ioof.org
- **Optimist International:** www.optimist.org
- **Order of the Eastern Star (Grand Chapter Order of the Eastern Star):** www.easternstar.org
- **Orioles (Fraternal Order of Orioles):** www.fraternalorderorioles.homestead.com
- **Police (Fraternal Order of Police):** www.grandlodgefop.org
- **Rainbow for Girls (International Order of the Rainbow for Girls):** www.iorg.org
- **Rebekahs:** www.ioof.org/rebekahs.html
- **Rotary International:** www.rotary.org
- **Shriners (The Shrine of North America):** www.shrinershq.org/ShrinersHQ
- **Veterans of Foreign Wars of the United States:** www.vfw.org

Most online sites related to fraternal orders provide historical information about the clubs and current membership rules. Although the sites may not provide you with actual records (membership lists and meeting minutes), they do give you an overview of what the club is about and an idea of what your ancestor did as a member. The sites also provide you with the names and addresses of local chapters — you can contact them to see whether they have original resources available for public use or whether they can send you copies of anything pertaining to your ancestor.

Having information about a fraternal order doesn't necessarily make a particular site the organization's *official* site. This is particularly true for international organizations. You may find Web pages for different chapters of a particular club in several different countries, and although each site may have some general club information in common, they are likely to have varying types of information specific to that chapter of the organization.

If you're looking for sites that contain information on fraternal organizations, you may want to try some of the comprehensive genealogy sites. If you can't find sufficient information there, try one of the general Internet search engines. To find information on fraternal orders through a general Internet search engine, try this:

1. **Open your Web browser and go to the AltaVista search engine page (www.altavista.com), or substitute the address of your favorite search engine.**

2. **In the Search box, type the name of a fraternal organization and click Find.**

   We're interested in finding information about the Knights of Columbus, so we typed that phrase in the Search box.

3. **On the search results page, click a link that interests you.**

   After you click Search, you see a page with the results of your search. Each result has the site's title and a brief abstract taken directly from the page, which you can use to determine whether the site contains information that you're interested in.

A Photo Is Worth a Thousand Words

In Chapter 2, we discuss the value of photographs in your genealogical research. But a lot of us don't have photographs of our family beyond two or three generations, though it sure would be great to find at least an electronic copy of a picture of your great-great-grandfathers. Such pictures may exist. Another researcher may have posted them on a personal site, or the photographs may be part of a collection belonging to a certain organization. You may also be interested in pictures of places where your ancestors lived. Being able to describe how a certain town, estate, or farm looked at the time your ancestor lived there adds color to your family history.

You can find various types of photographic sites on the Internet that can assist you with your research. Some of these sites explain the photographic process and the many types of photographs that have been used throughout history. Some sites contain collections of photographs from a certain geographic area or time period in history, and some sites contain photographs of the ancestors of a particular family. Here are some examples:

- **General information:** City Gallery's Learning page (`www.city-gallery.com/learning`) has a brief explanation of the types of photography used during the 19th century (see Figure 8-2), a photography query page, and a gallery of photographs from one studio of the period.

- **Photograph collections:** You can find general collections of images online at sites such as American Memory: Photographs, Prints, and Drawings at `http://memory.loc.gov/cgi-bin/query/S?ammem/collections:@field(FLD003+@band(origf+Photograph)):heading=Original+Format%3a+Photos+&+Prints`. You can find pictures also at sites that have a specific focus, such as the American West and Civil War (`www.treasurenet.com/images`), or images of people and places in Florida (`www.floridamemory.com/PhotographicCollection`).

- **Photograph identification:** The DeadFred Genealogy Photo Archive contains more than 99,000 photographs at `www.deadfred.com`. Each photograph includes descriptive information, including where the photograph was taken, the names of the subjects, and an approximate time frame (see Figure 8-3).

- **Personal photographs:** The Harrison Genealogy Repository site is an example of a personal Web site with a photo gallery: `http://free pages.genealogy.rootsweb.com/~harrisonrep/Photos/harrphot.htm`. The gallery includes the likenesses of several famous Harrisons, including Benjamin Harrison V, President William Henry Harrison, and President Benjamin Harrison.

Figure 8-2:
Find out about photographic methods of the past at City Gallery.

Figure 8-3:
An entry
on the
DeadFred
photograph
archive site.

To find photographic sites, you may want to visit one of the comprehensive genealogy sites or general Internet search engines.

Accessing Adoption Records

Adoption records are of interest to a lot of genealogists, including those who were adopted themselves, those who gave up children for adoption, and those who have ancestors who were adopted.

If you fall into the first two groups (you were adopted or gave up a child for adoption), some online resources may help you find members of your birth family. The online resources include registries, reference materials, advice and discussion groups, and information on legislation pertaining to adoption. Registries enable you to post information about yourself and your adoption, with the hope that a member of your birth family may see the posting and contact you. (Likewise, if you're the birth parent of an adoptee, you can post a message with the hope that the adoptee sees it and responds.)

Unfortunately, you won't find online sites that contain actual adoption records — for legal reasons, generally. Instead, you need to rely on registries and other resources that point you toward more substantial information about adoption. If you have a successful reunion with your birth parent(s) by registering with an online site, you can, with any luck, obtain information about their parents, grandparents, and so on — so that you know where to begin your genealogical pursuit of that family line.

Here are some online sites that have adoption registries, reference materials, advice and discussions, or legislative information:

✔ **Adoptees Internet Mailing List:** www.aiml.org

✔ **Child Welfare Information Gateway: Access to Adoption Records:** www.childwelfare.gov/systemwide/laws_policies/statutes/infoaccessap.cfm

✔ **AdoptionNetwork:** www.adoption.org

✔ **Adoption Registry Connect: Worldwide Adoptee and Birth Parent Search Database:** www.adopteeconnect.com/index.htm

✔ **About.com:** http://genealogy.about.com/od/adoption/index.htm

If you're interested in adoption records because you have ancestors who were adopted, finding information may be more difficult. Although some article- and blog-type sites exist that give general research information relating to adoption, we have yet to discover any sites specifically designed to aid in research for adopted ancestors. Most likely, you'll have to rely on the regular genealogical resources — particularly query pages and discussion groups — and the kindness and knowledge of other researchers to find information about your adopted ancestors.

If you're searching for general types of adoption resources, using a general Internet directory such as Yahoo! may be the best course of action. To find resources using Yahoo!, try this:

1. **Open your Web browser and go to Yahoo! at http://dir.yahoo.com.**

2. **Click the Society and Culture link in the left frame.**

3. **Click the Families link.**

Here's a second way to find items in Yahoo! (that may be a lot faster): Type a search term in the box near the top of the screen and have Yahoo! search for the topic. For example, you can type **Adoption** in the box and click Search, which produces a results page that has links to take you directly to the appropriate page in Yahoo! that contains adoption links.

4. **Under the Families category, click the Adoption link.**

This takes you directly to the adoption page — even though it's a few levels down in the directory's hierarchy.

5. **Click a link to another subdirectory in Yahoo! or a link to an Internet site that contains information that interests you.**

Descriptions follow most of the links in Yahoo! to give you an idea of what kind of information is on the sites. Figure 8-4 shows an example of a Yahoo! page.

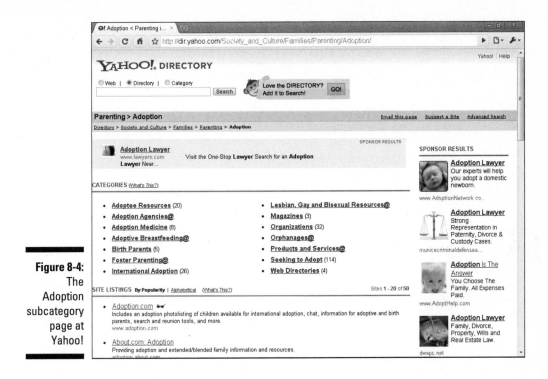

Figure 8-4:
The
Adoption
subcategory
page at
Yahoo!

Preparing to Be Schooled

Relatively few readily available records chronicle the early years of an individual. Educational records can help fill in the gaps. These records can take a number of forms, including enrollment records, transcripts, yearbooks, directories, and fraternity and sorority records.

The first step is to find out what educational institution your ancestor attended. If you're looking for an elementary or secondary school, you might visit the USGenWeb page (www.usgenweb.org) for the county where your ancestor lived to see whether information is available on the location of schools. If the USGenWeb page doesn't have the information, try to find the Web site of the local historical or genealogical society.

After you discover the name of the institution, find out who has the records for that school. Some schools — such as colleges and universities — have their own archives. For primary and secondary schools, you may need to contact the school district or the overarching parish. Or, if the school no longer exists, you need to find out where the records for that school were transferred.

To see whether a college or university has an archive, look at the list of archives at the Repositories of Primary Sources site (`www.uidaho.edu/special-collections/Other.Repositories.html`). If you're not sure where the records are located, you can use WorldCat, at `www.worldcat.org`, by following these steps:

1. **Use your Web browser to pull up `www.worldcat.org`.**

2. **In the search field, enter your criteria and then click Search.**

   We searched for Harvard enrollment records.

3. **Select a result that looks promising.**

   Figure 8-5 shows the results of our WorldCat search.

Turning to Bible Records

Bible records are a great source of birth, death, and marriage information for time periods before vital records were required. Because most Bible records are held by private individuals, it's sometimes difficult to locate them. Recognizing the importance of these records, groups have created Web sites to share the information contained in the Bibles. A few sites worth visiting are

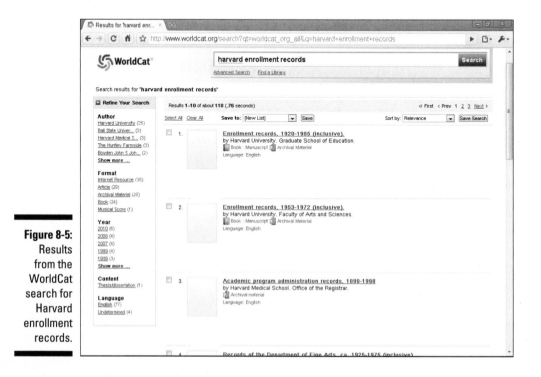

Figure 8-5:
Results
from the
WorldCat
search for
Harvard
enrollment
records.

- **Ancestor Hunt Family Bible Records:** www.ancestorhunt.com/family_bible_records.htm

- **Bible Records Online:** www.biblerecords.com

- **Family Bible Records in Onondaga County:** www.rootsweb.ancestry.com/~nyononda/BIBLE.HTM

- **Maine Family Bible Archives:** www.rootsweb.com/~meandrhs/taylor/bible/maine.html

Similar to looking for educational records, you can also find Bible records in some archives. You can use WorldCat (www.worldcat.org) to see what is available in different institutions. For details on how to use WorldCat, see the preceding section. Some subscription sites might also have Bible records. For example, Ancestry.com (www.ancestry.com) has Bible records from New York, Tennessee, Missouri, and Virginia, as well as a collection called Old Southern Bible Records.

Snooping through Great-Grandma's Diary

Another excellent source of information that can add color to your family history is a diary, journal, or memoir kept by your ancestor. Diaries and journals are books in which a person writes his or her thoughts and experiences, typically within a short time of events occurring. Memoirs are written reflections on one's life. Like Bibles and photos online, finding these personal memory keepers on the Internet is somewhat hit-and-miss. Individuals and organizations tend to place online digital images or transcriptions from these resources for their own family members or people from whom an organization has inherited the document. You can search for such records in the same way that you look for Bibles and photos: Look by location or surname using a site such as USGenWeb (www.usgenweb.org) or a search engine such as Google (www.google.com). Some example sites to check out, which may give you an idea of what you can expect from these types of records, are

- **Diaries, Memoirs, Letters, and Reports Along the Trails West:** www.over-land.com/diaries.html

- **Historical Journals and Diaries Online:** www.aisling.net/journaling/old-diaries-online.htm

- **Civil War Women: Primary Sources on the Internet:** http://library.duke.edu/specialcollections/bingham/guides/cwdocs.html

Nosing through Newspapers Records

A lot of the day-to-day details of your ancestor's life can be filled in by reading local newspapers. You can find obituaries, marriage announcements, social activities, and tax assessments information. Also, you can find background information on the locality that he or she lived in so that you gain a better perspective of your ancestor's life.

A lot of effort has been expended to digitize newspapers over the last few years. Ancestry.com (www.ancestry.com) has partnered with NewspaperArchive.com (www.newspaperarchive.com) to offer a collection of more than 1,000 newspaper databases online. The newspapers featured in the collection are digitized images that have been indexed by optical character recognition (OCR) — a software method in which letters in an image are translated into characters (typically letters of the alphabet) that a computer can read. Each page of the newspaper is searchable. When a search result is found, the text is highlighted on the page. The optical character recognition system doesn't always know the context of the words on the page — so the system sometimes generates false-positive search results. Figure 8-6 shows the interface for the newspaper collection at Ancestry.com.

Figure 8-6:
The Decatur Daily Review newspaper image at Ancestry.com.

WorldVitalRecords.com (www.worldvitalrecords.com) also has select newspapers from the NewspaperArchive.com site. In addition, it has newspapers from the SmallTownPapers.com (http://smalltownpapers.com/) site.

Several large newspapers have also begun to place their back issues online — often with a subscription service. For example, you can find the *Los Angeles Times* back to 1881 online at http://pqasb.pqarchiver.com/latimes/advancedsearch.html, the *Washington Post* from 1877 at http://pqasb.pqarchiver.com/washingtonpost/search.html, and the *Chicago Tribune* from 1852 at http://pqasb.pqarchiver.com/chicagotribune/advancedsearch.html.

You can find more about using newspapers in your research in Chapter 6.

Chapter 9

Fitting into Your Genes: Molecular Genealogy

In This Chapter

▶ Signing up for a DNA primer

▶ Determining the right test to use

▶ Searching for DNA sites

*I*t sounds like something right out of a crime scene investigation: You swab your cheek, send the sample to a lab, the results are analyzed, and presto! You find the identity of someone super-important. However, instead of identifying some master-minded criminal, you find the identity of that long-lost ancestor for whom you've been searching. Although the science behind molecular genealogy traces its roots to identifying individuals from crime scenes, it hasn't advanced to the point where you can simply take the test and watch your entire genealogy unfold.

Although *deoxyribonucleic acid (DNA)* testing is just one of many tools to use in documenting your research, it holds great potential for the future of genealogy. You may be familiar with the use of DNA testing in identifying the remains of Nicholas, the last Czar of Russia, and his family; in debating the last resting place of Christopher Columbus; or in identifying the true fate of Jesse James. The methods used in these investigations are the same methods that you can use to complement your documentary research.

In this chapter, we provide an overview of how DNA testing works, where you can order tests, and what to do with the information that you discover during the testing process.

Delving into DNA

Some people might think that we're attempting the impossible — explaining how DNA testing works in one mere chapter. However, we feel it is our duty to at least give you a basic introduction to genetic research so that you can use all the technological means available to you when digging for information on your ancestors.

You need an understanding of the terminology and how the testing process works to interpret your test results. If you find that our elementary explanations just whet your appetite, you can get a healthy dose on the subject with *Genetics For Dummies*, 2nd Edition, by Tara Rodden Robinson (Wiley).

A friendly word of caution

Before you embark into the world of molecular genealogy, we want you to consider two things. First, by taking a DNA test, you might find out something that you would rather not know. For example, some people have discovered that they're not biologically related to the family from which they've always claimed descent. Sometimes this occurs due to a "nonpaternal event," where the biological father was not the person listed on the birth record (this may have occurred in the immediate family or in a past generation). Others have discovered that they may not have the racial or ethnic composition that they've always identified themselves with. Although both situations are rare, you need to be prepared.

The second thing to remember is that molecular genealogy is a science, but not an absolute one. DNA test results show the probability that something is true. (*Probability* is the likelihood that a specific fact or outcome will occur.) Nothing is ever 100 percent certain. In addition, sometimes (but rarely) mistakes are made by the testing facility, or new research is discovered that changes the way that a test result is viewed. DNA testing for genealogy is still in its infancy and is going through some growing pains. As long as you can adapt to change and accept new technology, you'll be just fine in the world of DNA genealogy.

What can molecular genealogy do for you?

Have you ever thought about the applications of genetic testing in genealogical research? It's a brave new world in which some of your family riddles may be answered and the brick walls in your research could be torn down. Molecular genealogy offers hope in many research realms, not the least of which are

- ✔ Determining whether two people are related when one or both were adopted
- ✔ Identifying whether two people are descended from the same ancestor
- ✔ Discovering whether you are related to others with the same surname
- ✔ Proving or disproving your family tree research
- ✔ Providing clues about your ethnic origin

Getting down to bases

When we decided to conduct a molecular genealogy study on the surname Helm, we completed some basic research on genetics. While looking at the many resources available that describe deoxyribonucleic acid, or DNA, we found that one in particular contained a model that helped us understand the basics better. The resource was a publication called "DNA Program Kit," published jointly by the National Genome Research Institute, the United States Department of Energy, and the Science Museum of Minnesota. You can find this publication online at www.genome.gov/DNADay/DNA_Programming_Kit_Manual.pdf. We use a modified version of that model to help you understand the components of DNA that are used in molecular genealogy.

Being a family historian, most likely you've taken a research trip to a particular town to find the burial location for an ancestor. When you reached that town, your first stop was probably the local library. Entering the library, you quickly made your way to the reference room. You leafed through the reference room collection, looking for a cemetery index for that area. Finding an index, you located the chapter that contained a list of gravestones for the cemetery where your ancestor is buried. Thumbing through the chapter, you find your ancestor's name, which is typed with some combination of 26 letters (assuming that it contains no special characters and that the book is in English).

You can think about the components of DNA like the library example mentioned previously (see Figure 9-1 for a model of the components of DNA). The basic building blocks of humans are *cells* that function like little towns. Within each cell is a *nucleus,* which is the structure that contains all the DNA. This nucleus acts as the library for the cell. Within the nucleus is the *genome* (the complete set of instructions for how the cell will operate). You can think of the genome as the reference book collection of the library.

The human genome is comprised of 23 pairs of chromosomes. A *chromosome* is the container that holds the strands of DNA. Each type of chromosome has a different set of instructions and serves a different purpose. Sticking with our analogy, like a library's reference collection has several types of reference books, the genome has several types of chromosomes. Particular sections of a chromosome are called genes. *Genes* contain specific sequences of information that determine a particular inheritable characteristic of a human. Where a chromosome is the reference book, genes are the chapters in the book.

A particular gene can come in different forms called *alleles.* For example, the gene for eye color might come in a blue eye allele or a brown eye allele. To use our book analogy, a particular chapter of a book can be laid out in different ways. Alleles would be different layouts that a particular chapter could have.

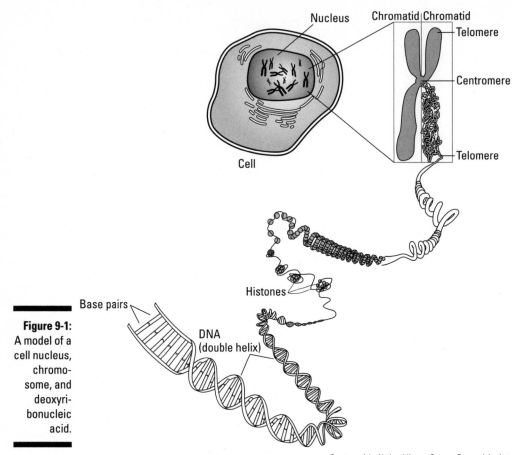

Courtesy of the National Human Genome Research Institute

Figure 9-1:
A model of a cell nucleus, chromosome, and deoxyribonucleic acid.

Genes are composed of *bases,* also called *nucleotides,* that form the "rungs" of the DNA "ladder" that hold the DNA molecule together. You find four types of bases: adenine (A), guanine (G), cytosine (C), and thymine (T). When forming the rungs of the DNA molecule, bases attach in only one way. Adenine always pairs with thymine on the opposite strand, and guanine always pairs with cytosine. The attachment of bases is called *base pairing.* The bases are the language of DNA. You read the sequence of the base pairs to determine the coding of the allele — just like reading the sequence of letters in a book forms a recognizable sentence.

Please understand that our DNA-library analogy is a very simplistic explanation of the molecular parts that are considered in genetic testing. DNA plays a much more complicated role in genetics than what we just covered. However, for the purpose of this chapter, our basic presentation on genetic structure should be sufficient for understanding the broader implications in DNA testing for molecular genealogy.

Selecting the Right Test for You

After you gain a basic understanding of molecular structure, you may find your curiosity piqued — are you ready to jump right in and gather DNA samples willy-nilly? Slow down! You have more to discover so that you don't lose time and momentum by submitting your swabs for the wrong types of tests.

Four types of tests are commonly available from DNA testing companies:

- **Y chromosome DNA testing:** Humans have 23 pairs of chromosomes. Of these 23, males and females have 22 pairs in common and one pair not in common. In that one pair, males have one X and one Y chromosome, whereas females have two X chromosomes. The Y chromosome DNA test explores the Y chromosome in this uncommon pair of chromosomes. As you might suspect at this point, this particular test is available only for men because females do not carry the Y chromosome. However, just because you — the reader — might be female, don't fail to read the following section on Y chromosome DNA testing. You can always have a male relative (such as your father, brother, uncle, or cousin) take this test for you to discover the hidden secrets in your familial Y DNA.

- **Mitochondrial DNA testing:** The mitochondrion is considered by some to be the "power plant" of the cell. (Remember, the cell is the basic building block of the human body.) It sits outside the nucleus of the cell, and it contains its own distinct genome — that means its genome is separate from the genome found in the nucleus of the cell. This distinct genome is known as mtDNA in genetic testing. The mtDNA is inherited only from the female parent, is passed to all offspring (male and female), and mutates (or changes) at a slow rate over generations. All of these aspects of the mtDNA make it good for identifying genetic relationships over hundreds of generations.

- **Autosomal DNA testing:** Autosomal DNA consists of 22 pairs of non-sex-specific chromosomes that are found in the cell nucleus — this means that they don't contain the X or Y chromosome. Autosomal DNA is found in males and females, and is the part of the DNA responsible for characteristics such as height and eye color. This DNA is inherited from both parents. Autosomal testing, also called admixture or biogeographical testing, is used to determine paternity, predict ethnicity, and diagnose potential health problems.

- **X chromosome DNA testing:** As we mentioned, males have one X and one Y chromosome, whereas females have two X chromosomes. This test looks at the mixture of the X chromosomes inherited over several generations.

Given the complexity of molecular research, we expect the tests to be complicated as well. Hence, each test warrants its own attention. In the next sections, we explore them in a little more depth.

Y chromosome DNA testing

In the preceding section, we introduced the concept that the Y chromosome DNA test examines the Y chromosome that men receive from their male ancestors. The Y chromosome is part of the one chromosomal pair that is not common between males and females; in males, the pair has an X and a Y chromosome, whereas in females, the pair has two X chromosomes. We also mentioned that this test is available only for men — although women can participate in Y chromosome projects by using a father, brother, or male cousin as a proxy (see Figure 9-2). Now it's time to get into the details of the test.

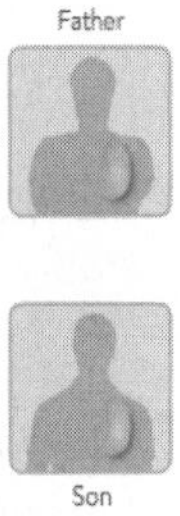

Figure 9-2:
A Y chromosome is passed from father to son relatively unchanged.

Father

Son

Courtesy of the Sorenson Molecular Genealogy Foundation,
the scientific backbone of GeneTree.com

"Junk" DNA is worth something

When scientists began studying chromosomes, they discovered that not all the base pairs were used as instructions for the cell. These *noncoding regions,* sometimes referred to as "junk" DNA because they seem to just be hanging around without helping guide the cell to fulfill its larger purpose, contain alleles that differ from person to person. This means that the junk DNA has characteristics that distinguish individuals from each other. Scientists soon began to use these alleles to identify individuals, especially in criminal investigations.

As more research was performed on the Y chromosome, scientists found that the noncoding regions could be used to define not only individual characteristics but also characteristics of larger populations into which individuals with these characteristics fit. In essence, they discovered how to determine what population a particular human was a member of by using the noncoding regions of the DNA. They also discovered that the Y chromosome changes (or mutates) very little or not at all between fathers and sons. Because the Y chromosome is passed only from father to son, it is useful for tracing the direct paternal line of an individual's ancestry (as illustrated by Figure 9-3).

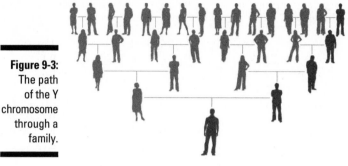

Figure 9-3:
The path
of the Y
chromosome
through a
family.

The testing process

The process of testing the Y chromosome starts with a man swabbing the inside of his cheek with a sample collection device that usually looks something like a Q-Tip cotton swab. The swab collects cheek cells, which serve as the source for the DNA. After the laboratory receives the swab, the DNA is extracted using a process called polymerase chain reaction (PCR). This process makes thousands of copies of the DNA so that it can be analyzed.

After the copies are made, sequences of DNA at specific locations on the chromosome are analyzed. These sequences are called *markers,* and the location of the markers on the chromosome is called the *locus* (or plural *loci*). The markers are read by the sequence of the bases. (Remember, as we mention in the section "Getting down to bases," earlier in this chapter, the bases are abbreviated A, G, C, and T). The sequence for the bases shown in Figure 9-4 are

```
ATGCTAATCGGC
```

Each marker is given a name that usually begins with *DYS* — short for DNA Y Chromosome Segment. When analyzing the markers, laboratory technicians look for the number of times that a segment of bases (usually three to five bases long) repeats. These segments of repeating bases are called *short tandem repeat polymorphisms* (STRPs).

Is your head spinning yet from all the definitions that we just threw at you? Think about the book analogy to recap what we just said in terms that we hope are easier to follow. Think of this book as the Y chromosome and this chapter as a gene on the chromosome. This page would be the locus where the segment is located — that is easily found by using the page number. The DNA Y Chromosome Segment is the following sentence:

I like this book VERY VERY VERY much.

The Short Tandem Repeat is the phrase *VERY VERY VERY* in the sentence — a set of letters that repeat.

Now see whether you can make sense of a real sequence of bases for the marker DYS393, keeping in mind that you can refer to our book example if needed:

> gtggtcttctacttgtgtcaatac AGAT AGAT AGAT AGAT AGAT AGAT AGAT AGAT AGAT AGAT AGAT AGAT AGAT AGAT AGAT atgtatgtctttctatgaga-catac ctcatttttggacttgagttc

To make it easier for you to see, we capitalized the letters and inserted spaces between the base segments composing the STR (which are AGAT). If you count the number of times the bases AGAT repeat, you'll find that the number of repeats for DYS393 for this individual is 15.

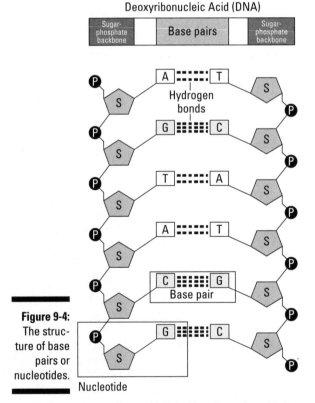

Figure 9-4: The structure of base pairs or nucleotides.

Courtesy of the National Human Genome Research Institute

Comparing the results

After the number of repeats within a marker is calculated, we can compare the results of that marker plus a few other markers to see whether two or more individuals are related. Most labs try to compare at least 12 markers. Table 9-1 shows a comparison between the markers of four individuals.

Table 9-1	A Comparison of 12 Markers for Four Individuals											
ID	DYS 393	DYS 390	DYS 19 /394	DYS 391	DYS 385a	DYS 385b	DYS 426	DYS 388	DYS 439	DYS 389-1	DYS 392	DYS 389-2
A	13	25	14	11	11	11	12	12	13	13	13	29
B	13	25	14	11	11	11	12	12	12	13	13	29
C	13	25	14	11	11	11	12	12	12	13	13	29
D	13	25	14	11	11	11	12	12	12	13	13	29
Modal	13	25	14	11	11	11	12	12	12	13	13	29

If you compare the results between individuals A and B in Table 9-1, you can see that they have the same number of repeats in 11 of the 12 markers. Only at DYS439 is there a difference in the number of repeats, commonly called a *mutation*. Based on this information, we would say that a genetic distance of 1 exists between these two individuals. At 12 markers, a genetic distance of 1 would indicate that these two individuals are probably related — however, testing more markers would certainly give a better indication of how closely they may be related. A higher probability exists that individuals B, C, and D are related, because they match on all 12 markers.

The result of a set of markers for an individual is called a *haplotype*. So, in the preceding chart, the haplotype for individual A is DYS393 – 13, DYS390 – 25, DYS19/394 – 14, DYS391 – 11, DYS385a – 11, DYS395b – 11, DYS426 – 12, DYS388 – 12, DYS439 – 13, DYS389-1 – 13, DYS392 – 13, DYS 389-2 – 29.

After you have haplotype results for an individual, it's important to get results from relatives of that individual. More specifically, it's important to get the haplotype results for relatives whose relationships can be documented by primary sources, including those in the extended family. These results help confirm the results of individual A and establish an overall specific haplotype for the family. For example, say that all the individuals in Table 9-1 are related, and the fact is well documented with primary sources. After analyzing the results, a *modal haplotype* can be calculated by looking at the number of repeats that have the highest occurrence for each marker. Because all the results are the same for 11 out of 12 markers, the modal values for these are the same as the number of repeats for that marker. That leaves only one marker to calculate — DYS439. The results for DYS439 include one 13 and four 12s. That makes the modal value for that marker 12 — because it appears the most. So, the row marked *Modal* in Table 9-1 shows the haplotype for Individual A's family.

The modal haplotype for a family can be used to compare that family to other families with the same surname to determine the probability that the two families are related. A good way to see these relationships is to join a surname DNA project — we talk about how to find these in the section "Helpful DNA Sites," later in this chapter.

Assessing the probability of a relationship

After the test is taken and the results compared, it's time to figure out the probability that two individuals are related. This probability is calculated by determining how often a change might occur to a marker over time. Fortunately, the testing companies calculate this for you and typically give you a tool (in the form of an online chart or written instructions) to compare two results.

Reviewing the data in Table 9-1, say that you want to determine how closely related Individual A may be to Individual B. To do this, you need to identify the *time to most recent common ancestor (TMRCA)* for the two individuals. The TMRCA is pretty much what it sounds like — a calculation to determine when two individuals may have shared the same ancestor. As you'll see from this example, the calculation is not extremely precise, but it is close enough to point you in the right direction as you begin looking for supporting documentation. By the way, if you want a more in-depth explanation of how TMRCA works, see the article by Bruce Walsh at http://nitro.biosci. arizona.edu/ftdna/TMRCA.html.

The easiest way to determine the TMRCA between two individuals is to use an online utility. If your testing company doesn't have one — or you're comparing results from more than one testing company — you can use the Y-Utility: Y-DNA Comparison Utility at www.mymcgee.com/tools/yutility.html. You have a lot of options with this utility, so we take it a step at a time.

1. **Point your Web browser to the Y-Utility Web site at www.mymcgee. com/tools/yutility.html.**

   The page has a number of options and ways of displaying the data. We'll adjust some of these to make it easier to see the results.

2. **Ensure that the Marker table includes those markers necessary for the calculation.**

   In the table at the top of the screen, you can see 100 markers. In this example, you'll be working with the first 13 markers from the left. Make sure that the following markers are checked Exists and Enable: DYS393, DYS390, DYS19/394, DYS391, DYS385a, DYS395b, DYS426, DYS388,

DYS439, DYS389-1, DYS392, and DYS 389-2. Be sure that DYS19b is not checked. You can leave the rest of the markers checked.

3. **Check the options that provide the appropriate calculation.**

   You are looking only for the TMRCA, so deselect the check boxes next to Ysearch, SMGF, Ybase, Yhrd, and Genetic Distance. Under the General Setup column, deselect the Create Modal Haplotype check box.

4. **Enter the marker values into the Paste Haplotype Rows Here field.**

   Make sure that you separate the values with a space, for example:

   ```
   A  13  25  14  11  11  11  12  12  13  13  13  29
   B  13  25  14  11  11  11  12  12  12  13  13  29
   ```

5. **Click Execute.**

   A new browser window appears with the calculation. In this example, the time to most recent common ancestor between Individuals A and B is estimated at 1,110 years (the box with the TMRCA contains a blue background).

Figure 9-5 shows the estimated TMRCA for Individuals A and B. Essentially, the results show a 50 percent probability that Individuals A and B shared a common ancestor within the past 1,110 years. So, as you can see, just testing on 12 markers doesn't give you conclusive evidence of how closely two people are related. However, it can certainly indicate that two individuals are not related — especially if more than 2 markers out of 12 do not match.

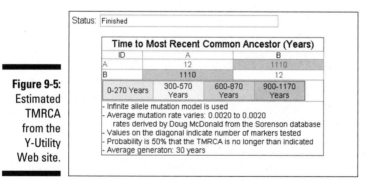

Figure 9-5: Estimated TMRCA from the Y-Utility Web site.

Haplogroups

We mention earlier in this chapter that haplotypes are a set of results of markers for a particular individual. When several similar haplotypes are categorized together, they compose a *haplogroup*. Haplogroups are useful for deep ancestry research (that is, research that is further back than the advent of surnames) and for placing a geographical context around the possible origin of the individuals in the haplogroup.

Y chromosome haplogroups are categorized by the letters A through R by the Y Chromosome Consortium (YCC). (The Y Chromosome Consortium is a group that studies and publishes findings about the Y chromosome. You can find out more about the group at http://ycc.biosci.arizona.edu.) These letter designations are based on mutations of certain locations of the Y chromosome. For instance, if an individual has a mutation at the M89 locus, that individual falls into a haplogroup between F and J. If the individual has a mutation at both the M89 and M170 loci, the individual is classified in the I haplogroup.

When you submit a sample to a DNA testing company, the results you receive usually include your haplogroup. You can then take that haplogroup and go to the National Geographic Genographic Project page to find out more about the origins of the haplogroup. Follow these steps:

1. **Point your Web browser to the National Geographic project site at genographic.nationalgeographic.com/genographic/index. html.**

   At the top of the blue portion of the page are links to the different sections of the site, including About Genographic, Atlas of Human Journey, Globe of Human History, Genetics Overview, Your Genetic Journey, and Project Updates.

2. **Click the Atlas of Human Journey link.**

   This page contains a timeline followed by an introductory paragraph about the atlas. Below the introduction in the black area are two buttons — Genetic Markers and Journey Highlights.

3. **Click Genetic Markers.**

   In the right column is a listing of haplogroups for both mitochondrial and Y chromosome. Scroll down to the Y chromosome area.

4. **Click the Y chromosome haplogroup that interests you.**

   We're interested in Haplogroup I, so we clicked the Y Chromosome Haplogroup I link.

Figure 9-6 shows a map of the migration path of Haplogroup I and some text describing attributes of the haplogroup. The haplogroup migrated from the Middle East into the Balkans and later into Central Europe.

Haplogroups can also be used to show the genetic distribution of individuals in a particular geographic area. For example, Doug McDonald maintains a map of the distribution of haplogroups at www.scs.uiuc.edu/~mcdonald/ WorldHaplogroupsMaps.pdf. So, if you're interested in finding out the distribution of Haplogroup I in Europe, you can match the color (pink) on the pie charts to determine how prevalent the haplogroup is in a particular area. From this chart, you can see that Haplogroup I has a strong concentration in Scandinavia and Northwest Europe. Another Y chromosome haplogroup map is located on the DNA Heritage site at `www.dnaheritage.com/ysnptree.asp`. This map is interactive and allows you to filter the map to show only the haplogroup that interests you. At the top of the map are letters representing the haplogroups. To filter the haplogroups, move your cursor over one of the letters. The map will show the distribution for only that haplogroup. Figure 9-7 shows the map for the distribution of Haplogroup I.

Because haplogroups are large collections of haplotypes, it is useful to break down haplogroups into subgroups that have common traits. These subgroups are referred to as *subclades*. Subclades can help genealogists get a clearer picture of the geographical setting of that portion of the haplogroup.

Although the typical Y chromosome test can suggest a haplogroup, it normally takes additional testing to confirm the haplogroup and a subclade to that haplogroup. In these additional tests, particular positions of the Y chromosome are examined for differences called *single nucleotide polymorphisms (SNPs)*, or "snips." Some SNPs are common and apply to a large population of people within a haplogroup. Other SNPs can be unique to an individual or a family — referred to as private SNPs. New SNPs are constantly being discovered, and that sometimes results in changes to the labels of subclades or the discovery of new subclades. To find the most up-to-date list of subclades, take a look at the International Society of Genetic Genealogy (ISOGG) Y-DNA Haplogroup Tree at `www.isogg.org/tree/Main06.html`.

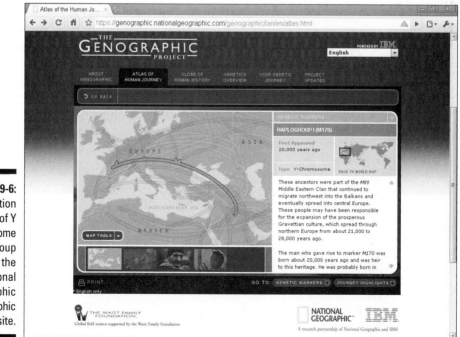

Figure 9-6:
Explanation of Y chromosome Haplogroup I at the National Geographic Genographic Project site.

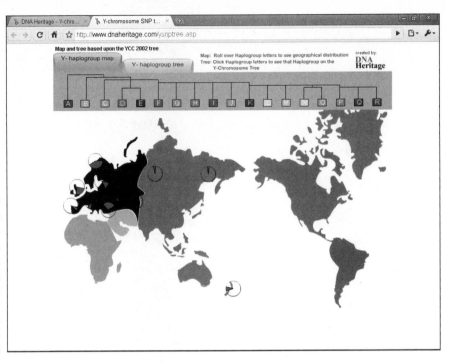

Figure 9-7:
Interactive
haplogroup
distribution
map at DNA
Heritage
filtered for
Haplogroup
I.

To illustrate how subclades work, look at our Haplogroup I example. As you can see from the haplogroup distribution map in Figure 9-6, Haplogroup I has a concentration in Northern Europe and a concentration in the Balkans. If you're in that haplogroup, you might be curious about which region your direct male ancestor came from. To find this out, SNP tests would be conducted on several areas of the Y chromosome, including those called M253, M307, P30, P40, S31, and P37.2. If a mutation is found at locus M253, M307, P30, or P40, the subclade is I1a — a subclade found in southern Norway, southwestern Sweden, and Denmark. If mutations are found at S31 and P37.2, the subclade is I1b1* — found in the western Balkans. Figure 9-8 shows the subclades of Haplogroup I.

After you discover the haplogroup of your results, you can join a Y chromosome project for a particular haplogroup. Through a haplogroup project, you might be able to find out more about the origins of the haplogroup or the subclade within the haplogroup and communicate with others who are studying the same genetic group. To find a project for your haplogroup, see whether your DNA testing company already has a project for it or do a search using a general Internet search engine, such as Google, for something like "Y-DNA Haplogroup I project."

Getting tested

Have you decided it's time to take the plunge and get a Y chromosome test? If you are female (or if you are a male but are not a direct-line descendant from the family for which you want to test), you need to find a male relative that is a direct-line descendant of the family you're researching. Then it's just a matter of selecting a testing company and following its instructions.

A number of testing companies offer Y chromosome testing. Some of these are

- **African Ancestry:** http://africanancestry.com
- **DNA Ancestry:** dna.ancestry.com/learnMorePaternal.aspx
- **DNA Heritage:** www.dnaheritage.com/ystr.asp
- **FamilyTreeDNA:** www.familytreedna.com
- **Genebase:** www.genebase.com
- **Oxford Ancestors:** www.oxfordancestors.com
- **Sorenson Molecular Genealogy Foundation:** www.smgf.org

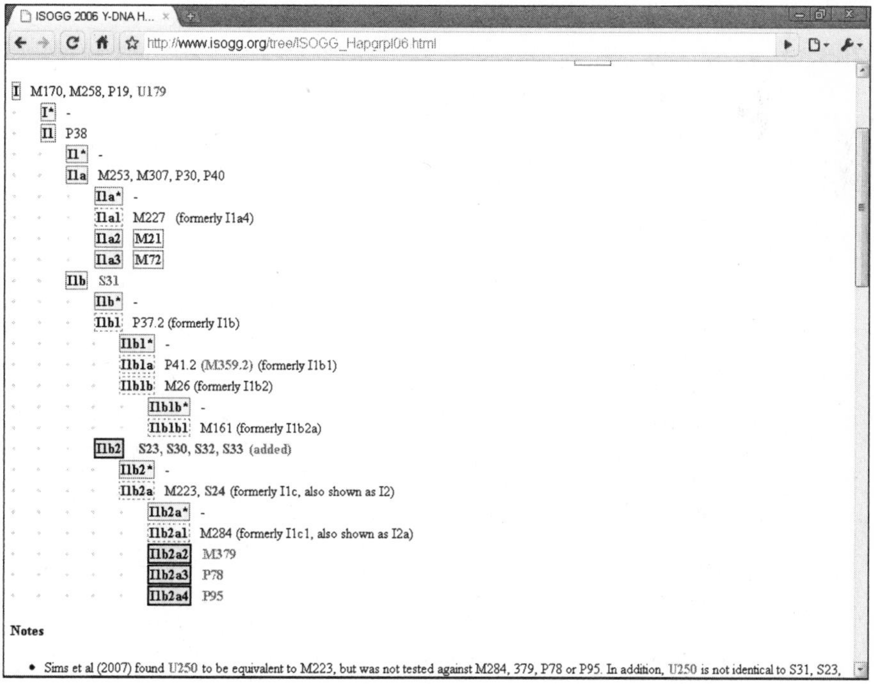

Figure 9-8: The subclades of Haplogroup I from the ISOGG Web site.

Locating others with the same results

Spending the money to perform a Y chromosome test doesn't do you much good unless you have something to compare the results with. To find others who have tested and received results, you should first look for a surname project currently under way for your direct male line. Some of the testing companies have established mechanisms for people to set up the projects that are housed on the testing companies' servers. For example, you can find a list of projects at the FamilyTreeDNA site at www.familytreedna.com/surname.aspx.

Even if you are a member of a surname project, you may want to distribute your results to a wider audience in the hopes of locating others with matching results. Some sites that you can use to "broadcast" your Y chromosome results are

- ✔ **Ybase:** http://ybase.org
- ✔ **Ysearch:** www.ysearch.org

If you don't want your results to be publicly accessible, you can use these sites to search for others with your same haplotype and contact them directly. Say that you want to see whether any matches exist for the surname Abell in Ysearch. Follow these steps:

1. **Open your Web browser and go to www.ysearch.org.**

   At the top of the page are blue tabs with labels such as Create a New User, Edit an Existing User, Alphabetical List of Last Names, Search by Last Name, Search for Genetic Matches, Search by Haplogroup, Research Tools, and Statistics.

2. **Click the Search by Last Name tab.**

   The resulting page contains two ways to search. You can search by entering a surname or by using a user ID. Also, the search can be limited to a specific geographic area.

3. **In the Type Last Names to Search For field, type the surname you're researching, type the two words in the Captcha box, and click Search.**

   Note that you can search for multiple names at the same time using commas to separate them. It is a good idea to do this if the last name has some common derivations. For the purposes of this example, type **Abell, Abel, Able.**

4. **Choose a match by clicking a link in the results table.**

   In our example, the results page shows six results. When we clicked the Abell result, the screen shows us brief information on each name, including an Abell from Maryland in Haplogroup I1.

5. Click the User ID link to see the DNA results for this individual.

Figure 9-9 shows the test results for this individual. You also find a link on the page where you can e-mail the individual who submitted the result to Ysearch.

Although you cannot add your own results to the database, you can search the Sorenson Molecular Genealogy Foundation Y-Chromosome Database at www.smgf.org/pages/sorensondatabase.jspx. The database allows searches by surname or by haplotypes. The results in the database include pedigree charts submitted by the participants of the study. Unfortunately, one limitation of the database is that you don't have a direct way of contacting the participant to share research findings. A few other searchable Y chromosome databases are also available. The Y Chromosome Haplotype Reference Database, at www.yhrd.org, allows you to see the distribution of a particular haplotype. However, it is a scientific database geared toward DNA researchers, so it doesn't contain a lot of information useful to genealogists. Oxford Ancestors also allows its database to be searched, if you log in as a guest. The database is located at www.oxfordancestors.com/content/view/72/105.

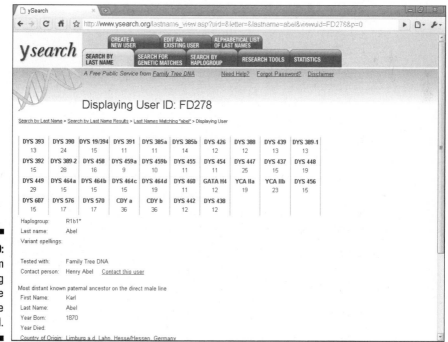

Figure 9-9: Results from Ysearch.org for the surname Abel.

Mitochondrial DNA testing

In the preceding section, we looked at Y chromosome DNA testing that assists in the genetic identification of the direct male line of a family. In this section, we look at mitochondrial DNA testing, which allows the identification of the genetic information of the direct female line of a family.

Remember from the beginning of the chapter that the mitochondrion is the "power plant" of the cell. It's outside the nucleus and has its own distinct genome, called mtDNA, which is inherited from the female parent by both male and female children (see Figure 9-10). Because it also mutates at a very slow rate, the mtDNA is good for identifying genetic relationships over many, many years and generations, as shown in Figure 9-11.

Figure 9-10: Mitochondrial DNA is passed from the mother to her children.

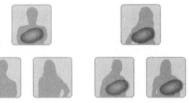

Courtesy of the Sorenson Molecular Genealogy Foundation, the scientific backbone of GeneTree.com

Figure 9-11: The path of the mitochondrial DNA through a family.

Courtesy of the Sorenson Molecular Genealogy Foundation, the scientific backbone of GeneTree.com

Testing method

For testing, mitochondrial DNA is divided into three regions — a coding region, a Hyper Variable Region One (HVR1), and a Hyper Variable Region

Two (HVR2). Genealogical tests are usually conducted on a sequence of Hyper Variable Region One or a sequence of both Hyper Variable Regions One and Two. Some testing facilities fully sequence the entire mitochondrial DNA; however, it is a fairly expensive test. The results from these sequences are compared to a sample known as the Cambridge Reference Sequence (CRS). The CRS is the mitochondrial sequence of the first individual to have her mitochondrial DNA sequenced. The differences between the sample and the CRS are considered mutations for the purposes of assigning a haplogroup to the sample.

How is this accomplished in practical terms? At the beginning of the chapter, we mention that DNA testing was used to identify the remains of the family of the last Czar of Russia. The results of the remains thought to be Czarina Alexandra were compared to Prince Philip and the results matched (Prince Philip and Czarina Alexandra were both descended from Queen Victoria). The results were listed as the following:

```
HVR1: 16111T, 16357C HVR2: 263G, 315.1C
```

Remembering back to when we talked about how DNA is coded (if you can't remember, don't panic — just look at the "Getting down to bases" section, earlier in this chapter), we mentioned that a DNA sequence was comprised of four bases: adenine (A), guanine (G), cytosine (C), and thymine (T). These same bases are used in sequencing mitochondrial DNA.

The first result for Czarina Alexandra was 16111T. This result is interpreted as the substitution of thymine in the location 16111 of the Hyper Variable One region. The second result translates as the substitution of cytosine at location 16357 of the same region. The next result, 263G, shows a substitution of guanine at location 263 in the Hyper Variable Two region. The fourth result is a bit different in that it contains a .1, indicating that an extra base was found at that location. This means that the fourth result shows that an extra cytosine is found at the 315 location in the Hyper Variable Two region. Based on the changes between Czarina Alexandra's sequence and the Cambridge Reference Sequence, her sample was classified in mitochondrial Haplogroup H.

Keep in mind that although they're named in the same manner, Y chromosome haplogroups and mitochondrial haplogroups are two different entities.

Making sense of the results

Mitochondrial DNA changes (or mutates) at a slow rate. This makes its uses for genealogical purposes very different than the uses for Y chromosomes, which change at a faster rate and can link family members together at closer intervals. However, mtDNA is useful for determining long-term relationships, as in the case of the Romanov family.

When two individuals have the same mutations within the Hyper Variable One region, it is considered a *low-resolution match*. If the individuals have a low-resolution match and are classified in the same haplogroup, there is about a 50 percent chance that they shared a common ancestor within the past 52 generations (or about 1,300 years). If they have a low-resolution match and the haplogroups are not the same, it is considered a coincidence, and the probability is that the two individuals did not share a common ancestor within a measurable time frame. Depending on your result set, you might get a lot of low-resolution matches. To see whether a connection really exists, it is useful to test both the Hyper Variable One and Hyper Variable Two regions.

A *high-resolution match* occurs when two individuals match exactly at both Hyper Variable One and Hyper Variable Two regions. Individuals having high-resolution matches are more likely to be related within a genealogically provable time frame. With a high-resolution match, there is about a 50 percent probability of sharing a common ancestor within the past 28 generations (about 700 years).

Testing companies

A lot of the same companies that provide Y chromosome tests also provide mitochondrial DNA tests. In fact, if you are male, you can have the tests performed at the same time on the same sample. Here are some places to consider:

- **African Ancestry:** http://africanancestry.com/matriclan.html
- **DNA Ancestry:** http://dna.ancestry.com/learnMoreMaternal.aspx
- **DNA Heritage:** www.dnaheritage.com/mtdna.asp
- **FamilyTreeDNA:** www.familytreedna.com
- **Genebase:** www.genebase.com
- **Oxford Ancestors:** www.oxfordancestors.com/content/view/35/55
- **Sorenson Molecular Genealogy Foundation:** www.smgf.org

Finding others with the same results

Similar to Y chromosome testing, you might want to post your mitochondrial DNA results to some public databases. One place to post results is mitosearch.org at www.mitosearch.org (see Figure 9-12). If you want to find results of mitochondrial tests performed by the Sorenson Molecular Genealogy Foundation, see the Mitochondrial Database at www.smgf.org/mtdna/search.jspx. To find more information on mitochondrial DNA scientific databases, check out MITOMAP at www.mitomap.org.

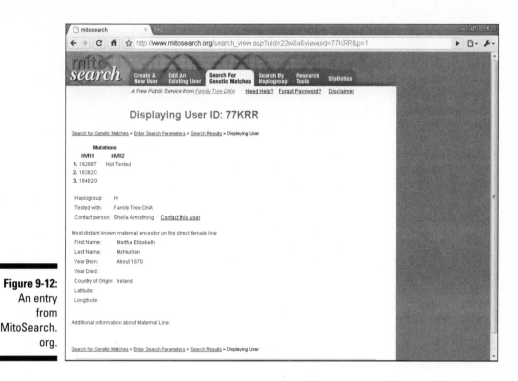

Figure 9-12:
An entry
from
MitoSearch.
org.

Autosomal DNA testing

A set of DNA tests that has received a lot of attention recently are autosomal tests (also known as admixture or biogeographical tests). Earlier in the chapter, we talked about 22 pairs of nonsex chromosomes found in the cell nucleus. These nonsex chromosomes are known as *autosomes*. Autosomes are found in both males and females and are the part of the DNA that is responsible for physical characteristics of an individual, such as height and eye color.

For each pair of autosomes that an individual has, one came from the father and the other from the mother. The process where a parent contributes half of his or her child's DNA, creating a new genetic identity, is called *recombination*. Similarly, each of the individual's parents received a set of autosomes from their parents and so forth through the generations, as shown in Figure 9-13.

Autosomal testing traditionally has been used for paternity testing, in forensic investigations, and to predict percentages of ethnicity for genealogical purposes. But recent work has expanded the use of autosomal testing within genealogy to test for relationships between individuals who have more recent common ancestors.

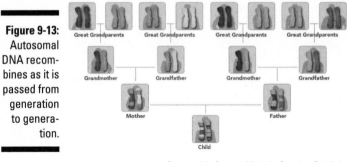

Figure 9-13:
Autosomal
DNA recom-
bines as it is
passed from
generation
to genera-
tion.

*Courtesy of the Sorenson Molecular Genealogy Foundation,
the scientific backbone of GeneTree.com*

Ethnicity testing

When forensic scientists began looking into DNA, they recognized that certain genetic markers were common to particular ethnicities. After enough
markers were identified with ethnicities, they could begin to assess what percentage of ethnicity a particular person might possess. Genealogists picked
up on this and believed that the same types of tests might be able to shed
some light on the ethnicities of their ancestors — especially in the areas of
identifying Native American, Jewish, and African ancestry.

The controversial weakness with autosomal testing is that the DNA in each
individual recombines differently. This means that two children born from
the same two parents could measure with different ethnicities because their
DNA does not recombine exactly the same way. Also, the percentages quoted
by testing companies can often have a significant error rate or change over
time as new research comes to light.

If you take an ethnicity test, you can expect to receive a copy of the
sequences examined and an interpretation of the results. The interpretation
usually comes in the form of a percentage of a certain ethnicity. For example,
you might receive results such as

> European: 92%
>
> Sub-Saharan African: 8%
>
> East Asian: 0%
>
> Indigenous American: 0%

Some companies now offer more in-depth testing of European ethnicities.
Results from these tests might look like the following:

> Southeastern Europe: 73%
>
> Iberian: 0%

Basque: 0%

Continental Europe: 6%

Northeastern Europe: 21%

If you are interested in taking an autosomal test, here are some companies to look at:

- ✔ **AncestrybyDNA:** www.ancestrybydna.com
- ✔ **DNA Tribes:** www.dnatribes.com
- ✔ **23andMe:** www.23andme.com/ancestry/origins

Relationship testing

As we mentioned, Y chromosome testing is useful for tracing the direct male line. Mitochondrial testing is good for tracing a direct female line. What about the people in between? Autosomal testing can be used to provide evidence for relationships between people who may share a recent ancestor, as shown in Figure 9-14.

Figure 9-14: People who are more closely related share more autosomal DNA than those more distantly related.

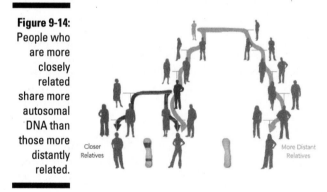

Closer Relatives

More Distant Relatives

Courtesy of the Sorenson Molecular Genealogy Foundation, the scientific backbone of GeneTree.com

How does it work, you ask? Within each generation, the autosomal DNA recombines using half of the DNA from each parent. Over time, the DNA contains more and more changes. By comparing the amount of similar DNA in two autosomal DNA samples, testing companies can suggest how closely two people are related.

For example, FamilyTreeDNA has introduced the Family Finder test. This test can be used to provide evidence on the relationship of two individuals if they are descended from the same great-great grandparent. The results of the test are kept in a database that is constantly searched for matches. According to FamilyTreeDNA, the Family Finder can detect 99 percent of a person's second cousins, 90 percent of third cousins, 50 percent of fourth cousins, and about 10 percent of fifth cousins. Another company that provides autosomal testing and matching of relatives is 23andMe, with its Relative Finder (www.23andme.com/ancestry/relfinder).

Because the recombination of autosomal DNA is random, an autosomal test might fail to recognize cousins. This is because a person does not necessarily inherit exactly 25 percent of his or her DNA from each grandparent. Plus, due to the random inheritance of DNA, nothing guarantees that two cousins would inherit enough of the same DNA to appear as a match.

X chromosome DNA testing

X chromosome testing can fill in some of the gaps between what Y chromosome and mitochondrial testing can show. As we mentioned, females have two X chromosomes and males have one X and one Y chromosome. The mother's X chromosomes act like autosomes in that the two X chromosomes recombine, and one X chromosome is passed from the mother to each child, regardless of sex. The father passes a copy of his X chromosome only to his daughters. Because he only has the one X chromosome, no recombination takes place (see Figure 9-15).

By looking at the X chromosome, relationships can be established for a larger population of individuals that share genetic material than can be traced through Y chromosome or mitochondrial testing (see Figure 9-16).

Figure 9-15:
Mothers pass a recombined X chromosome to their children. Fathers pass a non-recombined X chromosome only to their daughters.

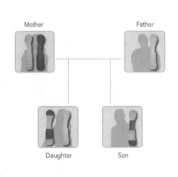

Courtesy of the Sorenson Molecular Genealogy Foundation, the scientific backbone of GeneTree.com

Figure 9-16:
X chromosome testing can link a larger population of individuals than Y chromosome or mitochondrial testing.

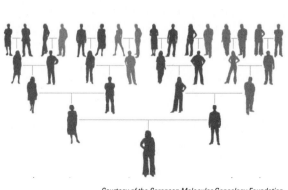

Courtesy of the Sorenson Molecular Genealogy Foundation,
the scientific backbone of GeneTree.com

Finding Helpful DNA Sites

Within this chapter, we were able to cover only the tip of the iceberg in using DNA testing for genealogical purposes. Some Web sites can provide additional information to help you decide whether DNA testing is useful for your research or to keep abreast of the current developments in DNA research.

If you're looking for some basic information on using DNA testing in genealogy, see the International Society of Genetic Genealogy DNA-Newbies page at www. isogg.org or at the Sorenson Molecular Genealogy Foundation's Why Molecular Genealogy page at www.smgf.org/pages/why_genetic_genealogy.jspx. The Sorenson Molecular Genealogy Foundation has some videos on its site that provide a clear and concise explanation of the fundamental concepts of molecular genealogy.

Because DNA testing methods and capabilities change on a frequent basis, it's a good idea to consult some sites that provide updates on the technology and issues related to using the technology. A couple of sites to consult include the Genealogy-DNA mailing list archives at http://lists5.roots web.com/index/other/DNA/GENEALOGY-DNA.html (you can also subscribe to the mailing list from this page) and the Genetic Genealogist blog at www.thegeneticgenealogist.com.

Part IV
Share and Share Alike

The 5th Wave   By Rich Tennant

"Tell the boss the 'Begets' aren't cutting it.
The people are demanding online access."

In this part . . .

Discover how to maximize your online research by effectively using as many resources as possible. This part addresses sharing information with others using reports, GEDCOM files, Web pages that you create yourself, and genealogical networking sites, as well as how to coordinate your research efforts with those of others. Along the way, you also find out a little history about GEDCOM and the best way to respect others' privacy and copyrights.

Chapter 10

Help Wanted!

*Y*ou can think of genealogical research as a journey. You may begin the journey by yourself, but after a while, you discover that the trip would go a lot faster if you have someone along for the ride. In your genealogical journey, these travel partners can take various forms — a single individual researching the same family, a research group searching for several branches of a family in which you're interested, or a genealogical society that coordinates the efforts of many people researching different families.

You may be saying, "A research mate sounds great! But where can I find one of my own?" Lucky you — in the next few pages, we explore just that. We look at ways that you can find (and keep) research partners, as well as ways that research groups and genealogical societies can help you meet your research goals.

Getting Out of Your Comfort Zone

We think it's a natural instinct to want to do all your own research. After all, that way, you have a sense of control over how the research is conducted, whether it's documented correctly, and what piece of information you get next. For you, it may even be comfortable to be alone in your quest. We understand that you may feel this way, but we're here to tell you that it's time to step outside your comfort zone. Although researching alone some of the time is great, don't try to do all the research yourself. As you'll discover, an awful lot of people out there are digging for answers, and it would be a shame for you not to take advantage of the work they have performed and vice versa.

We can't emphasize enough the benefits of sharing genealogical data. Sharing is the foundation on which the genealogical community is built. For example, when Matthew began researching his genealogy, he went to the National Archives, Library of Congress, and several regional libraries and archives. Along the way, he found a few books that made a passing mention of some of his ancestors, and he discovered some original records that helped him put some pieces together. It wasn't until he shared his information online that he began to realize just how many people were working on his surname. During the month following the creation of his Web site, he received messages from 40 other Helm researchers — one of whom lived in Slovenia! Although not all these researchers were working on Matthew's specific branch (only 2 of the 40 were directly related), he received valuable information on some of the areas on which other researchers were working. Matthew may never have known that some of these researchers existed had he not taken the first step to share his information.

By knowing the family lines and regions that other researchers are pursuing, you can coordinate your efforts with theirs — not only sharing information you've already collected but also working together toward your common goal. Maybe you live closer to a courthouse that holds records relating to your ancestor than does a distant cousin with whom you're communicating online. Maybe the cousin lives near a family gravesite that you'd like to have a photo of. Rather than duplicating efforts to collect the court records and photographs, you can make arrangements for each of you to get the desired items that are closest to you and then exchange copies of them over the Internet or through traditional mail.

The Shotgun Approach

You're probably wondering how to find individuals with whom to share your information. Well, you could start by going through telephone books and calling everyone with the surname that you're researching. However, given how some people feel about telemarketers, we don't recommend this as a strategy.

Sending mass e-mails to anyone you find with your surname through one of the online white-pages sites, networking sites, or online social circles is similar to the telemarketing strategy we've just warned you against. We refer to this mass e-mail strategy as the *shotgun approach,* and many people refer to it as spamming. You shoot out a bunch of e-mail messages aimed in various directions, with hopes of successfully hitting one or two targets. Although you may find one or two people who answer you in a positive way, a lot of people may find such unsolicited e-mail irritating. And, quite honestly, gleaning e-mail addresses from online white pages is not as easy as it was even just a few years ago. Most of the online directories that allow you to search for e-mail addresses no longer give the precise address to you. Rather, they either enable you to send an e-mail from their site to the individual, leaving it up to the recipient to respond to you, or they require you to purchase the specific information about the person from them or one of their sponsors. This is their way of protecting that person's online privacy, and for some, it's a means to earn money as well.

Instead of spending hours trying to find e-mail addresses through online directories and following a three- or four-step process to send an initial message to someone, go to a site that focuses on genealogy to find the names of and contact information for researchers who are interested in your surname. This is a much gentler, better way to go about finding others with the same interests as you.

Also, note that we aren't saying that e-mail directories don't have a function in genealogy. E-mail directories can be a good means for getting in contact with a relative whose e-mail address you've lost or one you know is interested in your e-mail.

Making Friends (and Keeping Them) Online

One place to begin looking for others who are doing similar research is the Roots Surname List (`http://rsl.rootsweb.com`), one of the oldest genealogy resources on the Internet. The site, shown in Figure 10-1, consists of a list of individuals, the surnames they're researching, and where on the planet those surnames are found. Other places to find fellow researchers include query pages on the Web, newsgroups, mailing lists, and social networking sites. (We delve into using general networking sites such as Facebook and genealogy-specific networking sites such as Geni.com in Chapter 11.)

After you identify some potential online friends, send them an e-mail message introducing yourself and briefly explaining your purpose for contacting them. Be sure to include a listing of the ancestors you're researching in your e-mail message.

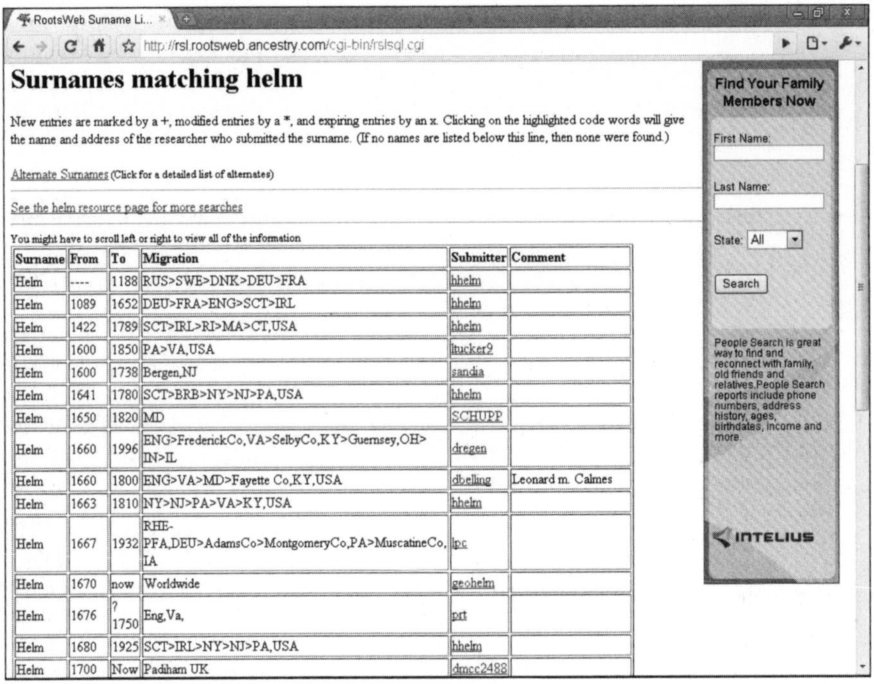
RootsWeb Surname Li...

http://rsl.rootsweb.ancestry.com/cgi-bin/rslsql.cgi

Surnames matching helm

New entries are marked by a +, modified entries by a *, and expiring entries by an x. Clicking on the highlighted code words will give the name and address of the researcher who submitted the surname. (If no names are listed below this line, then none were found.)

Alternate Surnames (Click for a detailed list of alternates)

See the helm resource page for more searches

You might have to scroll left or right to view all of the information

Surname	From	To	Migration	Submitter	Comment
Helm	----	1188	RUS>SWE>DNK>DEU>FRA	hhelm	
Helm	1089	1652	DEU>FRA>ENG>SCT>IRL	hhelm	
Helm	1422	1789	SCT>IRL>RI>MA>CT,USA	hhelm	
Helm	1600	1850	PA>VA,USA	ltucker9	
Helm	1600	1738	Bergen,NJ	sandia	
Helm	1641	1780	SCT>BRB>NY>NJ>PA,USA	hhelm	
Helm	1650	1820	MD	SCHUPP	
Helm	1660	1996	ENG>FrederickCo,VA>SelbyCo,KY>Guernsey,OH>IN>IL	dregen	
Helm	1660	1800	ENG>VA>MD>Fayette Co,KY,USA	dbelling	Leonard m. Calmes
Helm	1663	1810	NY>NJ>PA>VA>KY,USA	hhelm	
Helm	1667	1932	RHE-PFA,DEU>AdamsCo>MontgomeryCo,PA>MuscatineCo,IA	lpc	
Helm	1670	now	Worldwide	geohelm	
Helm	1676	? 1750	Eng,Va,	prt	
Helm	1680	1925	SCT>IRL>NY>NJ>PA,USA	hhelm	
Helm	1700	Now	Padiham UK	dmcc2488	

Figure 10-1: Example of the Roots Surname List for the Helm surname.

Before you rush out and start contacting people, however, we must offer the following sage advice:

- **Before sending messages to a Web site maintainer, look around the site to see whether that person is the appropriate one to approach:** More often than not, the person who maintains a Web site is indeed the one who is researching the surnames you find on that Web site. However, it's not unusual for site maintainers to host information on their sites for other people. If they do, they typically have separate contact addresses for those individuals and an explanation that they're not personally researching those surnames. Some even go so far as to post notices on their sites stating that they don't entertain research questions. So when you see a list of surnames on a site, don't automatically assume that the Web site maintainer is the person to contact. Look around a little to ensure that you're addressing the most appropriate person.
- **Make your messages brief and to the point:** E-mail messages that run five or six pages can overwhelm some people. If the person you send the message to is interested in your information and responds positively to you, you can send one or more detailed messages at a future date.
- **Ensure that your message is detailed enough for the recipients to decide whether your info relates to their research and whether they can help you:** Include names, dates, and places as appropriate.

✔ **Use net etiquette, or *netiquette,* when you create your messages:** Remember, e-mail can be an impersonal medium. Although you may mean one thing, someone who doesn't know you may mistakenly misinterpret your message. (For more on netiquette, see the nearby sidebar "Netiquette: Using your manners online.")

Netiquette: Using your manners online

Part of being a fine, upstanding member of the online genealogy community is communicating effectively and politely on the Internet. Online communication is often hampered by the fact that you can't see the people with whom you're corresponding, and you can't hear the intonation of their voices to determine what emotions they're expressing. To avoid misunderstandings, follow some simple guidelines — called *netiquette* — when writing messages:

✔ Don't send a message that you wouldn't want posted on a bulletin board at work or the library, or that you wouldn't want printed in a newsletter. You should expect that every e-mail you send is potentially public.

✔ Make sure that you don't violate any copyright laws by sending large portions of written works through e-mail. (For more information on copyrights, see Chapter 11.)

✔ If you receive a *flame* (a heated message usually sent to provoke a response), try to ignore it. Usually, no good comes from responding to a flame.

✔ Be careful when you respond to messages. Instead of replying to an individual, you may be replying to an entire group of people. Checking the To: line before you click the Send button is always a good idea.

✔ Use mixed case when you write e-mail messages. USING ALL UPPERCASE LETTERS INDICATES SHOUTING! The exception to this guideline is when you send a query and place your surnames in all-uppercase letters (for example, George HELM).

✔ If you participate in a mailing list or newsgroup and you reply with a message that is most likely of interest to only one person, consider sending that person a message individually rather than e-mailing the list as a whole.

✔ When you're joking, use smileys or type <grins> or <g>, but use these symbols sparingly to increase their effectiveness. A *smiley* is an emoticon that looks like :-). (Turn the book on its right side if you can't see the face.) *Emoticons* are graphics created by combinations of keys to express an emotion in an e-mail. Here are a few emoticons that you may run into:

:-)	Happy, smiling
;-)	Wink, ironic
:->	Sarcastic
8-)	Wearing glasses
:-(	Sad, unhappy
:-<	Disappointed
:-o	Frightened, surprised
:-()	Mustache

✔ **Don't disclose personal information that could violate a person's privacy:** Information such as addresses, birth dates, and Social Security numbers for living persons is considered private and should not be freely shared with other researchers. Also, we don't recommend that you send much personal information about yourself until you know the recipient a lot better. When first introducing yourself, your name and e-mail address should suffice, along with the information about the deceased ancestors you're researching.

✔ **Get permission before forwarding messages from other researchers:** Sometimes researchers may provide information that they do not want made available to the general public. Asking permission before forwarding a message to a third party eliminates any potential problems with violating the trust of your fellow researchers.

Joining a Herd: Research Groups

If your relatives are tired of hearing about your genealogy research trips or the information that you found on Great-uncle Beauford, but you'd like to share your triumphs with someone, you may be ready to join a research group.

Research groups consist of any number of people who coordinate their research and share resources to achieve success. These groups may start conducting research because they share a surname, family branch, or geographic location. Individuals who live geographically close to each other may make up a research group, or the group may consist of people who have never personally met each other but are interested in descendants of one particular person. Research groups may have a variety of goals and may have a formal or an informal structure.

A good example of a research group is one that Matthew discovered shortly after he posted his first Web page many years back. An individual who was researching one of his surnames on the East Coast of the United States contacted him. After exchanging a few e-mails, Matthew discovered that this individual was part of a small research group studying the origins of several different branches of the Helm surname. Each member of the group contributes the results of his or her personal research and provides any information that he or she finds, which may be of use to other members of the group. Over the years, the group has continued to work together and expanded their efforts. The group as a whole has sponsored research by professional genealogists in other countries to discover more about their ancestors there, and they've spun off a more formal research group that focuses solely on molecular research (DNA-based) of the Helm bloodlines. The vast majority of the communication for these two research groups is through e-mail.

You can find an example of an online-based research group at the William Aaron Saunders Research Group site (www.wasrg.org). The mission of this group is to collect and share genealogical data and stories relating to William Aaron Saunders (cir. 1735 VA to cir. 1785 NC). The site is constructed to help Saunders/Sanders researchers collaborate with each other. It has sections containing information about the research group members, family groups, stories, photos, and GEDCOM files. It also has links to other Web sites that have information about some of the same ancestors that are studied through the research group.

To find research groups, your best bet is to visit a comprehensive genealogical Web site or a site that specializes in surnames, such as the GeneaSearch Surname Registry at www.geneasearch.com/surnameregister.htm or SurnameWeb at www.surnameweb.org.

The following steps show you how to find groups pertaining to a surname on the site:

1. **Launch your Web browser and go to the SurnameWeb site at www.surnameweb.org.**

   After the page loads, you see a search field and the letters of the alphabet near the top center of the page.

2. **Click the letter of the alphabet that's the first letter of the surname that you're researching.**

   For example, say that the surname you're researching begins with the letter *P*. Find the link to the letter *P* and click it. This action brings up a Web page with the *P* index.

3. **Click the next level link corresponding to the first and second letter of the surname you are researching.**

   We selected the link labeled Po. You see a list of surname links that begin with the letters *Po*.

4. **Scroll through the list and click a surname link.**

   We want to find sites relating to the surname *Pollard,* so we clicked the link for the Pollard surname, which displayed a Results page entitled Pollard Surname Resource Center.

5. **Choose a site to visit.**

   Scroll down past all the links to search other commercial Web sites until you reach the links you're most interested in. We wanted to see the links that would take us directly to personal and group Web pages containing information about people named Pollard, so we selected the link titled Pollard Genealogy Web Pages under Pollard Surname Search.

In addition to using comprehensive genealogy sites and specialized surname sites, you can use other strategies to identify possible research groups. One way to find research groups pertaining to surnames is to visit a one-name studies index. You can find a list of one-name studies sites at the Guild of One-Name Studies page (www.one-name.org).

If you can't find an established online group that fits your interests, why not start one yourself? If you're interested in researching a particular topic, the chances are good that others out there are interested as well. Maybe the time has come for you to coordinate efforts and begin working with others toward your common research goals. Starting an online research group can be relatively easy — just post a message stating your interest in starting a group at some key locations, such as message boards, newsgroups, or mailing lists.

Becoming a Solid Member of (Genealogical) Society

Genealogical societies can be great places to discover research methods and to coordinate your research. Several types of societies exist. They range from the more traditional geographical or surname-based societies to *cybersocieties* (societies that exist only on the Internet) that are redefining the way people think about genealogical societies.

Geographical societies

Chapter 6 introduces geography-based genealogical societies as groups that can help you discover resources in a particular area in which your ancestors lived, or as groups in your hometown that can help you discover how to research effectively. However, local genealogical societies can provide another service to their members. These societies often coordinate local research efforts of the members in the form of projects. To locate geographical societies, follow our advice in Chapter 6 or check out the site of a genealogical-society federation such as one of these:

✔ Federation of Genealogical Societies, Society Hall page, at www.family history.com/societyhall

✔ Federation of Family History Societies, at www.ffhs.org.uk

These projects can take many forms. For example, the Illinois State Genealogical Society (www.rootsweb.com/~ilsgs) is working on several projects, including creating a database of county marriage records, updating a list of Illinois pioneers, forming a list of all cemeteries in the state (see Figure 10-2), and compiling indices of Civil War, World War I, and World War II certificates issued.

Fayette County   Updated 1/16/2003

NAME	ALIAS	OL	C	R	V	ST	SEC	TOWNSHIP	LOCATION	QTR QTR	QTR SEC
Abel						DE	02	Sharon		NW	SW
Adcock	Causey or Depew or Devore or Donelson			Y	Y	IN	17	Bear Grove		SW	NW
Ambuehl				Y	Y	AC	13	Lone Grove		NE	NE
Amish				Y		IN	17	Sefton		SW	SE
Ammerman				Y	Y	DE	18	Loudon		NW	SW
Antioch			Y	Y	Y	AC	22	Bowling Green		NW	NE
Arm Prairie			Y	Y		AC	35	Otego		SW	SE
Augsburg	Immanuel Lutheran		Y	Y	Y	AC	18	Wilberton		SE	SE
Austin					Y	DE	30	Carson		SW	NW
Bails					Y	DE	?	Bowling Green		?	?
Bear Creek				Y		AC	11	Pope		SE	SE
Beck				Y		IN	28	Ramsey		NE	NE
Beck Private	Snow			Y		IN	24	Bowling Green		SW	SW
Bethlehem	Brushy Point		Y	Y		AC	07	Bear Grove		?	SE
Big Spring					Y	DE	?	Carson		?	?
Biggs	Pratt			Y	Y	AC	21	Pope		SE	SE
Blankenship				Y		AC	15	Carson		?	NW
Boaz				Y		AC	36	Vandalia		NW	NW
Bob Doane				Y	Y	AC	25	Carson		NE	SE
Bolt				Y		AC	25	Ramsey		?	NE
Bolyard				Y		IN	28	Ramsey		SE	NW
Bone				Y		IN	32	Bear Grove		?	SW
Brackenbush				Y		IN	06	Shafter		SW	NE
Britton				Y	Y	IN	02	Kaskaskia		NE	SW

Figure 10-2:
Cemetery
entries for
Fayette
County,
Illinois, on
the ISGS
site.

Smaller groups of members sometimes work on projects in addition to the society's official projects. For example, you may belong to a county genealogical society and decide to join with a few members to write a history of the pioneers who settled a particular township in the county.

Family and surname associations

In addition to geographically based associations, you can find groups tied to particular names or family groups. Typically, they are referred to as — you've probably already guessed — surname or family associations or research groups.

Family associations also frequently sponsor projects that coordinate the efforts of several researchers. These projects may focus on the family or surname in a specific geographic area or point in time, or they may attempt to collect information about every individual possessing the surname throughout time and then place the information in a shared database.

You can find family and surname associations using the methods and Web sites recommended earlier in this chapter for finding research groups. In essence, the two types of organizations are similar — the main difference is whether formal meetings are held.

If a family or surname association isn't currently working on a project that interests you, by all means suggest a project that does interest you (as long as the project is relevant to the association as a whole).

Gathering Kinfolk: Using the Family Reunion for Research

You may have noticed that throughout this book, we strongly recommend that you interview relatives to gather information about your ancestors both to use as leads in finding records and to enhance your genealogy. Well, what better way to gather information from relatives than by attending a family reunion?

Family reunions can add a lot to your research because you find many relatives all in one place and typically most are eager to visit. A reunion is an efficient way to collect stories, photographs, databases (if others in the family research and keep their records in their computers), and even copies of records. You might even find some people interested in researching the family along with you. And a family reunion can be great fun, too.

When you attend your next family reunion, be sure to take along your notebook, list of interview questions (see Chapter 2, if you haven't developed your list yet), and camera. You can take some printed charts from your genealogical database, too — we bet that lots of your relatives will be interested in seeing them.

Rent-a-Researcher

A time may come when you've exhausted all the research avenues directly available to you and need help that family, friends, and society members can't provide. Maybe all the records you need to get past a research "brick wall" are in a distant place, or maybe you have too many other obligations and not enough time to research personally. You needn't fret. Professional researchers are happy to help you.

Professional researchers are people to whom you pay a fee to dig around and find information for you. They can retrieve specific records that you identify, or they can prepare an entire report on a family line using all the resources available. And, as you might expect, the amount that you pay depends on the level of service that you require. Professional researchers are especially helpful when you need records from locations to which you cannot travel conveniently.

When looking for a professional researcher, you want to find someone who is reputable and experienced in the area in which you need help. Here's a list of questions you may want to ask when shopping around for a professional researcher:

- ✔ **Is the researcher certified or accredited and, if so, by what organization?** In the genealogy field, certifications function a bit differently than in other fields. Rather than receiving a certification based on coursework, genealogical certifications are based on demonstrated research skills. You find two main certifying bodies in the field: the Board for Certification of Genealogists (www.bcgcertification.org) and the International Commission for the Accreditation of Professional Genealogists (www.icapgen.org). The Board for Certification of Genealogists (BCG) awards two credentials: Certified Genealogist and Certified Genealogical Lecturer.

  You might also run into some old certifications such as Certified Lineage Specialist (CLS), Certified American Indian Lineage Specialist (CAILS), Certified Genealogical Records Specialist (CGRS), and Certified Genealogical Instructor (CGI), which are no longer used by the organization.

  The credentials are awarded based on a peer-review process — meaning that a group of individuals possessing the credentials evaluate a research project of an applicant. The International Commission for the Accreditation of Professional Genealogists (ICAPGen) awards the Accredited Genealogist (AG) credential. The accreditation program originally was established by the Family History Department of the Church of Jesus Christ of Latter-day Saints. In 2000, the program was launched as an independent organization called ICAPGen. To become accredited, an applicant must submit a research project and take an examination. Accredited Genealogists are certified in a particular geographical or subject-matter area. So, you want to make sure that the accreditation that the researcher possesses matches your research question. Some professional researchers do not hold either of these credentials, but might hold a professional degree such as a Masters in Library and Information Science or advanced history degree from an accredited college or university. Depending on the research area, they could be just as proficient as a credentialed genealogist.

- ✔ **How many years of experience does the researcher have researching?** In general, we tend to think of a person as improving in knowledge and efficiency as he or she has more years of experience researching. But the answer to this question needs to be considered in context of some other questions. The researcher might have only a little time actually researching genealogies for others but might have an educational degree that required historical research experience.

✔ **What is the researcher's educational background?** The methods for researching and the type of reports that you can get from an individual can be directly influenced by his or her educational background. If the researcher has a degree in history, you may get more anecdotal material relating to the times and places in which your ancestor lived. If the researcher attended the school of hard knocks (and doesn't have a formal education per se but lots of experience researching), you may get specific, bare-bones facts about your ancestor.

✔ **Does the researcher have any professional affiliations?** In other words, does he or she belong to any professional genealogical organizations and, if so, which ones? Much like the question dealing with certification or accreditation, a researcher's willingness to belong to a professional organization shows a serious commitment. One particular organization to look for is membership in the Association of Professional Genealogists (www.apgen.org). The APG is an umbrella organization of all types of researchers and those providing professional services. It includes researchers credentialed under both BCG and ICAPGen, as well as other noncredentialed researchers. All members of the APG agree to be bound by a code of ethics and meet particular research standards.

✔ **What foreign languages does the researcher speak fluently?** This is an important question, if you need research conducted in another country. Some research firms send employees to other countries to gather information, but you need the reassurance that the employee has the qualifications necessary to obtain accurate information.

✔ **What records and resources does the researcher have access to?** Again, you want the reassurance that the researcher can obtain accurate information and from reliable sources. You probably don't want to pay a researcher to simply read the same documents that you have access to at your local library and put together a summary.

✔ **What is the professional researcher's experience in the area where you need help?** For example, if you need help interviewing distant relatives in a foreign country, has he or she conducted interviews in the past? Or, if you need records pertaining to a particular ethnic or religious group, does the researcher have experience researching those types of records?

✔ **How does the researcher charge?** You need to know how you're going to be charged — by the record, by the hour, or by the project. And it's helpful to know up front what methods of payment the researcher accepts so that you're prepared when payment time comes. And you should ask what you can do if you're dissatisfied with the researcher's services (although we hope you never need to know this).

✔ **Is the researcher currently working on other projects and, if so, how many and what kinds?** It's perfectly reasonable to ask how much time the researcher can devote to your research project and when you can get results. If the researcher tells you that it's going to take a year to get a copy of a single birth certificate from an agency in the town where he or she lives, you might want to rethink hiring that person.

✔ **Does the researcher have references you can contact?** We think that a researcher's willingness to provide references speaks to his or her ethics. And we recommend that you contact one or two of the references to find out what exactly they like about this researcher and whether they see the researcher as having any pitfalls of which you should be aware.

One way to find professional researchers is to look for them on comprehensive genealogy sites. Another is to consult an online directory of researchers, such as the Association of Professional Genealogists (www.apgen.org/directory/index.html) directory or genealogyPro (http://genealogypro.com).

Follow these steps to check the APG directory:

1. **Using your Web browser, go to the APG site at www.apgen.org.**

2. **Click the link from the list in the left column of the page under the Find a Specialist heading.**

   For example, we looked for a researcher who specializes in adoption.

3. **Click the link for a researcher who, based on the description posted, looks promising.**

   Figure 10-3 shows the researchers specializing in adoption.

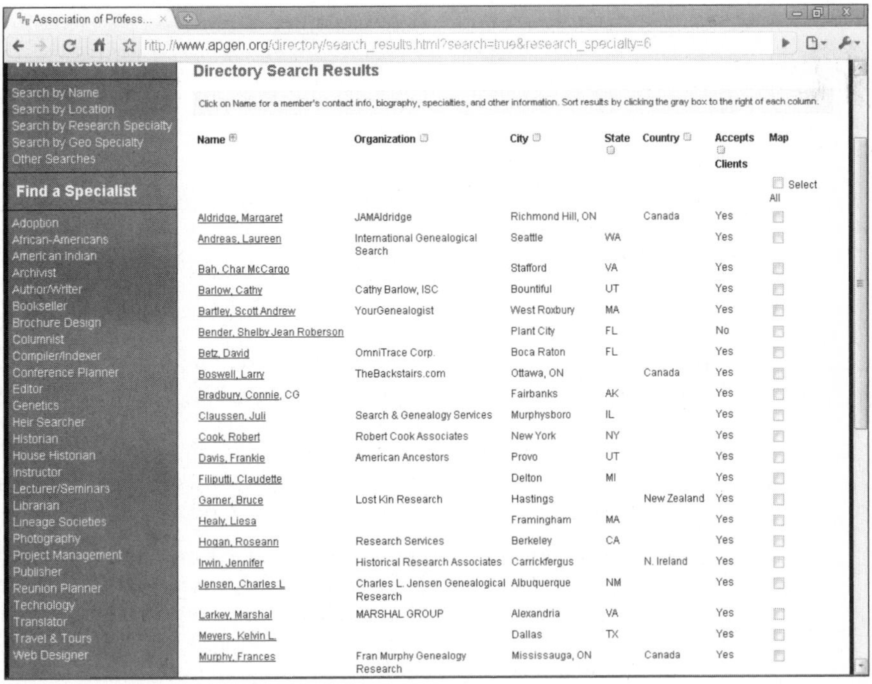

Figure 10-3: Researchers specializing in adoption at the Association of Professional Genealogists site.

When you find a professional researcher, make your initial contact. Be sure to be as specific as possible about your needs. That helps the researcher pinpoint exactly what he or she needs to do, and makes it easier to calculate how much it will cost you.

Chapter 11

Finding Your Online Home and Community

In This Chapter

▶ Helping other researchers

▶ Understanding the importance of sharing

▶ Networking for success

▶ Creating a home page or blog

▶ Using genealogical software utilities

▶ Generating reports

▶ Being a good citizen

You've loaded your genealogical database with information about your relatives and ancestors. Now you may begin feeling that it's time to start sharing the valuable information you discovered — after all, sharing information is one of the foundations of a solid genealogical community. When you share information, you often get a lot of information in return from other researchers. For example, shortly after we began the Helm/Helms Family Research Web page, several other Helm researchers throughout the world contacted us. We discovered that several Helm lines existed that we didn't even know about. Plus, we received valuable information on our own line from references that other researchers discovered during their research, not to mention that we made contact with some really nice folks we probably wouldn't have met otherwise.

You can find many online outlets for sharing information. In the not-so-distant past, our advice was to create from scratch and post your own home page (Web site) where you could open the doors to guests, inviting others to come to you for information and advice. But these days, much easier options exist than mastering HyperText Markup Language (HTML) and other coding programs. Online communities exist where all you have to do is use a template to create a snazzy-looking site. After your site is up and running, you can invite all your family and friends over. You can even make your site available to the general public so that others you don't know who might be researching the same families can find you on the Internet.

In this chapter, we focus on methods you can use to share information and explore networking sites, blogs, and even basic home-grown HTML Web pages (for the die-hard do-it-yourselfers) where you can post your information on the Web. Also we review how to use genealogical utility programs to help put content in specific formats on your site.

Why Would Anyone Want Your Stuff?

Why would anyone want my stuff? seems like a logical first question when you stop and think about making the many tidbits and treasures you collected available to others. Who would want a copy of that old, ratty-looking photograph you have of Great-grandpa as a dirty-faced toddler in what appears to be a dress? Nobody else wanted it in the first place, and that's probably how you ended up with it, right? The picture has sentimental value only to you. Wrong! Some of Great-grandpa's other descendants may be looking for information about him. They, too, would love to see a picture of him when he was a little boy — even better, they'd love to have their own electronic copy of that picture!

As you develop more and more online contact with other genealogists, you may find a lot of people who are interested in exchanging information. Some may be interested in your research findings because you share common ancestors, and others may be interested because they're researching in the same geographical area where your ancestors were from. Aren't these the same reasons that you're interested in seeing other researchers' stuff? Sharing your information is likely to encourage others to share theirs with you. Exchanging information with others may enable you to fill in some gaps in your own research efforts. Even if research findings received from others don't directly answer questions about your ancestors, they may give you clues about where to find more information to fill in the blanks.

Also, just because you haven't traced your genealogy back to the Middle Ages doesn't mean that your information isn't valuable. Although you should not share information on living persons without their explicit permission, you should feel free to share any facts that you do know about deceased ancestors. Just as you may not know your genealogy any further than your great-grandfather, someone else may be in the same boat — and with the same person! Meeting with that fellow researcher can lead to a mutual research relationship that can produce a lot more information in a shorter amount of time.

Share and Share Alike

So you're at the point where you recognize the value in sharing your genealogical information online. How do you begin letting people know what you have? Well, the first thing to do is to come up with a marketing plan for your information — much like a business does when it decides to sell a product.

Masterminding a surname marketing plan

A *surname marketing plan* is simply a checklist of places and people to contact to effectively inform the right individuals about the information that you have to contribute to the genealogy community. As you devise your plan, ask yourself the following questions:

- ✔ **What surname sites are interested in my information?** To find surname sites, see Chapter 4.

- ✔ **What geographical sites are interested in my information?** For geographical sites, see Chapter 6.

- ✔ **What association sites (both family and geographical) are interested in my information?** See Chapters 4 and 6 for association sites.

- ✔ **What general sites (such as query sites and GEDCOM collections) are interested in my information?** See Chapter 4 for some examples of these sites.

You may want to use all available Internet resources to let people know about your information, including your favorite networking site, mailing lists, newsgroups, a blog, and Web sites.

For example, April has information on a McSwain family. She knows that they lived in Madison, Estill, Jessamine, and Nicholas counties in Kentucky. To identify sites where she may be able to post this information, she looked for one-name study pages on the surname McSwain, personal pages that have connections to the McSwain family, and any mailing lists dedicated to discussing the family. She also tried to find sites for each of the four counties in Kentucky that the McSwains resided in. Then she searched for family societies or county genealogical or historical societies in Kentucky that look for information on their past inhabitants. Finally, she looked for general-query sites and GEDCOM repositories (more about GEDCOM later in this chapter) that may accept her information.

Contacting your target audience

After you write down the names and addresses of sites that probably attract an audience that you want to target, you need to notify them. Create a brief but detailed e-mail message to make your announcement. When you submit your message, look at the format required by each resource that you're contacting. Some *query sites* (places where you can post genealogical questions to get help from other researchers) also have specific formats, so you may need to modify your message for each of these sites. (For more information about query sites and posting queries, see Chapter 4.)

Here's a sample message to give you some ideas:

```
MCSWAIN, 1810-1910, KY, USA
I have information on the family of William McSwain of
Kentucky. William was born in 1802, married Elizabeth
Hisle in March 1827, and had the following children:
Thomas, Mary, Joseph, Sarah, Susan, Margaret, Elizabeth,
Nancy, and James.
```

Most people understand that you're willing to share information on the family if you post something to a site, so you probably don't need to say that within your message. Remember, people are more likely to read your message if it has a short-but-descriptive subject line, has text that is brief and to the point, and contains enough information for the readers to determine whether your information can help them (or whether they have information that can assist you).

Perfecting the Art of Networking

If you're an average person who likes to use the Internet to aid in your research but who doesn't have time to learn a whole computer programming language, the past few years have probably been like a dream to you. The growing number of Web sites intended to help people find other people with the same interests, talents, backgrounds, and locations is amazing!

It's hard to turn on the news without hearing some reference to one of these many networking sites — think Facebook and MySpace.com. Facebook (www.facebook.com) touts itself as a social utility meant to connect people with a common strand in their lives, whether that's working together, attending the same school, or living in the same or nearby communities. MySpace.com (www.myspace.com) is an online community where people with similar interests can interact. Although both of these popular networking sites have members with expressed interest in genealogy, we want to introduce you to networking sites with a more targeted focus on genealogy — after all, this is a genealogy-related book.

Like the number of networking sites in general, the number of genealogical-networking sites has grown at an incredible pace over the past couple of years. You might have heard of some of these:

- Geni (www.geni.com)
- Familyrelatives.com (www.familyrelatives.com)
- WeRelate.org (www.werelate.org)
- Famillion (www.famillion.com)
- OneGreatFamily (www.onegreatfamily.com)
- FamilyLink.com (www.familylink.com)

One curious but appropriate thing that we've noticed about the genealogy-based networking sites is that instead of starting a new member's profile with personal information about that member, the profile at many of these sites typically begins with a pedigree chart (also called a family tree). Another neat feature of some of these sites is that they use mathematical algorithms to link your tree(s) with trees that other people have submitted. In essence, this means they are trying to help connect you to others with the same family lines.

If you're looking to set up a genealogy-networking site where others can discover your family lines and contribute information directly to you in a public forum, Geni is one place to start. Here's what to do to get started:

1. **Using your Web browser, go to www.geni.com.**

   The Geni Web site is easy to figure out and has its claim to fame prominently displayed: "The world's largest free family tree."

2. **In the You — Start Here box, begin by clicking the option for your gender.**

3. **In the Your First Name field, enter your first name.**

4. **In the Your Last Name field, enter your last name.**

5. **In the Email field, type your preferred e-mail address.**

6. **Click the Start My Family Tree button.**

And voila! You have officially started your genealogical networking profile. Of course, your profile doesn't have much information of substance yet. It simply has your name, e-mail address, and gender — not enough to let others know who and where you're researching. So, you want to go ahead and enter a little more information:

1. **Starting with the My Tree tab in the Geni profile, click the parent whose information you are ready to add.**

   You can use the instruction dialog box that appears in the lower-center portion of the screen. Simply follow the instructions to add information about your parents. For this example, to enter information about your father, click the blue parental box above your box on the family tree. A dialog box appears where you can enter information.

2. **At the top of the box, select the Divorced check box if your parents are divorced.**

3. **In the First Name field, enter your father's first name.**

4. **If your father's last name is different from the one that automatically populates, fix it in the Last Name field.**

5. **Click the appropriate option to indicate whether your father is living or deceased.**

6. **If you like (and you have your dad's permission), type your father's e-mail address in the Email (Optional) field.**

   The e-mail address will be used to send this person an invitation to join Geni.com. Some relatives may consider these uninvited invitations to be spam, so be careful about entering other people's e-mail addresses at networking Web sites. For more information about protecting your relatives' privacy, be sure to read the section "Earning a Good Citizenship Award," later in this chapter.

7. **Click the More Fields link if you want to add more birth date information about your father, or click Add if you want to add only basic information.**

After you add information about a person using one of the boxes in the family tree, the box becomes activated and little yellow arrows surround it, as shown in Figure 11-1. You can click these arrows to navigate to that person's parents, spouse(s), and children to add more individuals to your tree.

The Geni site is impressive in the ways it helps you share your family tree research with others. Here's a quick overview of the various parts of the site:

- ✔ **Tree:** On this tab, you can view information about the family members included in the tree as a family tree (pedigree chart) or a list. You can navigate in the standard Geni.com format by clicking the yellow arrows and name boxes, or you can search by name in the Go To section.

- ✔ **More:** Several handy functions are accessible on the More menu. If you enter birth dates and anniversaries for your family members, the Calendar gives you a consolidated list that helps you remember special events. The Family Map shows you where your family members currently live and were born, if you include locations in the individualized data you record on the site. And the Discussion section allows you and visitors to your Geni tree to exchange written commentary on any topic you choose.

- ✔ **Profile:** The Profile section is where you can store data specifically about you — everything from your birth date and age, to educational information, to your work experience, to personal narratives about your life, aspirations, and research interests, or whatever you'd like to say about yourself in the free-form text boxes. This is also where you can track who you've invited to view and participate in your Geni tree. The data is sorted into five tabs: Overview, Info, Timeline, Discussions, and Sources. Depending on which setting you choose, various aspects of your profile may or may not be visible.

- ✔ **Photos:** Just as you would expect, the Photos section is where you can upload and sort photos into albums. You find various categories for your photos designated by content, such as whether you're included in the album, whether the photos are specifically of you, or which photos are your favorites.

- ✔ **Inbox:** The Inbox section is much like any other e-mail account. You have separate boxes for mail that has been received, sent, and saved.

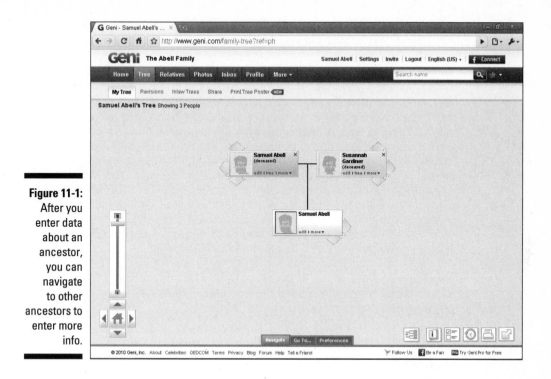

Figure 11-1:
After you enter data about an ancestor, you can navigate to other ancestors to enter more info.

It's worth noting that a few other sites that we would classify as social networking do not quite fit the family tree mold. They are interesting sites that we want to mention because they hold great potential in making your family history research a little more colorful and exciting. They are as follows:

- **Story of My Life (www.storyofmylife.com):** This is an online memoir site. You can record text narratives, videos, pictures, and even entire journals recounting anecdotal stories of your life. It's free to register and use the basic service, but if you want the Story of My Life Foundation to keep your stories forever, you have to pay a fee for Forever space.

- **Second Life (http://secondlife.com/):** Second Life is a three-dimensional (3-D) online world of digital neighborhoods. It is created by the residents and has imagery reflecting their personalities. Although its intent is not solely for genealogy, it does have interesting potential and applicability for genealogists. Imagine creating an environment to resemble your great-grandfather's world in 1850 Virginia. Or presenting an ancestor's experience on an orphan train to the western United States. Or simply a depiction of your family tree in 3-D. You lend your creativity to present your family history in new and exciting ways. The catch — a cost is involved for any services and functionality beyond the free basic membership.

Blogging for Attention

Blog is a common term around the Internet these days. But what exactly is a blog? *Blog* is an abbreviated name for a *Web log,* and it's just what it sounds like: an online journal or log. Typically blogs include narratives on whatever topic the blogger (the person who maintains the blog) feels like writing about. Therefore, genealogy blogs typically contain narratives on family history research. These narratives are much like the Web boards of years past, where people could go and post information about their research findings or needs, and others would post replies. The main difference is that the blogger typically updates the blog on a regular and frequent basis, anywhere from daily to weekly to monthly, and the blogger is the one who initiates the topics of discussion that are welcome on a particular blog. Some blogs even contain photos, video or audio clips, and links to other sites — all depending on the blogger's interests and abilities to include these things.

Blogs are available about all aspects of genealogy, including how-tos, news, ethnic-based research, surnames, conferences, technology, and document preservation.

Hunting blogs

Looking for genealogy blogs to aid in your family history research? A lot are available these days, and the number is growing rapidly. Of course you can find them by using a general Internet search engine such as Google.com. Or, you can use a couple of other simple options for finding blogs. The first is to visit the Genealogy Blog Finder search engine at `http://blogfinder.genealogue.com`. Here's how to use it:

1. **Open your Web browser and go to `http://blogfinder.genealogue.com`, as shown in Figure 11-2.**

2. **In the Search field, enter the name of the family or location you're researching.**

3. **Click Search.**

    You see a list of results with links to each. Click any that interest you.

If you're not sure of a spelling or if you just want to browse to see what's available, you can also use the menu system to navigate the Genealogy Blog Finder. All the topics under which the blogs are organized are accessible from the main Web page.

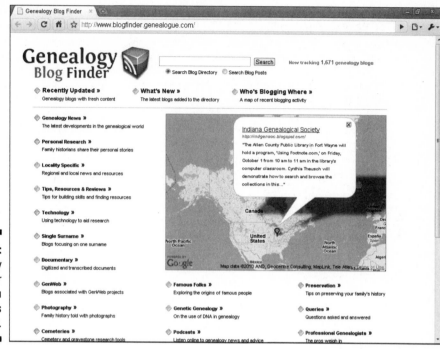

Figure 11-2:
Genealogy
Blog Finder
helps you
locate blogs
of interest.

A second, relatively simple way to find blogs is available. Go to one of the blog-hosting sites that we mention in the next section of this chapter and use the search functionality on the site to see whether any blogs are available through that service that fit your needs. For example, if you're looking for anything available on the Abel family in Fayette County, Illinois, you can search using the terms *Abel* and *Illinois* or *Abel* and *Fayette*. Although this method of searching is not difficult, it can become more time-consuming than the blog-specific search engine route.

Getting a blog of your own

If you're ready to start your own blog where you can share information about your research pursuits and genealogical interests, you have some options available. One is to use the blogging functionality at one of the popular networking sites — check out the section "Perfecting the Art of Networking," earlier in this chapter, for more information. Another option is to use a site specifically designed to host your personal blog. Three that come to mind are

✔ Blogger.com (www.blogger.com)

✔ Blog.com (www.blog.com)

✔ WordPress.com (www.wordpress.com)

Each of these sites offers easy-to-use instructions for creating your blog. You can choose from templates for the overall design at each site and privacy controls so that you can determine who has access to your blog and what levels of permission the user has (whether the user can just read your narratives or post replies, as well as whether he or she can contribute original narratives initiating online discussions). All three also offer the ability to post photos and files.

Here's a walk-through on how to set up your own blog at Blogger.com:

1. **Open your Web browser and go to `www.blogger.com`.**

   This opens the Blogger.com site. The site has several areas, including an online tour, a sign-in area for returning bloggers, and step-by-step instructions for creating a blog.

2. **Click the Create a Blog button.**

   This brings you to Step 1 in the Blogger process, which is to create a Google account. If you already have a Google account, it offers you the opportunity to log in using your existing account instead of creating a new one.

3. **In the Email Address field, type your current or preferred e-mail address.**

4. **In the Retype Email Address field, type the same e-mail address again.**

5. **Complete the Enter a Password field, typing a password that is at least eight characters long.**

   Remember that when setting up a password, you want to choose a combination of letters, numbers, or characters that won't be easy for others to decipher. We recommend that you do not use your pet's name or your mother's maiden name. Instead, it's better if you choose something that is not common knowledge about you — such as the name of your favorite book character with your favorite number on the end or a special text character such as $, #, or %. Click the Password Strength link, if you want Blogger.com-specific information about selecting a password. Blogger.com provides some excellent hints on making your password as safe as possible.

6. **In the Retype Password field, provide the same password again.**

7. **In the Display Name field, choose the name you want to show to others on the blog.**

   This is where you select an alias if you don't want your real name posted on the blog. You might choose to use just your first name, just your last name, or a nickname, or to select some new and random name that is catchy and fun.

8. **In the Birthday field, enter your date of birth.**

9. **In the Word Verification box, retype the word that you see above the field.**

   The letters and numbers are usually presented in a wavy, distorted way.

10. **Click the Terms of Service and read through them. If you agree to Blogger.com's terms, select the I Accept the Terms of Service check box. Then Click Continue.**

11. **In the Blog Title field, enter a name for your blog.**

12. **In the Blog Address (URL) field, type part of a Web address for your blog.**

   When choosing what to use for the section of the Web address that you get to designate, think about using something that fits with the title of your blog. For example, if your blog will be called Gerty's Genealogical Adventures, you might try using GenAdventure or GGAdventure in the URL.

   You see a Check Availability link below the blog address field; here you can see whether your preferred URL is already taken. If you click the Check Availability link and find that your choice is already taken, Blogger.com proposes some similar alternatives that are still available. You can choose to use one of the alternatives or start from scratch.

13. **In the Word Verification box, retype the combination of letters and numbers that you see above the field. Then Click Continue.**

   The letters and numbers usually appear wavy and distorted. After you click Continue, the next part of Step 2 appears; here you select the template to use in designing the look of your blog.

14. **Scroll through the list of templates, and select the one that you like best.**

   If you want to see the template a little bigger and better, click the Preview Template link below the template.

15. **Click Continue.**

   Congratulations! You've just created your blog. You get a message confirming that you have completed the blog-creation process, and you are now ready to begin posting to your blog.

16. **Click Start Posting Now to continue and begin adding content to your blog.**

   The next screen that opens has four tabs (Posting, Settings, Design, and Monetize) and a View Blog link. You need to navigate through this part of the site, providing the specific information that you want to include on your blog. Each of the tabs has several subtabs where you can control various aspects of your blog. The site is easy to use and intuitive by simply clicking through the tabs and subtabs. Here's a high-level description of what you can do in each tab:

- **Posting:** Compose narratives including research findings, your personal thoughts on how to research in certain areas, your opinions about new methods for researching, or recent findings on celebrity ancestries — pretty much whatever you think others would be interested in reading about you and your genealogy. Just keep in mind that if you make your blog available to anyone and everyone, you may get good and bad responses to your thoughts and opinions.

- **Settings:** Provide a description of your blog's intent, determine whether your blog is listed for public consumption, and choose some other editing settings, as well as set your preferences for archiving and e-mail, and assign permissions to others for using your blog. This is also where you can go if you decide to delete your blog — removing it permanently.

- **Design:** Edit the look of your blog, including the layout, colors, and fonts, or custom-write HTML or change templates.

- **Monetize:** Set up your blog to run advertisements and potentially bring in a little money if your viewers click the ads.

After you have your first blog set up, you're ready to start posting information about your genealogical insights and discoveries.

Building Your Own Home

When we wrote the first couple of editions of *Genealogy Online For Dummies,* the Web was a very different place. Networking sites and blogs were not commonplace. Back then, we were quick to recommend designing your own home page (or Web site, if you will) from scratch. These days, we recommend coding your own site in HTML (HyperText Markup Language) only if you are a die-hard fan of creating things personally.

If you are that type of person, but you're not sufficiently versed in coding HTML, we recommend that you tackle one or both of the following books before venturing into the world of Web-page design: *HTML, XHTML & CSS For Dummies,* 7th Edition, by Ed Tittel and Jeff Noble and *Building a Web Site For Dummies,* 4th Edition, by David A. Crowder (both published by Wiley).

Before you can build anything, you need to find a home (that is, a *host*) for it. Although you can design a basic home page on your own computer using no more than a word processor, others won't be able to see it until you put the page on a Web server on the Internet. A *Web server* is a computer that's connected directly to the Internet that serves Web pages when you request them using your computer's Web browser.

Commercial Internet service providers

If you subscribe to a commercial *Internet service provider (ISP)* such as AT&T, MSN, or Comcast, or if you subscribe to a local provider, you may already have a home for your Web pages. Some commercial ISPs include a specific space allocation for user home pages in their memberships, as well as some tools to help you build your site. Check your membership agreement to see whether you have space. Then you can follow the ISP's instructions for creating your Web site (using the service's page builder or editor) or for getting the home page that you've designed independently from your computer to the ISP's server. (If you didn't keep a copy of your membership agreement, don't fret! Most ISPs have an informational Web page that you can get to from your ISP's main page; the informational page reviews membership benefits.) You may as well take advantage of this service if you're already paying for it.

If your particular membership level doesn't include Web space, but the ISP has other membership levels that do, hold off on bumping up your membership level. You can take advantage of some free Web-hosting services that may save you money. Keep reading.

Free Web-hosting services

Some Web sites give you free space for your home page, provided that you agree to their rules and restrictions. We can safely bet that you won't have any problems using one of these freebies, because the terms (such as no pornography, nudity, or explicit language allowed) are genealogist-friendly.

If you decide to take advantage of Web space, remember that the companies that provide the space must pay their bills. They often make space available free to individuals by charging advertisers for banners and other advertisements. In such cases, the Web host reserves the right to require that you leave these advertisements on your home page. If you don't like the idea of an advertisement on your home page, or if you have strong objections to one of the companies being advertised on the site that gives you free space, you should find a fee-based Web space for your home page.

Here are a few free Web-hosting services that have been around for a while:

- ✔ Google sites (`www.google.com/sites`)
- ✔ Tripod (`www.tripod.lycos.com`)
- ✔ RootsWeb.com (`http://accounts.rootsweb.com/index.cgi?op=show&page=freagree.htm`)

Do you speak HTML?

HyperText Markup Language (or HTML) is the language of the Web. HTML is a code in which text documents are written so that Web browsers can read and interpret those documents, converting them into graphical images and text that you can see with a browser. HTML is a relatively easy language to learn, and many genealogists who post Web pages are self-taught. If you prefer not to read about it and teach yourself by experimenting instead, you can surely find classes as well as other resources in your area that could teach you the basics of HTML. Check with a local community college for structured classes, local genealogical societies for any workshops focusing on designing and posting Web pages, or the Web itself for online courses. Or, check out *HTML, XHTML & CSS For Dummies,* 7th Edition, by Ed Tittel and Jeff Noble.

Deciding which treasures to include

Although the content of genealogical Web pages with lots of textual information about ancestors or geographic areas may be very helpful, all-text pages won't attract the attention of your visitors. Even we get tired of sorting through and reading endless narratives on Web sites. We like to see things that personalize a Web site and are fun to look at. Graphics, icons, and photographs are ideal for this purpose. A couple of nice-looking, strategically placed photos of ancestors make a site feel more like a home.

If you have some photographs that have been scanned and saved as `.jpg` or `.gif` images or some media clips (such as video or audio files) that are in a format that meets the compatibility requirements for your Web-hosting service, you can post them on your Web site.

Just as you should be careful about posting factual information about living relatives, be careful about posting photos or recordings of them. If you want to use an image that has living relatives in it, get their permission before doing so. Some people are sensitive about having their pictures posted on the Web. Also, use common sense and good taste in selecting pictures for your page. Although a photo of little Susie at age 3 wearing a lampshade and dancing around in a tutu may be cute, a photo of Uncle Ed at age 63 doing the same thing may not be so endearing!

Including Your GEDCOM

Suppose that you contact others who are interested in your research findings. What's the best way to share your information with them? Certainly, you can type everything, print it, and send it to them. Or, you can export a copy of your genealogy database file — which the recipients can then import into their databases and create as many reports as they want — and save a tree in the process.

Most genealogical databases subscribe to a common standard for exporting their information called *GEenealogical Data COMmunication,* or *GEDCOM.* (Beware that some genealogical databases deviate from the standard a little — making things somewhat confusing.)

A *GEDCOM file* is a text file that contains your genealogical information with a set of tags that tells the genealogical database that is importing the information where to place it within its structure. For a little history and more information about GEDCOM, see Chapter 3. (Flip ahead to Figure 11-3 to see an example of a GEDCOM file.)

You may be asking, "Why is GEDCOM important?" It can save you time and energy in the process of sharing information. The next time someone asks you to send your data, you can export your genealogy data into a GEDCOM file and send it to him or her instead of typing it or saving a copy of your entire database.

Privatizing your database before sharing

If you plan to share the contents of your genealogical database online by generating and exporting a GEDCOM file, make sure that your file is ready to share with others. By this, we mean be sure that it's free from any information that could land you in the doghouse with any of your relatives — close or distant!

Some genealogical software programs enable you to indicate whether you want information on each relative included in reports and GEDCOM files. Other programs don't allow you to do this. This may mean that you need to manually scrub your GEDCOM file to remove information about all living persons.

After you have a GEDCOM file that is free of information about all living persons, you're ready to prepare it for the Web. You can choose from several programs to help you convert your GEDCOM file to HTML. GED2HTML may be the most commonly known GEDCOM-to-HTML converter available, and it's available for downloading at `www.starkeffect.com/ged2html`. Here's how to use it with your cleaned GEDCOM file:

1. **Open the GED2HTML program that you downloaded from `www.starkeffect.com/ged2html`.**

   A dialog box asks you to enter the location of your GEDCOM file. (You can browse if you can't remember the path for the GEDCOM file.)

2. **Type the path for your GEDCOM file, and then click Go.**

   A typical path looks like this: `c:\my documents\helm.ged`. GED2HTML runs a program using your GEDCOM file. You can watch it going through the file in a black window that appears.

3. **After the program is finished, press Enter to close the program window.**

   GED2HTML saves the output HTML files in a folder (appropriately called `HTML`) in the same directory where the GED2HTML program is saved.

4. **Use your Web browser to open any of the HTML output files.**

   After seeing what your output looks like and reviewing it to make sure that it doesn't contain any information that shouldn't be posted, you're ready to add it to your Web site (or link to it as its own Web page).

5. **Follow any instructions from your Web host, and upload your GED2HTML files to your Web server. Put any links to those files on your home page so that you can share your GEDCOM information online.**

   For example, suppose that GED2HTML saved an HTML-coded index of all the people in your GEDCOM file to a file called `persons.html`. After uploading or copying this file to your Web host's server, you can use a link command such as `<A HREF = "[directory path]/persons.html">` from your main home page to this index of persons to share it on the Web.

Generating GEDCOM files

Making a GEDCOM file using most software programs is quite easy. This is true for RootsMagic Essentials, too. If you have not yet downloaded and installed RootsMagic Essentials, flip back to Chapter 3. After you have the program ready to go, try this:

1. **Open RootsMagic Essentials.**

   Usually, you can open your software by double-clicking the icon for that program or by choosing Start➪Programs (or Start➪All Programs) and selecting the particular program.

2. **Use the default database that appears, or choose File➪Open to open another database.**

3. **After you open the database for which you want to create a GEDCOM file, choose File➪Export.**

   The GEDCOM Export dialog box appears.

4. **Choose whether you want to include everyone in your database in your GEDCOM file or only selected people. You can also choose the output format and what types of information to include. Then click OK.**

   If you choose to include only selected people in your GEDCOM file, you need to complete another dialog box marking those people to include. Highlight the individual's name and then select Mark People⇨Person to include him or her. After you select all the people you want to include, click OK.

5. **In the File Name field, type the new name for your GEDCOM file and then click Save.**

   Your GEDCOM file is created.

After a GEDCOM file is created on your hard drive, you can open it in a word processor (such as WordPad or Notepad) and review it to ensure that the information is formatted the way you want it. See Figure 11-3 for an example. Also, reviewing the file in a word processor is a good idea so that you can be sure that you included no information on living persons. After you're satisfied with the file, you can cut and paste it into an e-mail message or send it as an attachment using your e-mail program.

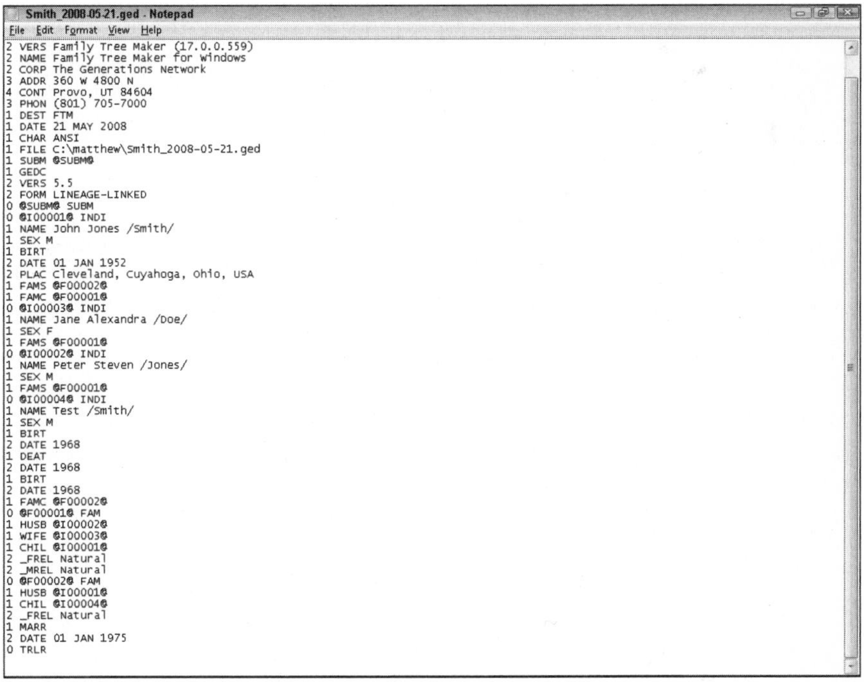

Figure 11-3: An example of a GEDCOM file opened in WordPad.

XML: GEDCOM's successor?

Although GEDCOM was designed to help researchers exchange information with each other using various genealogical software programs, it isn't necessarily the best way to present information on the Web. Over the past several years, people have tried to create a better way to display and identify genealogical information on the Web. Eventually, these efforts could produce the successor to GEDCOM.

One of the possible successors to GEDCOM is *eXtensible Markup Language,* more commonly recognized by the acronym *XML.* XML is similar to HyperText Markup Language (HTML) in that it uses tags to describe information. However, the purpose of XML is different than that of HTML. HTML was designed to tell a Web browser, such as Firefox or Internet Explorer, how to arrange text and graphics on a page. XML is designed not only to display information but also to describe the information. An early version of XML for the genealogical community was *GedML,* developed by Michael Kay. GedML uses XML tags to describe genealogical data on the Web, much like GEDCOM does for genealogical software. Here's an example of information provided in a GEDCOM file and its GedML equivalent:

GEDCOM:

```
0 @I0904@ INDI
1 NAME Samuel Clayton /
   ABELL/
1 SEX M
```

```
1 BIRT
2 DATE 16 Mar 1844
2 PLAC Nelson County, KY
1 FAMS @F0397@
```

GedML:

```
<INDI ID="I0904">
<NAME> Samuel Clayton
   <S>ABELL</S></NAME>
<SEX>M</SEX>
<EVEN EV='BIRT'>
<DATE>16 Mar 1844</DATE>
<PLAC> Nelson County, KY</
   PLAC> </EVEN>
<FAMS REF="F397"/>
</INDI>
```

XML, whether it's GedML or some other XML structure, promises an enhancement of the searchability of genealogical documents on the Web. Right now, it's difficult for genealogically focused search engines to identify what's genealogical in nature and what's not (for more on genealogically focused search engines, see Chapter 4). Also, tags allow search engines to determine whether a particular data element is a name or a place. XML also provides an efficient way to link genealogical data between Web sites, gives users more control over how particular text is displayed (such as notes), and allows genealogists to place information directly on the Web without using a program to convert databases or GEDCOM files to HTML. For more information on GedML, see http://users.breathe.com/mhkay/gedml.

Reporting Your Results

The purpose of finding an online community is to share information on ancestors or on geographical areas about which you have researched. It's hard to write and rewrite every detail in an e-mail message or online post. And while GEDCOM is a great option when two individuals have genealogical software that supports the standard, what about all those people who are new to genealogy and haven't invested in software yet? How do you send them information that they can use? One option is to generate reports through your genealogical software, export them into your word processor, and then print copies to mail (or attach copies of the word processing file to e-mail messages).

The process for generating a family tree or report should be similar for most genealogical software. Because we've explained in earlier parts of this book how to download and install RootsMagic Essentials, that's the software we use to demonstrate the process of creating reports. If you've not yet installed it or entered or imported some data into it, you might want to check out Chapter 3. It gives step-by-step instructions for entering all your detailed family information into RootsMagic Essentials.

Before you can generate a report, you have to find the person who will be the focus of that report. Here's a quick refresher on how to get to the appropriate person's record:

1. **Open RootsMagic Essentials and select the family file for which you want to generate a chart or report by highlighting the filename and clicking Open.**

   Usually, you can open your software by double-clicking the icon for that program or by choosing Start⇨Programs (or Start⇨All Programs) and selecting the particular program.

2. **Highlight the name of the person who will serve as the focus for your report.**

   On the Pedigree tab, highlight the name of the focal person of the family you select. For example, if Matthew wants to generate a report for his ancestor Samuel Clayton Abell, he highlights the Samuel Abell file.

3. **On the Reports menu, select a chart or report.**

   Some report types are not available in the RootsMagic Essentials version. You have to purchase the full product to generate them.

4. **Select the content to include in the report.**

   You can choose whether to generate the report on the current family or only selected people. You can also choose what information to include (such as spouses and children, photos, and notes) in the output. And you can manipulate some formatting options, such as layout, title, fonts, and sources.

5. **Click Generate Reports.**

   RootsMagic Essentials generates the report and displays it on your screen.

Earning a Good Citizenship Award

To be a good genealogical citizen, you should keep a few things in mind, such as maintaining privacy, respecting copyrights, and including adequate citations. In this section, we discuss these key topics.

Mandatory lecture on privacy

Sometimes, we genealogists get so caught up in dealing with the records of deceased persons that we forget one basic fact: Much of the information we've collected and put in our databases pertains to living individuals and thus is considered private. In our haste to share our information with others online, we often create our GEDCOM files and reports, and then ship them off to recipients without thinking twice about whether we may offend someone or invade his or her privacy by including personal information. The same thing goes for posting information directly to Web sites and in our blogs — we sometimes write the data into the family tree or include anecdotal information in our blog narratives without thinking about the consequences to living individuals. We need to be more careful.

Why worry about privacy? Ah, allow us to enlighten you. . . .

✔ **You may invade someone's right to privacy.** We've heard horror stories about Social Security numbers of living individuals ending up in GEDCOM files that are available on the Internet. We've also heard of people who didn't know that their biological parents weren't married (to each other, anyway) and found out through an online database. Your relatives may not want you to share personal information about them with others, and they may not have given you permission to do so. The same is true for photos and video clips. Just because you're gung ho to show the world the group photo from your family reunion does not mean that every one of your parents, siblings, aunts, uncles, and cousins feels the same way. So don't share the information or the image without the permission of everyone involved.

✔ **Genealogists aren't the only people who visit genealogical Internet sites.** Private detectives and other people who search for information on living persons frequently use genealogical databases to track people. They are known to lurk about, watching for information that may help their cases. Estranged spouses may visit sites looking for a way to track down their former partners. Also, people with less-than-honorable intentions may visit a genealogical Web site looking for potential scam or abuse victims. And some information, such as your mother's maiden name, may help the unscrupulous carry out fraud. For these reasons, it is illegal in some states and countries to share information about living persons on the Internet without first getting each person's written permission.

When sharing genealogical information, your safest bet is to clean out (exclude) any information on living individuals from your GEDCOM file or report when sharing it with others and include only the data that pertains to people who have long been deceased — unless you've obtained written consent from living persons to share information about them. By *long been deceased,* we mean deceased for more than ten years — although the time frame could be longer depending on the sensitivity of the information. You may also want to keep in mind that the U.S. Government standard dictates that no record covered under the Privacy Act is released until it's at least 72 years old.

Respecting copyrights

Copyright is the controlling right that a person or corporation owns over the duplication and distribution of a work that the person or corporation created. Although facts themselves can't be copyrighted, *works in which facts are contained* can be. Although the fact that your grandma was born on January 1, 1900, can't be copyrighted by anyone, a report that contains this information and was created by Aunt Velma may be. If you intend to include a significant portion of Aunt Velma's report in your own document, you need to secure permission from her to use the information.

With regard to copyright and the Internet, remember that just because you found some information on a Web site (or other Internet resource) does not mean that it's not copyrighted. If the Web site contains original material along with facts, it is copyrighted to the person who created it — regardless of whether the site has a copyright notice on it!

To protect yourself from infringing on someone's copyright and possibly ending up in a legal battle, you should do the following:

- ✔ Never copy another person's Web page, e-mail, blog, or other Internet creation (such as graphics) without his or her written consent.

- ✔ Never print an article, a story, a report, or other material to share with your family, friends, genealogical or historical society, class, or anyone else without the creator's written consent.

- ✔ Always assume that a resource is copyrighted.

- ✔ Always cite sources of the information in your genealogy and on your Web pages. (See the next section in this chapter for more information.)

- ✔ Always *link* to other Web pages rather than copying their content on your own Web site.

If you don't understand what copyright is or if you have questions about it, be sure to check out the U.S. Copyright Office's Home Page at www.copy right.gov. Two U.S. Copyright Office pages of particular interest at the site are Copyright Basics and Frequently Asked Questions (FAQs).

Citing your sources

We can't stress enough the importance of citing your sources when sharing information — online or through traditional means. Be sure to include references that reflect where you obtained your information; that's just as important when you share your information as it is when you research it. Not only does referencing provide the other person with leads to possible additional information, but it also gives you a place to return and double-check your facts if someone challenges them. Sometimes, after exchanging information with another researcher, you both notice that you have conflicting data about a particular ancestor. Knowing where to turn to double-check the facts (and, with any luck, find out who has the correct information) can save you time and embarrassment.

Here are some examples of ways to cite online sources of information:

- **E-mail messages:** Matthew Helm, [<ezgenealogy@aol.com> or 111 Main Street, Anyplace, Anystate 11111]. "Looking for George Helm," Message to April Helm, 12 October 2009. [Message cites vital records in Helm's possession.]

- **Newsgroups:** Matthew Helm, [<ezgenealogy@aol.com> or 111 Main Street, Anyplace, Anystate 11111]. "Computing in Genealogy" in soc. genealogy.computing, 05 June 2006.

- **Web sites:** Matthew Helm, [<ezgenealogy@aol.com> or 111 Main Street, Anyplace, Anystate 11111]. "Helm's Genealogy Toolbox." <genealogy. tbox.com> January 2004. [This site contains numerous links to other genealogical resources on the Internet. On July 12, 2010, located and checked links on Abell family; found two that were promising.]

  With a note like the preceding one in brackets, you expect that your next two citations are the two Web sites that looked promising. For each site, you should provide notes stating exactly what you did or did not find.

Although most genealogical software programs now enable you to store source information and citations along with your data, many still don't export the source information automatically. For that reason, double-check any reports or GEDCOM files you generate to see whether your source information is included before sharing them with other researchers. If the information isn't included, create a new GEDCOM file that includes sources.

Part V
The Large Genealogical Sites

The 5th Wave   By Rich Tennant

"That's strange — according to your birth certificate I got from Tommy's genealogy project, you're not the Queen of the Universe and Master of All Men."

In this part . . .

The chapters here focus on two of the largest online resources for family history research: Ancestry.com and FamilySearch.org. Both sites offer substantial collections of transcribed records and digitized images that can help in your genealogical research. Many of the resources at Ancestry.com are subscription based, whereas resources maintained by FamilySearch.org are free.

Chapter 12

Discovering Ancestry.com

Ancestry.com is probably one of the most recognized genealogical Web sites today. It's been around a while and has a substantial presence not only in the field of family history but also in mainstream media. It boasts the world's largest online collection of family trees and family history documents. One visit to the Web site shows you that Ancestry.com does, indeed, have a very large collection of digitized and transcribed record sets. What you may not realize upon first glance is that the site is also a great source of educational information and a networking site for family researchers. In this chapter, we take a closer look at what the site has to offer.

Touring Ancestry.com

You find a lot to see and use at Ancestry.com. Although the navigation tools are easy to use, a new user might be overwhelmed by the plethora of record sets. Additionally, it's not always clear which resources are available for free. But don't worry. We walk you through how to use Ancestry.com and determine what is available to help you on this resourceful site.

Climbing family trees in Ancestry.com

Ancestry.com offers the ability to enter your family tree information online. Then you can share with others as well as benefit from the many family trees that other people have uploaded and made available for your researching pleasure.

Start My Tree

The minute you arrive on the Ancestry.com home page (`www.ancestry.com`), you can jump right in and start creating your online family tree, as shown in Figure 12-1. The Start My Tree section, at the top of the page, enables you to add your information to the Ancestry.com collection of family trees so that you can connect with other, possibly related, researchers. Additionally, it's a mechanism for searching the site.

Figure 12-1:
Click the Start My Tree button to start sharing your family tree.

The best way to see how the Start My Tree section works is to use it. Follow these steps:

1. **Click the Start My Tree button.**

2. **Click the Add Yourself field.**

   The Add Yourself window pops up.

3. **Complete the Add Yourself area, providing your first and middle name, your last name, your gender, your birth date, and the place where you were born.**

   Remember to use your maiden name if you're female.

4. **Click Continue.**

5. **Click the field for your father, enter his information in the Add Father window, and click Save.**

   Upon saving your dad's information, the Save and Build Your Free Family Tree window appears. This window allows you to set the permissions for who can see your Ancestry.com family tree.

6. **In the Tree Name field, enter a name for your family tree.**

   The field contains a default name, such as Sanders Family Tree. If you want a different, more specific name, you need to overwrite the default value. For example, you might want to name this tree with both of your parents' surnames (Sanders and Cook Family Tree), or you might want to give it your full name because you are the starting point for the tree.

7. **If you don't want your name as entered in the tree provided, change the First Name and Last Name fields.**

   Your name as you entered it into the tree defaults into these fields. If you prefer to use a nickname or if you're entering the tree starting with an ancestor's name instead of your own, you may want to update these fields.

8. **In the Email Address field, provide your e-mail address.**

9. **Decide whether others are allowed to view your family tree.**

   If you want other Ancestry.com users to be able to see your family tree and contact you, select the box marked Allow Others to See My Tree as a Public Member Tree. If you are simply using this family tree information to search the Ancestry.com site and do not want to be contacted by others, deselect the box. Note that Ancestry.com follows privacy guidelines that do not make information about any living person available for viewing. This means that only entries who have death dates are displayed in the Ancestry.com family trees.

   Before you commit one way or the other to sharing your family tree, we recommend that you read through Ancestry.com's privacy policy. You can access it through the link on the right side of the Save and Build Your Free Family Tree box — it's next to the little padlock icon that says We Value Your Privacy.

10. **Click the Save My Tree button.**

    You are assigned a free Ancestry.com account, and the resulting page gives you a username and password. It also displays a larger view of your family tree, where you can continue completing fields for your other relatives, such as mother and grandparents. You can also navigate to see this family tree information in different layouts, such as a Family Group Sheet or a list of people in your tree. (For an explanation of a Family Group Sheet, flip to the glossary or refer to Chapter 2.)

After you create your family tree, Ancestry.com starts comparing your information to tons of data in its system. It looks for anything in its collection that might pertain to you and the ancestors about whom you provided information. This includes comparing your data to other family trees, as well as the indexes to records that Ancestry.com has. If it finds something that it thinks is a match, it will put a little green leaf (also known as a hint) in the upper-right corner of the box containing your ancestor's name. Click the leaf to see more information about the potential match.

Clicking the leaf to see a potential match does not necessarily mean that you'll get to see the actual record. In many cases, the records are part of Ancestry. com's subscription service, and you can't view the record without subscribing. The good news is that Ancestry.com offers a 14-day free trial of its subscription sections of the site. For more information about the free 14-day trial, check out the section "Examining the free resources," later in this chapter.

In addition to seeing your family history research online in the form of a tree, you can use the Ancestry.com family tree program to store more than just names, dates, and locations that you typically see on a pedigree chart (for descriptions of various charts, check out the glossary or Chapter 2). By selecting an individual from the list of people in the tree, you can add and view more detailed information, including facts and sources, notes, and contact information, and you can add media such as photos, videos, or audio clips, as shown in Figure 12-2. You can also view timelines. And you can add other family members related to this person directly from this view. As a bonus, if you use an iPhone, you can access your family tree information on the road through the Tree to Go application.

Growing different kinds of trees

When you set up a new tree, you can indicate whether you want the tree to be visible to the general public at Ancestry.com or restricted to only you. (You can change your mind at any time. Just click the Tree Settings link at the top of your tree and then click Privacy Settings to update who has access.) If you restrict your tree(s), the information is marked as a Private Member Tree — it is still indexed and can be searched, but others can't see the data without your permission. If you don't restrict access, your tree becomes available through the Public Member Trees, or Ancestry World Tree. Using the Family Trees or Search tabs, you can access different trees.

Private Member Trees

The Private Member Trees section of the Ancestry forest contains family trees in a special permissions zone. The trees are restricted in terms of who can see and add to them. You can choose to restrict your tree to only family members or other researchers that you identify. Likewise, if you have a relative who uses Ancestry.com, he or she might choose to allow you access to his or her tree without making the tree available to the general public. When you have access to a Private Member Tree, you get to the tree through the Private Member Tree link in the Family Trees tab.

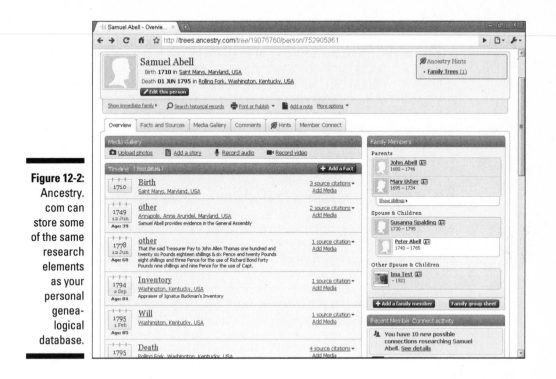

Figure 12-2:
Ancestry.
com can
store some
of the same
research
elements
as your
personal
genea-
logical
database.

Even though your Private Member Tree is restricted to you (the tree creator/ owner) and people that you authorize to access it, the data in your tree is indexed and can still be searched by other site users. If a search identifies a potential match to another user who is not allowed access to your Private Member Tree, that user is given a link to contact you. You'll get an e-mail through Ancestry.com and then have the opportunity to respond and share information if you choose to do so.

Public Member Trees

The Public Member Trees section allows you to search for matches in and view any tree that has been designated as public access. Select Public Member Trees from the Search tab to use the search form. From the Public Member Trees page, you can also access other card catalogs of family trees that are open to everyone: Ancestry World Tree and OneWorldTree.

The Ancestry World Tree is the collection of family trees that you and other users have submitted. It uses trees like the one you created earlier in this chapter and contains around 400 million names.

Ancestry.com's OneWorldTree is a project with the goal of linking everyone in the world through their family trees. Using algorithms to evaluate the family tree(s) that you enter at Ancestry.com, the site tries to make connections

between families and link the trees. It uses names, dates, and locations to identify potential matches among family trees. It's a creative way to give researchers
leads of where to look for records and to make contact with other researchers.

Although OneWorldTree can provide leads and potential links between families, we always strongly recommend that you follow up by finding primary
sources to substantiate these leads before you make the final claim that two
families are related by a single link. For a quick refresher on the importance of
using primary sources, peek at Chapter 1.

Searching Ancestry.com's vast collection

In addition to using your family tree on Ancestry.com as a basis for searching
for information and records (see the previous section for more information
about using Ancestry.com family trees), you can search for pertinent records
in the collection in two other ways.

The first way to search is to scroll down to the middle of the Ancestry.
com home page until you see the Search the World's Largest Online Family
History Collection section. You can complete the Search for an Ancestor box
and then click the Search button to run a standard search of the site. Even
if you know only a name and a possible location, this search function can
be useful. For example, April ran a quick search using the first name Foster,
the last name McSwain, and a death location of Oklahoma to see whether
Ancestry.com had anything on one of her great-grandfathers. Sure enough,
the search yielded four exact matches and more than 89,000 potential
matches or leads. We might add that the first few potential matches were
relatives of the Foster McSwain she was looking for.

The second way to search is to use the drop-down Search menu at the top of
the Ancestry.com home page. Clicking the Search drop-down menu enables
you to select which types of records you're looking for. Your options are
Search All Records; Census and Voter Lists; Birth, Marriage, and Death;
Public Member Trees; Military; Immigration and Travel; and Card Catalog.

To search for a particular type of record, follow these steps:

1. **Click the Search menu in the toolbar at the top of the Ancestry.com
   home page and select Birth, Marriage, and Death.**

   The Birth, Marriage, and Death Search page opens.

2. **Enter your search criteria in the form.**

   The criteria that you can use for this search includes First and Middle
   Names, Last Name, Birth information (date and location), Lived In
   (Residence) location, Death information (date and location), information

about family members (relationships and names), Marriage information (date and location), a More field (where you can enter keywords to use in the search), and Gender.

For our example search, April is looking for birth information about her great-grandfather, William Henry Reese. On the search form, she enters **William Henry** for First and Middle Names, **Reese** for Last Name, **Texas** for Lived In (Residence) and Death location (because she's heard from family members that he died in Texas), and **Male** for Gender.

3. **Click the Search button.**

   The search ends on the results page, with more than 400,000 potential matches among all the birth, marriage, and death records in Ancestry.com's holdings. We clicked the Narrow by Category link for only Birth, Baptism, and Christening records to reduce the number of results. We can then scroll through the list and select the results that look promising. When searching like this, you might need to return to relatives or notes to see whether you can further limit your search results by using a city or county name for any of the locations or approximate dates for the life events.

Taking your Ancestry.com tree to go

If you're an iPhone user, you can use a handy little application to see your Ancestry family tree on the go. The app is called Tree to Go, and it accesses your Ancestry.com account and downloads the data in your family tree.

You can scroll through the list of people in your family tree in a list format and view the specific data for an individual in a form that looks a lot like a family group sheet. The individual form includes standard data: full name, birth information (date and location), death information (date and location), and names of parents, spouse(s), and children. Each family member name in the individual form links to the individual form for that relative.

The downloaded family tree includes photos, information about specific events, and notes. In addition, you can edit the entry and add to the tree. You can update information about any specific ancestor who is in the file: Upload photos or take new photos with your iPhone to attach to the family tree file; add information about spouses, parents, and children to an existing entry; and add new individuals to the application.

Any data you add to Tree to Go on the road automatically uploads to your account on Ancestry.com so that you have an almost-immediate backup of newly acquired research findings when traveling.

Browsing the collection

Everywhere you look on Ancestry.com, you can find links to collections of records and information by category or topic. If you scroll down to the bottom of the main home page, you find the Explore Centuries of Resources section. This section is a basic overview list with links to examples of the record sets that fit in the particular category. The category choices are as follows:

- ✔ Census Records & Voter Lists
- ✔ Immigration & Emigration Records
- ✔ Family Trees
- ✔ Newspapers & Periodicals
- ✔ Court, Land, Wills & Financial Records
- ✔ Maps, Atlases & Gazetteers
- ✔ Birth, Marriage & Death Records
- ✔ Military Records
- ✔ Photos and Images
- ✔ Directories & Member Lists
- ✔ Stories, Memories & Histories

In addition to the links to the example record sets, each category has a link to see all the records for that specific area. Clicking that link takes you to a page where you can search the entire categorical collection for records of interest. The search page also identifies Featured Data Collections, which have recently been updated or which are free for a limited time. (For more information about how to access the free indexes or records, check out the next section.)

Examining the free resources

Ancestry.com is a subscription site and uses the revenues generated through subscriptions to increase its collection of genealogically focused databases of records and indexes. However, the site makes some of its databases in each of the categories identified in the preceding section available to use for free. Often these are new record sets that the site is introducing or indexes that have been updated recently. They are called Featured Data Collections.

The catch to accessing these free Featured Data Collections is that you are still required to have an Ancestry.com account. You can set up a free account when you create an Ancestry.com family tree (see the "Start My Tree" section, earlier in this chapter, for more information). In addition to allowing you access to the featured, free databases, a free account enables you to maintain and share your family tree online, upload photos and documents to support your family tree, and allow relatives to access your tree too.

Another option for viewing Ancestry.com resources for free is to sign up for a 14-day free trial. This gives you an account through which you can access not only the Featured Data Collections but also all the record sets and collaboration tools for either the United States or the World collection. The catch to the 14-day free trial is that you are required to provide credit card information and, if you do not contact Ancestry.com before the expiration of the free trial period, you will be charged for the regular subscription at the end of the 14 days.

Considering a subscription

Ancestry.com offers various subscriptions. Currently, it has annual and monthly subscriptions, and you can choose to have access to only records for the United States or access to records from all over the world. To find out more about the subscription options, click the Subscribe button in the upper-right corner of the Ancestry.com pages.

The subscription information includes prices and lengths of service. A handy chart is available so that you can easily compare what you get for the three levels: the free guest account, the United States record set, and the World record set.

Collaborating

If you're reading through this chapter section by section, you've already discovered that one of the main ways that you can collaborate with others on Ancestry.com is to create and share your family tree(s). But this is not the only way that you can make connections with other users and contribute to the overall site. Other sections of Ancestry.com encourage cooperation in the genealogical community. You can find these resources under the Collaborate link on the menu bar. They are as follows:

✔ **Recent Member Connect Activity:** This notification tells you what other members with similar interests have done lately. You set the Recent Activity filters to limit what you want to see in terms of activity and then let the Ancestry.com site go to work. Say that another user accesses a record that you've recently used or that someone makes a family tree connection to one of your trees. Ancestry.com notifies you so that you can get in touch with that person, should you choose to do so.

✔ **Message Boards:** The Ancestry.com message boards are like a great big bulletin board where people post notes about their research and others can post responses. More than 17 million posts are currently on more than 161,000 boards. Because these numbers can be a little daunting, you can use a search engine to do the looking for you. (For more information about message boards in general, flip to Chapter 4.)

✔ **Ancestry World Archives Project:** This project is a worldwide endeavor in which people all over transcribe and contribute indexes for record sets that Ancestry.com digitizes and posts online. The user-contributed indexes are available for free.

✔ **Member Directory:** Looking for other Ancestry.com members with interests similar to your own? You can search for them in the Member Directory section and make contact with them directly or though Ancestry.com.

✔ **Public Profile:** The last option under Collaborate is really more about you. This is your public profile — how others see your information when searching for friends through Ancestry.com. Use this option to specify certain interests and identify families that you are researching so that others can adequately find you through one of the search mechanisms.

Finding other services at Ancestry.com

Ancestry.com is a company of many services. In addition to offering the online databases and helping people make connections through research, it offers other fee-based services that you might find interesting or useful.

Linking to others through DNA testing

Ancestry.com offers three types of DNA testing: a paternal lineage DNA test (also called a Y chromosome test), a maternal lineage DNA test (also called an mtDNA test), and a paternal and maternal lineage DNA test. To get a better understanding of DNA testing and how it helps with genealogical research, turn to Chapter 9. To find out more about Ancestry.com's DNA tests and the cost, check out `http://dna.ancestry.com/buyKitGoals.aspx`.

Publishing your memoirs

If you want to publish your genealogical findings or if you want to create a keepsake book for the grandkids, be sure to check out the Publish section of Ancestry.com. In addition to books, the section offers calendars and posters. The site offers help in the form of online samples and tutorials.

Browsing the AncestryStore

Just as it sounds, the AncestryStore is an online retail establishment associated with Ancestry.com. It offers all sorts of genealogical books and software. You also find historical maps — international, military, and United States.

Looking to hire an expert

If you're at a point in your research that you need some professional help —
we mean professional help of the research variety, not therapy — you might
be happy to know that Ancestry.com offers to help you connect with an expert.
The experts are identified in six areas: custom research, record lookup, language translation, ask an expert, record pickup, and local photo. If you're thinking about hiring a researcher, review Chapter 10 for additional advice.

Peeking at the Learning Center

The Learning Center at Ancestry.com has an assortment of online tutorials
and articles to help researchers do all sorts of things. You find instructions
on how to use different parts of Ancestry.com (such as building an online
tree), as well as blank forms and charts that you can download. Also you can
find an Ancestry blog, a FAQ section, and a Wiki, where users can contribute
helpful advice.

RootsWeb.com at a Glance

RootsWeb.com is a well-established online community for genealogists. It's
been around for a long time and has gone through various renditions. Several
years ago, it became part of the Ancestry.com family and has remained
closely associated with Ancestry. Whereas Ancestry.com relies heavily on
subscriptions to keep its collection growing, RootsWeb.com relies heavily on
the generosity of its users to give their time, energy, and personal resources
to make genealogical data available for free for all to use.

Users can contribute to RootsWeb.com by submitting transcriptions of books
and records, sharing their family trees in the WorldConnect Project (a database of family trees that now has more than 575 million names in it), participating in the RootsWeb Surname List, or RSL (a registry of surnames being
researched worldwide and how to contact those researching the names),
and posting messages and responses to the message boards and mailing lists
hosted by RootsWeb.com. RootsWeb.com also offers Web hosting, where you
can build your own genealogy Web site.

To experience RootsWeb.com, point your browser to `www.rootsweb.`
`ancestry.com`. The directory on the home page gives you a quick and
comprehensive look at what RootsWeb.com has to offer, as shown in Figure
12-3. Click any of the links to discover how you can contribute to the various
RootsWeb.com projects.

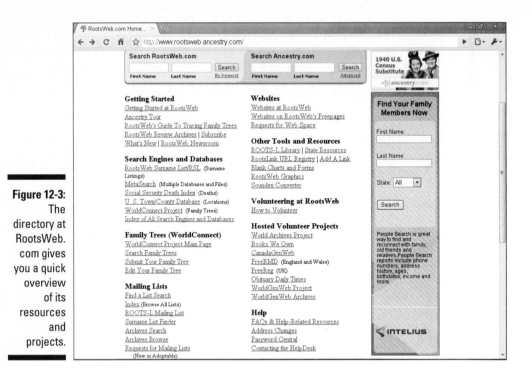

Figure 12-3:
The directory at RootsWeb.com gives you a quick overview of its resources and projects.

Ancestry.com outside the United States

When you first access Ancestry.com, the example databases that are listed and some of the other resources on the site may be configured for United States researchers. However, don't be misled. Ancestry.com has an excellent selection of resources for researchers with interests outside the United States.

The fastest way to find international collections at Ancestry.com is to go to the bottom of the Ancestry.com home page, at www.ancestry.com, and look for the little drop-down box at the lower right. Initially, the box says Ancestry.com. If you click the drop-down arrows, you can select a link for an international version of the Web site. The countries represented are United States, United Kingdom, Canada (English), Canada (Français), Australia, Deutschland, Italia, France, Sverige, and China.

If you want to quickly see all of Ancestry.com's data holdings for one of the countries for which it has a site, you can select the Card Catalog under the Search menu. For example, Figure 12-4 shows the Card Catalog for the Ancestry.de Web site with resources pertaining to Germany. You see the entire collection, including the title of the database, the category of the collection in which the record set belongs, and the number of records in the database.

Searching on the international versions of Ancestry.com works the same way as searching in the United States version of the site. So if you need a refresher on how basic navigation of Ancestry.com works, you can flip back through parts of this chapter that cover searching and entering your family tree.

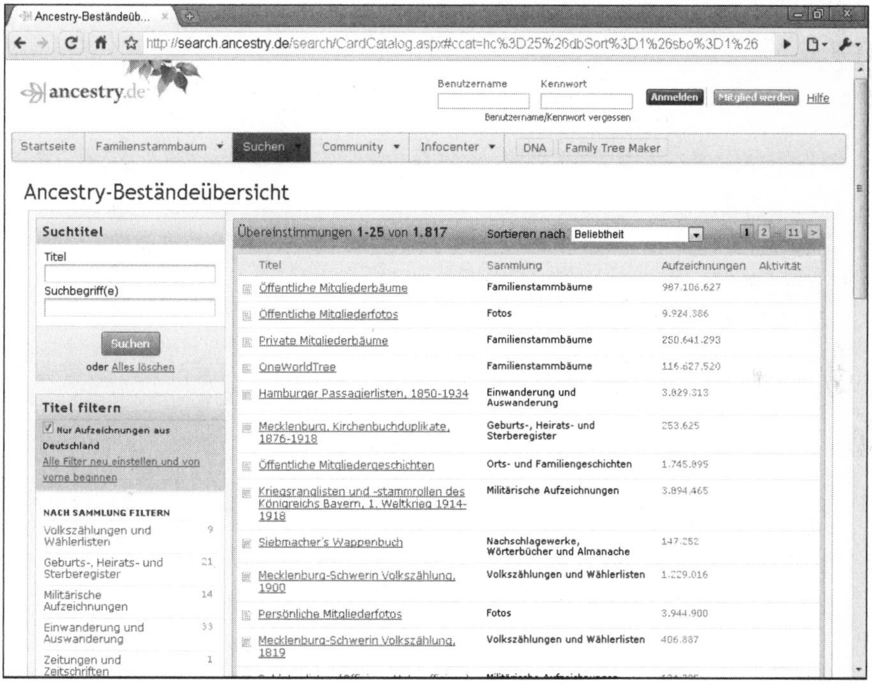

Figure 12-4:
The
Ancestry.de
card
catalog.

Chapter 13

Exploring FamilySearch

In This Chapter

▶ Searching for index entries and records

▶ Finding out more about the libraries and centers

▶ Anticipating changes to the site

*F*amilySearch is a service of the Church of Jesus Christ of Latter-day Saints and is intended to help people discover more about their family history, as well as to connect with other researchers and family members. The online component of FamilySearch, located at www.FamilySearch.org, is open to everyone regardless of religious affiliation. The records are also available through the more than 4,600 Family History Centers in 132 countries, which are also open to the public.

As we are writing this edition of *Genealogy Online For Dummies,* the FamilySearch.org site is preparing to undergo major changes. According to the FamilySearch Public Affairs department, the site will have an all-new look and feel, as well as enhanced functionality. The new FamilySearch.org is in a beta testing phase, so we will provide information on both the current FamilySearch.org as well as the new and improved site based on what we've seen through the beta testing.

Introducing the Current FamilySearch.org

FamilySearch.org is an easy-to-navigate site that offers lots of leads to genealogists. You can search a collection of indexes of family history data, access online classes, read up on what's new at FamilySearch, and download Personal Ancestral File (PAF), which is a free genealogical program. The following sections take a closer look at the databases and image collections available at FamilySearch.org.

Searching in the indexes

When you visit FamilySearch.org, the first thing you probably notice is the search form. This search identifies entries in the FamilySearch collection of birth, marriage, death, census, church, and other indexes that match your search criteria.

The search identifies potential matches in the following indexes:

- **International Genealogical Index (IGI):** A list of births and marriages of deceased individuals reflected in records collected by the Church of Jesus Christ of Latter-day Saints.

- **Ancestral File:** A database created and maintained by the Church of Jesus Christ of Latter-day Saints with millions of names available in family group sheets and pedigree charts.

- **Military Index:** A list of those killed in the Korean and Vietnam Wars.

- **Social Security Death Index (SSDI):** An index of those persons for whom Social Security death claims were filed with the United States government.

- **Pedigree Resource File:** Index of user-contributed family trees.

- **Vital Records Index:** Index of birth, marriage, and death records.

- **U.S. Census Records:** These are indexes of the various U.S. censuses that are available to the public. For more information about census records, review Chapter 5.

- **Family History Library Catalog:** This entry is just what it sounds like — the library card catalog for the Church of Jesus Christ of Latter-day Saints Family History Library.

Here's how you search in FamilySearch.org:

1. **In the Search Records for Your Ancestors section, enter your search criteria.**

   Include as much information as you can. The fields you can complete are First and Middle Names, Last Name, Life Event, Year, Year Range, Country or Region, and State.

   For our example search, April is looking for any information about her great-grandfather, Foster McSwain. In the search form, she enters Foster in the First and Middle Names field (using only the one name because she doesn't know Foster's middle name), McSwain for Last Name, United States for the Country or Region, and Oklahoma for the State.

2. **Click the Search button.**

   The results page is sorted by the index in which the record was found, and the overall results are numbered so that you can easily scroll through and see what's available. If a link looks promising, click it to see more information about the file, including where to find it on microfilm. If an online image is available that matches the record, you'll find another link that you can follow. Note, though, that sometimes the image is available from a fee-based or subscription site. Oftentimes, the results have simply the index information, so you have to use the data as a lead for where to look for the original record.

Using the Record Search Pilot

The regular search function at FamilySearch.org helps you locate entries about your ancestors in indexes. But your goal is to find actual records for your relatives that can prove their life events and show that they truly lived at a particular place at a certain time. Another search section at FamilySearch.org does just this. Choosing Record Search Pilot from the Search Records menu at the top of the site takes you to the Discover Your Ancestors search form. The results from this search include the name of the potential match, the type of record or index, the events recorded and the location, the names of the spouse and children if any exist, and the names of the parents if applicable. If a digital image of the record is available online, a link to the image is also included, as shown in Figure 13-1.

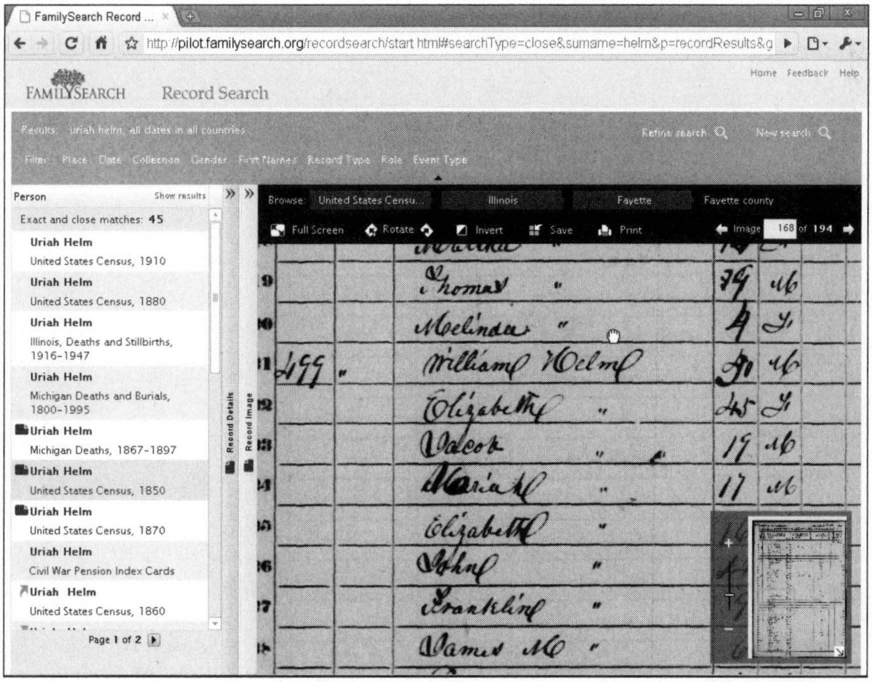

Figure 13-1:
You can access digital images through the results page.

Examining other resources

FamilySearch.org provides more than just indexes and records. The site also has informational and educational resources to help you in your research.

Catching up on FamilySearch news

You find a section on the FamilySearch.org home page that contains articles and press releases pertaining to FamilySearch. You can read here to see what's coming and when, in terms of improvements to the site. You can also find general articles about records resources.

Learning from online classes and resources

Looking for more help in determining how and where to research? Look no further. The FamilySearch.org site has online classes that are offered for free. You find many useful topics, from geographical-based researching (such as newspaper research in the United States and researching Polish people who were displaced), to a beginner's series of courses, to general how-to classes (such as how to read handwritten records or how to use research logs). Additionally, the site has information on upcoming workshops and special events.

Downloading Personal Ancestral File and forms

Personal Ancestral File (PAF) is a free genealogical database that you can download from FamilySearch.org. It enables you to enter and maintain data on your ancestors that you collect in your genealogical pursuits. For more information about how a genealogical database works, check out Chapter 3. If you want to produce colorful charts using your genealogical data in PAF, you can also find a companion program to download at FamilySearch.org.

Sharing your genealogical data

You can register with FamilySearch.org and share your genealogical database contents to be part of the Pedigree Resource File. You should follow the instructions on the Web site. FamilySearch.org discusses getting permission from living relatives and cleaning up the data to protect privacy, and then saving the file in the GEDCOM format. For more information about generating GEDCOM files from your personal database, flip to Chapter 3. After you share your file, it will be added to the Pedigree Resource File, where others can search and access the data. Additionally, copies of the Pedigree Resource File are archived in special vaults in Utah for long-term preservation.

Peeking at the new and improved FamilySearch.org

In the not-too-distant future, you can expect to see some changes at the FamilySeach.org site. It will look a little different, and some of its functionality will be improved. Eventually, you will see the new functionality at the `www.FamilySearch.org` Web address. But until beta testing is complete and the site is fully up and running, you can sneak a peek at `https://beta.familysearch.org/`, shown in Figure 13-2.

Searching at FamilySearch.org will be the most changed item. You'll be able to restrict your search by category (Historical Records, Trees, Library Catalog, or All Collections), and the criteria you can use will vary slightly with each category. Other parts of the site will be modified a bit. For example, the Learn section will undergo changes that enable you to search for online courses, research aids, and other educational resources, as well as collaborate online with other researchers. FamilySearch.org will also offer a Research Wiki. And finally, you'll be able to log in to all parts of the site with a single sign-on.

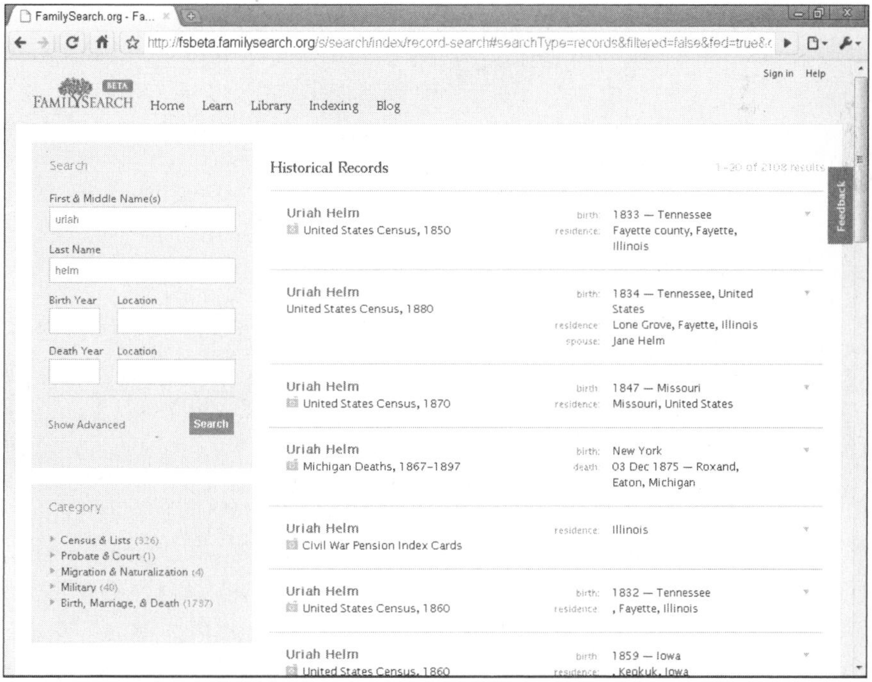

Figure 13-2:
The beta version of the new Family Search. org site.

Giving Back through FamilySearch Indexing

FamilySearch Indexing is a project through which volunteers help transcribe records from all over the world and submit them for posting on the Web site so that others can access them for free. It's a simple process. FamilySearch obtains the records and digitizes them. You download copies of the digital images to your personal computer. Then using special online software, you index the data in the digital records. The result — a searchable index — is made available to the public free of charge.

For more information about the FamilySearch Indexing project, go to `www.familysearch.org/eng/indexing/frameset_indexing.asp`.

Part VI
The Part of Tens

The 5th Wave   By Rich Tennant

"Hold your horses. It takes time to locate the ancestors for someone of your background."

In this part . . .

Ah, The Part of Tens — a staple of the *Dummies* books. Use these chapters as quick references when you're looking for the following:

- ✔ Items to think about when you travel for research

- ✔ Things to ponder when designing genealogical Web pages

- ✔ Places to visit when you need a bit of help with your research

- ✔ Tips for making the most of your research

Chapter 14

Ten Tools for Your Researching Travels

*R*esearching your family history online may jump-start your genealogical pursuits, but at some point, you'll want to make a pilgrimage to your ancestor's birthplace, travel to another location to get original records or pictures, or attend a family reunion to meet some primary sources in person. In this chapter, we discuss ways you can make your trip easier by planning your travels and taking along a few aids.

Planning Your Trip Using the Web

A wealth of information is available to help you plan your travels — and it's all at your fingertips! You can surf the Web to check out hotels and motels, car-rental agencies, airlines, restaurants, grocery stores, local attractions, and a host of other services related to research trips and vacations. Two sites that provide links to all sorts of travel-related information are MapQuest (`www.mapquest.com`) and the Yahoo! Travel section (`http://dir.yahoo.com/recreation/travel`). Each has sections for transportation, lodging, dining, and a variety of other things you need while traveling. You can even use MapQuest to plan your route if you're driving in North America.

Follow these steps to get driving directions from MapQuest:

1. **Using your Web browser, go to the MapQuest site (www.mapquest.com).**

2. **Click the Directions tab.**

   The Directions page appears, offering two columns of boxes to complete.

3. **In the first column, complete the fields indicating your start location or where this part of your journey will begin.**

   You can type the name of a business in the optional Find a Business field, if your starting point is a commercial place. Or, you can enter a street address in the Address or Intersection field.

   Type the city from which your journey is to begin in the City field. Type the state or province from which you'll begin your trip in the State field. You can type the zip code too, but it is not required.

4. **In the second column, complete the fields indicating your destination or end location.**

   The destination fields are titled just like the starting fields and accept the same type of information.

5. **Click Get Directions.**

   MapQuest determines the directions from your starting point to your destination. If MapQuest can't determine a route for you, it provides an explanation and recommends revising your direction information.

Narrowing Your Target

Before you jump in the car and start heading out, you should do a little research on the places you plan to visit. Fire up your computer at home and check the days and hours that repositories you plan to visit are open to the public. Review their holdings to determine exactly what types of records you are looking for at particular locations. And review their rules and policies — you do not want to haul in all your gadgets if they allow you to bring only paper and a writing utensil.

If you're traveling during cold months, you might want to see whether your destination offers lockers or a coat closet to store your jacket, umbrella, or backpack. If you plan to spend an entire day in one location, you might want to see whether it has a cafeteria or food court where you can purchase lunch, or whether it has a designated place where you can eat a lunch you bring with you. You can iron out all sorts of details before you embark on your journey.

If you're traveling within the United States, the USGenWeb Project (www.usgenweb.com) provides links for every state and details on many of the resources that are available.

Remembering Your Laptop or Notebook

It would be frustrating if you reached your destination and found that you didn't have any of your past findings and leads for research on this trip with you, and you couldn't remember much about the ancestors you set out to research. It's easy to get caught up in packing and meeting departure times, and to forget some of the most important things you need to have with you. We don't expect you to have all your research memorized, so be sure to set your laptop computer or your notebook containing your genealogical database and all your family charts, pictures, and notes in an obvious place so that you don't forget to take it along. You could even keep a printed copy of the directions you just received from MapQuest (see the "Planning Your Trip Using the Web" section, earlier in this chapter) with your laptop or notebook so that you don't forget them either.

Opting for an iPad

Although having your notebook or laptop computer with you is handy, these days you have a smaller, lighter option: the iPad. If you're like we are, you were probably wondering what all the hype was over the iPad. You need only to play with one to discover many of its possibilities for genealogical travels. You can find numerous iPad applications that are handy on the road:

- **GEDCOM viewers:** See the contents of your genealogical database in a chart format (review Chapters 3 and 11 for quick refreshers on GEDCOM).

- **Photo storage:** Take digital copies of your family-related pictures or scanned images of records with you. This feature is especially nice at a family reunion, where you can either set photos to play in a slide show on the iPad for everyone to see or sort through them to reminisce with your relatives.

- **Map applications:** No need to carry printed copies of the maps you downloaded plotting your trip. And if you get lost, you can find your way back to the main road.

- **Banking interfaces:** Transfer money between accounts or assess whether you're staying within your budget.

- **Text editors:** Take notes of the things you find in your on-site research.

- **Web browsers and e-mail access:** Stay connected to everything you use in cyberspace from home while on the road. If your iPad has service through a wireless phone network (or you've rigged it to use your cellular phone as a modem), you can access the Internet from almost anywhere in the United States.

Flashing Your Treasures

Our title for this section caught your attention, didn't it? Well, it's really not risqué — we're talking about flash drives (also sometimes called thumb drives or jump drives). Flash drives are inexpensive devices that store from 2GB (gigabytes) to 32GB of files, presentations, music, and photos. They plug into the USB port on any computer and transfer files from one location to another quickly. Most flash drives fit on your keychain, so you can carry them almost anywhere.

A flash drive is a wonderful gadget to have if you're going to share your genealogical treasures with others at a family reunion or society meeting or if you plan to give a presentation at a genealogical meeting or conference.

Capturing a Picture-Perfect Moment

If your mother is like April's mother, she drilled into your head when you were young that you should always carry a camera with you. It doesn't have to be a digital camera, although we highly recommend it. The point-and-click digital cameras have come down a lot in price over the past few years, and they are small and handy to have around for many reasons — photos at family reunions, pictures of headstones in cemeteries, or snapshots of the family homestead or some landmark near it. (We won't mention how we know that they are also great to have on hand if you get into a car accident while on your genealogical excursion.) If you're visiting a library or archive that allows you to bring your camera inside with you, it might even be used to photograph documents.

Be sure to take plenty of film for your traditional camera or an extra memory card or stick for your digital camera, and extra batteries.

You might have a camera with you at all times in the form of your cellular phone. We have to admit that we were skeptical about cellular phones with built-in cameras when they were introduced. However, we have grown to understand the practical applications that such a gadget offers. The ability to take photos on a whim is a luxury that truly can benefit a genealogist.

Using Your Cell Phone as a Cell Phone

In the preceding section, we talk about using your cell phone as a camera. But you should take your cell phone with you on your research jaunts and ensure that it is charged at all times so that you can use it as a phone, too. We probably don't have to explain that you will want it if you have an emergency while traveling. A cell phone is also useful when you need to call a relative or research buddy if you have questions about a particular ancestor that you're researching in a location away from home.

For example, a few years back, we were visiting a cemetery that we had never been to before and were having trouble locating Matthew's ancestor because of conflicting information in the family file. It was a wonderful convenience to be able to call his aunt and ask her for clarification rather than having to travel home to phone her or waiting to see her and then making a return trip to the cemetery at a later date.

Positioning Yourself for Success

If you've had the opportunity to work much with land records, you know the difficulty in translating the land descriptions into an actual place on the ground. One way to help you find a specific location is to use latitudes and longitudes.

Latitude is the distance of a point either north or south of the equator, and *longitude* is the distance of a point either east or west of the prime meridian. If you want a primer on latitude and longitude, we recommend visiting the WorldAtlas.com site at `www/worldatlas.com/aatlas/imageg.htm`.

In genealogy, you might encounter latitude and longitude associated with descriptions of historical landmarks, land measurements, and burial locations, among other things.

Global positioning systems (GPS) pick up satellite signals that determine your precise location in terms of latitude and longitude. They're also designed to guide you to specific locations based on latitude and longitude. This feature is useful if you're looking for a plat of land where your great-great-grandfather lived but all the natural markings have changed over time.

You find many varieties of GPS devices — from handheld systems, to navigation systems built into cars, to cellular phones that can give you position readings. Although handheld GPS devices and automobile navigation systems can be expensive, cellular phones with built-in GPS are common and a good alternative. So check your cell phone to see whether it has positioning capabilities before rushing out to buy a GPS device.

Diversifying Your Currency

If you travel for pleasure or business much, you know it's a good idea to have various forms of currency with you. Traveling for genealogical pursuits is no different. You should carry some cash, not only in the form of paper money but also in coins. Change is often needed for toll roads, parking meters, and copy machines in libraries and archives. These days, credit cards are more readily accepted at institutions such as courthouses, libraries, and archives, so you may not need to carry oodles of cash — in fact, for safety reasons, we do not recommend carrying a lot of cash. It doesn't hurt to carry a checkbook or at least one or two checks in your wallet or pocketbook. Some courthouses still accept checks, and many genealogical and historical societies are happy to take them.

If you're planning to travel to another country, you probably won't be able to pay in your own currency. You'll need to have some money converted to the resident currency of the country you're visiting. You might want to check out a currency converter such as XE: Universal Currency Converter (www. xe.com/ucc) or the Yahoo! Finance Currencies Center (http://finance. yahoo.com/currency-converter). These sites enable you to predict costs in your own country's currency based on the current exchange rates.

Have Scanner, Will Travel

At first, it may sound a bit strange to say that you should take your flatbed scanner with you on your travels. However, many document repositories now allow you to bring in a small scanner with your laptop.

Scanning the documents that you discover on location saves you the cost of having them reproduced on a copier and saves you time that you'd typically lose waiting for a staff member to copy the document (if it is a large document that requires staff copying). Be sure to check the policies of the repository online to make sure that it allows a scanner on-site before trying to bring it into the repository.

When it comes to scanners, the catch is whether you have one that is small and lightweight enough to carry with you. Some flatbed scanners are thin and light but are still cumbersome to carry because of the size of the bed. This type of scanner might be a viable option if you're carrying a large computer bag or backpack. But it's likely that you'll want a handheld type of scanner. We recently discovered a wand-style, handheld scanner called the Magic Wand PDS-ST410A-VP that seems made for on-site researching. It's about 10 inches long and less than 2 inches wide and deep, so it fits nicely in a bag. The scanner stores the images to a microSD card, making it easy to swap out the card when scanning lots of documents. You can find out more about the Magic Wand at www.vupointsolutions.com/PDS-ST410-VP.asp.

Chapter 15

Ten Design Tips for Your Web Site or Blog

In This Chapter

▶ Designing an attractive but useful site

▶ Posting information carefully and ethically

▶ Conducting quality control checks

*Y*ou've probably seen them: Web pages that look like the maintainers simply copied someone else's site and then plugged their surnames into specified spots and maybe changed the background color of the page. Typically, such pages don't contain much information of value — they're simply lists of surnames with no context and maybe lists of links to some of the better-known genealogical Web sites. Some might say that these sites are clones. We agree. You don't want your genealogical Web site to contain almost exactly the same information as sites created by others. You want your site to be unique and useful to other genealogists so that a lot of people will visit your site and recommend it to others. At the same time, you don't necessarily want your site to be overwhelming complicated or ugly. The same thing goes for your blog — you don't want your blog to sound just like another's. So what can you do to avoid the genealogical Web-site ruts that some genealogists find themselves in? In this chapter we offer a few ideas and places to get help.

Be Unique

Please, please, please tell us that you want to set your home page apart from all other genealogical Web sites. You don't really have to be told not to copy the content from other sites, right? But when you design your site, the pressure is on, and coming up with ideas for textual and graphical content can be difficult. We understand that this pressure can make it tempting for you to take ideas from Web sites that you like.

Although you can certainly look to other sites for ideas about formatting and content, don't copy the sites verbatim! Web sites are copyrighted by the person(s) who created them — even if they don't display a copyright notice — and you can get in trouble for copying them. (See Chapter 11 for more information about copyrights.)

The other reason you shouldn't copy other Web sites is that you want your page to attract as many visitors as possible — and to do this, you need to offer something unique that makes it worth people's time to stop by. After all, if your site has the same information as another site, people have no particular need to visit your page. For example, because several comprehensive genealogical sites already exist, posting a Web site that merely has links to other genealogical pages doesn't make much sense. Likewise, if you're thinking about making a one-name study site for a surname for which four or five one-name study sites already exist, you may want to focus your home page on another surname you're researching.

Be creative. Look around and see what existing genealogical Web sites offer, and then seek to fill the void — select a unique topic, name, or location that doesn't have much coverage (or better yet, that doesn't have any coverage). If you want to post a surname site, think about making a site for your surname in a particular state or country. Or, think about posting some transcribed records that would benefit genealogists who are researching ancestors from a particular county.

If you find it challenging to come up with enough unique and original content for your site, consider involving others in your efforts. You can turn to relatives or other researchers who are interested in the same family lines as you — perhaps someone who doesn't have Internet access with whom you correspond, or others who have access but don't have the time or motivation to create their own sites.

Include Surnames and Contact Info

If the purpose of your blog or Web site is not only to share your collection of genealogical information but also to get information from others, be sure to include a list of the names you're researching. And don't be stingy with information. We encourage you to share at least a little information about your ancestors with those surnames. Just a list of surnames alone isn't going to be helpful to visitors to your site, particularly if any of the surnames on your list are common — Smith, Johnson, Jones, Martin, and so on.

An online version of the information contained in your GEDCOM file (a text file that contains the contents of your genealogical database, created using GED2HTML or another similar program — see Chapter 11 for more information) will do because it includes an index of surnames that people can look through, and also has information about your ancestors with those surnames.

Also be sure to include your name and e-mail address so that people know how to get in touch with you to share data.

If you're comfortable doing so, you can include your mailing address on your Web site so that those who don't have e-mail access can contact you. Or, if you're not comfortable providing such personal information but you want other researchers to be able to contact you, you may want to consider getting a post-office box that you can post on your Web site and use for receiving genealogy-related mail.

Make Your Site Attractive, not Flashy

Choose your colors and graphics wisely! Although using some color and graphics (including photographs) helps your Web site stand out and makes it more personal, be careful about using too much color or too many graphics. By *too much color,* we mean backgrounds that are so bright that they almost blind your visitors (or make the rest of the site hard to look at) or backgrounds that drown out the colors of your links. You want your site to be appealing to others as well as to you; before using neon pink or lime green, stop and think about how others may react. The especially good news here is that if you use a networking site such as Geni, you can choose from standard templates using subdued, easy-to-look-at colors and fonts. The variety of templates gives you an opportunity to distinguish your site from others without being fully responsible for determining the layout and formatting.

The more graphics you use and the larger they are, the longer a computer takes to load them. And animated graphics are even worse! They take a long time to load and can make your visitors dizzy and disoriented, if you have several graphics moving in different directions at the same time. Graphics files aren't the only factor that affects how quickly computers load files. The amount of bandwidth of your Internet connection and the amount of space available on your hard drive also affect download time. Waiting for a page to load that has more graphics than useful text content is frustrating. You can pretty much bet that people won't wait around, so concentrate on making your page as user-friendly as possible from the beginning. Use graphics tastefully and sparingly.

If you have a lot of family photos that you really want to share, put each photo on its own page and provide links to the photo pages from your home page. This way, visitors who aren't interested in seeing the photos don't have to wait for the images to load on their computers just to view the other contents of your site, and visitors who are interested in a particular image don't have to wait for all the other photos to load.

To shrink the size of the graphics on your Web site, try using a *graphics optimizer* (a tool that formats your graphics to make them load faster in someone's Web browser) such as NetMechanic GIFBot, available at www.netmechanic.com/accelerate.htm.

Be Careful What You Post

Be careful and thoughtful when designing your Web site and posting information contributed by others. Don't post any information that could hurt or offend someone. Respect the privacy of others and post information only on people who have been deceased for many years. (When in doubt, a good conservative figure to use is 25 years.) Even then, be cautious about telling old family stories that may affect people who are still alive. (For more information about privacy, see Chapter 11.)

Cite Your Sources

We can't stress enough that you should always cite your sources when you put genealogical narrative on your blog or Web site, or when you post information from records that you've collected or people you've interviewed. That way, people who visit your page and get data from it know exactly where you got the information and can follow up on it if they need or want to. (Also, by citing your sources, you keep yourself out of trouble because others may have provided the information to you, and they deserve the credit for the research.)

Realize that Not All Web Browsers Are Created Equal

Web browsers interpret HTML documents differently depending on who created the software. Also, some Web browsers have HTML tags that are specific to the browser. So, although you may create a Web site that looks great using Microsoft Internet Explorer, it may look off-center or somewhat different when using Google Chrome or Apple Safari. Because of this problem, try not to use tags that are specific to any one browser when you create your Web site. For that matter, whenever possible, test your page in several browsers before posting it for public access. Better yet, use a testing service that allows the "experts" to look at your page and give you feedback. The Yahoo! HTML Validation and Checkers page at `http://dir.yahoo.com/Computers_and_Internet/Data_Formats/HTML/Validation_and_Checkers` provides a decent list of programs that check your Web site and notify you about broken links.

Another consideration when designing your Web page is to make your Web pages readable by screen-reading browsers. Screen-reading browsers allow visually impaired researchers to access information on the Web. To see whether your content is accessible, you can find scanning utilities at WebsiteTips.com, at `http://websitetips.com/accessibility/tools`.

Check and Recheck Your Links

If you include any links to other sites on your blog entry or Web site, double-check them. Make sure that the links work properly so that your visitors don't have problems navigating to sites that you recommend or getting to other pages on your site. A lot of genealogical Web sites tend to be transient — the maintainers move them for one reason or another, or take them down entirely — so you should also check back periodically (once a month or so) to make sure that the links still work.

If you have a lot of links on your Web site and don't have the time to check every one yourself (which is a common scenario), look to the Yahoo! HTML Validation and Checkers page at `http://dir.yahoo.com/Computers_and_Internet/Data_Formats/HTML/Validation_and_Checkers`. It links to a list of programs that check your Web site and notify you about broken links.

Market Your Information

After you put together your Web site and post it on your provider's server, or create your blog, you need to let people know that the site or blog exists so that they can stop by and visit, as well as contribute. How do you do this? We recommend that you follow some of the same tips in Chapter 11 for marketing the research that you've performed on your surnames (using mailing lists if the site deals with particular surnames or geographic areas). In particular, one of the best ways to promote your Web site is to register it with several comprehensive genealogical Web sites that receive a lot of traffic from people looking for genealogy-related pages.

Also, most of the major search engines have links to registration or submission pages within their sites that enable you to submit your URL. To save time, you can visit Addme.com (`www.addme.com/submission.htm`) and click Free Search Engine Submission to forward your Web site information to 20 search engines for free.

Help Others

Don't go overboard patting yourself on the back on your blog or Web site — you know, promoting your home page or blog for the sake of receiving awards from other sites, magazines, societies, or other sources. Post your genealogical site or blog with the intent of helping other genealogists and encouraging a sharing genealogical community. If you use the majority of your page to advertise your awards and beg people to vote for your site in popularity contests, you lose a lot of valuable space that could be used to post information useful to genealogists. And you may lose credibility with your visitors, causing them to turn away — which defeats the purpose of self-promotion in the first place.

We're not saying that you shouldn't acknowledge awards that your site or blog receives if it has good and sound genealogical content. We recognize that it's good business to give a little traffic back to the sites, magazines, societies, or other sources that send visitors your way by awarding your page some honor. You can acknowledge the honors you receive in a tasteful and humble manner. Don't plaster the graphics for every single award across the top of your page. Rather, set up a separate Web page for awards and provide a link from your home page so that those who are interested in seeing your honors can go to that page.

Get Help

Chapter 11 provides a lot of information about why you would want to create a Web site or blog, and gives you ideas of what to include. However, it does not bestow upon you all the knowledge that you need to program a Web site. For that, we defer to two other *For Dummies* books that deal with that topic: *HTML, XHTML, & CSS For Dummies,* 7th Edition, by Ed Tittel and Jeff Noble, and *Building a Web Site For Dummies*, 4th Edition, by David A. Crowder (both published by Wiley).

You have other ways to discover how to do fancier things with your Web site. Check out community colleges in your area or workshops offered by local libraries or genealogical societies. Community colleges and workshops often offer classes or sessions on how to build a Web site, walking you through the basics of HTML — what the tags are, how to use them, and how to post a Web site.

The following online sites are additional resources for designing and programming Web pages:

- ✔ **About.com's Personal Web Pages section:** `http://personalweb.about.com`
- ✔ **Web Building Tutorial:** `www.w3schools.com/site/default.asp`

Chapter 16

Ten Helpful Sites for Searching

In This Chapter

▶ Finding how-to sites

▶ Getting help in the form of lookups

▶ Subscribing to mailing lists

Do census records make you feel senseless? Panicked at the idea of using Soundex? Just plain confused about where to start? These ten sites may relieve some of the anxiety you feel toward researching your genealogy.

Ancestry.com Learning Center

`http://learn.ancestry.com/Home/HMLND.aspx`

Although the purpose of Ancestry.com Learning Center is to offer subscriptions to online data, the site also offers some good articles and video tutorials. The video tutorials cover topics such as Get Started, Home Sources, and All About Me. The Learning Center provides free forms and charts, descriptions of historical record types (including census, military, and vital records), as well as advice on how to use the various resources on Ancestry.com.

One area you might want to investigate is the Article Archives area, where you can find articles on many research topics. These articles come from a variety of sources, including Ancestry Magazine, Ancestry Weekly Discovery, Ancestry Monthly Update, Ancestry Archive, Videos, Webinars, Ancestry World Archives, and Project Newsletter.

FamilySearch Research Wiki

`https://wiki.familysearch.org`

With nearly 40,000 articles related to genealogical research, the FamilySearch Research Wiki is an invaluable guide to assist you with your research. (By the way, a *Wiki* is a collaborative Web site where users provide definitions and information about a topic.) Whether you are looking for guidance on a specific locality, a type of record, or an ethnic group, or you need general help with research, you should be able to find an applicable article. The site is set up like a typical Wiki and is maintained by the genealogical community at large. If you're new to genealogical research, try starting with the How-to Pages for Family History located at `https://wiki.familysearch.org/en/How-to_Pages_for_Family_History`.

If you have a specific topic that you've researched and it's not listed on the Wiki, you can create a login and share your knowledge with the rest of the genealogical community through the Wiki.

Roots Television

`www.rootstelevision.com`

Roots Television contains free videos on a variety of genealogical topics. To see the video lineup, click the Program Guide link on the main page of the Web site. You can find excerpts from the *Ancestors* television series, lectures from genealogical conferences, and instructional videos.

Genealogy Today: Online Guide to Genealogy

`www.genealogytoday.com`

Genealogy Today's Online Guide to Genealogy (located on the left side of the home page, near the bottom) contains tips for experienced and newbie researchers alike. The guide is divided into four categories: Getting Started, Family History, Research Tools, and Advanced Topics. Mixed with the articles are suggestions on how to use the site's other resources to contribute to your research success. Under Advanced Topics, try the News Center link, which reports on new genealogical resources. The link to the GenWeekly newsletter offers insight on research geared toward researchers with all levels of experience.

GeneaSearch

`www.geneasearch.com`

GeneaSearch offers help in the form of lookups (a service in which others will look up information for you in geographic locations that you can't easily access) and online resources. Some of the online resources are a surname registry, military rosters, transcribed records, directories, obituaries, family newsletters, information about researching female ancestors, and a beginner's guide.

GEN-NEWBIE-L

`http://lists.rootsweb.ancestry.com/index/other/Miscellaneous/GEN-NEWBIE.html`

The GEN-NEWBIE-L mailing list is a forum for individuals who are new to computers and genealogy and are looking for a place to discuss a variety of topics in a comfortable environment. To subscribe to the mailing list, follow these steps:

1. **Open your favorite e-mail program and start a new e-mail message.**
2. **Type** Gen-Newbie-L-request@rootsweb.com **in the Address line.**
3. **Leave the Subject line blank and type only the word** subscribe **in the body of your message.**

   Make sure that you turn off any signature lines present in your e-mail.
4. **Send your e-mail message.**

Soon you will receive a confirmation message with additional details on unsubscribing from the mailing list (if you want to do so down the road) and other administrative items. If you have questions about the mailing list, consult the GEN-NEWBIE-L home page for help. If you've asked questions, you can search the archives of the mailing list from the mailing list's home page to see whether your questions have been answered.

National Genealogical Society

`www.ngsgenealogy.org`

The National Genealogical Society (NGS) is an organization for individuals whose research interests include the United States. At its Web site, you can find information on the society's home-study genealogy course, how to start your genealogy research, research services, the society's library catalog, and conferences. The site also has information about membership — no surprise there — and does a good job of keeping visitors abreast of genealogical news and events. You even find a "bookstore" that carries a lot more than just books on its virtual shelves. Recently, NGS posted a free online Family History Skills course available to its members.

ProGenealogists

www.progenealogists.com/resources.htm

ProGenealogists is a professional genealogical research firm. It provides a number of research services, for a fee, and it can access records and researchers from around the world. In addition to providing research services, ProGenealogists has posted several resources, including a list of links to online databases, how-to articles, a citation guide, resources related to specific countries, blank forms, lists of journals and magazines, genealogy news, and research tools.

Getting Started in Genealogy and Family History

www.genuki.org.uk/gs

The GENUKI (U.K. and Ireland Genealogy) Web site provides a list of helpful hints for starting out in genealogical research. The extensive list covers the following elements (and more): deciding the aim of your research, using Family History Centers, joining a genealogical society, tracing immigrants, and organizing your information. You also find a list of reference materials — should you want to read more about the topics GENUKI discusses.

About.com Genealogy: One-Stop Beginner's Genealogy

http://genealogy.about.com/library/onestop/bl_beginner.htm

If you're looking for information on a range of genealogical topics, hop over to the About.com Genealogy site. The One-Stop Beginner's Genealogy section of the site has a large collection of articles categorized by subject: Articles and Tips, Learning Corner, and Tools and How-To. You find many subcategories under each of these topics as well. Some of the resources in these categories include information on surname origins, mistakes you can avoid, a genealogy chat room, and publishing your family history.

Chapter 17

Ten Tips for Genealogical Smooth Sailing

In This Chapter

▶ Enhancing your genealogical research

▶ Collaborating with other researchers

▶ Avoiding pitfalls

*Y*ou want to make optimal use of your time when researching your genealogy — online and offline. Being time-efficient means planning well and keeping organized notes so that bad leads don't distract you. Making the most of your time also means staying motivated when and if a bad lead has distracted you. Your genealogy research is worth continuing. This chapter offers some tips to help you plan, organize, and execute your research.

Start with What You Know

When you begin researching your genealogy, start with what you know — information about yourself and your immediate family. (Sure, this concept seems basic, but it's worth repeating.) Then work your way back in time, using information from relatives and copies of records that you obtain. Solving the mystery of your heritage is easier if you have some clues to start with. If you begin directly with your great-great-grandpa and all you know about him is his name, you may get frustrated very early in the process — especially if Great-great-grandpa has a relatively common name such as John Sanders or William Martin! Can you imagine trying to track down records on *all* the John Sanderses or William Martins who turn up in one year's census? (We believe in thoroughly covering the basics, so if you want to hear this again, go to Chapter 1.)

Get Organized

The better organized you are, the more success you're likely to have with your research efforts. If you know ahead of time where you stand in researching your family lines, you can identify rather quickly which records or other materials you need to find about a particular surname, location, or time frame. Knowing your gaps in information enables you to get right down to the nitty-gritty of researching instead of spending the first hour or two of your research rehashing where you left off.

To help yourself get organized, keep a *research log* — a record of when and where you searched for information. For example, if you ran a Google (www.google.com) search on the name Emaline Crump on January 1, 2010, and found 13 pages that you wanted to visit, record that in your research log. Also record when you visited those pages and whether they provided any useful information to you. That way, the next time you're online researching your Crump ancestors, you know that you already ran a Google search and visited the particular resulting pages, so you don't have to do it again. (Of course, you may want to repeat the search at a future date to see whether any *new* Crump-related sites turn up. Again, your research log can come in handy because it can remind you of whether you've already visited some of the resulting sites.)

You can print a copy of a research log at the Church of Jesus Christ of Latter-day Saints site at http://lds.org/images/howdoibeg/Research_Log.html.

Although this particular log is intended for offline research, you can modify it for your online pursuits — substituting the URL of a site you visit for the Location/Call Numbers section of the form. Or you can find a *research table* (which is basically a research log by another name) at the Genealogy.com site at www.genealogy.com/00000002.html?Welcome=1016426690.

A few other options are to create your own research log with a plain notebook or a spreadsheet on your handy-dandy computer, or to use an already-prepared form that comes with your genealogical database (if available).

Here are two Web sites that can give you pointers on organizing your paper-based sources:

- ✔ **Getting Organized:** www.genealogy.com/getting_organized.html
- ✔ **Organizing Your Files:** https://wiki.familysearch.org/en/Organizing_Your_Files

Always Get Proof

Unfortunately, not all researchers take the same amount of care when gathering sources and presenting the fruits of their research. So it's not a good idea to trust that everything that other researchers print or post is an undisputable fact.

Always be a little skeptical about secondhand information and seek to get your own proof of an event. We're not saying that if Aunt Dorothy gives you a copy of Great-grandma's birth certificate that you still need to get your own copy from the original source. However, if Aunt Dorothy merely tells you that Great-grandma was born in Hardin County, Kentucky, and that she knows this because Great-grandma said so, you do need to get a copy of Great-grandma's birth certificate or some other primary record that verifies this fact.

Even when using primary sources, evaluate the information that you find on each record. If the information does not add up, the record could be wrong. If you suspect this is the case, it's a good idea to find another record that can help clear up the inconsistency.

If you assume that everything you hear or read is true, you're likely to get distracted frequently by bad leads. You could end up tracing an entire branch of a family that you're not even related to. And just think of all the time you could have spent working on your own family line!

For more information on how to evaluate sources, see the Evaluation of Evidence page at the ProGenealogists site at `www.progenealogists.com/evidenceevaluation.htm`. Also, see the Genealogical Proof Standard page at the Board for Certification of Genealogists site, at `www.bcgcertification.org/resources/standard.html`, for information on how to effectively use proof in your research.

Always Cite Your Sources

Always — and we mean *always* — cite your sources. We can't say this enough! In other chapters (Chapter 11, for example), we explore why citing your sources is a smart thing to do when sharing your genealogical information with others. We also touch on the importance of citing sources for your own research — so important, in fact, that we reiterate the point here. Make sure that you know where, when, and how you obtained a particular piece of information about your ancestors just in case you ever need to verify the information or get another copy of the record. Doing so saves you a lot of grief. It also brings you greater respect from others for your efforts.

Although you can find entire books on citing sources, if you're in a hurry and need quick advice, take a look at the Citation Guide at the ProGenealogists site (www.progenealogists.com/citations.htm). The guide includes a good introduction to citation formats for both online and offline sources. When you have the time, you should delve into the definitive work on genealogical source citations — *Evidence,* by Elizabeth Shown Mills (published by the Genealogical Publishing Company).

Focus, Focus, Focus

If you're trying to remember all your ancestors in all your family lines and research them all at the same time, you're bound to get confused and burned out! Focus on one or two branches at a time. Even better — focus on one or two people within a branch at a time. By maintaining a tight focus, you can still find information on other relatives in that branch of the family and collect records and data that pertain to them — without driving yourself crazy.

Share Your Information

One of the best ways to facilitate getting genealogical information from others is to share some information first. Although most genealogists are generous people, some still believe in protecting their discoveries like closely guarded treasures — it's "every man for himself" in their minds. However, after they realize that you want to *give* information as well as receive it, some of them lighten up and are much more willing to share with you. By sharing information, you can save each other time and energy, as well as begin to coordinate your research in a manner that benefits both of you.

The Internet has proven to be an invaluable resource for genealogists by providing easy access for unconditional and conditional sharing of information among genealogists. Those of you who are willing to share your knowledge can go online and post information to your heart's content. And in return, simply ask the researchers who benefit from your site to share their findings with you. And if you are a more apprehensive about sharing your knowledge, you can post messages describing what you're looking for and state that you're willing to share what you have with anyone who can help you.

You have several different ways to share your information online. We cover many of these methods in various chapters of this book. You can share in one-on-one e-mail messages, networking sites, mailing lists, newsgroups, and Web pages — just to name a few.

Join a Society or Research Group

You've probably heard the phrase "Two heads are better than one," right? Well, this theory holds true for genealogy. Joining a society or a research group enables you to combine research efforts with others who are interested in a particular surname or geographic location, so that together you save time and energy obtaining documents that benefit everyone. A society or research group also provides you with a support group to which you can turn when you begin to get discouraged or whenever you want to share a triumph.

You can find genealogical societies and research groups in several ways. Check out your favorite comprehensive genealogical site and look under both the category that lists societies and the place category for the location where you live. Or, if you're interested in finding a society in the United States, take a look at the Federation of Genealogical Societies home page at www.fgs.org (which identifies member societies by location) or the USGenWeb Project at www.usgenweb.org (which links to state pages that identify resources for the state and its counties).

If you're interested in finding a society in a country other than the United States, check out the WorldGenWeb site at www.worldgenweb.org to link to resource pages for the region that you're researching. These resource pages should include at least general information about societies in the area.

Attend a Conference or Workshop

Conferences and workshops hosted by genealogical societies can be a great resource. They can help you get organized and find out how to research a particular place or look for specific records, and motivate you to keep plugging along with your research even if you have days when you feel like you haven't accomplished a thing. Conferences and workshops also enable you to meet other researchers with whom you have something in common, whether it's researching a specific surname or geographic location, or just research in general. Being in the company of someone with whom you can share your genealogical successes and failures is always nice.

Typically, conferences and workshops offer sessions that instruct you on various traditional researching topics such as the following:

- Using local libraries and archives
- Finding and using land records
- Obtaining vital records
- Converting Soundex codes and using the census
- Publishing a genealogical report or book

And most workshops offer some computer-based components such as the following:

- ✔ Using genealogical software
- ✔ Designing and posting your own genealogical Web page
- ✔ Joining online societies and mailing lists
- ✔ Presenting overviews of the Internet's genealogical offerings
- ✔ Using a computer in general

You can use your trusty computer and Internet connection to find genealogical and historical conferences and workshops in your area. The Federation of Genealogical Societies (`www.fgs.org/calendar/index.php`) provides information about conferences coming up in the next few months. For events in the United Kingdom, look at GENEVA: the GENUKI calendar of Genealogical Events and Activities (`http://geneva.weald.org.uk`). You can also use these sites to get the word out about a conference or workshop that you're helping to plan!

Attend a Family Reunion

Family reunions enable you to see and share information with relatives you haven't seen in a long time and to meet new relatives you never would have known. Although we cover family reunions in more detail in Chapter 10, we want to reiterate here that reunions are a wonderful opportunity to build your genealogical base by just chatting with relatives about old family stories, ancestors, and so on. Although a reunion doesn't feel like a formal interview, it can give you much of the same information that you would receive if you sat down and formally interviewed each of the people in attendance. Taking along a tape recorder or video camera is a good idea because you don't have to worry about writing down everything your relatives say right at that moment — you can just sit back and enjoy talking with your family. Plus, your genealogy records are greatly enhanced by audio or video. (When you're going to tape a conversation, make sure that you have the permission of the relatives you plan to record and that you set aside *lots* of time later to transcribe the tapes if you don't attach them directly to your genealogical database as media files.)

Family reunions also offer you the opportunity to share what you know about the family and exchange genealogical records and reports. If you know ahead of time that several of your relatives are also into genealogical research, you can better plan with them what records, pictures, reports, and other resources to bring. If you're not sure that any of your relatives are into genealogical research, we recommend that you take a notebook with some printed reports and maybe a narrative family history or genealogy (if you've put one together) that you can share. Remember, your work doesn't have to be complete (in fact, it probably won't be) or perfect in grammar for others to enjoy seeing what you've collected.

To find out about family reunions, watch the family association and one-name study Web sites of the surnames you're researching. Typically, this type of Web site has sections set up for reunion announcements. Also, see the *Reunions* magazine site at `www.reunionsmag.com`.

Planning a reunion can often be a challenging experience. Fortunately, software is available to help you with all the details. Family Reunion Organizer by RootsMagic, Inc. is just such a program. You can find a demo copy of the software at `http://family-reunion.com/organizer`.

Don't Give Up

You're going to have days where you spend hours at the library or archives — or on the Internet — with no research success whatsoever (or so you may think). Don't let those days get you down, and certainly don't give up! Instead of thinking about what you didn't discover about your ancestors on such days, think in terms of what you *did* find out — that your ancestors were not in that record for that particular place at that particular time. By checking that record, you eliminated one more item on your to-do list. So the next time you get ready to research, you know exactly where *not* to look for more information.

Glossary

Abstract: A brief overview or summary of what a document or Web site contains.

Adjutant General's report: Published account of the actions of military units from a particular state during a war.

Adoption: To legally be declared part of a family into which you were not born.

Ahnentafel: A well-known genealogical numbering system in which there is a mathematical relationship between parents and children. The word itself means ancestor and table in German. Also referred to as the Sosa-Stradonitz system of numbering.

Albumen print: A type of photograph that was produced on a thin piece of paper coated with albumen and silver nitrate and usually mounted on cardboard; typically taken between 1858 and 1910.

Allele: The form a gene takes that drives human characteristics such as eye color.

Ambrotype: A type of photograph that was printed on thin glass and usually had a black backing; typically taken between 1858 and 1866.

America Online: A popular commercial Internet service provider. Also referred to as AOL.

Americanized: The process of changing one's surname (last name) to make it easier to pronounce or as the result of a misspelling on a record when an immigrant entered the United States.

Ancestor: A person from whom you are descended.

Ancestor chart: A chart that runs horizontally across a page and identifies a primary person (including that person's name, date, and place of birth, date and place of marriage, and date and place of death), his or her parents, then each of their parents, and so on until the chart runs off the page. Usually called a pedigree chart.

Ancestral file: A database created and maintained by the Church of Jesus Christ of Latter-day Saints, with millions of names available in family group sheets and pedigree charts; part of the FamilySearch collection of CD-ROMs, which are accessible at Family History Centers. See also *Family History Centers* and *Family History Library*.

AOL: See *America Online.*

Archive: A physical location where historical documents and records are stored.

Autosome: One of the 22 non-sex chromosomes in the cell nucleus.

Banns: See *marriage banns.*

Baptismal certificate: A certificate issued by a church at the time of baptism; sometimes used to approximate a birth date in the absence of a birth certificate.

Bases: Also called nucleotides. Rungs of the DNA ladder that hold the molecule together. Four types exist: adenine, guanine, cytosine, and thymine.

Bibliography: A list of books or other materials that were used in research; also a list of books or other materials that are available on a particular topic.

Biographical sketch: A brief written account of a person's life.

Biography: A detailed written account of a person's life.

Birth certificate: A legal record stating when and where a person was born.

Blog: An abbreviated name for a Web log, which is an online journal or log of the author's interests and activities.

Blogging: The act of recording your thoughts, opinions, news, or research findings in a Web log.

Bounty land: Federal land given to a person in exchange for military service or some other civic service.

Brick Wall Syndrome: A situation when you think you have exhausted every possible way of finding an ancestor.

Browser: See *Web browser.*

Bureau of Refugees, Freedmen, and Abandoned Lands: Established in 1865, the bureau had programs to assist ex-slaves after the American Civil War. Also called Freedman's Bureau.

Cabinet card: A larger version of the carte-de-visite photograph; typically taken between 1865 and 1906.

Canon code: A code that explains the bloodline relationship in legal terms by identifying how many degrees of separation (or steps) exist between two people related by blood. Canon law counts only the number of steps from the nearest common ancestor of both relatives.

Carte-de-visite: A type of photograph that was a small paper print mounted on a card; collections were usually bound together in photo albums. Typically taken between 1858 and 1891.

CD-ROM: Acronym for Compact Disc–Read-Only Memory; used in your computer's compact disc drive. A CD-ROM stores large amounts of information (including multimedia) that can be retrieved by your computer.

Cells: Basic building blocks of the human body.

Census: The counting of a population undertaken by a government.

Census index: A listing of people who are included in particular census records, along with references indicating where you can find the actual census records.

Census return: The record or form on which census information is collected. Also called a census schedule.

Census schedule: Another term for a census return form.

Charter: A formal or informal document that defines the scope of a newsgroup.

Chromosome: The container that holds the strands of deoxyribonucleic acid (DNA); each chromosome has a different set of instructions and serves a different purpose.

Cite: To name the source of some information and provide reference to the original source.

Civil code: A code that explains the bloodline relationship in legal terms by identifying how many degrees of separation (or kinship steps) exist between two people related by blood. Civil law counts each step between two relatives as a degree.

Civil records: Government documents that contain information on the civic duties of your ancestors, proceedings of municipal governments, or any other records of your ancestors' interaction with the government; often found in local and state archives or courthouses.

Civil registration: Primary record of a vital event in life: birth, death, or marriage; for the most part, originals are kept by local governments. Also called vital records in the United States and Canada.

Compiled genealogy: An online or print publication of one's genealogical findings. It can be a traditional narrative or a lineage-linked database.

Comprehensive genealogical index: A Web site that identifies a large number of other genealogical sites that contain information on a number of families, locations, or a variety of other genealogy-related subjects.

Conscription: Also called draft; this is the act of enrolling people for compulsory service in the military.

Cookies: Pieces of information sent to your computer by other computers when you visit certain Web pages. Generally, cookies are used for navigation or by commercial sites that want to rotate banner advertisements for you so that you don't get tired of the same advertisement.

Copyright: Copyright is the exclusive right of a creator to reproduce, prepare derivative works, distribute, perform, display, sell, lend, or rent his or her creations.

County clerk: The clerk of the county court that records or maintains records of transactions and events in that county. Sometimes called the county recorder.

Cyber society: A genealogical or historical society that exists only on the Internet.

Cyberspace: A slang term for the Internet.

Daguerreotype: A type of photograph that required a long exposure time and was printed on silver-plated copper; typically taken between 1839 and 1860.

Database: A collection of information that is entered, organized, stored, and used on a computer.

Death certificate: A legal record stating when and where a person died.

Declaration of intent: A sworn statement by a person who intends to become a naturalized citizen of the United States.

Deed: A document that records the transfer of ownership of a piece of property or land.

Degrees of separation: The number of steps between two people who are related by blood.

Deoxyribonucleic acid (DNA): Part of your molecular structure that determines your characteristics.

Descendant: A person who descended from a particular ancestor.

Descendant chart: A chart that contains information about an ancestor and spouse (or particular spouses, if there was more than one), their children and their spouses, grandchildren and spouses, and so on down the family line; usually formatted vertically on a page, like a list.

Diary: A book containing one's innermost thoughts and findings in life.

Digest mode: An option for receiving postings to some mailing lists in which several messages are batched together and sent to you instead of each message being sent separately.

Digital camera: A camera that captures images to computer memory instead of to film. You can then download those images to your computer.

Digitized record: A copy or an image of a record that has been made using electronic means.

Directory: A collection of information about individuals who live in a particular place.

Divorce decree: A document that legally ends a marriage.

Download: Getting a file (information or a program) to your computer from another computer or electronic device.

Draft: Also called conscription; this is the act of enrolling people for compulsory service in the military.

Electronic mail: Messages sent from one person to another electronically over the Internet or an intranet. Also called e-mail.

E-mail: Short for electronic mail.

Emigrant: A person who leaves or moves away from one country to settle in another country.

Emoticons: Graphics created by combinations of keyboard keys to express an emotion within a message.

Enumeration district: The area assigned to a particular enumerator of the census.

Enumerator: A person who collected details on individuals during a census.

Estate: The assets and liabilities of a person who dies.

Evernote: A software-based filing cabinet to help you organize notes, photos, and documents.

Family association: An organized group of individuals who are researching the same family.

Family association site: A Web site that's designed and posted by an organization devoted to researching a particular family.

Family group sheet: A summary of a particular family, including biographical information about a husband, a wife, and their children.

Family history: The written account of a family's existence over time.

Family History Centers: Local branches of the Family History Library.

Family History Library: The main library of the Church of Jesus Christ of Latter-day Saints. The Family History Library, in Salt Lake City, Utah, has the world's largest collection of genealogical holdings, including print sources and microfilmed records, as well as records and other information shared by genealogical researchers worldwide.

Family History Library Catalog: A listing of records (books, films, microfiche, CDs, cassette tapes, videos, and microfilms) available at the Family History Library in Salt Lake City, Utah; part of the FamilySearch collection of CD-ROMs, which are accessible at Family History Centers.

Family outline: Also called an outline report; a list of the descendants of a particular ancestor.

Family reunion: A gathering of people who share ancestors.

FAQ: Acronym for Frequently Asked Questions.

FHC: Acronym for Family History Center.

FHL: Acronym for Family History Library.

Flame: An online verbal (written) attack.

Flash drive: A tiny device that stores 2GB or more of data (files, presentations, photos, and music). Also called a thumb drive or a jump drive.

Forum: A subject-specific area where members post messages and files.

Fraternal order: A service club or organization of persons.

Freedman's Bureau: Abbreviated name for the Bureau of Refugees, Freedmen, and Abandoned Lands.

Freedman's Savings and Trust Company: Established in 1865, this was a bank for ex-slaves.

Freeware: Software that you usually obtain and use for free by downloading it from the Internet.

Frequently Asked Questions (FAQs): A Web page or message posted to a mailing list or newsgroup that explains answers to the most-asked questions of that particular Web site, mailing list, or newsgroup. Usually serves as a starting point for people who are new to a site or resource.

Gazetteer: Geographical dictionary that provides information about places.

GEDCOM: Acronym for GEnealogical Data COMmunication. This is a standard file format used for exporting and importing data to and from genealogical databases.

GENDEX: An index of online genealogical databases that comply with the GEDCOM-converted-to-HTML indexing format.

Gene: A section of a chromosome that contains specific sequences of information that determine a particular inheritable characteristic of a human.

Genealogical database: Software in which you enter, store, and use information about ancestors, descendants, and others relevant to your genealogy.

Genealogical Data Communication (GEDCOM): The standard file format for exporting and importing information among genealogical databases; intended to make data translatable between different genealogical software programs so that you can share your family information easily.

Genealogical Proof Standard: Developed by the Board for Certification of Genealogists, this standard is a system of five steps meant to prove that a particular event happened.

Genealogical society: An organized group that attempts to preserve documents and history for the area in which the society is located. A genealogical society often has a second purpose, which is to help its members research their ancestors.

Genealogically focused search engine: A program that indexes the full text of Web sites that are of interest and value to genealogists, and allows you to search the index for particular keywords.

Genealogy: The study of ancestors, descendants, and family origins.

Genome: A complete set of instructions for how a cell will operate.

Geographic-specific Web site: A Web site that has information pertaining to a particular locality (town, county, state, country, or other area).

Geographical information systems (GIS): Software that allows you to create maps based on layers of information.

Glass-plate negative: A type of photograph made from light-sensitive silver bromide immersed in gelatin; typically taken between 1848 and 1930.

Global positioning system (GPS): A satellite system that receives and sends signals to a receiver, enabling the person controlling the receiver to determine his or her exact geographical coordinates.

Haplogroup: A grouping of several similar haplotypes.

Haplotype: A set of results of genetic markers for a particular individual. Haplotypes are used to compare the results of two or more individuals to determine genetic distance.

Helm Online Family Tree Research Cycle: A five-phase research model that explains the ongoing process of genealogical research. The five phases are planning, collecting, researching, consolidating, and distilling.

Henry System: A widely used and accepted genealogical numbering system that assigns a particular sequence of numbers to the children of a family's progenitor and then to subsequent generations.

Historical society: An organized group that attempts to preserve documents and history for the area in which the society is located.

Home page: The entry point for a Web site.

HTML: Acronym for HyperText Markup Language.

HyperText Markup Language: The programming language of the Web. HTML is a code that's translated into graphical pages by software called a Web browser.

IGI: Acronym for International Genealogical Index.

Immigrant: A person who moves to or settles in a country.

Immigration record: A record of the entry of a person into a specific country where he or she was not native-born or naturalized.

Index: A list of some sort. An index can be a list of Web sites, types of records, and so on.

Interface: An online form or page.

Interlibrary loan: A system in which one library loans a book or other material to another library for a person to borrow or use.

International Genealogical Index (IGI): A list of births and marriages of deceased individuals reflected in records collected by the Church of Jesus Christ of Latter-day Saints. The International Genealogical Index is part of the FamilySearch collection of CD-ROMs, accessible at Family History Centers.

Internet: A system of computer networks joined by high-speed data lines called backbones.

Internet service provider (ISP): A company or other organization that provides people with access to the Internet through a direct connection or dial-up connection.

Intestate: The estate status of a person who died without leaving a valid will.

ISP: Acronym for Internet service provider.

Jump drive: See *flash drive*. Also called thumb drive.

Junk DNA: A noncoding region of a DNA strand.

Kinship report: A list of family members and how they relate directly to one particular individual in your database. Kinship reports usually include the civil code and canon code for the relationship to the individual.

Land grant: Permission to purchase land or a gift of land in exchange for military service or other civic service.

Land patent: A document that conveyed the title of a piece of land to a new owner after that person met required conditions to own the land.

Land record: A document recording the sale or exchange of land; most land records are maintained at a local level where the property is located.

Lineage-linked database: A database that is organized by the relationships among people about whom information is stored in the tables.

Listowner: A person who oversees a mailing list.

Listserv: A software program for managing electronic mailing lists.

Locus: The specific location of a marker on a chromosome. Plural is loci.

Lurking: Reading messages that others post to a mailing list or newsgroup without posting any messages of your own.

Maiden name: The surname with which a woman is born; sometimes reflected as née on records and documents.

Mail mode: The method for mailing lists in which each message is sent to you separately as it's posted.

Mailing list: An e-mail exchange forum that consists of a group of people who share common interests; e-mail messages posted to the list come directly to your e-mail address in full-format (mail mode) or digest mode; the list consists of the names of everyone who joins the group. When you want to send a message to the group, you post it to a single e-mail address that subsequently delivers the message to everyone on the list.

Manumission papers: Documents granting slaves their freedom.

Marker: A sequence of DNA at a specific location on a chromosome.

Marriage banns: A proclamation made in front of a church congregation expressing one's intent to marry.

Marriage bond: A financial contract guaranteeing that a marriage was going to take place; usually posted by the groom and another person (often the father or brother of the bride).

Marriage certificate: A legal document certifying the union of two individuals.

Marriage license: A document granting permission to marry from a civil or ecclesiastical authority.

Maternal: Relating to the mother's side of the family.

Metasearch engine: A site where you can use a single interface (or online form) to conduct searches using several different search engines at the same time.

Microfiche: A clear sheet that contains tiny images of documents, records, books, and so on; you must read it with a microfiche reader or other magnifying equipment.

Microfilm: A roll of clear film that contains tiny images of documents, records, books, and so forth; you must read it with a microfilm reader.

Military index: A list of those killed in the Korean and Vietnam Wars; part of the FamilySearch collection of CD-ROMs, which are accessible at Family History Centers.

Mitochondrion: The power plant of a cell; sits outside the nucleus and contains its own genome.

Modem: A piece of equipment that allows your computer to talk to other computers through a telephone or cable line; modems can be internal (inside your computer) or external (plugged into one of your computer's serial ports or cards).

Moderator: A person who determines whether a post to a newsgroup or mailing list is appropriate and, if so, posts it.

Mortgage: Legal agreement to repay money borrowed, with real property as collateral.

Muster record: A type of military pay record reflecting who was present with a military unit at a particular time and place.

Mutation: A difference in the number of repeats within a genetic marker from one generation to another.

Naturalization: The official process of becoming a citizen or subject of a particular country in a manner other than birth in that country.

Naturalization record: The legal document proving that one is a naturalized citizen.

Netiquette: Simple guidelines for communicating effectively and politely on the Internet.

Networking site: A Web site intended to help people find other people with the same interests, talents, backgrounds, and locations.

Newbie: A person who is new to the Internet or other technology.

Newsgroup: A place to post messages of a particular focus so that groups of people at large can read them online; messages are posted to a news server which, in turn, copies the messages to other news servers.

Nucleotides: Also called bases. Rungs of the DNA ladder that hold the molecule together. Four types exist: adenine, guanine, cytosine, and thymine.

Nucleus: The center of a cell that contains the deoxyribonucleic acid (DNA).

Obituary: An account of one's death that usually appears in a newspaper or other type of media.

One-name study: A page on the Web that focuses on research involving one particular surname regardless of the geographic location in which it appears.

Online: Gaining access to and using the Internet or something that is available through the Internet.

Online database: A collection of tables containing data that is accessible through the Internet.

Orphan: An infant or a child whose parents are both deceased. In some earlier times and places, a child was considered an orphan if his or her father had died but the mother was still living.

Outline report: Also called a family outline; a list of descendants of a particular ancestor.

Passenger list: Listing of the names of passengers who traveled from one country to another on a particular ship.

Paternal: Relating to the father's side of the family.

Pedigree chart: A chart that runs horizontally across a page, identifying a primary person (including that person's name, date and place of birth, date and place of marriage, and date and place of death), his or her parents, then each of their parents, and so on until the chart runs off the page. Sometimes called an ancestor chart.

Pedigree resource file: An index of user-contributed family trees maintained by the Church of Jesus Christ of Latter-day Saints.

Pension record: A type of military record reflecting the amount of a pension that the government paid to an individual who served in the military. Pension records also showed the amount of pension paid to the widow or orphan(s) of such an individual.

Personal genealogical site: Another name for a personal Web page that contains information relating to a person's or family's ancestry.

Personal Web page: A page on the Web that was designed and posted by an individual or a family. It may also be called a personal genealogical site.

Petition for land: An application that your ancestor may have filed for a land grant.

Plat map: A map of lots within a tract of land, usually showing the owners' names. Also spelled platte map.

Platinum print: A type of photograph with a matte surface that appeared to be embedded in the paper. Images were often highlighted with artistic chalk, giving the photo a hand-drawn quality; typically taken between 1880 and 1930.

Primary source: A document, an oral account, a photograph, or any other item that was created at the time a certain event occurred; information for the record was supplied by a witness to the event.

Probability: The likelihood that a specific fact or outcome will occur.

Probate: The settlement of one's estate after death.

Probate records: Types of court records that deal with the settling of an estate upon one's death. Probate records include contested wills and will readings; often the file contains testimonies and the ruling.

Professional researcher: A person who, for a fee, can research your genealogy — particular family lines — or obtain copies of documents for you.

Progenitor: The farthest-back ancestor you know about in a particular family line.

Query: A research question that you post to a particular Web site, mailing list, or newsgroup so that other researchers can help you solve your genealogical research problems or challenges.

Recombination: The process by which a parent contributes half of his or her child's DNA, creating a new genetic identity.

Research groups: A group of people who coordinate their research and share resources to achieve success.

Research log: A record of where and when you searched for information. Also called a research table.

Research table: See *research log.*

Robot: A program that travels throughout the Internet and collects information about sites and resources that it comes across. Also called a bot or spider.

RootsMagic Essentials: A trial version of a popular genealogical database.

Roots Surname List (RSL): A list of surnames, their associated dates, and locations accompanied by the contact information for persons researching those surnames that is maintained by RootsWeb.com.

RSL: Acronym for Roots Surname List.

Scanner: A device that captures digital images of photographs and documents to your computer.

Search engine: A program that searches either a large index of information generated by robots or a particular Web site.

Secondary source: A document, an oral account, or any other record that was created after an event took place or for which information was supplied by someone who was not an eyewitness to the event.

Server: A computer that makes information available for access by other computers.

Service record: A type of military record that chronicles the military career of an individual.

Shareware: Software that you can try before you pay to license and use it permanently; usually you download shareware from the Internet.

Short tandem repeat polymorphisms (STRPs): Segments of repeating bases in DNA.

Shotgun approach: A bad idea; the process of sending mass e-mails to anyone you find with your surname through one of the online white pages sites.

Single nucleotide polymorphism (SNP): A variation in a DNA sequence in which a nucleotide differs between two individuals or in a paired chromosome for a single individual.

Site: One or more Web pages; also called a Web site.

Smartphone: A cellular phone that can connect to the Internet and has more computing capability than a regular cellular phone.

Snail mail: Mail delivered by hand — such as U.S. Mail.

Social Security Death Index: An index of those persons for whom Social Security death claims were filed with the United States government. Although a few records in the index predate 1962, most date from 1962 to the present.

Sosa-Stradonitz System: See *ahnentafel.*

Sound card: An internal computer device that enables you to hear the audio features of software or audio files that you download from the Internet.

Soundex: A system of indexing the U.S. federal census that groups names that sound alike but are spelled differently; the Soundex code for a name consists of a letter followed by three numbers.

Source: Any person or material (book, document, record, periodical, and so on) that provides information for your research.

Spam: Unsolicited junk e-mail that tries to sell you something or offers a paid service.

Spider: A program that travels throughout the Internet and collects information about sites and resources it comes across. Also called a robot.

Spreadsheet: A worksheet that allows you to arrange data and track in a particular format.

Stereographic card: A type of photograph that was paired and rendered a three-dimensional effect when used with a viewer; developed in the 1850s.

Subclade: Subgroup of a haplogroup.

Subscription database: An online database that is accessible if you subscribe to it.

Surname: A last name or family name.

Surname marketing plan: A checklist of places and people to contact to effectively inform the right individuals about information that you would like to contribute to the genealogy community.

Survey: A detailed drawing and legal description of the boundaries of a land parcel.

Tax record: A record of any tax paid, including property, inheritance, and church taxes. Most taxes were collected at the local level, but some of the records have now been turned over to government archives.

Tertiary source: A source of information that is not considered primary or secondary.

Thread: A group of messages with a common subject on a newsgroup.

Thumb drive: See *flash drive*. Also called jump drive.

Tintype: A type of photograph that was made on a metal sheet; the image was often coated with a varnish; typically taken between 1858 and 1910.

Tiny tafel: A compact way to show the relationships within a family database. Tiny tafel provides a Soundex code for a surname and the dates and locations where that surname may be found according to the database.

Toggling: The process of flipping back and forth between open programs on your computer by using the Alt and Tab keys in Windows, or the Application Switcher on the Mac.

Tract book: A book that describes the lots within a township or other geographic area.

Transcribed record: A copy of the content of a record that has been duplicated word for word.

Uniform Resource Locator (URL): A standard online address provided for resources on the Web.

URL: Acronym for Uniform Resource Locator.

USGenWeb Project: Online project that provides a central resource for genealogical information (records and reference materials) pertaining to counties within states in the United States.

U.S. Colored Troops database: An online database of information on more than 230,000 soldiers of African descent who served in the U.S. Colored Troops; part of the Civil War Soldiers and Sailors System sponsored by the National Park Service.

Video-capture board: A device that enables your computer to import images from your video camera or VCR.

Visa: A document that permits a noncitizen to live and travel freely in the United States.

Vital record: Primary record of a vital event in life — birth, death, or marriage; for the most part, local governments keep the originals. Often called civil registrations outside the United States.

Vital records index: An index of birth, marriage, and death records maintained by the Church of Jesus Christ of Latter-day Saints.

Warrant: A certificate to receive land when your ancestor's petition for a land grant was approved.

Web: A system for viewing and using multimedia documents on the Internet; Web documents are created in HyperText Markup Language (HTML) and are read by Web browser programs. Also called the World Wide Web.

Web browser: Software that enables you to view HTML documents on the Internet.

Web log: An online journal or log of one's interests and activities. Also see *blog*.

Web page: A multimedia document that is created in HTML and is viewable on the Internet with the use of a Web browser.

Webmaster: A person responsible for creating and maintaining a particular Web site.

Web server: A computer connected to the Internet that serves Web pages when you request them using your computer's Web browser.

Web site: One or more Web pages created by an individual or organization; also called a site.

Wiki: A collaborative Web site where users can contribute information on a particular subject.

Will: A legal document that explains how a person wishes his or her estate to be settled or distributed upon death.

Witness: One who attests that he or she saw an event.

Word processor: Software that allows you to write and edit text.

XML: A specialized computer code, similar to HTML, that uses tags to describe information. The broader purpose of XML is not only to display information but also to describe the information.

Index

• *I* •

• N •

• S •

• T •

Apple & Macs

iPad For Dummies
978-0-470-58027-1

iPhone For Dummies,
4th Edition
978-0-470-87870-5

MacBook For Dummies, 3rd
Edition
978-0-470-76918-8

Mac OS X Snow Leopard For
Dummies
978-0-470-43543-4

Business

Bookkeeping For Dummies
978-0-7645-9848-7

Job Interviews
For Dummies,
3rd Edition
978-0-470-17748-8

Resumes For Dummies,
5th Edition
978-0-470-08037-5

Starting an
Online Business
For Dummies,
6th Edition
978-0-470-60210-2

Stock Investing
For Dummies,
3rd Edition
978-0-470-40114-9

Successful
Time Management
For Dummies
978-0-470-29034-7

Computer Hardware

BlackBerry
For Dummies,
4th Edition
978-0-470-60700-8

Computers For Seniors
For Dummies,
2nd Edition
978-0-470-53483-0

PCs For Dummies,
Windows
7 Edition
978-0-470-46542-4

Laptops For Dummies,
4th Edition
978-0-470-57829-2

Cooking & Entertaining

Cooking Basics
For Dummies,
3rd Edition
978-0-7645-7206-7

Wine For Dummies,
4th Edition
978-0-470-04579-4

Diet & Nutrition

Dieting For Dummies,
2nd Edition
978-0-7645-4149-0

Nutrition For Dummies,
4th Edition
978-0-471-79868-2

Weight Training
For Dummies,
3rd Edition
978-0-471-76845-6

Digital Photography

Digital SLR Cameras &
Photography For Dummies,
3rd Edition
978-0-470-46606-3

Photoshop Elements 8
For Dummies
978-0-470-52967-6

Gardening

Gardening Basics
For Dummies
978-0-470-03749-2

Organic Gardening
For Dummies,
2nd Edition
978-0-470-43067-5

Green/Sustainable

Raising Chickens
For Dummies
978-0-470-46544-8

Green Cleaning
For Dummies
978-0-470-39106-8

Health

Diabetes For Dummies,
3rd Edition
978-0-470-27086-8

Food Allergies
For Dummies
978-0-470-09584-3

Living Gluten-Free
For Dummies,
2nd Edition
978-0-470-58589-4

Hobbies/General

Chess For Dummies,
2nd Edition
978-0-7645-8404-6

Drawing
Cartoons & Comics
For Dummies
978-0-470-42683-8

Knitting For Dummies,
2nd Edition
978-0-470-28747-7

Organizing
For Dummies
978-0-7645-5300-4

Su Doku For Dummies
978-0-470-01892-7

Home Improvement

Home Maintenance
For Dummies,
2nd Edition
978-0-470-43063-7

Home Theater
For Dummies,
3rd Edition
978-0-470-41189-6

Living the
Country Lifestyle
All-in-One
For Dummies
978-0-470-43061-3

Solar Power Your Home
For Dummies,
2nd Edition
978-0-470-59678-4

Internet

Blogging For Dummies,
3rd Edition
978-0-470-61996-4

eBay For Dummies,
6th Edition
978-0-470-49741-8

Facebook For Dummies,
3rd Edition
978-0-470-87804-0

Web Marketing
For Dummies,
2nd Edition
978-0-470-37181-7

WordPress
For Dummies,
3rd Edition
978-0-470-59274-8

Language & Foreign Language

French For Dummies
978-0-7645-5193-2

Italian Phrases
For Dummies
978-0-7645-7203-6

Spanish For Dummies,
2nd Edition
978-0-470-87855-2

Spanish
For Dummies,
Audio Set
978-0-470-09585-0

Math & Science

Algebra I
For Dummies,
2nd Edition
978-0-470-55964-2

Biology For Dummies,
2nd Edition
978-0-470-59875-7

Calculus For Dummies
978-0-7645-2498-1

Chemistry For Dummies
978-0-7645-5430-8

Microsoft Office

Excel 2010 For Dummies
978-0-470-48953-6

Office 2010 All-in-One
For Dummies
978-0-470-49748-7

Office 2010 For Dummies,
Book + DVD Bundle
978-0-470-62698-6

Word 2010 For Dummies
978-0-470-48772-3

Music

Guitar For Dummies,
2nd Edition
978-0-7645-9904-0

iPod & iTunes For
Dummies, 8th Edition
978-0-470-87871-2

Piano Exercises
For Dummies
978-0-470-38765-8

Parenting & Education

Parenting For Dummies,
2nd Edition
978-0-7645-5418-6

Type 1 Diabetes
For Dummies
978-0-470-17811-9

Pets

Cats For Dummies,
2nd Edition
978-0-7645-5275-5

Dog Training For Dummies,
3rd Edition
978-0-470-60029-0

Puppies For Dummies,
2nd Edition
978-0-470-03717-1

Religion & Inspiration

The Bible For Dummies
978-0-7645-5296-0

Catholicism For Dummies
978-0-7645-5391-2

Women in the Bible
For Dummies
978-0-7645-8475-6

Self-Help & Relationship

Anger Management
For Dummies
978-0-470-03715-7

Overcoming Anxiety
For Dummies,
2nd Edition
978-0-470-57441-6

Sports

Baseball
For Dummies,
3rd Edition
978-0-7645-7537-2

Basketball
For Dummies,
2nd Edition
978-0-7645-5248-9

Golf For Dummies,
3rd Edition
978-0-471-76871-5

Web Development

Web Design
All-in-One
For Dummies
978-0-470-41796-6

Web Sites
Do-It-Yourself
For Dummies,
2nd Edition
978-0-470-56520-9

Windows 7

Windows 7
For Dummies
978-0-470-49743-2

Windows 7
For Dummies,
Book + DVD Bundle
978-0-470-52398-8

Windows 7 All-in-One
For Dummies
978-0-470-48763-1

Wherever you are in life, Dummies makes it easier.